SHOOTIN' THE SH*T WITH
KEVIN SMITH

SHOOTIN' THE SH*T WITH KEVIN SMITH

THE BEST OF SMODCAST

ISBN-13 9781845764159

Published by
Titan Books
A division of
Titan Publishing Group Ltd
144 Southwark St
London
SE1 0UP

First edition September 2009
1 3 5 7 9 10 8 6 4 2

The publishers would like to thank SModcast producer Ken Plume for his invaluable help with this book.

Visit our websites:
www.titanbooks.com
www.quickstopentertainment.com/category/smodcast/

A CIP catalogue record for this title is available from the British Library.

Printed and bound in the United States of America

BOOBERTY!

SHOOTIN' THE SH*T WITH
KEVIN SMITH
THE BEST OF SMODCAST

Illustrations by Michael Macari

TITAN BOOKS

DEDICATION

For Jen — because she lets me candidly share with strangers so much of my life. It doesn't sound like a big deal 'til you realize it's *her* life as well. I have a very cool wife, is what I'm saying.

SPECIAL THANKS

Ken Plume — SModcast's own Jam Master Jay, the mix-master general, whose audio presence, sadly, doesn't translate to print. But aurally? Without him? We sound empty.

Elliot Greenburg — He taught Scott and I how to use the equipment — very important and necessary step in podcasting or any electronic venture.

Ming — Who always makes sure Scott and I are floating somewhere through cyberspace.

CONTENTS

From SModcast 01: Fisting Flipper 3
How the name SModcast was created

From SModcast 02: A Dubious Superpower 3
The Alanis Morissette mugging story

From SModcast 04: Can I Get a Witness? 7
Kevin's shame at jerking off on a nude Jen's calf

From SModcast 05: Nipples You Can Hang a Coat On 10
Kevin and the YMCA

From SModcast 09: Red, White, But Never Blue, eh 13
Dogs and sex

From SModcast 10: Eating a Chicken's Soul 19
Weight loss and population control

From SModcast 10: Eating a Chicken's Soul 21
Does a chicken have a soul?

From SModcast 11: A Fistful of Shame 27
Sundance and Cannes

From SModcast 12: A Fat Kenickie 34
Kevin's high school theater experience

From SModcast 13: SFodcast (or SWodcast) 41
Walt's flea market story

From SModcast 14: On Guard For Thee 53
Malcolm's pinky betting fiasco

From SModcast 15: Pretty-Good Worker 61
The Helen Keller conversation

From SModcast 19: We Owe It All to Nook-Nook 85
A Nook-Nook tribute

From SModcast 21: Little Outhouse On the Prairie 86
Wiping technique

From SModcast 23: Good Vibrations..88
Malcolm floods the Rumson house

From SModcast 23: Good Vibrations..90
Kevin sees Chay's boob and then runs

From SModcast 25: Lynching Vixen 91
Bryan Johnson trying to pep-talk strippers.

From SModcast 26: Beware the Hobo..92
Bryan Johnson's scorpion story

From SModcast 28: Scottacita Wants a Carnita!...94
Lard conversation

From SModcast 29: Harry Scotter..95
Bertie Bott's beans in the ass

From SModcast 30: Smith & Wesson...96
Tales of Crime and Punishment

From SModcast 31: Loneliness of the Long Distance Mosier 99
The Jesus list

From SModcast 34: Jersey Justice League..103
An act of tenderness with Walt

From SModcast 37: In a Row? 104
Jennifer Connelly remakes Scott Mosier

From SModcast 38: Leeroy Jenkem! 109
Defending Kevin's honor

From SModcast 39: Of Berries and Twigs 113
Scott Mosier discovers the true nature of Alex Mosier

From SModcast 40: Ned Smitty 115
The Ned Smitty routine

From SModcast 40: Ned Smitty ... 122
Kevin finds out he's foppish

From SModcast 42: SMerry Christmas ... 123
Scott is told he will raise the second coming of Christ

From SModcast 45: End of the SMod-fast ... 130
How long before a stranded Kevin and Scott would fuck?

From SModcast 46: Mr Deaves Goes to Town ... 135
"Where's my shirt?!"

From SModcast 50: Gnome Alone ... 138
Kevin and Walt discuss what Mewes would do for a comic

From SModcast 52: The (c)Rapture ... 142
What if Jesus came back?

From SModcast 53: Meat Curtains ... 168
The steak tartare story

From SModcast 54: SModder's Day ... 171
Kevin describes to Harley the concept of a mix tape

From SModcast 56: And Now a Word ... 173
Scott's harrowing highway tale/vs. Make-a-Wish

From SModcast 57: Terrorist Pizza ... 201
Gordo, the righteously indignant Canadian

From SModcast 57: Terrorist Pizza ... 210
Kevin explores the world while high

From SModcast 59: Frosh Meat ... 227
Initiation and night baseball

From SModcast 60: The Clone War ... 233
Pillow Babies and Stalin's ape-man army

From SModcast 60: The Clone War ... 238
Cloning debate and Walt's loneliness

From SModcast 61: "Bridge Beach!" 267
The infamous Bridge Beach story

From SModcast 62: The Human Quilt 271
Confronting the Foreigner dude in the cereal aisle

From SModcast 63: SMod-Kushed 281
Hitler's dog engineering program and the Nazi stink

From SModcast 64: Farewell and Adieu 290
Scott's shark tale

From SModcast 64: Farewell and Adieu 296
The brain transplant

From SModcast 65: Captain Kev and Mister Scott 303
Harley turns to Satan

From SModcast 66: Sleipnir the Conqueror 306
Origins of Santa Claus and Satan Claus

From SModcast 69: The Talking Cure, Pt. 2 319
Rate Your Libido or *Watch My Dumbass FUCK!!!*

From SModcast 69: Talking Cure, Pt. 2 321
BOOBERTY!

From SModcast 69: Talking Cure, Pt. 2 324
Hero, question mark?

SModcast 72: Hello Dere! 331
Bryan witnesses a very odd fight at the teen club

From SModcast 78: For Today's Elegant Man 333
Jaundice and *Star Wars*

From SModcast 80: RIP 334
The future dies

Kevin Smith
Scott Mosier
37
BEAN-N-GONE
COFFEE SHOP
Shootin' the Shit

est.2007

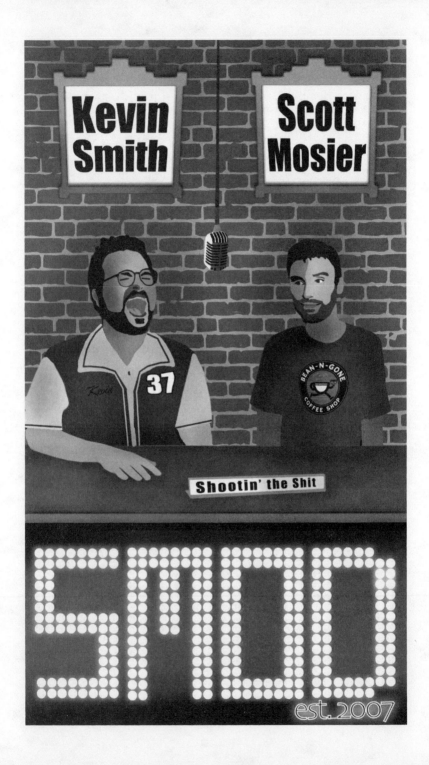

INTRODUCTION

Don't be fooled by my name on the cover. I didn't write this.

Well, I wrote *this* — the intro. But the rest of it? I didn't write it. I didn't even transcribe it from the original recording.

There is no author, really, and yet, somehow, I'm not a plagiarist. If I'm guilty of anything, it's simply wanting to talk to Mosier more. That's the not-so-secret origin of SModcast, the podcast I do (almost) every week with my longtime friend and producer, Scott Mosier: it was born out of a desire to spend time with Mos in a non-work capacity.

I first met the young Scott Mosier way back in 1992 on our first day at the Vancouver Film School. In contemporary parlance, he looked like that kid from *Twilight* all the 'tween girls cream over. But back in '92? He just looked like Luke Perry.

At first glance, I assumed I wasn't gonna like him. "Look at this fuck," I muttered to myself, mean-mugging Mosier during our class orientation. "All leather-jacket-wearing, well-groomed, dual citizenship-carrying cool, who's probably never had to beg for a handy. I hate him."

Within the first two weeks of school, we were coupled-up for a class exercise that eventually forced us into conversation. I wish I had total recall of the exact words we exchanged (I like to remember it as Ben Kenobi introducing us, *à la* the *Phantom Menace* trailer; the *trailer*, okay? Not the actual movie), but I know where the conversations eventually went: hysterical, interesting, fucked-up places. For the next five months, Mos and I spent lots of time together, bonded by a similar sense of dry humor and, every once in a while, dopey outsiders-dying-to-get-in industry *faux*-speak (for a short film project, we named our production company Post Party at Spago's — a joke which wasn't even that funny then, and certainly shows its age now).

I dropped out of film school midway through the eight-month program, but

Scott (and our longtime cinematographer Dave Klein) stuck it out. Months later, they both joined me in New Jersey to shoot a no-budget flick about a guy who works in a convenience store.

From the moment *Clerks* was picked up by Miramax, Scott and I became inseparable. The mini-major would send me to fifteen or twenty festivals over the next few months and Scott attended every one of them with me. We flew all over the world, showing our flick, Q&A-ing afterwards, building a city-by-city awareness for our theatrical release date in the fall.

Understand if you will that it was an age of magic and wonder: our first film had been picked up by *THE* premiere art-house distributor of the era, and we were being courted for more work by other studios as well. I had a dream, and Mos helped me forge it into reality. I was longing to be "heard" — to get *my* voice out there. And this veritable stranger I'd known less than a year helped make it happen. Do you understand what a gift that is — aiding someone on a vision quest? I loved the man about as much as you *can* love someone you have no interest in fucking. Scott was my hetero life-mate.

After the January '94 to November '94 *Clerks* film festival road show, the flick came out — thus signaling not only the end of our grass roots tour, but the start of our next movie as well: *Mallrats*. After that, there was *Chasing Amy*, *Dogma*, *Jay and Silent Bob Strike Back*, etc. And with each flick, we began spending less and less time together outside of work. The majority of our conversations became project related and we afforded ourselves very little time to simply hang and be friends like we used to. I got married in '99, he did the same a few years later, and then the time we spent together outside of work pretty much ground to a halt altogether.

And that's the way it went for a while. Until I had the idea.

I'd often wished I'd taped an interview with my father before he died. Shit, just a recording of his voice, even — so generations from now, our family could possibly hear the gentle inflections of the patriarch. But more than that, I wish I had him telling some *stories*. I could've maybe gotten him to spin some yarn about a time long before I was even a late-night urge in the fall of '69 (I was born August, '70); just a record of who he *really* was, y'know?

And that, in turn, got me wondering how many more people I was ever going to lose without putting 'em on wax, so to speak. I couldn't shake the idea that all of these characters in my life had millions of unrecorded stories about who they are, as well as the mundane events that shaped them.

So with very little fanfare, I asked Mos if he wanted to start doing a podcast together for one of my websites, quickstopentertainment.com, with the idea being that it'd give us at least an hour a week to hang out and bullshit about anything but our work. Surprisingly, the normally press-and-public shy Scott said yes. Even more surprisingly, he came up with the name; a name I immediately wanted to hug.

SModcast.

And so, on February 1, 2007, Mos and I sat at a poker table in the Los Angeles View Askew office at Sycamore and DeLongpre, in a Chaplin bungalow behind the old United Artists lot, and started talking. And by the night of February 5, 2007, that idea I'd had started to bear fruit.

"I never knew Mosier was so funny," the listeners would write. "Scott's fucking quick, man." Or "I love the voices Scott does. His characters are hysterical." And every once in a while: "Scott's even funnier than Kevin."

I'd had this idea about how to thank my friend for helping me get my voice out there all those years ago, and the idea was to put *his* voice out there, so everyone would know what *I've* known for fifteen years: he's an amazingly interesting and quick-witted guy you'd wanna sit around and bullshit with.

And then, SModcast evolved: when Mos wasn't available, I brought on *other* people I'd always found really funny and fascinating who normally never found themselves in front of a microphone. I was simultaneously proudly pulling back the curtain on the folks who made me who I am, *and* digitally insuring that I'd always have their wonderful stories preserved, in their distinctive voices.

And best of all? It was all free. No money, no problems. And since no commerce was involved, it never became a business. And since no business was involved, it remains an oasis: a place where me and Mos (and others) can shoot the shit. For posterity, as it were.

So am I the author of all the text that follows? God, no. They're conversations, full of give and take. I didn't write for these rich individuals; they all speak for themselves.

But technically? Podcasting with pals was my idea. So, yeah — I'm kinda the author of this book.

I just didn't write it.

Kevin Smith
27 July 2009

Welcome to SModcast

Key:

KS: Kevin Smith
SM: Scott Mosier
WF: Walt Flanagan
BJ: Bryan Johnson
MI: Malcolm Ingram
JS: Jennifer Schwalbach
HS: Harley Smith

From SModcast 01: Fisting Flipper
How the name SModcast was created

KS: Welcome to SModcast, where I, Kevin Smith, and my good friend and producer Scott Mosier, sit around and add to the detritus or the wasteland of podcasts that are out there. We thought about calling it 'yet another podcast' but SModcast, which Mosier came up with, was good. Explain that title.
SM: It's really clever. Your last name is Smith and my last name is Mosier. And I took the first letter off of our last names and then put them together and took the 'p' off the podcast.
KS: Wow. I really thought more went into it than that. But you know what, it works. It's cute. It's a fun word to say. SModcast.
SM: It rolls off the tongue.
KS: Like Zamboni. It's just fun to say.
SM: Yeah.

From SModcast 02: A Dubious Superpower
The Alanis Morissette mugging story

KS: There was one time me and Alanis Morissette were working on *Dogma*, and it was one of our days off. It was a Saturday or Sunday. We worked six-day weeks on that movie!
SM: We did.
KS: I guess it was a Sunday. Me and Alanis were just walking around, bullshitting and whatnot, and just got further and further from the hotel, into areas where probably it wasn't a good idea to be walking around after dark. And in moments like that, my fucking radar goes off. I'm one of those people who just suspects everybody wants to commit a crime if they're on the streets at night — white, black, Asian… I don't give a fuck — everybody. If you're on the streets in a downtown area after dark, it isn't a well-lit area and you're up side streets and shit — chances are, I feel, you're up to no good. So we're walking down one of those fucking streets and I notice this dude across the street. There's nobody else, dude — fuck, it's like *28 Days Later*, where a man wakes up and he's walking across the bridge and nobody's there. It's fucking empty. Street lights only. And there's a dude on

the other side of the street — shady looking character, ratty-assed clothes, who crosses the fucking street to be on our side of the street. And immediately my fucking Spider-sense starts tingling. I have no fucking superpowers, you know? Spidey starts tingling and he can fucking shoot some web and fucking punch somebody. *My* Spider-sense starts tingling, and I'm like, "I'm going to have to offer to suck this guy's dick…"

SM: That's your superpower. [Laughs.]

KS: My superpower is like, "I'll suck your dick if you let us go."

SM: You'd have to do it well.

KS: Oh yeah. "I'm a master cocksucker, let us live," that kinda thing. So, I see this dude cross the street, and he's walking directly towards us, making eye contact. We're on his fucking radar at that point. And she don't fucking notice, because Alanis is a real "up with people" kinda person, where everyone is inherently good.

SM: She's not suspecting.

KS: Oh, she's *so* not suspecting. I don't know how that girl has got so far in life without something horrible happening to her. 'Cause she just trusts everyone. And also, even if we *were* to get killed or something, Alanis would be the person sitting there going, "Well, it's probably our fault." Like, she would cognitively reframe the whole thing to be our fault or society's fault. Never like, "This dude's killing us — it's his fault." It's everyone else's fault. Blame doesn't go where it belongs 'cause she just likes people. She trusts them. So the dude is coming at us and Alanis is yammering away, and I'm kinda half in the conversation at that point, because the other half of me is focusing on the dude that's rapidly getting closer and closer, and the distance between us is shrinking. And I'm just scared shitless, you know? 'Cause I'm like, "What am I going to do?" I'm so not the fucking brave dude.

SM: And you're not *that* confident about sucking his dick! [Laughs.]

KS: [Laughs.] No. I mean, I can do an able-bodied job, a yeoman-like job, but I think he might still rob us anyway!

SM: You don't know if you can save your life with your mouth.

KS: No! If I could suck a cock to save my life or her life… Maybe mine, maybe if he's like, "Alright, that cocksucking was worth *you* getting a mild whoop ass, but I'm going to kill her." And I'd be like, "Why didn't you ask her to suck your dick? She's a chick!" Also, he didn't look like he was in the mood for a cocksucking anyway — he looked like he wanted something from us. You can tell, you get a vibe, man.

SM: Yeah.

KS: That dude had a vibe like he wanted something from us, and we were *definitely* the focus of his attention. He crossed the fucking street! So I'm like, oh my god. He's getting closer and closer, and she's just talking. Finally I'm like, "A, do you see this?" And she says, "What?" And I'm trying to talk about the dude without the dude noticing, because he's getting closer. And she's like, "So?" And I said, "He crossed the street to be on our side of the street," and she's like, "What? Are you worried?" She's Canadian and there's no crime in Canada. She's not on the same page. But literally, I'm almost crying at this point, so she's sensing that something's wrong. I'm maybe a couple of inches shy of pissing my pants, because I'm like, "What do I do?" I'm not strong enough to whoop ass on this dude!

SM: You're not like Mewes.

KS: Mewes is the kinda guy that if someone started shit with him, Mewes would throw down. There was this dude that came up to Mewes in a bar and said, "Were you in that movie *Clerks*?" and he was like, "Yeah." And the guy punches him in the face. Mewes just turns around, grabs a pool stick and starts beating on the motherfucker. And he's got some boys there, so they all jump in and start kicking this dude's ass. But even without his boys, Mewes is, "If you're going to hit me, I'm going to hit you back really, *really* hard." I'm *so* not that guy. If you hit me, I'm going to cry.

SM: [Laughs.] I'm going to cry on your fist.

KS: Exactly. If anything, your fist will slip off my face, based on the fucking Niagara Falls pouring from my eyes. I am such a pussy. And I'm like, "I can't protect myself, let alone me and this fucking girl." And this girl's got like the biggest album on the fucking planet at that time. And I'm thinking, all the headlines are going to read "Alanis Morissette, Friend, Die 'Cause Pussy Don't Do Shit."

SM: [Laughs.] "Man Covered In Tears And Urine."

KS: [Laughs.] "Shit, Urine And Tears: Body Found Beside Her. Heavy-Set Gentleman Did Nothing"! So I'm like, "We're dead!" I remember saying to her, "This is fucked up. We're going to get hurt right now, I know it." And the dude smokes right up to us, man, and he says "Hey." And I said, "Hello…" And she's like, [in a chirpy voice] "Hi!" because she's that kinda person. And he said… "I was wondering if you guys wanted to buy a

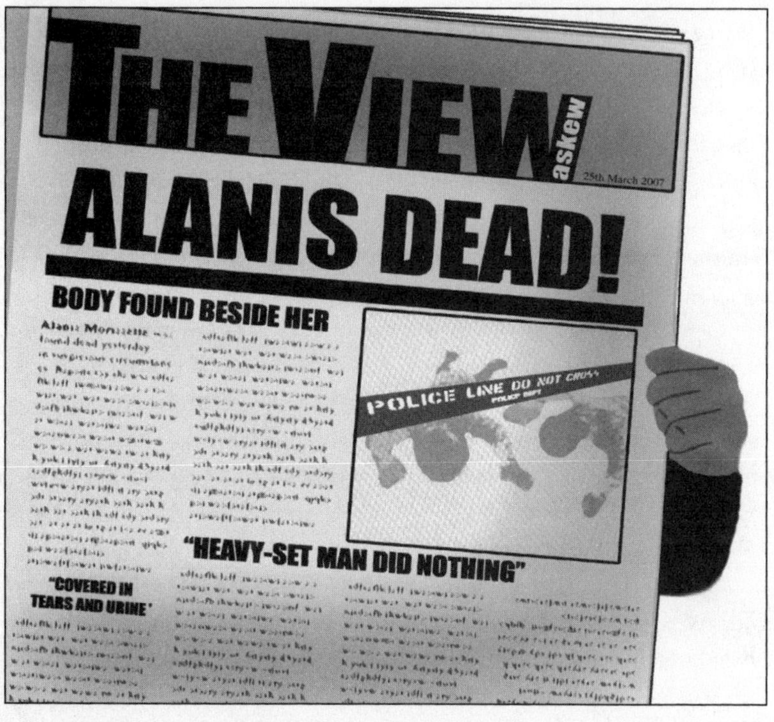
THE VIEW
askew
25th March 2007
ALANIS DEAD!
BODY FOUND BESIDE HER
POLICE LINE DO NOT CROSS
"HEAVY-SET MAN DID NOTHING"
"COVERED IN TEARS AND URINE'

magazine?" You know, I feel like that statement was the opening salvo to me going, "Huh?"

SM: "I would *love* to buy a magazine!"

KS: "Which one? Is it *Boy's Life*? Is it *Highlights For Children*?" But was still kinda tight about it. I'm so ashamed to admit it — and I didn't *immediately* push Alanis into the dude and run away, but I *did* separate myself from her. I was in fight or flight mode, and I was going to hope that she was going to run too — but I was a couple of steps away from her, you know? The fucking chivalry thing would have been me putting myself between her and harm's way. But I'm like, "Fuck it, she's a tough broad, she sings about blowing dudes and beers" — I'm fucking running and hoping that she's smart enough, 'cause she's a smart chick, too — to run, maybe in the other direction, rather than us ganging up on the dude, because two against one… and who knew if he had someone in a side alley, or what? So I'm not at ease. But Alanis just goes with it, and she says, "Well, what one?" The dude

reaches into his fucking jacket, and at this point, I'm like, "Here it comes," it's a knife, it's a gun, I don't know what it is, it's a rusty fucking razor. It's something bad. And the dude *literally* pulls out three magazines. And it's three magazines that he probably lifted off a newsstand, because it was *Good Housekeeping* and fucking *Womenswear Daily* or something. We gave the dude five bucks, he gave us the magazines, and that was the end of it. And I could tell that if I had had *any* shot of getting together with Alanis Morissette, because this was prior to me getting together with Jen, really — if I had any shot with her, it probably went out the window that day.
SM: It collapsed right there.
KS: Because I think she might have sensed, "You were totally about to let me get attacked!"
SM: You were about to run from *Good Housekeeping* magazine. [Laughs.]
KS: Totally! It was horrifying!

From SModcast 04: Can I Get a Witness?
Kevin's shame at jerking off on a nude Jen's calf

KS: I was struck by the notion this weekend that no matter how much I've been able to accomplish with my career professionally, that personally it doesn't fucking amount to a hill of beans. Some people assume that because you make movies and shit you're on easy street, life is great, and it's not. I still have trouble getting laid, that kinda thing. I got done with my Q&A at the New York Comic-Con and I was gonna head down to Jersey to play some poker, and Jen was staying in the city to go out. So I get back to the hotel room and she's in the shower, it's one of those glass doors. And suddenly I was like, "I'm going to get laid, she looks good to me right now." Normally she does all the time, she's naked.
SM: Wet, soapy?
KS: Totally. Well not soapy. It's not like I want to get soap in my cock or something like that, because that burns. But I was totally like, "I want to try and get one off before I get on the road and shit." Because there's still a part of me that's like, you're married and whatnot and you love who you're with, but there're still always that male part of you that's like, "I would like to fuck and then move on pretty quickly," rather than lay around and cuddle and

chitchat and bullshit. Sometimes you just want to fucking snap one out and then fucking go on with your day in a real caveman kinda way. Not where you want to drag her by the hair—

SM: The quest for fuck.

KS: But I don't want to make love. There's no quest for fuck. I just want to fucking shoot one and go. So she was getting ready for her shindig, to go out, so she's like, "I don't have the time." I threw it out there and I'm not subtle about it and shit like that, I'm like, "You want to bone?" Not really the way into a woman's panties.

SM: No.

KS: Even if you're married to her. They do still like to be romanced a bit. But I knew the clock was against me on this one. And she was like, "No. I got to get ready. Later on, maybe tomorrow when we come back and you pick me up then we can totally do it because I want to do it, but I have no time." And I'm so not the force-the-issue kinda guy so I wasn't like, "No, we're doing it." But I was still disappointed and I was still ready to go because she looked good and shit. So she's getting ready, and does this ever happen to you, it's such an embarrassing, desperate sexual act, where you're like, "I'll just jerk off and you watch"? Have you ever been that guy who's done that?

SM: Nah, I haven't quite done that.

KS: I've done that many times in my life, where it's like I just wanna…

SM: You wanna be interactive…

KS: I want to cum so badly and yet you want to be interactive, you don't want to fly solo and shit, and jerk off into a fucking sock, but you want someone to be involved.

SM: It's kinda sexy.

KS: It's kinda sexy a little bit.

SM: For you to cum and her to be in the room.

KS: It's dirty enough and you're there but it is so stupid to be like, "I'm going to jerk off and you can watch." If the roles were reversed and she's like, "I'm going to rub one out and I want you to watch," I'd be like, "Argh, I guess."

SM: "Is this leading to something?"

KS: Exactly, there's always the whole thing of, if you're rubbing one out will I eventually get to fuck you?

SM: And she's like, "No."

KS: Yeah, that would be the kinda thing. But for me if I was like, of course in the back of your mind you're always like, "While I'm jerking off she can get turned on and then want to fuck." But not when she's getting ready, she's not thinking about that. So we're in the bathroom and I throw that out there and she goes, "Well, I don't really have the time." So I said, "What if you just took off your robe?" Because she's getting all prepared in the mirror, wearing this robe, "What if you just took off your robe and I jerked off here in the bathroom looking at you?" And she's like, "If you want, go ahead." She's putting on her make-up. So fucking sad, the more I think about it, but I was so desperate to fucking get it off. So she drops her robe and is naked, I'm in the bathroom still trying to figure out whether I'm going to commit to this kinda thing, because we've been married for close to eight years, but at the same time that could be the thing where she's like, "Look, I always thought you were a loser and had good intentions but come on dude, you're going to fucking tug one out and crack one on my fucking leg while I'm getting ready in the bathroom mirror? That's just insane. Have a little self-respect." But I didn't have any, so I fucking—

SM: You did it?

KS: I totally did it dude. I dropped down to my knees and I'm behind her and she's literally not really paying that much attention to me, putting on her make-up, doing her mascara and shit like that. I get down on my knees, I drop my fucking drawers, I start tugging one out just staring at her asshole and the back of her pussy, you know, that back view. And in order to do that you've got to spread the cheeks a little bit, but I only jerk off one hand so it doesn't matter. But at the same time I'm spreading her cheeks and pushing her a little bit, and she's like, "I'm putting on my mascara, don't forget." I'm like, "Alright." So it's real clinical, not very sexy, but it was kinda weird and hot at the same time, and like a sick fucking degenerate mutt I'm just on my knees staring at her asshole and the back of her pussy from behind jerking off, tug one out all the way to fruition. I don't think I'd gotten laid for like two days or something so I had a nice pent up fucking 'pchoom!' kinda load that hit her leg, and I fucking feel bad for anyone that uses that bathroom after us at that hotel room, because it went right on the rug too. And then afterwards I just felt like such a scumbag. I can't believe I couldn't just wait and I succumbed to the filthy fucking urges, desperate sickening urges to "just let me jerk off while I'm here." It was kinda hot though. It would be like if you could jerk off in a strip club, because you're getting to look but

you're not allowed to touch, because she wasn't going to fuck and I was hoping that she'd get turned on enough to be like, "Oh, fuck it, let's do it."
SM: But she didn't.
KS: So I was left to my own devices and had to take matters in hand. But it was so sad really in some weird way. But she was nice about it, she didn't make me feel sad about it, she said, "That was kinda sexy." But I think she might have just been saying that so I didn't take that drive down to Jersey going, "What *happened* to me? I really let myself go in every way, I have no self-respect whatsoever, I can't stop fucking eating and I've fallen to jerking off on my wife's fucking calf." It's weird the depths you'll plumb, human sexuality, just to fucking get one off or whatnot.
SM: When it gets in your head and you've got to get it out.
KS: Yeah, and granted it's kinda tame in comparison to how some fucking filthy animals conduct themselves. And serial killers, some of them kill because it pleases some sort of sexual urge, and it's not even predicated on a sexual act, but for some reason they can't get off unless there's death involved. So I'm not there yet.

From SModcast 05: Nipples You Can Hang a Coat On
Kevin and the YMCA

KS: My first and only gay experience was at a YMCA. And when I say gay experience, I don't mean I wound up sucking cock — I wound up getting my cock sucked. Nah, I didn't wind up doing anything, but I joined the YMCA for CAM 2 [weight training based on air pressure resistance], I was like, that sounds awesome. It made it sound easier for some reason, because you don't have to lift weights. It's air! Air doesn't weigh that much — I'll be in shape in no time! So I joined this higher level, because you can join on the standard level — they had a pool, there was a basketball court, they had an indoor running track, and that was over the basketball court.
SM: Mine had that.
KS: The indoor track? I remember that, that was kinda cool, man. You could jog inside.

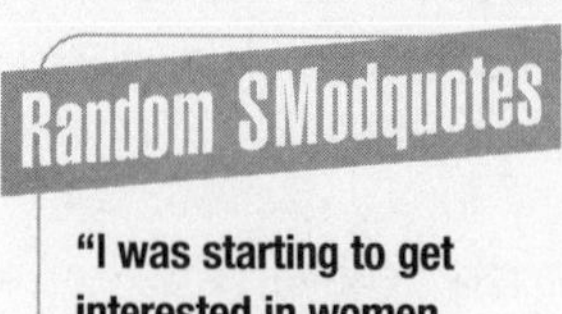

"I was starting to get interested in women. Naked women... That weren't my Mother!"

But if you went up a level it got you into CAM 2, and it had nicer locker rooms and they had a steam room and a sauna and a Jacuzzi and shit like that. I was eighteen, maybe nineteen, and I had a little extra scratch, so I went and joined, and I was in one of those phases where, “I'm going to get into shape.” It's a phase I fucking pass into at least once a year every year of my fucking life. And so I joined the YMCA and went to do the CAM 2 and shit like that, and I was like, “I'm going to use the fucking Jacuzzi, I've never had much hot tub experience.” We didn't have one in our house, and we didn't know anyone with a hot tub, so I thought, fuck it. So I went in, and the locker rooms made me uncomfortable to begin with, because dudes feel free to walk around…

SM: It's a fucking sausage party.

KS: Oh my god, it was a total sausage party — there were dicks everywhere.

SM: There's wieners and there's hair…

KS: Totally. And I'm not comfortable letting my dick out there in the world, even before I had something of a profile where people would go, “Hey! Silent Bob's got a little dick!” I just didn't want anyone going, “Hey! That random fat dude's got a little dick!” So I went into the Jacuzzi wearing a bathing suit. I did a little work out and I was sitting in the Jacuzzi relaxing and whatnot, and it's a hot tub, so it blows bubbles and shit. And this other motherfucker, who did *not* have a bathing suit on, gets in the hot tub. And I didn't think much of it. I was a little like, “Dude, put on a pair of trunks, would you?” But whatever, that's what they do in a locker room. The hot tub's not very big, and he doesn't sit across from me, which I thought, “Well, maybe he doesn't want to because then we have no choice but to lock eyes,” and fucking fall in love and fall like lovers into the tidal pool! So he sits kinda near me, which I'm cognitively reframing in my head as him not wanting to stare directly at me. They had little seats built in within the tub itself.

SM: Was it round or square?

KS: It was roundish *and* squarish. Maybe octagonal would be the best description. So the dude sits next to me, and I didn't think much of it beyond, “You don't want to stare at me.” Maybe a minute later… hand on my fucking leg! And, you know, you have to react in a split second with shit like that. The first thing that went through my head was “Oh, this dude hit me with his fucking foot,” but it wasn't a foot, it was a sustained grip on my leg. It wasn't an accident. Clearly this dude made a fucking move. The whole thing lasted about three seconds before I was able to put it together and react, but I got the distinct impression that it was a pass. Only a retarded person wouldn't understand that it was a pass! Dude had his hand on my fucking leg! And it didn't do a slide straight to my dick or anything like that, but it was firmly on my upper thigh. And I was up like a shot and out of the fucking hot tub!

SM: Did you look back at all?

KS: In regret, you mean? Or like, "Hey, let's go to dinner, let's move a little slower?"

SM: Did you look at him?

KS: Well, I got a bead on him when he got in the tub, so I knew what he looked like. I could still kinda picture him in my head. He was a skinny dude, had an afro but for a white dude — some people call it a jewfro, that kinda thing… I got a bead on him, what he looked like, but he didn't occur to me as gay.

SM: But I mean, there's the moment — he puts his hand on your leg, you take three seconds to be like, "Hand on my leg, this isn't an accident. This guy is making a gay pass at me, I'm not necessarily interested in that," so you get out. But from the moment that the hand hit your leg, did you look at him? Say anything?

KS: No, I didn't make eye contact. And I know there are people — like Mewes would fucking *hit* somebody if they did that to him. Or somebody would say, "What the fuck?" Mine was just…

SM: You should have done *Invasion of the Body Snatchers*!

KS: [Laughs] Yeah, like with an open gaping maw, and pointing and shit! I just got up — I remember I got up like a shot, and it was kinda embarrassing, because you're in the middle of a wet slippery tub, so I then tumbled down onto my knees into the water and got up and tried to keep my cool and got out, but didn't say anything. I mean, now if that happened in my life I might be like, "Oh dude, I'm just tubbing."

SM: Not even angry, just, "Hey, I'm just here for the water."

KS: Exactly, "I'm just lying here for the cum…"

SM: And then he's like, "Well, then do you mind if I just jerk off…"

KS: Yeah, and I'm like, "Uh… sure, I guess, I mean — nobody's around… Feel free. I mean, if you think I'm sexy, yeah…" It's weird, because in the moment I was not flattered by it at all. Now in life, I might be a bit more flattered by the whole thing. I might think, "Maybe he's a fan." A very touchy fan, who wants to fuck. But then it was just weird and awkward, and I remember going down to the desk. I immediately got my fucking gear on. I put my clothes on over my bathing suit because I was like, I don't want to hang out in this locker room because I don't want to have an awkward conversation. Not that I thought the dude was like, "I ain't taking no for an answer."

SM: And puts his hand on your leg again!

KS: Or on my fucking neck, and pushes me to the ground and jerks off on the back of my fucking head! But even if the guy was going to come over and say, "Hey, I'm sorry," I didn't want to be there. So I got dressed and went downstairs. I stopped going to the Y, and then I lost my job, so I was like, in need of scratch, and so I went back to the Y.

SM: You were looking to get paid!

KS: I was! I was like, I'm going to get some fucking money out of these motherfuckers! So I went back to the Y and said, "I want to cancel my membership to the health club." And they said, "Oh, OK, so we can do that right now." And I said "Yeah, and I was hoping to get reimbursed because I've only really used it twice." And they were like, "Well, it's non-refundable membership." So I said, "Alright, well here's the thing, I was in the hot tub and some dude made a pass at me and put a hand on my leg." And I remember the dude I was talking to at the counter was just looking at me, like, "Nobody wants to fuck you. I ain't buying this." This was like, a real 'mouse in my beer bottle' or 'fly in my salad' kinda thing. The dude just wasn't buying it, but I'm like, "I'm telling you dude, it's true." And he's like, "Well, we don't really have a policy in place for that kind of thing." What the dude didn't say was, "Motherfucker, it's the Y — of *course* somebody made a pass at you in the men's locker room! That's what happens, for Christ's sake!"

From SModcast 09: Red, White, But Never Blue, eh.
Dogs and sex

KS: We got a dog [Scully, a Labrador], and after a week or two weeks we were like, "What a pain in the ass man, we've got to get another dog to hang out with this dog, so that this dog will leave us alone." So then we went to a pure breed kennel in Middletown to find a puppy. It didn't say "Pure breed kennel" it said something like, "Puppy world" or some such shit. It wasn't at a mall. Your mall dogs generally come from puppy farms and shit like that.

SM: Inbred?

KS: Yeah, a lot of mum fucked brother or son.

SM: Yeah, it's just a disgusting hillbilly…

KS: Redneck pups. Then they have the audacity to charge what they charge. So we went to this pure breed kennel and they had a fucking swarm of gorgeous lab puppies. Jen found one and immediately fell in love with it. We wanted to get a boy because we had a girl, Scully, so we wanted to get a boy, Mulder. We're huge *X-Files* fans. A little gay, but whatever. She liked this puppy so much so we're like, "Alright, let's get it." I went over to the counter, slapped it up on the counter and said, "How much?" And they were like, "Four thousand dollars." I was like, "You are out of your fucking mind! Who charges for a dog, man? They're running around, they're free, the dog is like air, you can't charge…"

SM: You can go back to *The Hills Have Eyes* kennel and get a fucking dog over there.

KS: Totally, I'll go get a bunch of dogs. I'll buy the store for four grand! But she loved the dog so much, and it was right in the beginning of our relationship and she was pregnant, so what was I going to say? "No"? What a bad precedent that would have set, we barely knew each other at that point. So I had to fucking pony up. Worth every penny. A world of difference between a six hundred dollar mall dog and a four thousand dollar kennel dog. That four thousand dollar kennel dog, Mulder, is so human it is insane. I think he's pure bred between a human being and a yellow lab. He's just so sensitive and good-natured, he's never the dog in the garbage can. That's Scully. Scully is the one that would eat out of the toilet, just eat fucking shit if somebody doesn't flush it, which bums me out so much. Mulder won't touch it. Mulder is not fucking beggy or shit like that, if you're like, "Mulder!" he's very easily shamed. If you go, "Ooooo!" then he'll just shrink. The worst thing you could do to that dog is go, "Ooooo!" You never have to hit that dog, so good-natured we never got him fixed. I was like, "Don't do that, don't take the man's nuts away. Give him his nuts." And for years, we've had Mulder for almost eight years now…

SM: Well, at four thousand dollars, his nuts are worth a couple of hundred bucks.

Random SModquotes
"Better a gay Batman
than no Batman at all."

KS: Totally! What am I going to do? Toss those nuts away? I mean, let them hang, let them be there. Dude never showed an interest in sex. Scully was fixed, so she never went into heat. We had another dog a year later, a chocolate lab which we named Louis, and she got fixed and has never been a problem. So all these years, the only time I ever saw Mulder show an interest in sex, because some dogs hump beds and legs and shit like that, was when Eliza Dushku brought her dog over one day. It was a boy dog and Mulder was all over him, followed him everywhere and at one point tried to get up on the back of him. So I was like, "Awesome! We've got a gay dog! We've got ourselves a gay dog, he don't care about pussy and shit." But then if you've lived with Scully, as the only female you know for five or six years, and you're like, "If this is what the female world has to offer me…"

SM: "I don't want to fuck that bitch!"

KS: "No, my god! I'd rather fuck this strange male dog if I've got to fuck anyone." He'd never shown an interest in sex once, never been a problem, never once, *never* been a problem. Then last July, the wife went away for a bit and me and the kid had been talking about wanting to get a Dachshund, a wiener dog, just because they're funny looking. And Jen was, "Never, no way. We've got three dogs, that's enough." And as soon as she was out of town I was like, "Fuck it. Let's go get a Dachshund." So we went to the mall, which was such a mistake, because around here that was the only place I knew where to find a dog. We found ourselves a little Dachshund, bought it. Not a bad price, comparatively, but still fourteen hundred bucks seems like a lot of money for a little fucking… just for a joke, right? To be like, "Ha ha, look at you, you look like a wiener." Brought it home, named it Shecky. Wife came home, was very pissed about the whole thing but got over it. Shecky's just a holy terror. Rotten little… loves me but just a rotten dog, chewing up things. A puppy, just chewing things she shouldn't chew. Terrorizing the other dogs because she's young and they're older and she just wants to play. She did not bring out the vitality of the other dogs. The other dogs were like, "Jesus! *Another* dog?"

SM: "When are we going to die?"

KS: "I guess you're really pressing the point here, but everything was good with the two of us, then you got a third but the third doesn't bother us too much. But now you've got this fucking thing..." All she does is jump up and bites their ears and then gravity pulls her back to the ground because she can't fly. They're just dragging this dog around by their ears. She terrorizes Mulder, jumps up, grabs his ears, will run over and hump his head. I guess dogs do that for dominance because I've seen Scully do that to Mulder. Every once in a while, Mulder is on the floor and Scully will pimp by, she'll stop and will literally hump his head and then walk away.

SM: It's about submission.

JS: Yeah, it's about, "Who's the boss? I'm the boss! I can fuck your head at any time, I won!" And Mulder never seemed to care. He was like, "Whatever. Like any marriage, you give the woman the illusion of power." And that's what I think Mulder does, "Yeah, you're in charge. It's your world." This little dog started humping his head too and he was just like, "Look, I'll take it from the big one but come on! This fucking thing? I've got this thing beat by a mile, even with three paws tied behind my back." But still would let it kinda go. Shecky went into heat and started having the dog period, which is fucking gross, but she started out with the little blood drops, they call it spotting. We're like, "What's wrong with Shecky?" And someone was like, "Well, she's in heat." So when they're in heat you can't fix them until after the heat is done. Jekyll and Hyde with fucking Mulder. Suddenly the scent of puss in the air sent this dog *over the edge*. I've never seen this dog behave like this, it was like a completely different dog. Just fucking went crazy. He just had his nose buried in her fucking crotch, always following her, nose up the ass and shit like that. Then he managed to fuck this little dog. Now we don't have a Dachshund that's a grown up Dachshund, we've got a miniature Dachshund so it's even smaller than the normal Dachshund. She was born in July and it's now March so that's seven or eight months old. But I guess, if there's grass on the field fucking play ball. This dog wound up fucking that little dog. We didn't catch him, we didn't see him in the act, but we saw the aftermath which was that little dog's little puss was *wrecked*. The biggest flappiest fucking meat curtains you've ever seen in your life. Her puss dragging across the floor. You never notice dog puss anyway. The only time you notice dog genitalia is if it's a boy and the red thing is out and you're like, "Put that shit away!" But all of a sudden we were like, "Oh shit, oh my god!" There's Shecky's lab, labia just dragging across, leaving a snail trail along the floor! He got the fuck in there and my wife went crazy. My wife is a massive fucking feminist and she took it in this real personally offended kinda way of like, "How dare he force himself on her!" I'm like, "Hey man, it's the animal kingdom, that's what they do." She was like, "Fucking *men*!" She was saying after that, "I'm sure Mulder hates himself. I'm sure Mulder's like, 'I hate this little dog but I would never fuck it, I can't but I *have* to, I have no choice. Puss is in the air, I've got to do what I've got to do.'" You're talking about a dog who's dick is bigger than the entire little dog it was fucking. Just wrecked, totally wrecked! Then it raises the question of if she gets pregnant what the fuck kinda gross unholy progeny are going to pop out of that little dog? Little lab puppies with long bodies and massive heads that just drag across the floor, they can only walk in circles using their head as a pivot point, like when Santa's Little Helper had puppies, like this weird mix breed. At first I was like, "There's no way! They can't have puppies." Then somebody who was a dog trainer told me, "They can totally have puppies."

SM: Sperm is sperm, egg is egg…

KS: Sperm is sperm, totally. But it was crazy man. We had to put Shecky in a cage, and Mulder would fucking hump the cage. There was so much cum all over this dog. It was crazy dude. I bathed the dog. We have a service that comes to the house and once a month basically they pull up in a van, plug into your hose and then bring your dogs into their van and wash them up and stuff. It's like getting the dogs all spiffing but you don't have to leave the house. But the little dog, it's like a hundred bucks and we're not going to waste that money on the little dog. So I take the little dog in the shower with me every once in a while. So I'll go take a shower and the first thing I'll do is soap the dog up and wash the dog then she just sits there whilst I finish my shower. We've got a lot of room in the shower. It's weird, so I keep my back to her. I don't want her looking at my dick and judging me. Like, "Look at you! Fucking Mulder's dick is bigger than yours." So I had to take her in the shower twice in the span of a week because she was caked with fucking dog spunk. It was the most disgusting thing I ever saw. Mulder just could not control himself. It was like watching nature in a way that I'd never seen it, up close and personal man. He was howling and doing shit that was completely uncharacteristic. This dog barely makes a sound, Mulder's not a barker or a growler. He would just sit there outside the cage just howling.

SM: Just going crazy.

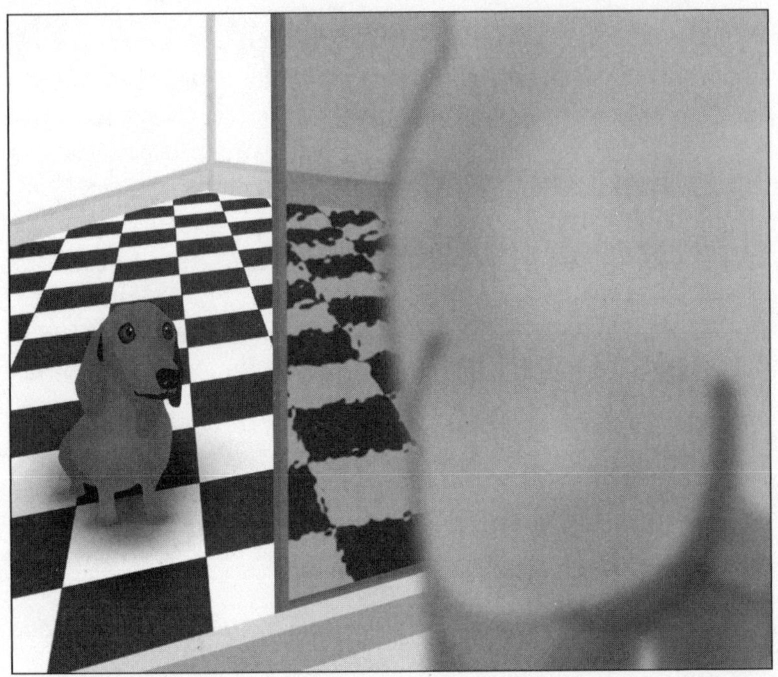

KS: And she must have gotten into it! Who knows? Maybe she got into it and that's how he got to fuck her in the first place. I saw her present to the dude. Where she was pushing down on the front part of her long ass body and pushing her ass up in the air with the tail out giving him the puss. He went over and was hovering over her and I had to break them apart and shit. One part of me just wanted to watch. I was like, "This will be fucked up man! Watching a big dog fuck a little dog."

SM: Get some popcorn?

KS: Totally! I'm going to call some friends and be like, "You've got to see this!" But I had to break them up, I felt bad for the little dog. Even though she was presenting, going "Do it! Do it, Mulder!" I was like, "You don't want this done. This is a horrible thing. He is way bigger than you man." This dog trainer told me that when they fuck, the dog dick goes in the dog puss and then when the dog cums the penis enlarges, so they end up in this weird twisted position, he can't just withdraw. They wind up ass to ass, like in fucking *Requiem for a Dream*, "Ass to ass!" They wind up ass to ass for him to dismount, to dislodge. This dog and this dog ass to ass, it's such an unpretty sight. This little dog, I'm serious, is about half the size of Mulder's head. The idea of something that big going into something that small, whilst entertaining to watch, is something I couldn't abide by. It's the craziest thing I've ever seen in my life. Jen was like, "See, I told you to have Mulder fixed. You fucking said no and see what happened." I'm like, "You can't blame the motherfucker for that mess. It's not his fault. I know that dude hates himself." Now Shecky is out of heat and now they can be in the same room and it ain't no big deal, but you know Mulder is sitting around going, "I can't believe I fucked it. I hate that little dog."

From SModcast 10: Eating a Chicken's Soul
Weight loss and population control

KS: If people want to attract me as a reader, it would be like, "You know who's got the biggest dick in Hollywood? Liam Neeson!" It's that shit you hear where you're kinda, "Really? Liam Neeson?"
SM: Someone's on a semen diet!
KS: Oh, I would read that in a heartbeat. I'd be like, "Who's eating cum? And does it work?" 'Cause I'd be—
SM: Would you?
KS: Oh, if it was a guaranteed way to lose weight, you eat the sperm and the sperm just eats the food that's in your stomach. [Laughs.] And it's like having a tapeworm of sorts? Oh, I would be fucking eating *so* much cock. I think I'd get a pass from my wife. Though I'm sure she'd be like, "Look, why don't you eat your own cum? Why should you eat someone else's dick for it?" But I'd be like, "I need more!" because I'd obviously only be able to generate so much cum in a day…
SM: You could ask some friends, as opposed to immediately putting a dick in your mouth.
KS: That's true. "Everyone jerk off into a cup and let me bukkake that shit."
SM: I'd pitch in.
KS: I'd appreciate that. That'd be weird, though.
SM: I'd pitch in, but like, on my own.
KS: You wouldn't stand around with a bunch of dudes, circle-jerking off into

a cup?

SM: No, I couldn't do that.

KS: Well, first off, let's say I eat a whole pizza, how much cum would I have to eat? In this science fictional world where sperm will eat the contents of your stomach before you digest it…

SM: While nurturing your body…

KS: Yes, you're full of nutrients but you're not storing the fat. The body's not storing the sugar.

SM: Gotcha. Your body's eating the existing fat.

KS: And for some reason you're not digesting the sperm, they're just swimming out of your system. What a glorious world that would be.

SM: Well, let's see — how many of those [slimming] shakes do you have a day?

KS: I drink five or six of those shakes a day, and they're 180 calories a pop.

SM: But the actual size — what if you had to drink five cartons?

KS: Five cartons? Do you know how much cum that would take? Every dude I know — and I'm talking about, "Hey, I met George Clooney once" — *every* dude I know wouldn't fill one!

SM: OK, three. Well, here's the other side of it. Let's say you and I discovered this today, it's like, "Are you kidding me?"

KS: How did we discover it? The backstory is more interesting than the actual weight loss! "How did you guys figure it out?"

SM: There'd be a giant press conference: "How did you guys figure this out?" and we'd be like, "Oh well, you know… just eating each other's cum…"

KS: Well, that's the thing — do we tell them all? Do we have a press conference and tell them all about it? Or do we keep it to ourselves, and market it, don't tell people what's inside it? Make it holistic — you don't have to go in front of the FDA with a holistic or organic drug. Like, Echinacea and shit like that. We'd just say "all natural!" But do we bother telling the world, or do we just take advantage? "Fuck this, let's just jerk off and sell it!"

SM: Well, if the results were fucking amazing then you could tell people. And I guess we're talking amazing results. But it would eliminate part of your male market.

KS: Why? Look, I'm a fat man — I fancy myself as a lover of women. I would not be put off by the notion of drinking male cum. [Laughs.] Let's just make it very clear to everybody, because some dudes would want to dupe themselves, "Well, it just says cum — could be chick's cum!"

SM: But you have to admit that we live in a society where certain people would just not…

KS: You mean like conservatives and whatnot?

SM: Yeah.

KS: Yeah, because, like, "That could be a baby."

SM: Yeah — there you go.

KS: I appreciate their position. Actually, I don't appreciate it. I respect that they have their position, but not every fucking sperm becomes a kid. And you're telling me that these people have never jerked off or never had sex in their lives just simply to enjoy it? It's just sex for procreation? Every time George Bush has had sex with his wife, it's just been to make a kid? They've only had sex twice, then? No, of course, they enjoy having sex. And sometimes the sperm just doesn't do what it's supposed to, it doesn't go anywhere. Why not go in my belly and make me thin?

SM: And think about the economic benefit — think of how many people are qualified? I mean, it is a male job, but think of all the guys in the world — you don't have to go to college.

KS: You could be homeless, and do it. I could roll up to a homeless guy and say, "Would you mind if I gave you ten dollars to put your dick in this cup?" And you know, you might want to test it…

SM: [Laughs.] You could be a little more selective!

KS: [Laughs.] I know, but ten bucks is a steal, man. I bet it would have an effect on the population, too.

SM: Because there would be so much.

KS: So much cum would be going into rich people's stomachs.

SM: Men are going to be like, "I'm not going to fuck — this is worth money!"

KS: "This is pearly white gold!" I would do it in a heartbeat, and I wouldn't think twice about it.

From SModcast 10: Eating a Chicken's Soul
Does a chicken have a soul?

KS: The way we see a bear or a shark, do you think that's the way chickens look at human beings? That there's a communicado that goes in the chicken world where they're like, "If a human's coming at you, pick up a bike, make yourself look big."

SM: Well they don't have any arms really. I think that's why chickens run, if you walk in chickens don't like—

KS: So they've got the fight or flight response, they've got the flight aspect.

SM: It's like, "There's something large coming in here, we've got to move." Or if you bring food they're still timid, but some birds will come and eat out of your hand. I mean they still have senses to sense the difference between us coming in there and say a coyote or something.

KS: Right.

SM: But to a chicken we're just a big huge thing.

KS: What's the difference between a human and a coyote to a chicken? Both of us are coming to eat him, the coyote sooner rather than later.

SM: Well if you have a chicken coop, you're just coming in to get eggs, you're not slaughtering them in front of everybody.

KS: But isn't there a part of them that's like, "Protect the young! They're taking our babies!"

SM: I don't think chickens—

KS: You don't think chickens have emotions?

SM: The chicken brain is not the most developed.

KS: I gotta imagine the chicken has to have emotions, the chicken has to feel like—

SM: Or you *want* to think?

KS: I really do! Part of me wants to and a part of me doesn't want to, because I eat a lot of chicken. But part of me wants to believe that the chicken is sitting on a bunch of eggs and then some asshole comes in and is stealing them—

SM: Like naming them?

KS: Totally! This will be Herbert, this will be George, this would be Francis.

SM: Most people who eat chicken tend to not think that they have emotions, usually it's people who don't eat meat who have the impression that—

KS: A chicken has a soul.

SM: Yeah. The media is just that they're dumb fucking things pecking around, shooting out eggs.

KS: Yeah, I'm a happy medium where I've got to believe that there's more going on in a chicken.

SM: You want to eat their soul!

KS: “Here it comes, it’s the fat soul sucker! Hide the babies! Oh, he’s back! He took Bertha!” Yeah, I don’t want to necessarily eat their souls, but I have a hard time thinking the chicken is just sitting there, “Gooup! Bweurr!”

SM: That’s hard to imagine!

KS: Christ man, you’ve got to think like it’s a living being, it has a brain, a higher function. If we were a jellyfish-eating world, I’d be fine. A jellyfish does not have a brain or a spine. I still don’t understand how a jellyfish works. I was at the aquarium with the kid and I read something like, “The jellyfish has no brain, no heart, no spine.” I’m like, “The jellyfish is like me!” But I have those things, but in theory I’m spineless and heartless and brainless. But this thing literally has — how does that fucking thing exist? It’s a freak of nature, just this thing that lives and eats other things but it doesn’t have a brain, it doesn’t have a heart and it doesn’t have a spine. What the fuck makes a jellyfish work?

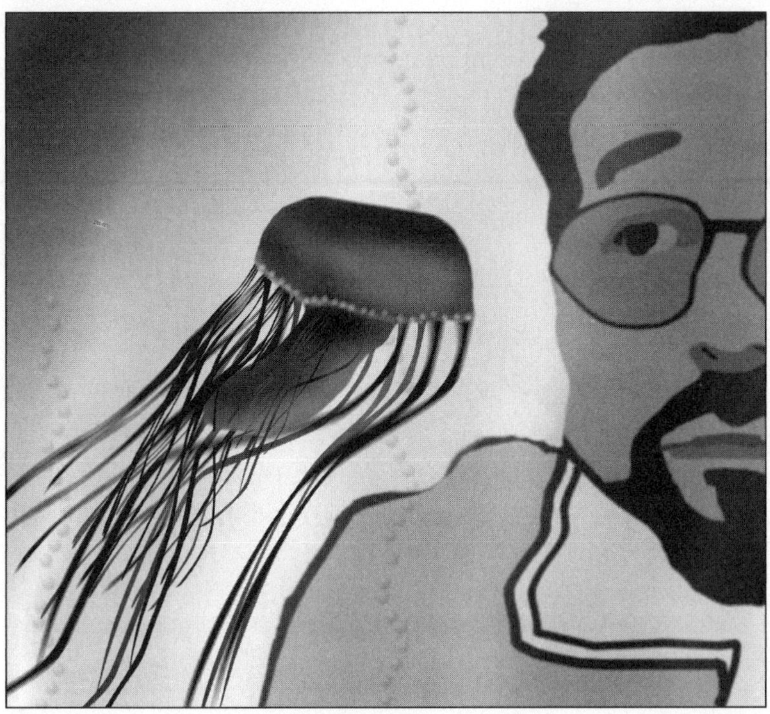

SM: It's an arrangement of cells. Look at bacteria. Bacteria is a living thing, but they don't have spines and brains.
KS: No brain whatsoever?
SM: If a jellyfish doesn't have a brain, I'm going to vote for bacteria not having a brain.
KS: Yeah, a jellyfish is weird. So I could see a jellyfish just be "Brrruep!" just floating in the ocean, "Beurrp! Brrrp brre" — Even that's giving it too much, 'cause there's an inflection in "Brrreup Be Brreup Be."
SM: It'd be robotic. It'd be "Brrrrrrb Brrrrb."
KS: No man, they don't even make noises. But a chicken, there's got to be like, when you leave and the chickens are alone there must be like, "Hey, what's up? How are you?" "We're still alive, we're still doing it, they haven't eaten us yet. Let's work on our escape plan like *Chicken Run*, like the dream, the Aardman animation."
SM: I'd say that it's proof positive that they don't fucking do that.
KS: Why?
SM: Well, I mean I've never heard of them doing that. In the age of the Internet we should do the research, and maybe someone can write in with their stories of chickens fucking doing elaborate escape plans.
KS: I'm not even looking for that. I'm looking for, has anyone ever buried a mic in a chicken coop? Not let them know, like built a chicken coop with a microphone in it, hidden, throughout the place, a bunch of mics and then brought the chickens in there and be like, "We're just going to eat your eggs and that's it and then maybe we'll eat you sometime or whatever." Just treat them like normal chickens — don't let them know that the jig is up — and then walk away and then see if the chickens say anything when the door closes.
SM: In English?
KS: Wait a good minute. Whatever, any language. Even if they spoke Chinese I think it would be wicked if they were suddenly like [whispering] "They're gone. ['Chinese'] Tonking Tonking." Yeah, I'd take that. But still you'd get somebody to translate it to find out what chickens say to one another. And the conversations they would have, like just, "Look at my dick. Look at my chicken dick." Whatever, I don't need them formulating fucking math equations but if I could relate to a chicken a little more—
SM: Would you eat them then?

KS: No! I would stop eating them. I'd be like, "Holy shit, these things talk, they know English, they've just been waiting all this time to pull the whole *Planet of the Apes*."

SM: But if we found out that chickens were just like, "Hey Fred, how you doing?"

KS: "Hey Fred, look at my dick. Watch me jerk off." I imagine a dirty chicken…

SM: Dirty chickens! If that did happen then I don't think you would want that because you would have nothing to eat!

KS: No, I would eat box cereal.

SM: You'd eat box cereal?

KS: I would live off fucking Kellogg's.

SM: What if you found out, if we mic'd the grain…

KS: And they spoke?

SM: Yeah.

KS: Then I'd have to re-evaluate.

SM: You know what is funny about corn is that they think that most sugar based cereals are heavily corn based.

KS: Yeah, that's when they grind them up. I'll eat corn when you grind it up. But it's that texture. If you grind it and dry it up, yeah I'll eat cornmeal. I'll eat that raw. Just give me a fistful of cornmeal and I'll eat it. Like a chicken would, that's why I relate to the chicken very much.

SM: And what you're hoping is that you could be left in the coop and be like, "Let me see your dick!"

KS: Totally! I would like to go incognito into a chicken coop and rattle large chickens—

SM: You're a chicken fetishist!

KS: Look, let's not be ridiculous. You don't even need to be in a big chicken outfit. Let's say they built into the coop a place where I could put just my head, my body's outside the coop resting comfortably, my head is sitting on a nest. And you know like we know some special effects dudes, they decorate my head, they do me up so I look like a chicken.

SM: But your face is like the belly.

KS: Yes, but I'm wearing white contact lenses so it just blends in with the feathers and shit like that. So I'm totally undercover, I'm not dressed like a giant chicken where they might be like, "Come on dude, try a bit harder."

But I do blend. Then they fucking start talking, and talking about showing their dicks.

SM: It's like, "Look at the new guy."

KS: Totally, yeah.

SM: "Show us your dick!" And you're like, "They didn't put a dick on me!"

KS: "Why didn't they think of that?" How long would I sit in that coop listening to the conversation? Like I think the first time a chicken said something I'd be like, "Aha!" And they'd be like, "Oh shit!"

SM: "The jig's up."

KS: "Caught."

SM: See, I would imagine that if chickens could talk, in a world where chickens could talk, they're smart enough.

KS: And we're not talking about "Bwarp!" We're talking about—

SM: "Look at my dick."

KS: "Devils tied up the Series 2-2." Like they're interested in the shit we are.

SM: I think that if they had the power to do that, one of them would have been like, "Stop fucking eating us." Like in the world where chickens could talk and they loved their babies and all the rest of that stuff, then why wouldn't it occur to them to be like, "Look, look, stop eating our children!"

KS: How do you know they haven't? How do you know that some chicken hasn't said that on a farm to Farmer John and Farmer John was just like, "Oh my god, if the word gets out that chickens are almost human-like, I got no work."

SM: I'd say Farmer John's first reaction would be like—

KS: "Satan is in this chicken!"

SM: He could be scared of demon-possession, or, he'd try to make a buck off of that. I'm sure he'd make more fucking money off his talking chickens than out of his fucking eggs.

KS: Yeah but let's say he's got the talking chicken and he's like, "I'm going to take the talking chicken out into the world." And the chicken is around the microphone, "Finally I have a forum, a platform, to address the world!" Like, "Look, we all talk, all of us chickens talk. I'm not the only one. Farmer John can't get rich off me because all the chickens talk." Farmer John is fucked. If he had thought ahead he'd be like, "If I let people know that chickens talk, if I spill the beans, my livelihood is killed."

SM: Well, the chicken would lie. The chicken would be like, "I'm the only one that talks."

KS: Until he gets in front of a microphone?

SM: Yeah.

KS: Wow! That is presupposing a world in which not only can the chicken speak, but it's devious!

SM: The chicken would be. It's sitting around the coop all day.

KS: That's true.

SM: I'm going to bet on the chicken. I'm going to bet on the super brain chicken that's smart enough to know that the revolution's going to start, but that if he fucks it all up… He'd be better off being the celebrity chicken fighting for his cause than just going out there and being, "Hey man, we all fucking talk, Farmer John. We're all fucking talking — mostly about our dicks."

KS: "But still, so do you." In a world where the chickens reveal themselves to be—

SM: Highly intelligent.

KS: Higher brain function animals, how long before we stop eating chicken the world over? Because it's not like immediate, it's not like *Happy Feet*, like, "Oh shit, that penguin is dancing, let's stop fishing the ocean."

SM: I'd say that the immediate reaction is that a lot of people would stop, and a lot of people would just start killing them out of fear.

KS: Because if it can speak, then it can plan. If it can plan, then we're next!

From SModcast 11: A Fistful of Shame
Sundance and Cannes

KS: Do you still like going to film festivals?

SM: Not really.

KS: Why?

SM: Usually it's not that much fun. There are a few festivals that are fun, because you can go and actually get into movies, actually watch some movies. And then once you leave the movie it's like the festival doesn't take over the town. Toronto was kinda fun. But I don't know, it was really fun when we were doing it before, on *Clerks* and stuff like that, that was really fun. I always remember that.

KS: That, and you remember when we went back to Cannes with *Clerks 2*?

SM: Yeah.

KS: That sucked ass for the majority of the week that we were there and then when we finally screened, then it rocked. Getting that standing ovation, bitch.

SM: *Clerks 2* was great, but it's still work, I'm there to find out the fate of the film, not to go see movies.

KS: Well some people like going to parties and shit.

SM: Yeah, that's the other side of it.

KS: You remember when we went to Sundance? That might be the last time I spent any amount of time getting drunk. We went to Sundance and we went for the whole thing.

SM: '94.

KS: So our movie didn't screen until a few days into it.

SM: Yeah.

KS: Probably like the halfway mark or something like that. So for the first few days that we were there, I remember that all we did was drink.

SM: We'd go and drink.

KS: We'd go and see movies and drink. I remember going to see *Backbeat* and getting drunk. And then going to see *Go Fish* and then getting drunk. Just doing a lot of drinking.

SM: We were drinking, probably anxiety.

KS: Yeah. And also we just didn't know how to carry ourselves, didn't know what we were supposed to be doing and whatnot. And also we didn't expect to get picked up but we were like, "This is awesome to be here." And we spent that whole first year with *Clerks* going around from festival to festival. We went to so many fucking festivals, we went to at least twenty to thirty. Went to Cannes of course, we went to any number of places, tonnes of festivals. But Toronto I think wrapped it up, it might have been the last one before the movie came out. But do you remember we went to Germany at one point? We were supposed to go to London and we got to Newark airport, we were about a half hour/forty-five minutes before the flight was supposed to take off, and they were like, "We're not going to let you on."

SM: "You've got to be here an hour before." It was like the international terminal was closed at that point.

KS: Yeah, nobody was there. And then the plane sat on the tarmac for another hour and a half or something like that.

SM: Yeah.

KS: We didn't get to go to London that time. But we took Bryan with us.

SM: To Munich.

KS: We were going to take him to London.

SM: Yeah.

KS: And then we couldn't go so we said, "Fuck it, we'll take him to Munich." And based on the festivals that we had gone to, you and I, they would offer us separate rooms, some places, because I was like, "Well, Scott's got to go" ... and I guess they didn't normally, back in the day Miramax didn't do that and they were just, "Well, just the director goes because the festival pays for it." But I was like, "Well, Scott's got to go." So I'd bring you and you'd stay in my room essentially, but it was our room. But all the places we went, like remember when we went to Japan, Tokyo? We went to the Tokyo Sundance and the room was fucking massive.

SM: It was huge.

KS: It had those no-fog mirrors in the bathroom and the toilet did shit to your ass and we were like, "What a world of wonders this is!" But every place was huge, so when we were going to Munich we were like, "Let's bring Bry." And they were like, "Um, you guys want more than one room?" And we didn't want to be pushy — we'd got our foot in the door and we didn't want to get thrown out of the business — so we were like, "No, we can all fit in one room." And that was the first time we got into a room that was so fucking small.

SM: It was super-small.

KS: The German idea of air-conditioning hopefully has gotten better, but back then it was basically a fan with an ice-cube in front of it. And three bodies in a tiny room in August with lame-ass air conditioning, it was fucking terrible. And the mini-bar, the soda was warm.

SM: None of it was cold.

KS: The Coke didn't even taste like Coke, it tasted like water with a black crayon in it, *hot* water with a black crayon in it. And it was just so cramped and horrible. It was the only festival that I remember that *Pulp Fiction* played at after Cannes, because Harvey decided, based on the Cannes win, to pull it out of every festival that they had scheduled it for. But Quentin really wanted to go to the Munich Film Festival, because I guess he'd been there with *Reservoir Dogs*, so he wanted to go with this one. This was the only one he went to post-Cannes with *Pulp Fiction.* So he was there, and we hung out with him, but he was in a different fucking world altogether. I remember we were bored and searching for shit to do and Mosier hooked up with the *jungfrau*, what was the chick's name? You don't even remember, that's sad. I remember the name of every person that ever looked at me naked and you're just like, "Nah."

SM: I'm not indifferent about it, I'm trying to remember.

KS: We called her *jungfrau*, which meant—

SM: For years you guys always called her *jungfrau* so when I think of her, I just think of *jungfrau*.

KS: Didn't it mean virgin or young lady or something like that?

SM: Yeah.

KS: But she taught us a little German. *Obdachlos*.

SM: Homeless people.

KS: But she took a real shine to fucking Mos, so Mos was hanging out with her a lot, getting fucking busy with this Kraut broad, this *fräulein*.

SM: That's how I wrote about her in my diary.

KS: "Dear Diary, plunged into the Kraut broad. It was awesome. With my Brat." Me and Johnson, left to our own devices, like Johnson of course wanted to go to a death camp.

SM: Yeah.

KS: Dachau.

SM: But literally the hotel room was so small, it was that point where I was like, "Hey, you guys wanna *not* be in the room?"

KS: Totally, and we're like, "Yeah, I guess we want to go to a death camp." And this wasn't even, I mean they're all death camps, but Dachau was more prison camp, work camp. But there were ovens. But it was like German people don't really like to talk about the Holocaust and [sarcastic] I'm *sure* that when Americans get there that's all they want to talk about.

SM: I remember that when you go to a festival usually you have a handler, you have somebody—

KS: Like, "What do you want to do? You want to go to some places? We can hook you up." And we were like, "Yeah, we want to go to Dachau." And they were like, "Hmm, no. You don't. You really don't."

SM: I remember her specifically saying, "You don't want to go there right before a Q&A, you'll be all depressed."

KS: We had to come back and intro the film and do a Q&A and whatnot and she was just like, "You know, when you come back from there you're not going to feel very funny, and it'd probably be best to go another day." And I was like, "Well, this is the only day we can go really." Which was kinda not true, but we really wanted to go. They wouldn't hook us up with a ride, so we took a cab out there. And I remember the taxi driver walked around with us and his English was poor but our German was worse, so he wound up hanging out with me and Johnson, because you can't always catch a cab out of Dachau.

SM: Exactly, it's not like the airport.

KS: Exactly! They don't have them all lined up and shit. And it's a very sobering affair as you'd imagine. That's the one with "*Arbeit macht frei*," "Work will make you free," above the gates. We were walking around with this cab driver in a pretty solemn place, I mean even as much of a joker as Bryan is, you couldn't have a sense of humor in that place.

Random SModquotes

"A weird guy in a big chef hat and a mustache came up to me and said he was gonna fuck my wife in the ass, but he gave me some great canned food."

SM: Yeah.

KS: We were walking around with this dude going like, "So, did you have relatives who…?" And he said, "I think. I think." And we asked, "Did they ever tell you about it?" "In school they teach and we'd learn but no talk. They teach." He was basically trying to communicate that — you imagine that in Germany they must sit around and go like, "God, we feel like such assholes" — but they put the past in the past, and try to move on. And every time an American arrives over there we're like, "Let's dredge up your horror."

SM: "You guys are fucked up! Why did you do that? God damn you're fucked up!"

KS: It was pretty sobering. Then we went back and did the Q&A and I was still able to be witty and whatnot. I just didn't really address like, "Hey, I just got back from Dachau and boy am I fucking tired!" The other thing we did in Munich was that Johnson had a camera, and apparently in Europe people just like to lay out naked.

SM: Yeah. There's a river that went through Munich and so it's hot and it was summer so there's lots of… I do remember, that like three fucking thirteen-

year-olds, we fucking scrambled up the rocks of the beach—
KS: To look at naked *fräuleins*, and took pictures too.
SM: Which ultimately means you're looking at boobs and you're looking at fucking dicks. Because inevitably you see a lot of skin and you just look over and sometimes it's a girl and sometimes it was a dude.
KS: Most times it was a dude. There was one chick who looked like she was a burn victim or something and that was kinda a turn-off, we were trying to see some naked boobs and be like, "I don't want to see *those* naked boobs." That was sobering, that was solemn as well. Kinda like going to Dachau. But it was just a horrible fucking trip to be crammed into that tiny hotel room. Fucking three of us, I remember we were so bored one night that me and Johnson started throwing glasses out the window.
SM: I remember that.
KS: We were on the sixth floor and just started whipping glasses out of the window.
SM: I'd been out and I think I came back and you guys are giggling.
KS: You're like, "What have you guys been doing?" "We've been whipping glasses out into the back alley and they've been breaking." And you're like, "Yeah, I've just fucked some German broad." And we're like, "Oh well, not all of us are that lucky." That was a weird era, that whole '94-'95. It's going back over a decade now. I was living at the Universal Hilton [in L.A.], both of us were. First we were staying at Jim Jacks' when we were doing the post-production, then he finally got tired of us and moved us up to the Universal Hilton.
SM: Yeah.
KS: The one that looks like a lot of glass. I started going out with Joey [Lauren Adams] at that point and so I was living there and dating her until we were done with the movie, and then I would go back home. Such a weird… really a lifetime ago. Since then I've got married, had a child, I never go back there, unless there's some kinda speaking gig. I stayed there once in 2001 when we came out to do *Jay and Silent Bob Strike Back*, before I moved into the rental house, we stayed there one night. But doesn't it seem like such a long time ago now at this point?
SM: It does seem like a long time ago.
KS: Is there shit that will bring you right back to it? Like whenever I hear 'Kissed by a Rose', the Seal song, which was in *Batman Forever* which was out

that summer, that immediately takes me back to that place. Not in a sentimental, I miss it, kinda of way, but it'll just take me back to that time and place, that headspace where I was then. Because you've got to remember it's a period before *Mallrats* came out and the studio was like, "This movie is going to make a lot of money, this movie—"

SM: "This is going to be *huge*."

KS: "We're going to be fucking rich, we're going to be famous, we're gonna be…" And then the movie comes out and then fucking nothing.

SM: "We're not rich, we're not famous."

KS: We weren't rich or famous.

SM: I remember that was the year that *Braveheart* came out.

KS: Was it? '95?

SM: I just remember Dave and I, you were with Joey, and Dave and I were for some reason at the hotel and we walked up to City Walk and saw *Braveheart*.

KS: Was a lot of City Walk-ing in those days.

SM: Yeah, 'cause it was very close by.

KS: Do you ever miss that period? Because now you're an old man, you've been doing film for like thirteen years at this point.

SM: I am.

KS: Do you ever miss the days of wide-eyed wonder: "I can't believe this is what we get to do for a living!" Because now we acclimate so quickly that it's, "Now this is what I do." And after you've been doing it for ten years, in our case thirteen, it's just like, "This is what I do for a living." And you still appreciate it but you're not like, "I can't believe this is happening to me!"

SM: Yeah.

KS: Because it's like, "Well, you better believe it, because it's been going on for a while." Do you ever miss that?

SM: Not really. Nah. The bridge between being that way and then where I feel I've arrived at now — not that it's not exciting — but that I like feeling acclimated to it, I like feeling that this is what I do, and I feel more comfortable with what I do, and more confident with what I do, so I don't know, I don't really—

KS: You don't live in the past?

SM: No. Not at all.

KS: You're a real today guy. Not even a forward-looker, just—

SM: I'm really bad about anything from the past, any box of shit, you're like, "Hey, it's a box of shit from ten years ago!" I'm just like, "Uh."
KS: Oh, to me it's treasure. "What would be in this box? Holy shit, look at this!" I still have all my notes from high school and shit.
SM: I think my mom has a box of shit at her house that she's always like, "What do you want to do with it?" And I'm like, "Ah, nothing."
KS: You're not even remotely interested in delving into it and finding the young Scott Mosier contained therein?
SM: Mostly it's sports trophies, and she has my Varsity Letterman jacket and I'm always like…
KS: Wear it bitch! That'd be hot if you walked around in your Varsity Letter jacket. People would be like, [enthusiastic] "What's that all about?"
SM: And I'd be like, "Meh, I went to high school."

From SModcast 12: A Fat Kenickie
Kevin's high school theater experience

KS: When I was in high school, what shows was I in? Well, when I was in grade school, 8th grade we did *A Man for All Seasons,* kinda bashed through a shortened version of it. I played Cromwell. That's not musical, that's just straight drama. Freshman year I was in *Damn Yankees,* I played Rocky and we sang 'The Game', a song about fucking but you don't say fucking, but it's all using baseball metaphors to describe the act of fucking, and just when you're about to fuck you can't do it because you've got to keep your head in the game. *Damn Yankees* is the show where 'You've Got to Have Heart' came from, [starts to sing]…
SM: Yeah, yeah.
KS: That's probably the most famous number from that show. But there's a song that the baseball team, the players, sing, that's called 'The Game' where they talk about how they're about to fucking get laid but then [singing] "They thought about the game…" And they couldn't do it because essentially you've got to hold onto your Chi for the game.
SM: Thought so.
KS: But considering that the play was done in the late '50s, early '60s, or something like that, it's pretty risqué.

SM: Talking about holding your nut.
KS: Exactly, it's pretty much about just don't fucking—
SM: [singing] "Hold your nut."
KS: Yeah, today it's a bit more blatant. If I were to do the musical it would be like, [singing] "You can't cum in her mouth until the game is over," you know. And people don't like to see that, they like their shit a little more subtle, they like inferences. Sophomore year in high school me and Ernie O'Donnell and Mike Belicose were big kings of the stage, which could get you laid back in those days. We didn't have a football team at our school.
SM: Got ya.
KS: The biggest sport was basketball, they had a baseball team of course, cross-country was real big. But no football, so you didn't have any 300-pound muscle-heads going, "Fucking drama-fag!" and putting you into a locker or something like that. It was actually kinda cool to be in the play.
SM: Nice.
KS: And so the next year I think we got a little full of ourselves, because we had kinda small roles in *Damn Yankees* that we character-ed it up a little bit. Ernie did the Billy Crystal 'Old Jewish Man' character, like, "Give me a C, a bouncy C" from *Saturday Night Live* circa '86 or '87, no '82, '83. I just did a kinda Bronx accent and really hammed it up and whatnot. So the next year we were like, "We'll be the fucking *stars* of the shit." Then there was this woman, this teacher Mrs Crowley who was very pear-shaped, very, very big thighs — and that's coming from a dude with big thighs himself — who took over the show, and was very mean. She didn't really appreciate our sense of humor. We were mounting *Our Town*. When you're doing the high school show you want to do a musical because they're kinda fun. *Our Town* is such a sober, somber piece about life and death in a small town, a New England town, with ghosts. There are no sets, basically the stage manager is the narrator, but is called the stage manager, and he comes out and describes the whole set, it's almost like a Beckett play, there's nothing up there.
SM: Yeah, yeah.
KS: But it's a Thornton Wilder play. It's very Spartan in its approach. At one point people die in it and they go sit in these upright chairs representing the graves and it's just not… wonderful piece but—
SM: It's not a song about [singing] "I almost came, but I gotta do the game!"
KS: There's no holding-your-nut songs. It was a real drop off for me in

sophomore year. Ernie and Mike as well. Not Mike so much, because Mike couldn't care less. But me and Ernie were like, "Really? This? There's nothing fun about this, you can't make it fun." You can't make *Our Town* funny. You can't get in there—

SM: You could try.

KS: Like moxie it up with an old Jewish accent and people be like, "What? It's New England, what are you talking about?" So I remember Ernie got a smaller part and he was outraged by it. I got a big part, the stage manager, the narrator part, and you narrate the whole fucking show. You don't interact with the other actors, you're just the guy that stands there.

SM: With the audience?

KS: "This is Grover's Corner" or whatever, going through the list and shit. But in solidarity with Ernie, who really hated Mrs Crowley and didn't like the fact that he didn't get a big part, I dropped out of the show.

SM: Wow.

KS: And the rumor at that point was that Mrs Crowley, this was going to be her last year at school so she wasn't going to do the show next year. So we were shoving that in their face going like, "You ain't gonna be here next year so fuck it man, we're dropping out."

SM: "Boycotting this year."

KS: Boycotting the show, won't matter next year, we'll have killer parts. But Mrs Crowley hung out and did the show the next year. So Ernie wouldn't even audition because he's like, "Fuck it, she's never going to give us parts." But I'm like, "Well, maybe we should forgive and forget." And I went up for it, because well what else did I have? I ain't playing fucking sports, I have the fucking stage and that's it.

SM: You were the king.

KS: I was the king of the Hudson Theater scene. So the show they were doing was *You're A Good Man Charlie Brown*. Now *You're A Good Man Charlie Brown* is a *Peanuts* show, it's all about the *Peanuts*. It's a musical about the *Peanuts*. You've got your Charlie Brown, Sally, Linus, Lucy, Schroeder, and those are the big parts, that's really it. Snoopy of course. And Snoopy's big number is 'Suppertime'. But six parts essentially. Parts were given in order of class hierarchy, if you were a senior you were getting better parts, and if you were fucking freshman/sophomore, supporting roles. So there was only one senior that year and it was this dude John Manigrasso, who was another big star of the Hudson Theater stage.

SM: Got ya.

KS: Really talented dude. He wound up naturally playing the part of Charlie Brown. That leaves me, and I wasn't even gunning for Charlie Brown, and nor was I gunning for Snoopy, I was looking for Schroeder.

SM: Schroeder.

KS: 'Cause I thought Schroeder had a pretty cool part, and I figured I couldn't aim high because Mrs Crowley was going to be like, "Fuck you, I'm not casting you as Snoopy. Who ever heard of a fat Snoopy? You could be Garfield. If we were doing a Garfield show you'd sit there and talk about how much you fucking love lasagna." So I went for Schroeder. I was dating Kim Walker at the time, I figured she'd get Sally and she wound up getting Lucy, which is kinda the female lead. I wound up getting cast in the chorus. This show doesn't even have a chorus.

SM: They created a chorus?

KS: They created a chorus just to fucking… she stuck me in a chorus, like a chorus of one, where essentially I would join the cast and sing full numbers when the whole cast was singing. Other than that, I wasn't allowed to fucking go out there.

SM: Were you in a costume?

KS: Nah, you wear pretty primary stuff. Charlie Brown wore the zigzag shirt of course.

SM: They didn't even bother trying to make you one of the other random

looking characters?

KS: Dude, I was like, "Make me fucking Franklin! I'll put on some black face, I'll do some Franklin!" And that was met with disapproval. I didn't mean it in a racist way but I was like, "Let's stay true to the comics."

SM: That's why you weren't—

SM: Yeah, I might have fucking busted my chances a little bit. But I was like, "Give me Pig-Pen, I'll filthy it up and shit." See that would have been the ideal role for me. Pig-Pen who wasn't physically dirty but just came out and was like, "Look at my dick," and said dirty things, so like staying in the spirit but deviating. Mrs Crowley didn't want to deviate. She wanted to stick with the text. So this chick, I forget her name, she was like a freshman, she wound up getting the role of Snoopy, the plum part in the show. It was a real kinda like, "Fuck you. I'm not even going to cast you as Snoopy, you're as low as a junior at this point. You've got one more year to do a show, next year is your senior year. And then presumably you're done with shows for the rest of your fucking life, because you're not going to go anywhere because you're from Highlands." There was that kinda tone, approach to it. She cast me as chorus, gave a fucking freshman the part of Snoopy. I was flabbergasted. But I stuck with it. Ernie was like, "Fuck her man, just quit the show. We did it last year." I'm like, "Nah, I'm going to stick with it." So I stuck with it and played a chorus member, you know. Not in an egotistical or blow-hardy way, but like… Come on dude — did you ever hear of the chick who played Snoopy in the Henry Hudson 1987 production of *You're A Good Man Charlie Brown*? Fuck no!

SM: Well I did, just now. That's about it.

KS: But she didn't really go on to light the world on fire. I fucking made a few pictures and shit.

SM: Well, at that point you were just a guy who crossed Mrs Crowley.

KS: Pretty much.

SM: Who bailed on her *Our Town*.

KS: I've got to give it up to her, she was a real, it took her a year, but she got payback. Because I quit *Our Town* two weeks from the fucking show.

SM: She must have been pissed. Because she gave you what she thought would be like the—

KS: The fuck you part.

SM: No, in *Our Town*.

KS: Oh, she gave me the plum part in *Our Town*, totally.
SM: She's like, "I believe in you." And then you're just, "Fuck this!"
KS: Yeah and I was like my boy Ernie, because Ernie didn't get a part.
SM: Got to play the fishmonger.
KS: Yeah, I hitched my wagon to the wrong star in that case. And then the chick who I'd wind up dating later in the year, Kim Walker, she wound up taking the stage manager part. And in *You're A Good Man Charlie Brown* she wound up being Lucy. She got a big number to sing and whatnot.
SM: So you stuck with the chorus part?
KS: Stuck with the chorus part, and there was this one unifying moment as there is so often in theater. You know what, I was wrong. Kim did not play Lucy, she played Sally. This chick Danielle played Lucy. Danielle Chevelier. She was good too, she played it real blousy and big-mouthed and shit, the way Lucy is. But as a chorus member you're also a fucking stagehand, so you're moving the doghouse in and out, whenever Snoopy's not on, they move the doghouse off. Other shit gets moved out. So we're moving the doghouse from stage to backstage and to be fair everybody on the cast helps move shit when the curtain closes and the lights go dark; we help move shit because we didn't have a lot of stagehands. Danielle Chevelier is fucking holding up her end, there are four people moving the doghouse, it's pretty heavy. We put it down and "bam!" glass on her finger, lacerates, cuts that shit open and she's bleeding. And you're talking about a high school sophomore girl who sees blood, fucking "Waaah!" And went screaming from the backstage area immediately to the bathroom. Wise choice. But crying, panicked. And she's supposed to do the scene.
SM: What do you do?
KS: What the fuck happens? What do you do? So I went out and just improvised. Snoopy's onstage at this point and Snoopy's waiting for Lucy, to have the scene with Lucy. Charlie Brown is onstage too. So I go out and grab a clipboard and I'm like, "I'm looking for a Snappy." And they're like, "Err, Snappy? We don't have a Snappy. We have a Snoopy. Who are you?" I'm like, "I'm the Dogcatcher." And we just riff a fucking two, three-minute interlude.
SM: Waiting for?
KS: Yeah, just cracking jokes, dog jokes and shit like that. But it was the only time I got some fucking play in *You're A Good Man Charlie Brown*. Didn't get any credit for it. It wasn't like Mrs Crowley was like, "Good job."

SM: "You saved us."

KS: Yeah.

SM: Did you just do it, or was there a moment of, "Someone's got to do something!"

KS: It was, and being that it was a high school musical we were all like, "Someone's got to do something!" Like in a very affectedly gay voice. Once she left and she's supposed to be onstage, I'm like, "What are we going to do?" I mean you don't want to stop the show, it's not like she lost a finger.

SM: The show must go on.

KS: That's what they say. Our motto at the Hudson Repertory Players was "The show must go on." So I just kinda, quick thinking, ran out. There was a part of me that was just like, "Here's my fucking chance!"

SM: Yeah.

KS: Mrs Crowley looked at me like I'd dropped the doghouse on Danielle's finger on purpose. In a real *All About Eve* kinda way. So I could go out there and steal the show and whatnot. But I didn't, it just happened and I just went up there.

SM: And then she re-entered the show as Lucy with a band-aid?

KS: Yeah, she came back with a really good ad-lib, if you know the show, where she's like, "What is everyone standing around for? What, is it suppertime?" And 'Suppertime' is the big Snoopy number. So the audience was like, "Aahh!" They all applauded. Then the show went on as normal. But I took that chorus part and did the grind, 'cause I'm like, "Crowley is going to stick around, senior year she's going to be in charge of the play so—"

SM: You wanted to make up for your indiscretion.

KS: Yeah, make up for my rebellion so I can get a good part. Senior year Crowley doesn't do the show, Mr Rogers does the show so it didn't matter, I didn't have to fucking *mea culpa mea culpa*, didn't have to go through purgatory and shit. We did *Grease*, Ernie got to play Kenickie. So Ernie got to say "fuck you" to the stage twice and still got to play the lead senior year. He got to play Danny Zuko, I'm sorry. Then I got the role of Kenickie. Jeff Conaway in the movie. But in the show, in the play, Kenickie gets to sing 'Greased Lightning'. In the movie John Travolta as Danny Zuko sang 'Greased Lightning'. In the play, the stage version, Kenickie sings it. So imagine me, the most heavy-set Kenickie that ever tread the boards, in a leather coat that barely covers my fucking gut, wearing a white t-shirt, which sometimes the coat would come off and I'd got a pack of cigarettes rolled in my white t-shirt sleeve and you see stretch-marks down my… just the most unsightly Kenickie that ever took the fucking stage. Having to get up there and do 'Greased Lightning' and do it justice, because that is the number that everybody knows from *Grease*. They know 'Summer Loving' but they know 'Greased Lightning'. Ernie was pissed he didn't get to sing 'Greased Lightning', but he made up for it as he got to dance and shake his booty and shit in that number. And I didn't. I mean I fucking shake my booty when I fucking take a step, I can't help but shake the booty, the flab just keeps going. But it was a weird experience having to be the dude who sings the big number.

SM: The big showstopper.

KS: And being aesthetically not what people are used to seeing. Nobody wants to see a fat Kenickie.

From SModcast 13: SFodcast (or SWodcast)
Walt's flea market story

KS: We were talking about what's hot and what's not at a flea market these days. The thing that everybody's selling is VHSs.

WF: I think hot is the wrong term, they're just bountiful at flea markets at this point in time.

KS: And going into that day shopping yesterday you could not have imagined that you would have wanted to purchase a VHS. What on earth could make you buy a VHS? Nothing.

WF: I don't think there was anything that I would say, "Oh my god, I need that VHS!"

KS: Cut to, we're walking down one of the aisles and there's this seventy-five year-old woman running a table. The way this place is set up is it's indoor and outdoor, it's like a big parking lot.

WF: A big football field.

KS: A big football field, yeah, way bigger than a parking lot, but it's all dirt. And they have these round cement bases that they just throw picnic table-tops on top of, and you rent that space for like ten bucks a day or something.

I think that's the figure that somebody quoted at us yesterday. And you just bring shit there to sell. And when I say shit I mean shit, like the fucking mishmash of product on any given table, there's almost no theme. Every once in a while here's a dude selling all DVDs or here's a dude selling all tube-socks but generally it's just like—

WF: Crap.

KS: Oh my god, it's like here's a little food scale that looks like we rescued it from the Nor'easter of '92, it's rusty and wet and it's going for seventy-five cents. Right next to it is a doll missing an arm. Right next to it is—

WF: A computer from 1982.

KS: It is! It's just insane man. It's like somebody's garage sale, somebody who goes to garage sales and when the garage sale is done and the people are like, "This will never sell, let's just throw it out," these people collect it all and bring it to the flea market to sell. It's insane the kinda shit that you can buy there. We're walking past the table, this seventy-five year-old woman has her truck behind her, she has an array of shit on the table, just crap where you're like, "This will never sell, nobody's ever going to buy this. You're living in hope and dying in despair. There will never be a consumer for any of this." There are five videotapes on the table. That's it.

WF: In a Tupperware bin.

KS: Just a complete after-thought, but fucking one of the tapes, which attracts Flanagan like a magnet, is a New Jersey Devils—

WF: It's a New Jersey Devils tenth anniversary history.

KS: A look-back.

WF: Yeah, a look-back on the first ten years of the New Jersey Devils.

KS: And you'd never seen it before?

WF: Never, and I'm a big Devils fan, I collect a lot of Devils paraphernalia and I have never ever seen this tape before.

KS: So that's a Christmas-like moment. That's why people go to flea markets, to find that thing that they didn't know they were looking for, that ultimate treasure. So it stands to reason with all video tapes being cheap at this point that it's going to be relatively inexpensive, but whatever the price is going to be, Flanagan will probably pay it because he's never seen this tape and wants this tape and he can add it to his Devils collection. So we ask the lady, "How much for the Devils tape?" And she says, "Two bucks." And Walter goes, and I won't even try to lay inflection on it if it wasn't there, Walter goes, "I'll give you fifty cents." And the woman, it looked like Walter was like, "I'm going to drop my balls in your mouth. How about that? That's my offer. My offer is this, nothing but a fucking tea-bag." She went like *white*, she aged two years right in front of us. It was immediately like, "Fifty cents? You're crazy!"

WF: I didn't even know what I'd said...

KS: I remember, you were like, "Come on, fifty cents! Nobody's gonna buy this."

WF: Yes, that's what I said.

KS: You were like, "Fifty cents," and she was like, "You're so rude, that's so rude." And Walter's holding the tape and he's gone, "Alright, seventy-five cents?" And then she puts her hand on the tape and says, "I'm not selling it to you." And starts a tug-of-war with Walter.

WF: She starts a tug-of-war and I'm like, "OK, I'm sorry. I'll give you five dollars."

KS: It wasn't even "I'm sorry" yet.

WF: Didn't I apologize?

KS: Not yet. You got there. But at first you thought she was kidding around.

WF: Yeah, I thought she had recognized you, and was doing a little something.

KS: Auditioning?

WF: Well not auditioning, but I thought she was just playing a gag.

KS: And me as the eyewitness. I'm like, "This lady is seriously mad. She might have a stroke she's so fucking pissed." I'd never seen anything like it in terms of watching the elderly get angry, except maybe in a movie or something like that. If you ever saw *Marathon Man*, at the beginning there's an old Jewish guy who's pissed off because he recognizes a dude who probably worked at a Nazi death camp, and he starts chasing him down the street.

WF: I remember that one.

KS: It was crazy man. She goes, "I'm not selling that to you," and she starts tugging away. Walter won't let it go. So at this point he's pretty much involved in a tug-of-war, almost a fucking shoving match, with a seventy-five year-old woman. And then Walter caves and goes, "Ah OK, I'll give you

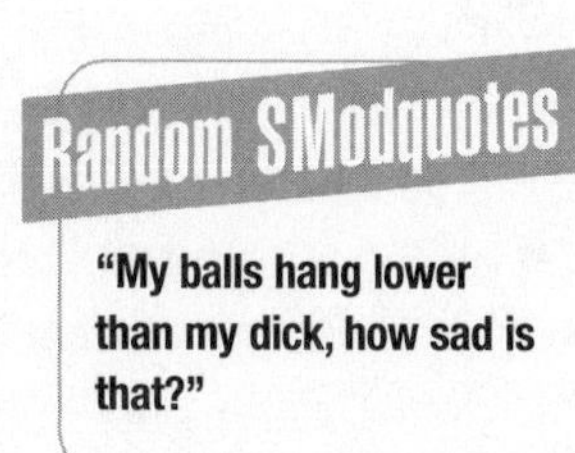
Random SModquotes
"My balls hang lower than my dick, how sad is that?"

the two dollars for it." She goes, "I'm not selling it to you," yanks it out of his hand, thus proving she's stronger than Walt, takes two steps back towards where her truck is, opens the car door, hurls the tape in, slams the door and stalks two feet away, turning her back on us. "I'm not selling it to you, you're crazy," she's going. That's when you suddenly go to five bucks with it. So suddenly at this point you're willing to pay 150 percent more than the original asking price just because you tried to haggle her down to the most insulting fucking price you could have offered.

WF: When I realized she was serious I was getting angry because I didn't think I was in the wrong. When you go to a flea market you play the game, you do not pay what they tell you.

KS: Yes. Haggling is expected.

WF: That's the whole fun of it. Or else I'm just going to go to Sears or JC Penny.

KS: Where you would never find that tape.

WF: Or eBay. And I'll pay whatever. But that's the charm, the allure, in my opinion, of a flea market.

KS: She was not held-sway by that allure at all.

WF: No, and I felt she was wrong in not partaking in the expected banter between customer and seller.

KS: She wasn't playing. She wanted two dollars for it and was hell-bent on getting two dollars. So Walter then... and I'm standing there watching this whole thing and trying not to laugh, but inside smiling ear to ear because I'm like, "Classic." Walter then takes it into the completely unexpected arena of jumping from a five-dollar offer to a *fifty*-dollar offer for the tape. Walter goes, "I'll give you fifty dollars for it. How about that? Fifty dollars?" Now if this woman made fifty dollars in four months of that flea market I'd be shocked, if she told me, "I've made fifty bucks over four months." There's no way, at the prices she was selling, and the crap she was selling. That fifty dollars, that's what you *dream* about on the other side of that flea market table, that somebody's going to come along and purchase something for that much money. Or you're sat there going, "I hope I make fifty dollars today." That would be an amazing day at the flea market. Pay ten bucks for a table, walk away with forty bucks, that's awesome. Fifty dollars he offers her, and to her fucking credit — man, you had incensed her so much—

WF: She wouldn't budge.

KS: She wouldn't fucking budge.

WF: I was never going to pay her fifty bucks.

KS: "I know what you can do with your fifty dollars." And Walter goes, "What?" And she goes, "You put it in your pocket and get out of here. You're rude. You're crazy, just rude. That's rude, fifty dollars? I'll give you fifty cents…" And Walter is pleading at this point going, "Come on, fifty dollars. Fifty dollars for that tape!"

WF: I was apologizing.

KS: He was. I'm sitting there going, "He seriously wants to give her fifty dollars for this tape! This could be fantastic."

WF: But inside I was setting her up to be like, "OK, I'll get the tape out of the car," and I wanted her to break her moral high ground that she felt she was on, and then I was going to be, "You're out of your mind if you think I'm going to give you fifty dollars for this tape."

KS: You were going to add insult to injury! You already insulted her once but if she did cave and go, "Fine, give me the fifty dollars," you would've been like, "You stupid fucking whore! I would never pay fifty dollars for that tape!"

WF: I definitely would've been, "You're out of your mind if you think anybody's giving you fifty dollars for this, I'll give you a dollar."

KS: She stuck by her guns with integrity like you read about.

WF: In the end she definitely would not budge. She played me.

KS: She did. She had your number. Thankfully Malcolm saunters up like, "What the hell is going on here?" Malcolm had seen the escalation from a few tables down, and he saw the tug of war and he saw the ire on her face and the shock on Walter's face. So Malcolm tried the pre-emptive buy where he's like, "Well, sell it to me." She's like, "You're just going to give it to him." "Nah, I don't know these guys, I want it, sell it to me." And she's like, "Nope, nope, nope," and she left it in her car. Then she went to the car, we started leaving the tables and she went back to the car to grab the tape and put it on the table. And we walked two tables down just going, "Can you believe that?" Malcolm wound up buying it, but she wouldn't sell it for the original two dollar price, she wound up selling it for five. For that outrage she wound up making 150 percent profit on something that cost her nothing. I'm sure she didn't buy that tape herself because you even asked her, "Are you a Devils fan?" You approached it from the angle of like maybe there's a fellow fan here and I insulted her as a Devils fan. Walter goes, "Are you a Devils fan? Because I'm a Devils fan. If you're a big Devils fan and I offered you fifty cents and you didn't take it because you're a Devils fan and I've insulted you—"

WF: "I can understand that."

KS: Yeah, you were ready to back down there.

WF: I'd have deserved the tongue-lashing.

KS: She was like, "Meh," she didn't know who the Devils were. She didn't even know what a videotape was. She just knew that it was a fucking rectangle that she wanted two dollars for. So Malcolm winds up buying it for five bucks because she was like, "I know you're going to give it to him so I'm going to charge you five," and Malcolm wound up taking it. Did you watch the tape?

WF: I watched it last night.

KS: And?

WF: It wasn't worth five dollars.

KS: Was it worth the fifty cents originally offered?

WF: It definitely would have been worth fifty cents. It definitely would have been worth two dollars. Maybe the story was worth five dollars, but the actual tape was a one-time viewing only.

KS: What astounded me about the entire flea market process was, like you said, you go in expecting people to play the game. The idea is you go, "Here's the set price," "I'm gonna go way lower, you're going to go higher than that but lower than what you're asking, and we'll settle somewhere in the middle." That wasn't even the only time that day that somebody said no to a lower offer. Later on there was a pin, we walked past somebody's table, another fucking terrible diaspora mish-mash of fucking the worst crap that you could imagine... that dude actually had the food-scale which you picked up and I was like, "What the fuck!? What does he want that for? Why would he even be interested in it?" Did he think that it was something that it wasn't? Clearly it was a food-scale. I'm like, "If Walter wants a food-scale I'm going to buy him a brand new one, if he's going to start measuring out his food. But not on this rusty-assed, disease-ridden, germ-ridden thing." This dude had on the table four pins, like oversized pins that you stick on your jacket. One of them was "I like Ike," shit like that. But one of them — the odd one out of the bunch because three were political buttons — one was a giant "Where's the Beef?" pin.

WF: With the old lady's face.

KS: With Clara Peller, the chick who was the old lady [in the Wendy's commercial]. Immediately we were like, "We've got to get that and make Malcolm wear it." So Walter asks the dude, "How much for this?" and he goes, "I give you two for five dollars." Walter goes, "Well, I don't want two, I just want this pin," and the guy's like, "Three dollars," and Walter goes, "Ah, I'll give you a dollar," which was overpaying in and of itself, but he goes, "No, no. Is too popular, I couldn't take no dollar." I was crazed! I'm like, "Wouldn't you rather have gotten rid of that thing so you didn't have to pack it up in your sad little fucking flea market kit and lug it back to your garage for the next weekend where you're going to unpack it, lay it out there and watch it not sell again? Wouldn't you rather walk away with cash money, like a buck maybe, pay a couple of tolls on the fucking turnpike for that?"

WF: I would.

KS: You could pick up a bottle of soda, any number of things, but this dude wasn't letting it go, he wanted minimum three dollars for that pin. Like as if that pin had the cure for cancer, or a cure for a small dick, "Oh no this is worth something." Like, "To who buddy? How long has this been sitting here?" There was like this crappy framed collection of three elephants, I don't even know how to describe it but they were kinda in a window box thing, and I was like, "My kid loves elephants man, I wonder how much that is?" Walt says, "Do you want me to find out?" I said, "Yeah, I don't know." I was already thinking if I brought that home my wife would be like, "Where did *this* come from? This looks fucking filthy, this looks like it came from the pit of Hell." So Walter asked and I was like, "I'd give him five bucks for that," and Walter calls it that he's never going to let that go for five, that's easily ten bucks. You asked the dude and it was thirty! Thirty dollars and it's just like, "Dude!" We didn't even haggle with him, you can't talk sense to a man who's going to charge thirty dollars for that thing. He acted like it was a one-of-a-kind thing and in point of fact he was right, that probably doesn't exist anywhere else in the world any more because everyone threw theirs out years ago. They bought it at a fucking Caldor store back in '82, in the bad arts section next to the plumbing supplies, and long since destroyed. That may very well be the only one left in the world. But nobody's going to pay thirty bucks for that.

Random SModquotes

"Why the fuck would you give a kid gold, frankincense, and myrrh? Give the kid a bond."

WF: Not in Englishtown.

KS: Anywhere! The only place you'd get thirty bucks for that is if the world was wiped out by nuclear war and the next fucking beings that inhabited the planet or arrived on the Earth were archeologists and they fucking dug it out of the earth and were like, "This is a relic from an ancient past." Then maybe somebody would be like, "I'll give you thirty dollars for it." It was crazy how much. Nobody wanted to haggle. Everybody had gold and they wouldn't let it go for a little less.

WF: Your words cannot do justice to how much shit is on that field.

KS: It's crazy.

WF: It's crazy and wonderful all at the same time.

KS: That's the best part of it. It really is just like if you buy nothing, which is impossible, as we learned, because we were looking at the crap and there was talk of, "Will anybody buy anything?" And I was, "I can't see myself buying anything." I did wind up buying shit. Like I saw a set of car mats, *Simpsons* car mats circa '92 or '89-'92 when they were making lots of *Simpsons* paraphernalia, and the price on them was forty bucks, which is what someone had paid to buy them from Target or somewhere, and I was like, "I'd like these, these are kinda cool." Then I had a moral dilemma because my kid got me car mats that say "Daddy Man" on them, personalized car mats, for father's day two years ago and it would be a shitty move to suddenly replace them with *The Simpsons*. She'd be like, "Where are my car mats?" and I'd be like, "Well, I like Homer." But I was thinking, "I've got to find out," and my ceiling was ten bucks; if he'll give these to me for ten bucks then we'll do it. The forty-buck price tag on it was there from the store, not from it being in this dude's inventory, his fucking garage sale inventory for the last ten years. I was like, "No way," based on what had fucking been going on throughout the beginning of the day, so the dude comes over and I ask, "How much are these?" and he says, "Eight bucks." "Fucking sold!" I had to buy it, but was immediately filled with pious remorse as I walked away going, "Well you know Bryan is a big fan of *The Simpsons*, maybe I give them to Bryan? But then Bryan doesn't have a car, Bryan drives a motorcycle. OK, I know I'm going to face down the wife over this, "Where are the Daddy Man car mats?" "Oh, what? I'm just rotating, just changing them." I feel a fight coming on that one. But you can't walk out of there without buying something. Even if you could, even if you had the will power, let's say you went with no money so you couldn't make any purchases, it is worth the trip alone just to fucking see the collection of the bungled and the botched, the people that make up not just behind the counter but in front of the counter, the people who are selling and the people who are buying. Who are these fucking people? And haven't they heard of eBay?

WF: I can't agree more, it is so worth it. How long did it take us to cover it?

KS: [Explodes] Four Hours!! We were there for four hours! The first twenty minutes I was going, "I don't know how long we can keep doing this." In my mind driving here I was, "This is going to be wonderful," then I have twenty minutes and it's just a sea of crap and shit! There's nothing, it's like being lost in Highlands, the fucking rendering plant at the bottom of Miller Hill, where all the fucking shit was stored, all the sewage, it was like being trapped in that place where everywhere you look, you throw a rock, you hit shit. It's just nothing but shit, no gold. There was a dude who was selling comic books, selling coins, selling old money, old Deutsche Marks from World War Two—

WF: Hockey cards.

KS: Hockey cards, weird collection of bullshit. But he had a box of *Venom* comics, he'd pooled *Venom* comics because Venom's in *Spiderman 3*, so he had a box that was *Venom* comics. It said "*Venom*!!!" with three exclamation points after it, and the price was three for five dollars or one for two bucks.

WF: No it was three for five, that's what the deal was.

KS: So Walter goes through the box and finds a bunch of stuff because he can bring it back here for the store and throw 'em up on a wall or put 'em on eBay, because right now there's an interest in Venom so he can make a profit on them. So he grabs a pile of them.

WF: Forty-five dollars' worth.

KS: Spends ten minutes searching through them and picking out the choice ones, there's no rhyme or reason from my perspective. I'm watching him pick them out and I'm like, "Why that one over that one?" But he was going through it as if he was like, "... if I can connect these two chromosomes I'll have a new genome!" Some bizarre science that I couldn't understand. So he comes up with a collection that's forty-five dollars' worth, the dude counts it

out and Walter's "How much?" and the dude says—
WF: "Forty-five, I'll take forty."
KS: And Walter, in his inimitable fashion, goes, "Would you take thirty?"
WF: I didn't say, "I'll give you thirty," I said, "Would you take thirty?"
KS: Because the old lady was pissed about that, she referenced the fact that you told her what you were going to do, not "would you mind taking" or "can I offer you fifty cents" with "look, my daughter has leukemia and I need as much money as I can get, but I want this tape as well, it will put a smile on her face." She hated that you came at her with, "I'm going to give you fifty cents you old woman, and you're going to like it because you can buy a can of dog food and eat it! Because that's what the elderly eat!" That's what pissed her off. You were in the wrong on that one.
WF: I was in the wrong on that one. I think I did phrase that wrong. Like I said, I hadn't been there in two years and I think that I should have come at her with more of an offer.
KS: More honey, than vinegar. You catch more flies with honey than vinegar. You told her what she was going to be doing and she was, "I'm seventy-five and you're telling me nothing!" I'm sure that if she rolled up her sleeve she might have had a tattoo on her arm and be, "You're just like the Nazis, telling me what's going to happen!" So with this dude you take the approach of "Would you take thirty?"
WF: Right.
KS: Ten dollars less than the price that the dude quoted, which granted was five dollars less than what he could have charged, based on the price he put on the box. So he's already cutting you a break of five, but still, thirty bucks is thirty bucks. He had multiple copies of them, it's not like, "These are my only copies of eight or nine or ten Venom comics that I have, if you take them I'm done." He had multiple copies of each issue that Walter pulled out. Walter goes, "Will you take thirty?" and the guy goes, what was his terminology?
WF: "They're going too good right now, they're selling too well. I can't afford to let them go."
KS: [Incredulous] Nobody was around this guy! They're going too good to who? He meant that they're going too good right now if you buy them. It was insane. Walter is "Nah, forget it" and just bought three instead. The dude kept stating his case as you guys were exchanging cash, "Yeah, they're just

moving too well with the movie and whatnot, so…" I was *flabbergasted*, "Dude you're not going to make thirty bucks all day." Granted he was five bucks closer to the thirty bucks because you bought three comics. But thirty bucks cash and you don't have to lug this shit back home, that's a little less stock that you have to worry about somebody else knocking over, spilling shit on it. It's not like they take the best care of all the products there either. Those comic books were in pretty good condition, bagged and boarded, but Malcolm was on the hunt for records, and it looked like people had taken a piss on the records and put them out in the sun and then put them on the table and charged you.

WF: What about the astounding comment from one of the record vendors at the flea market that there's a high level of theft.

KS: That was awe-inspiring. I didn't know what to make of that. I don't know what I was more taken aback by, the fact that they revealed that there's high theft and that there's tonnes of shoplifting going on, not just shoplifting but fucking con-man artists coming into this joint, and the dude's relating tales of, "We'll have one kid come up to the counter and spill something while another kid takes shit," and I'm like, "What is this, the 1930s? This shit would be valuable to a kid who's like, 'Let's go play stickball!' What kid is going to want any of the crap you're fucking selling?" I bought a record there or something.

WF: The Muppets?

KS: A *Sesame Street* record. So I don't know if I'm more astounded by the tale of shoplifting, or the dude relating it looking like he'd had a tongue cut out in a Vietnamese prisoner camp. He looked like he'd been through the shit. Didn't have that fucking thousand-yard stare but looked just, "I'm a broken human being and the fucking Viet Cong stole my tongue." He was just [mumbles tongue-lessly], "Yes, there are a lot of thefts, people taking stuff."

WF: And the wife.

KS: And the wife would chime in! I didn't know who to look at more because she looked like she got hit by a fucking truck too. It's wonderful that these two people found each other, but it's also hellish that this is how they spend their weekends, sitting here worrying, guarding their shit from being stolen by people. Your heart goes out. Who's stealing this shit!?

WF: Exactly.

KS: If somebody's like, "This is treasure, I've got to get my hands on this by

any means necessary."
WF: But the lengths that he said that they would go through, the actual ruse, "They spill a soda and whilst we clean it up they steal something."
KS: "It's like something out of Dickens dude! I'm surrounded by Artful Dodgers and I have to guard my shit. You don't understand." But I didn't understand that until his fucking wife translated it. The whole time I'm staring at this dude's mouth going, "I'm pretty sure his tongue was cut out. Oh my god, this is horrible." It was mind-bending. At one point we finally got into the dire situation where there was this horrible life-size green, I don't know if it's a bunny or a dog—
WF: It was a dog.
KS: A dog, maybe one you would have won at the Boardwalk in '82 and it was over-stuffed at the Boardwalk and after fucking fifteen years—
WF: It had evaporated.
KS: All the stuffing had gone down to its fucking feet like it had phlebitis and it almost looked like a bunny costume, but really it was supposed to be a stuffed animal. So I go, "How much is that going to be?" and I said, "Malcolm, I dare you to go over and offer two bucks for it. If you can get that thing for two dollars, I'll give you twenty dollars." So Malcolm goes over and asks, "So how much for the giant dog?" And the lady's like, "It's five dollars. Five dollars and it's all yours," which is a reasonable price if it wasn't so fucking germy, disease-ridden and old.
WF: That's a big if.
KS: A massive if. So Malcolm says to the lady, "Would you take two?" And she goes—
WF: "Look how big it is!"
KS: Immediately. "Look how big it is!" It's like, "Lady, fucking fifty pounds of human waste is still human waste, you don't get more money on it, it's like being the tallest midget. Come on, it's diminishing returns." So Malcolm spills the beans and says, "My friend bet me twenty dollars that I couldn't get it for two," and she's like, "Oh, I'll sell it to you then. You gonna kick me back into your twenty dollars?" And he's "Yeah." But he didn't. Then Malcolm is walking around wearing this thing around him like he's Kraven the Hunter with the lion's fucking pelt around his neck for three aisles before Walter goes, "Man, that thing is just so old and germy and it's on your neck." I don't know if it was the power of suggestion or it took three aisles for the

mites and the fucking whatever was living in that thing to start soaking into Malcolm's neck, and Malcolm suddenly just ditches it on a spare table, one of the empty tables there, goes to the bathroom and washes his hands thoroughly and washes his neck. It was such an eye-opener, but it was so worth the trip.

WF: They're all like that, great entertainment.

KS: I told my wife about it, regaling her with the tales of the adventure I'd had: "You missed out!" And she couldn't get past the idea that I went to a flea market: "You hate old things." "No, but there was a time when I liked going to flea markets and shit," and I'm telling the stories and she's, "He fought a seventy-five year-old woman over a videotape!?" She did not see the allure in it at all.

From SModcast 14: On Guard For Thee
Malcolm's pinky betting fiasco

MI: I don't even know the name of the Canadian Prime Minister right now!

WF: What?!

KS: Get the fuck out of here dude! Come on, you're Canadian.

WF: How do you feel Canadian? You're like, "I feel so Canadian right now." How can a Canadian make the comment "I feel so Canadian" and yet not know who his leader is?

MI: [Embarrassed pause.]

KS: Caught, bitch, caught! You're like, "Ah, you guys. You're being judgmental."

WF: It's not Paul Martin?

MI: No it's not Paul Martin. If you give me a minute, I'm really over-tired.

WF: What, a minute to go over to the computer and fucking type it in?

KS: Can you imagine? Short of my daughter, you ask any American, "Who's the President of the United States?" they'll be able to tell you, whether they agree with his politics or not.

Random SModquotes

"It's just got to be an unpleasant experience because at the end of it, it culminates with somebody essentially dick sneezing into your mouth."

WF: Why do you think it is that you can't remember?
MI: I'm really over-tired and essentially—
KS: Oh man, if they'd just fucking freed me from a death camp and I was starving and I weighed eighty pounds, I was all bones and shit, and I'd been beaten and I thought I was going to die every day, and their first question was, "Who's the president of the United States?" I'd be like, "Is it still 2007?" If it was yes, then I'd be, "Then it's George W. Bush."
MI: This is really sad and depressing actually.
WF: I guess it really shows how influential or how important Canada's leaders are.
MI: That's exactly it. You know it actually is Paul Martin. I keep thinking of Mike Harris, and had a conversation with someone about Mike Harris in the past twenty-four hours. But it is Paul Martin. He was over there for the summit.
KS: You're sure?
MI: I'm absolutely 100 percent that it is Paul Martin.
KS: That was a showstopper to me. That boggled my mind. That is bizarre that you're just like, "Err, I'm not real sure who the PM is." You just came from Toronto two days ago!
WF: You don't vote?
MI: I vote in local politics. Carl Ray is our local Member.
WF: He's the mayor?
MI: No, he's the local Member of Parliament. So I do know the local politics, but I guess on a broader scale… if you asked me a few days ago I might have known. I know the tired thing isn't going to work with you, but I've slept four hours in the past three days.
KS: That is such bullshit dude.
WF: You've been up forty-four hours?
KS: And even if you'd been up forty-four hours, you're starting to lose details?
MI: Yeah.
KS: "I'm real hazy." "Malcolm, what gender are you?" "Err, give me a minute because I… Let me reach in my pants, I haven't slept in three days, I'm not quite sure."
MI: You get caught in a brain-fart because you don't want to say, "Oh yes, it's that guy," and then you fuck it up totally. But in that process—

KS: Malcolm, a brain-fart is, "Who is that dude who sat next to me in social studies," or, "Who taught civics in my junior year?" That's a brain-fart.
WF: "Who's the leader of the country I live in?"
KS: "My home and native land? I'm not quite sure. Let me get back to you because I'm just really sleepy." That is priceless dude. That is classic Malcolm Ingram right there.
MI: My parents would be so proud. I'm so happy I've been on this SModcast, I'm telling you.
KS: I'm sending this right to your mom, "You've got to school this motherfucker!" and she's like, "Oh, he'd be able to tell me where the nearest gay bar is I'm sure, but he can't tell me who the fucking PM is! You're an embarrassment Malcolm, an embarrassment to me as a mother and as a Canadian."
WF: Were you in Canada when Ottawa made it?
MI: I was in Canada, but I'm not a hockey fan.
WF: Is Toronto upset or happy that they're in?
MI: They'll take Toronto as their team. They'll root for Ottawa—
WF: As the Canadian team?
MI: Yes, as the Canadian team. Geographically they would also have rooted for Buffalo because the J-route is really close.
WF: They wouldn't root for Montreal?
MI: They would.
WF: I thought with Montreal it's very—
MI: There's competition and it's against, as you go further south I imagine the fans of the—
KS: You don't know what you're talking about do you? At this point now everything you say I call into question. You're like, "The more southern you get the more errr… I'm really tired! Please stop grilling me!" You're acting like we've got you like it's *Midnight Express* and we just pulled you off the tarmac with all the drugs and kept you up for hours asking you questions like, "Where did the drugs come from?" "I don't know! I don't remember!"
MI: It really feels exactly like that though. It's not a good feeling.
WF: We could get on our high horse and say we know the President and Vice-President, but if you were to get into the real nitty-gritty I probably wouldn't know.
KS: But that's fine. I've got no argument with that. You ask me, "Who's the

Secretary of Defense now?" I'd be like, "It was Rumsfeld but now he left and I don't know who took his post after that." But Jesus Christ, the President of the United States!? The equivalent is the PM of Canada. You *have* to know that, that's a no-brainer.

MI: I could tell you all the Prime Ministers when I was growing up. Pierre Trudeau and Brian Mulroney.

WF: Did they do great things?

MI: Yeah. Pierre Trudeau was a really great Prime Minister.

WF: So I guess Paul Martin has done *nothing*. He hasn't made any fucking difference.

MI: Paul Martin really hasn't. Chrétien was the last Prime Minister I can really remember.

KS: Who?

MI: Chrétien, Jean Chrétien. Those were really good Prime Ministers.

WF: How long has Paul Martin been Prime Minister?

MI: He's been Prime Minister probably about three years now. I can tell you George Bush, Condoleezza Rice, I could tell you the American side but you guys, would you have known the Canadian Prime Minister?

KS: No, but I'm not Canadian. So I can hit you with, "Well I know Pierre Trudeau was once and Brian Mulroney was once, I don't know who the current PM is," but I'm not expected to know. If I was well-read and kept up with current world affairs and didn't have my head up my own ass going, "What do Jay and Silent Bob do today?"… As a well educated person I guess I should know, but come on, it's not my back yard, it's not where I live, it's not my home and native land so I'm not supposed to know who the PM is. That's your job. I just have to know who the President of my country is.

MI: But is there a responsibility to know who the Prime Minister is?

WF: Who's the leader of Great Britain?

MI: Tony Blair.

WF: He knows Great Britain's but he doesn't know his own country!

MI: But I'll admit that Canada is incredibly ineffectual.

WF: Boring. He's a boring Prime Minister.

MI: He's a boring Prime Minister who really hasn't done that much.

WF: He has no real juice?

MI: No. Right now with Bush in power, Canada is cowering to America.

KS: You just took this to a political place... You're going to get back on that plane, land at fucking Pearson in Toronto and they're going to be like, "Oh, here he is. Doesn't even know who the PM is and then says he's doing a bad job, eh? Get back to the States Hollywood!" I hope your PM does an interview where he's like, "I saw [Malcolm's film] *Drawing Flies* and it sucked, it left no impression whatsoever." You're all over the place on this one man. "I saw a rod. No it wasn't a rod, it was a UFO."

MI: Never once did I say, "I saw a rod," it was a UFO.

WF: Has there ever been a female Prime Minister?

MI: No. [Pause.] Kim Campbell, there *was* a female Prime Minister.

KS: When was that?

MI: That would have been in the '90s. She wasn't Prime Minister for very long.

KS: Why not?

MI: She was a woman. Nah, hey—

WF: [Gasps.]

KS: Oh my god, dude. We've offended the entire country of Canada as well as women everywhere.

MI: That was a joke. There was a big smile on my face and I knew exactly what I was saying.

KS: They can't see the smile on SModcast sir. For all they know, based on the bullshit you've been slinging, this guy is a fucking ignorant hate-tank. Do you think any Canadians who listen to this will give you shit for that, serious anger, "What the fuck" patriotic "You're un-Canadian" or would they just raz you, "You fucking dumbass how do you not know who the PM is?"

MI: I think it's more of a stupid dope thing than actually a political thing. I hope anyway. Brain-farts man. Although I can't even say it's a brain-fart, right? It's ignorance I guess.

WF: In America if someone doesn't know who the President is you just think they're a mental fucking patient.

MI: But it does say a lot. In Canada the Prime Minister isn't on TV all the time, it's really different. Especially with Paul Martin, if that is his name. The only time you see Paul Martin is when he's kissing Bono's ass, that's basically the time that our Prime Minister will make the news.

WF: I am pretty sure that Paul Martin is not still the Prime Minister.

MI: No, he is absolutely 1000 percent the Prime Minister.

WF: Because I kinda remember that they didn't make the joke any more,

about Paul Martin's—
KS: So you know the name Paul Martin why?
WF: Because there is a Devils defenseman called Paul Martin on the team and they would always make the joke, "Not the Prime Minister but the player," and they stopped making the joke because Paul Martin wasn't the Prime Minister any more.
MI: Can I vindicate myself by saying that I'll cut off my little finger right now if it's not Paul Martin, I'm so sure that it's Paul Martin.
WF: We gotta have that on a fucking camera though.
MI: I am so sure that it's Paul Martin that I would cut off my finger. I don't know why I couldn't think of it.
WF: I remember them talking about it in the Devils telecast who the new Prime Minister was, and it wasn't Paul Martin.
MI: It *is* Paul Martin though.
WF: I'm just saying I don't think it is, but you're Canadian, you *know*.
MI: Well obviously I didn't know, but it absolutely is Paul Martin.
WF: Kevin is googling the Canadian Prime Minister right now!
KS: Do you have a knife on you? The Prime Minister of Canada is Stephen Harper, sir.
[Stunned silence.]
MI: I quit. I fucking quit. I quit.
WF: He was elected just in 2007, right?
MI: 2006 probably.
WF: 2006? I remember them talking about it on the Devils broadcast that they couldn't make that lame joke any more.
KS: You literally just hit the floor. You are just the king of "I'm gonna throw my balls out there and make the most insane statement, I'm so cocksure I will cut off an appendage if the PM is not Paul Martin! Who? Stephen Harper! My god! Oh, Jesus! Don't make me cut my little finger off! That's my jerk-off finger!"
MI: That's my thing, I tried to vindicate myself and I'm astounded. But the thing about it is that I can honestly say that… Oh god!
KS: But you seemed so sure after a certain point. "It is, it is Paul Martin. It is Paul Martin, it is." You talked yourself into believing that Paul Martin was the—
WF: It's like the equivalent of one of us maintaining that Clinton is still the President.

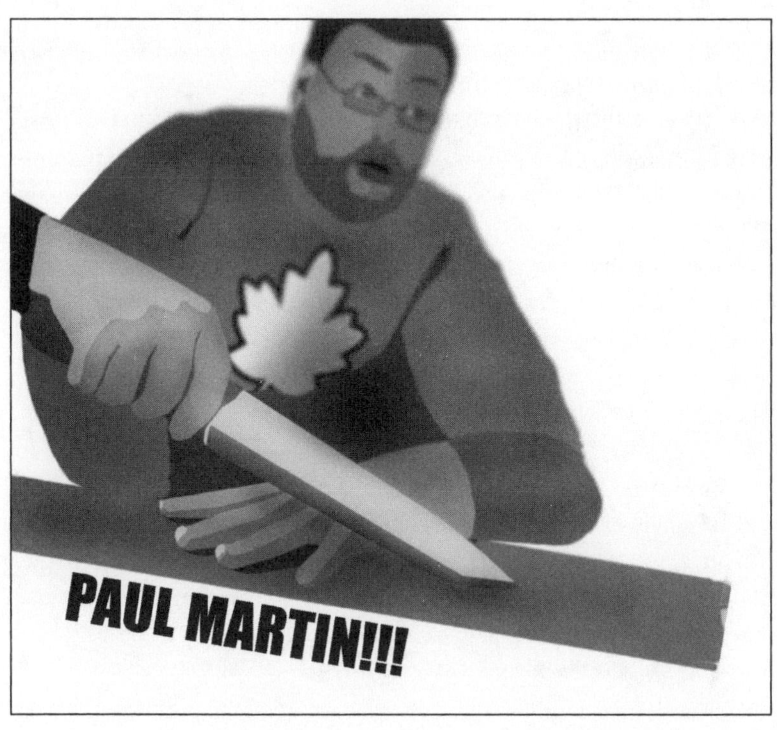

KS: “Nah, I’m serious. He took us to war. When he said we’re going to get Osama Bin Laden, it’s Clinton. It’s Clinton, Clinton, Clinton, Clinton.” “It’s Bush.” “Ah, Jesus! That’s right, it’s Bush. I’m sorry.”

MI: The thing about it is that Paul Martin I remembered from the G8 which happened very, very recently, it was last year. I guess that whilst I’ve been in the States we’ve elected a new Prime Minister and his name is Stephen Harper.

KS: Unless he was elected Friday night when you arrived it is inexcusable that you didn’t know the name of your PM, sir.

MI: I haven’t been in Canada all that much. To be fair, in the past six months, the past year and a half, I haven’t been in Canada all that much.

KS: So I go overseas to do a tour of duty in London for something, I’m still keeping up with who the President of the country is. Even if I’m not voting in the elections I’m like, “Who’s President? Right on. Good to know.” Because I’m from America.

MI: But ultimately, I'm going to get killed for this, not by you guys, American policy affects us a lot more than Canadian policy.
KS: I agree sir. That's why Walter and I don't know the PM of Canada is Stephen Harper, and that's why it's OK that we don't know. You're from Canada dude! There is no fucking excuse for why you don't know who the PM is. It's your country. You can throw out the whole, "Well, America sets the tone," and that's fine but you're from there dude.
MI: One thing that really shames me, and that means I need to be more proactive, is that one thing I do know about Stephen Harper, I do remember now, is that we just had the big AIDs summit in Toronto and Stephen Harper wouldn't come out and address, he was too busy. Bill Clinton was there, Bill Gates was there. It was a big conference and Stephen Harper claimed that he was too busy to come and show up for it, so it's fucking insane and so stupid that I couldn't remember his name. He does have some influence on things that are important.
KS: Why have you got to bring SModcast down? We were having a good time, razzing you, blasting your nuts about not knowing—
WF: That was a calculated move—
KS: Oh it really was.
WF: —to get you off his nuts!
KS: Oh, you're not as dumb as the guy you were ten minutes ago, the dude who didn't know who the PM was. "How do I get myself out of this hole? Oh, I'm going to introduce the human Holocaust. Well you know, because of AIDs a lot of people die and perhaps we shouldn't be laughing at simple things like me maybe not knowing who the PM is because AIDs is a much bigger issue." You're saying that the PM didn't go to an AIDs conference at all.
MI: No, he said he was too busy. There was a huge, huge fucking summit that was in Canada. It was last summer and he didn't show up.
KS: That must have been covered in the news, yes? To death, that would have to be the top story on the front page of *The Globe and Mail*.
WF: "Stands up AIDs community."
KS: Yeah, "Harper says 'Fuck You!'" That's a big story. Probably covered as first leading story on the news that night?
MI: The synapses obviously weren't firing, but when his name came up I was, "Oh shit, that's the guy!" And I remembered that at the time it made me

feel horrible to be Canadian that our Prime Minister wouldn't attend that. It was despicable.
WF: Hey, he dissed the AIDs community. You just dissed him on SModcast.
KS: I'd say you're even. I think it's funny how you're saying, "Look here, not knowing the PM is pretty bad but what he did is an egregious error that is unforgivable. He's the bad guy here! I shouldn't have to know his name, he's a fucking hate-tank! He hates people with AIDs so band together, let's all not know his name together!" Oh Malcolm, you're priceless.
MI: Hopefully there's a lesson we learned in this somehow. Hopefully through this horrible experience, maybe some Canadian out there is listening to this and starts to examine our political culture.
KS: And hopefully some Canadian out there listening to this will show up at your apartment door and beat your ass to a pulp. "You fucking un-Canadian, un-patriotic motherfucker, eh!?" [Makes sounds of Malcolm being beaten to a pulp.]
MI: This SModcast is ending with you saying you want to see me be physically mutilated?
KS: You want to go out on a high note instead?
MI: Anything but that. Are you inviting people to do physical damage to me now for this?
KS: No, I don't wish any harm on you, on anyone. No one should punch Malcolm. But if I see you and you've got a big welt on your face then I don't think I'll even have to ask, I'll assume that it was a fiercely, fiercely patriotic Canadian who thought that you just needed to be taught a lesson.

From SModcast 15: Pretty-Good Worker
The Helen Keller conversation

KS: We were talking about something last week at dinner which I thought was a pretty interesting topic, and we should revisit it here. My wife's been reading my kid these books — you know my wife's a real hardcore feminist and whatnot. And you know, mostly your history books are about dudes who did shit, but she found a series of graphic novels — illustrated stories, history stories — of female-driven stories. So, you've got your Eleanor Roosevelt, you've got your Molly Pitcher, and you've got your Helen Keller.

Random SModquotes

"You suck someone else's dick, technically, if you're a guy, technically, yes that's gay. You suck your own dick? Not gay. Just masturbation. Risky, chancy, not very tasty masturbation."

SM: Mm-hm.

KS: And we've joked about Helen Keller in *Clerks 2* and whatnot, but it wasn't until Jen was talking about the story of Helen Keller, having just read it to Harley like three times… 'cause the kid was like… you know, a kid can't get their head around the concept of deaf, dumb and blind. I know you're not supposed to say 'dumb' any more, you're supposed to say 'mute,' but when I was a kid they called it 'deaf, dumb and blind.' I was like, "Was the kid impressed by that story, the story of the miracle worker?" and Jen said, "No, the kid was more panicked about, 'How can I catch this? I don't wanna wake up deaf, dumb and blind, I don't want to fucking wake up and suddenly… you know, can I catch it from somebody at school, how does one transfer this?'" And we had to explain, normally it's a condition one's born with, or a physical defect or something like that, a birth defect. But the story of Helen Keller really sparked my imagination inasmuch as, I *cannot* fucking understand it at this point. And I've been criticized a few times for SModcast because I really kinda let my ignorant flag fly, 'cause I'm not very shy about being like, "I don't know shit about this subject, *you* tell me." And you generally seem to know a lot more about things than I do. So… the story of Helen Keller is this chick who's born deaf, dumb and blind, she can't hear, she can't see, and based on that she can't speak beyond that "euurh-urh" you know, that kinda thing. And Annie Sullivan comes along, the miracle worker, and finds a way to not only communicate with this kid, who they had written off as just like, "she's a monster."

SM: Wild, feral.

KS: Totally, almost an animal. And Annie Sullivan found a way to communicate with her, taught her sign language, gave her a language and taught her to communicate, and as we know Helen Keller went on to write things, she went on to meet Presidents and shit like that. But… the reason they call that story, the movie, *The Miracle Worker*, is because the fact that Annie Sullivan was able to accomplish that was nothing short of amazing, and the fact that Helen Keller was able to accomplish what she did was nothing short of amazing. Particularly that period of time, I'm sure now it's a lot different. I started thinking, "Do you think it was true? Do you think, maybe" — and I put this out there and got heat for it — I was like, "Maybe it was like a case of..." You know, they credit her with writing inspirational things and I think she maybe wrote a book, or, she did writing, Helen Keller did, later on, after she had her language skills and whatnot. And I was like, "Do you think it was really her, or do you think somebody just wrote the book and said like, 'No, Helen did this man, isn't it amazing?'" Like, was it a case of hype, or... I don't know enough about this subject, maybe I shouldn't be talking about it, but I'm always kinda interested in like, is it true? In a world where people manufacture hype all the time now, it would be tough to have anybody believe the story of *The Miracle Worker*, about, you know; this chick has no visual impetus, no aural — A-U-R-A-L, of the ear, impetus — and yet learned to speak, and learned to communicate. And you're born into a world with no visual or aural stimuli. How do you communicate with that person?

SM: How would you... I don't know. I've never read the writings of Helen Keller, so...

KS: But she's written stuff. You go to the Internet, and pull up quotes, famous quotations, and Helen Keller has said some pretty amazing things. I mean you've got a Mark Twain quote on your desktop computer screensaver. She's said quotes like that, where you're like, "that's fucking impressive" considering that, you know, everyone wrote this broad off as a coyote at one point. I can't get my head around it, and it makes me... of course, being that we live in a cynical age and I'm like, "Well, maybe it wasn't true."

SM: Maybe she just had bad vision.

KS: Or maybe no, maybe she didn't do any of the things that people said that she did, maybe she didn't learn to speak, she didn't learn to write, Annie Sullivan didn't really break through...

SM: They just kept her in her room.

KS: Yeah, they just told people, because that's the days pre-Internet, pre-TV News... they had printed news but you could just tell people shit and people would buy it. You could be like, "Hey man, this chick taught this deaf, dumb and blind chick to speak and now she can communicate."

SM: But didn't she go meet the President?

KS: I don't know, did she?

SM: I don't know, I'm like... You're a couple of strokes ahead of me...

KS: The kid's book.

SM: There's stuff going on…

KS: Well, it's not unheard of that a President of this country would, you know, lie. Or keep some sort of subterfuge going, or create subterfuge. I think it's naïve to be like, "Well, if she met a President, and the President vouched for it, it must be true."

SM: I'm saying that if she attended public events, like she went to meet the President, and obviously the whole point of her meeting the President is that it's something that would be covered in the press. Like, people were there, fucking Newsreel and shit.

KS: Totally, Newsreel, to put the word out there, because it's an inspiring story. But maybe they pulled the President aside ahead of time, and were like, "OK look…"

SM: "She'll probably bite you."

KS: Yeah — "Look, she's as feral as a fuckin' coyote, I swear to you, she's wild and she smells of poo. But just… let's keep this going."

SM: "Just squirt her with this water bottle."

KS: Yeah, "And keep it going. And in fact this isn't really Helen Keller, this is an actress pretending to be deaf, dumb and blind, but it's an inspiring story, and we want to inspire people to reach for better, reach for more, and prove themselves, or not give up on the handicapped," or something like that, so, you know, "Let's keep this thing going." And if you're the President, and somebody said that to you, would you be like, "Fuck that, I'm telling everybody that you're lying, you're lying about Helen Keller." You'd be like, "No, this is a good thing for the country, to think that something like this could be done, it makes the impossible seem achievable," and shit like that. I don't know… I'm not like, seriously sitting here doubting it, going, "This is all horseshit, you've all been lying about Helen Keller."

SM: Just proposing the idea…

KS: And I only propose this idea, or my incredulity about the subject, based on the fact that I just don't understand how you communicate with somebody who cannot hear or see. Like, how do you fucking explain 'elephant' to Helen Keller, without having an elephant there? If you had an elephant — 'cause she was very tactile — you took her to an elephant and you were like, making her feel it and shit, there's the trunk, and then you write the word, you sign the word 'elephant' in her hand — then she's got some basis, she's like, "OK, so an elephant is this… thing that's bigger than me…." I mean, that's the thing, she can't even in her mind go, "It is a thing," she doesn't have the word for thing, she had no language whatsoever, so, it boggles my mind. Like, how do you explain… Annie Sullivan had to give this woman, this Helen Keller chick, every piece of language she ever had. Like, you think about if you have a kid… to me it would have been akin to teaching Wolfie to fucking speak, by taking his paw and fucking… At least Wolfie would have the edge, inasmuch as Wolfie could see shit, and hear shit, and you could scream like, "ELEPHANT!" in his ear and he'd be like, "Alright, I get it, I get it." But like, it's… I just don't understand. It'd be like… I had a kid, I still have a kid, it was very easy to explain 'elephant' to her. I showed her a picture of an elephant, and then we were halfway there. And then I would say, "elephant," and she would say, "rehrenfent," and over time she got to the pronunciation, but she had a visual picture, an image. Helen Keller had no visual image or reference for any of the things, you can't explain… how do you give somebody a sentence, like, "The quick brown fox jumps over the lazy dog," when she doesn't know what any of those things are?

SM: Like we said the other night, you immediately jump to 'elephant', which is like the first thing, the miracle worker's like, "forget about the fork, forget about 'air'…"

KS: "'Water'."

SM: "'You', 'me'. Let's go to the elephant."

KS: If you've never seen one, and you can't hear a description of what an elephant is, how do you get your head around like, "There's this massive lumbering form on four legs, that has a big nose, and it eats peanuts, and you know… very big, big as a house, you know, friendly in disposition unless you get them pissed off and then they trample on you and people hunt them for their ivory…" It's like, all that information that I just fucking conveyed right there, you need reference points for everything. Including the articles, like just 'the', 'a', 'an', shit like that.

SM: Well, there's probably a lot of text about the case that would explain all this.

KS: [Laughs] I really should just turn to the fucking Wikipedia and read about it but I thought maybe you would have the answers.

SM: I mean, I think there's two things. One, the difference between Helen

Keller and Wolfie is probably that, as somebody who is like us, she probably had an intense desire to understand what was going on.

KS: Who, Helen Keller?

SM: Yes.

KS: How do you know that?

SM: Well, if it's true, and if you're not right that it's a vast conspiracy…

KS: You're just saying based on the fact that she was starved for any sort of stimuli besides like, "Here's food," they'd put food in front of her and she'd eat it, or pooing and peeing or whatever…

SM: Based on just being a human being.

KS: "I've gotta get out of this fucking box."

SM: Yeah, based on like, being a human being.

KS: But does she even know she's a human being? She has no basis for comparison.

SM: But I'm not saying that she's sitting there going, "I want to… I am a human being and I therefore don't understand," it's sort of like, you are *something*, with a mind.

KS: Right. But how does one feed that mind? If you can't see, and you can't hear. And it's not as if I'm saying, "I don't understand why blind people don't fucking kill themselves right now." Usually, you have one sense to rely on… visual or aural stimuli are very important. It's one thing to be able to feel shit, but you know, if you're deaf, you look at the world around you, and somebody could be like, "tree" and kinda write the word 'tree'. And if you're blind, people can tell you, "OK an elephant is this big gray thing…" Although you wouldn't say "gray", 'cause the blind person would be like, "Thanks, that helps." But it's like, "It's bigger than a dog, you know what a dog feels like, right? An elephant is like a thousand dogs put together, and it has a very long nose…" So you could talk to them. But somebody who has no means of receiving information beyond me taking the palm of their hand and pressing letters into it… They don't even know what letters are! I mean it just boggles my fucking mind! It leads me to believe — or not believe, but think…

SM: It's the moon landing.

KS: It's a fucking hoax! It's the moon landing! It's just like, it's a very inspiring story that perhaps led to the greater good. Like, now you can teach deaf children, or blind children, or deaf and blind children to communicate.

I mean, shit, they can teach gorillas to communicate with sign language. But they can see. Not blind gorillas, but you know…

SM: You can't get over the one… the inch at the beginning.

KS: Yes.

SM: Which is like, if she understood… I mean ultimately it's like, if you're blind, you're still not… you're taking all the information through…

KS: Through one other sense. Primarily one other sense, what you're hearing.

SM: Yes, exactly. And what you're feeling.

KS: I don't think that's an unfair assumption to make. I understand that, you know the tactile sense is very important. And I've said tactile three times now, that's the fourth. Being able to touch something, lay hands on it, is important.

SM: It gives you texture, and it can give you size, and make-up, and…

KS: But she doesn't even know what 'size' is, dude, she has no basis for comparison for size, because she doesn't know what the concept of 'small' or what the concept of 'big' is. Like, pre-Annie Sullivan you sit Helen Keller in front of a house, you might as well sit her in front of a dog house, she can't see it. I mean, you put her hand on it, but she's feeling wood, and then you put her hand on the house, and that feels like wood, too. Like, what's the diff? And she doesn't even know what wood is. It boggles my fucking mind. I can't believe I've gotten to like, age thirty-six, I'll be thirty-seven in a few months, and I still don't fucking… I've never really given it much thought. Because it's one of those things you just buy. Like, when you're a kid you're like, the story of Helen Keller, she was deaf, dumb and blind, and then Annie Sullivan came in and taught her how to read and communicate, and broke through somehow, and you're like, "Wow, that's fucking cool, man, that's great." And you just buy it, you never stop to think, "How the fuck was that possible, and did it really happen? And if it did happen, why the fuck didn't they make an even bigger deal of it than they did?" I understand they wrote a book about it, and she was celebrated…

SM: You weren't really around at that point.

KS: I wasn't, but that's something… we should have a Helen Keller Day, if it's true. And more than that, we should have an Annie Sullivan Day, because it's one thing to be the person trapped in a world without visual or aural stimuli, and learning to communicate somehow through rudimentary, or even evolved means… But to be the person that's like, "I'm gonna teach this person language."

SM: "I'm going to have the patience."

KS: "I'm going to have the patience," and who knows how long it fucking took, but to be able to take somebody's hand, and press your fingers into it, and give them an alphabet that they'd never had before. You know, it's one thing… I've watched the development… I was around for my own development, from a child to reading and math and shit like that, but I've been able to watch it with Harley, and it's always astounding to me, to be like, "One day this kid didn't read, and now this kid knows how to fucking read." Like, she sounds shit out, and… she can read anything at this point. You know, there are words of course that give her trouble, like I threw 'xylophone' at her and she's like [makes muted quizzical noise], and I'm like, "I'm smarter than you." But you know, generally she can get through anything. And so watching that was amazing. I cannot get my head around what it must have taken to give Helen Keller language skills. Communication skills. Did you ever think about it? I feel like I'm stoned. Like, it sounds like a conversation you have when you're stoned where you're like, "Helen Keller, you know, didn't know shit, and then, now she *knows* shit. Shit!" It just boggles my mind.

SM: I don't know enough… like I said, I have a hard time believing it's a hoax. I mean, to me…

KS: Do you think it was like in the least bit exaggerated, like perhaps she gave her very rudimentary communication skills but she's not really responsible for the quotes that are attributed to her or, you know…

SM: Well, once she had the ability to speak, she had the ability to think.

KS: She didn't speak, though.

SM: Well, to communicate. Once she was able to communicate, if she created those quotes… I mean look, she's a person that should be able to say it, she went through some fucking shit…

KS: Yeah, she could drop some wisdom on me. Helen Keller's the type of person, if you were ever feeling blue, you'd just spend thirty seconds with her and you're like, "Alright, I have perspective back."

SM: Yeah, "I didn't have it that hard."

KS: Right, "I guess my shit's pretty easy."

SM: But, deep down in my mind I still think that for all, you know, being

deaf, dumb and blind… it had to have been just the fact that somebody reached out to her and *tried* to communicate with her, must have engaged her mind.
KS: Right.
SM: Where it's like, nobody *ever* engaged her mind before. Now I'm making it up because I don't know, but I assume that *somebody* actually attempted to engage her mind. Where the rest of the people were just like, "Fucking Jesus."
KS: "Just put food in that hole and then clean the poop out of that hole."
SM: Yeah, "Wash her off, put her to bed." But somebody actually tried to engage her mind, and like, something has to kick in, something has to click in, where it's the desire to like… it's like a kid, it's like a baby. John Gordon has a baby, and I was over his house, and the kid's crying. And they say, "It wants to eat, it wants to sleep, it's, you know, pooped his diaper."
KS: The crying is something, it's a message. They don't just do it for the fuck of it.
SM: The crying is, with no form of communication, that's the one thing they can do, and they're doing it in order to be like, "I want you to pay attention to me, because I…" Well, sometimes they just cry, but that may be because they have an upset stomach, and they don't know anything to do, it's like you can't help them, but that's their form of communication. So even at that point, that baby, that three-month-old thing, it still has mind functions in that way, where it's trying to be understood. So it's like, in that capacity, here's a girl who is sort of in a state of arrested development, but is still craving that same thing, which is just like… could you imagine, you're trapped in this world, but you know there are people around? I know that she doesn't understand the concept of 'people'…

Random SModquotes
"The Magellan of unspeakable acts."

KS: Right.
SM: But her mind has to adapt certain things, it's like, "Somebody comes and takes me here." She doesn't have the language to say that, but it's like, you still…
KS: But she doesn't even have 'somebody'. She has no… what kinda thought process can you have when you don't have words and you don't have visual

stimulus? That is the thing that's puzzling to me…

SM: But the words are ultimately a way of describing what's happening.

KS: Sure, but you have to… you get a word-picture in your head. I say "butterfly," one of two things happens: you see a butterfly, or you see the word 'butterfly' in your head. But you get a picture, you get a mind-image. This chick had no mind-image whatsoever.

SM: But as a child, as a baby, if you liken it to that — the baby cries and something happens.

KS: Right, but a baby can see shit.

SM: But it doesn't matter if they can see it, it's just like, the baby cries and it gets the bottle, the baby cries and this happens. It's not like the baby's sitting there in his mind… what you do is, you keep putting everything into words, where it's like the baby's going, "If I cry, then blah blah." They don't know the word for 'cry', they don't know the word for 'bottle'.

KS: It's just instinctual.

SM: Yeah, they don't have any language. They're just trying to communicate.

KS: So, you're going on record as saying that Helen Keller is a big fat baby?

SM: She was.

KS: That's very disrespectful. Helen Keller achieved many, many things…

SM: Trying to push out your idea that it's all fake, and making me the bad guy.

KS: I mean, I'm really astounded and kinda insulted, we should end SModcast now. You don't make fun of Helen Keller. Helen Keller apparently lived with Annie Sullivan the rest of her life.

SM: I'd buy that.

KS: I mean, right? Like, who else could she talk to?

SM: Well, obviously they developed a way to communicate that was something specific to them, I'm sure somebody else could try to add sign language. But also, I'm sure that it's like… think about it, the bond that was established between those two must have been incredible, on both sides. Once again, to me, to have somebody step forward and actually try to engage you must have been… you know, why would it occur to you to be like, "Alright, I'm gonna move on."

KS: Yeah, totally. And if you're Annie Sullivan, you can't quit that job, because you're that person's only link to the world.

SM: 'Cause you've got to get to 'elephant'.

KS: Exactly. You're like, "One day I'm gonna fucking explain 'elephant' to this deaf, dumb and blind motherfucker, she's trying my patience." She must have gotten to 'elephant'. 'Cause we were trying to figure that out, the other night, and in a world where she's met Presidents, I'm sure they took her to the circus and let her feel an elephant and be like, "There's an elephant." Could you imagine how much of her time she spent feeling shit, and then having it spelled out in her hand? That is an amazing fucking life to me, a life that was written off, probably, originally, and her parents were like, "Jesus Christ, what are we gonna do? There's nothing *to* do." Like, you didn't know that she was blind or deaf for fucking years when she was a kid, 'cause they probably couldn't diagnose that thing early, and then when she figured out you're like, "What do we do?" You're talking about, like, I think it was the 1800s or something like that, maybe early 1900s…

SM: Probably 19…

KS: I guess maybe early 1900s. What, were they cavemen, or something? Like, this story was passed down from cave wall to cave wall? And, you know, you're just at a loss. It's not like, let's say you have a kid that's born physically challenged, can't walk or something like that, you're not like, "Alright, let's dash it on the rocks," or something, you're like, "We can still communicate with the kid, we can still nurture…"

SM: Well, at that point there had been blind people, people that had been blind, and I'm sure at that point…

KS: There must have been people that were born deaf and blind prior to Helen Keller.

SM: I'm sure that like, if you look at a majority, a lot of them were probably put in institutions and stuff like that. Because nobody…

KS: They didn't know what to do with them.

SM: Yeah. That's why the book isn't called *The… Pretty-Good Worker.*

KS: [Laughs.] That's classic. I remember, we were talking, we were having the same conversation with John Gordon at dinner, and John Gordon looked at me, like just fucking *aghast*, when I was just like, "Maybe it was all a hoax…" and shit, and he was just like, "What are you, a Holocaust denier?" And I was like, "No, dude, I don't deny the Holocaust, 'cause I can understand man's aggression toward man." I mean, I don't condone it, but I get it, I've seen fucking people hit people and I get aggression…

SM: And that happens all the time…

KS: Totally.

SM: You get genocide all over the place.

KS: That, and just how something steamrolls from like, "The Jews got more than we got, let's get rid of the Jews and take what they got." That's just fucking silly, stupid, evil human nature, greedy, wanton… I cannot, I have no way to wrap my head around somebody who is practically in a fucking Skinner box from day one, who suddenly develops language, and when I say "suddenly," who knows how long it took? I really should read that little comic book. Or perhaps branch out and read a novel about it, or you know, a text of some sort.

SM: If anybody needs to read that book…

KS: It must be me… It's so weird because until it was brought up, I just… you just buy that story. It's one of those stories that you're just like, "Yeah, I see no reason to disagree with this. I'm a child…" You're trusting, you're very naïve, so you don't know about how duplicitous people can be, or how people will spin something to be a bit more than it means, or what really was, history is all a sense of perspective, shit like that — so when they tell you George Washington was a good man who founded the United States, first President of the United States of America, you're like, "Right on, George Washington, good man." And then years later somebody's like [horror-filled whisper], "But he owned slaves." And, "He probably fucked around on his wife." You know, shit like that comes later. Helen Keller is one of those things where you're like, "Alright man, this deaf, dumb and blind chick learned to communicate and she had some…"

SM: [Whisper] "She owned slaves."

KS: Right, nobody told me that yet. Where they're like, "Helen Keller had slaves…"

SM: "Blind slaves…"

KS: She subjugated those, as she felt subjugated by… But, I just don't, for some reason it suddenly became tough to get my head around how that possibly could have happened.

SM: It's that initial stage of, once you accept the fact that she could be spoken to on her hand, then you're like — you get it, you're fine.

KS: And then don't you feel a degree of shame, 'cause the shit I do with my hand is so lame in comparison.

SM: You speak to your dick.

KS: I put my cock in it, exactly. It's like, I'm the miracle worker for my cock, you know, where I put my hand on my dick and I 'make things happen'. It's like a magic wand and I make a dick-sneeze into my Y-fronts...
SM: You explain to it what an elephant is.
KS: Totally. I'm like, "Check this out, this is an elephant. This is how an elephant jerks off." This chick like, through her hand, and through Annie Sullivan's hands, was able to open up a world that had not existed up until that point.
SM: But, she created... Helen Keller's world is still very... it's individual to her.
KS: Right.
SM: It never became what it is to you and me. It just didn't.
KS: Right, we're probably... we're way better than Helen Keller is what you're saying.
SM: Yeah.
KS: Fuck her, we got a lot going on. How come they don't write books about us? No, I get it, basically the spectrum of our experience is far greater than Helen Keller would ever know.
SM: Yeah. It's like she never, even with all that stuff, she never arrived to that place where it's like...
KS: She never made a movie with a donkey show in it, is what you're getting at.
SM: No, she never did that.
KS: So we got that over Helen Keller. I never met her and I don't know anybody that did, and her communication skills were rudimentary at best, but still amazing considering what her starting point was.
SM: Yeah. But... I'm not saying, "Hey, if you can't see, life really fucking sucks," I'm just saying that like, obviously, it still is different, it just has to be different.
KS: It's one thing if you can't see, but you can hear. And it's another thing if you can't hear, but you can see. You're hamstrung to a large degree but not fucking like, completely cut off from the world. I mean, thank god she had limbs and wasn't a Thalidomide baby, how would Annie Sullivan have communicated with this person?
SM: On her belly.
KS: And then people would have been like, "That's just creepy. Stop touching

her belly."

SM: To me it's still part of the human condition that it's just like, even with those two things against her, her brain was still functioning in the same way, as any child out there, like your kid now. They just want to understand, they want to engage in everything, they want to understand what this is and what that is, and while she can't process it the same way that we do, it's like, she still has a mind, and she's able to process, she's just going to process it in a different way. She can't process it like a blind person, she can't process like a deaf person, she has to process it through feel… but she still has a brain, she still has a mind.

KS: Do you think she probably never got laid, though, you imagine?

SM: Ah, you know, maybe. Maybe, maybe that was part of the…

KS: That's not part of the… they don't talk about that.

SM: That's not like a quote?

KS: It's not in the kids' book, I'll tell you that much. Like, on page thirty-five they're like, "Later in life, she got fucked hard."

SM: Helen Keller quote number 135: "Ohh, god, that was good."

KS: "It feels good in the ass."

SM: "I like the ass better."

KS: That must… that would be terrifying. You'd imagine that was probably shut down to her. I can't imagine Helen Keller ever had sex. At that point you're like, "Whatever, who needs sex." This woman learned to communicate, she learned…

SM: Once she'd learned about the elephant…

KS: Out of the chasm, the cone of silence, utter silence, and once she learned about the elephant, where do you go from there? But she must have had like, urges…

SM: Masturbated?

KS: She must have touched it. Probably. And then somebody has to explain that to her. Could you imagine the uncomfortable conversation with Annie Sullivan where she's printing in her hand…

SM: "Did you wash your hand?"

KS: She's like, "Which hand did you use, Helen?" And Annie Sullivan having to sign on her hand, "Well, that's natural, and you do it, and just don't tell me about it. I don't want to know about it, Helen."

SM: "Just don't do it in public."

KS: "You're thirty-five, would you fucking move out, get your own place, I'm trying to get something going here with a man!" I think Annie Sullivan got married, and actually had a husband, you know, it's like when you marry Annie Sullivan…

SM: You marry Helen Keller.

KS: You marry Helen Keller, to some degree. Easy to fuck round Helen Keller though, I'd imagine. It's not like they were like, "We gotta keep it quiet." They probably fucked right in front of her. Annie Sullivan could still be doing sign language on her hand while her husband's reaming her from behind…

SM: I'm sure that never happened.

KS: You know, they might have. People are weird. They might have been like, you know she's like, "What's your fantasy John, what did you ever want? Tell me something you've never done before you want to do," like a three-way or something like that. He's like, "I've always wanted to fuck you while you did sign language with Helen, right in front of her but she don't know about it." And Annie's like, "I've gotta get a divorce. You're a horrible human being."

SM: I don't know, I mean I also don't know the story, now I'm curious, I want to find out, maybe she did…

KS: SModcast opens up doors, is what I'm getting at.

SM: You just ask questions, though.

KS: We do, we pose questions and then you go out and find information… I can't imagine that it didn't spark anyone else's imagination the way it sparked mine recently. Where I'm just like, I never really thought about it, beyond what I was told. I just bought the story. And now I'm like… And this is weird, because I'm somebody who believes in God, there's more proof that Helen Keller accomplished the things that she did.

SM: That's pretty goofy.

KS: I'm sitting there going, "I don't know if Helen Keller really did learn to speak or communicate, but there *is* an invisible man, who lives up in the air, and [slips into Southern accent] he watches over us and he created squirrels and me 'n' you…" It's strange, I really do take a big leap of faith on God, but Helen Keller I'm like, "I don't know, where's the proof?"

SM: I haven't read it in detail either.

KS: Gotta find out more.

SM: I don't know whether or not she *ever* had sight, or hearing? I don't know the story.

KS: No. Again… there is a *children's* version of it in my house and I haven't taken the time to look at it — but the story I remember from grade school was: born deaf, dumb and blind. She didn't lose it, maybe it was one of those Rubella things like you saw on *Little House on the Prairie*, whatever, like how Laura Ingalls' sister Mary lost her sight, she could see, and then she went blind one day because she got Rubella or Scarlet Fever or some such shit. But I always heard that she, Helen Keller, was just born deaf, dumb and blind. It always takes me to... remember the video, the Metallica video? I forget which one it was… it wasn't 'Enter Sandman' it was uh… that song… But they used footage from the movie *Johnny Got His Gun*, where the dude — it's disturbing footage, I think it's like a World War Two movie or post-World War Two movie about a dude who gets his arms and legs blown off, he can't communicate any more, I don't even know if he can hear any more, he's just basically a head and a body and he has a cone on his face for some reason, he can't see, and they have this footage of him, and they inter-cut it with the dialog… it was such a twisted video, especially when juxtaposed against a Metallica song, but an even more twisted movie, I would imagine.

SM: I've never seen it.

KS: I never saw it either, but I mean I saw the footage in that video and I was just always like, what a weird predicament to be in. Like, one day you could communicate and walk around and shit like that, and then you just can't. And yet he was still hearing people around him, he was still… you're trapped in your own body. And I guess kinda that's what Helen Keller was, but I mean, was she truly trapped? 'Cause you can't feel trapped unless you know freedom, and she never really knew freedom of expression, inasmuch as being able to speak beyond the grunts and the fucking yelling and the throwing. I remember the movie, she threw a lot of shit. I remember seeing it when I was a kid and I was like, "Man, I would get in trouble for that kinda shit."

SM: All I remember of the movie, the way they play it is that…

KS: Which movie? 'Cause there were two, there was one where Anne Bancroft was the Miracle Worker, she was Annie Sullivan, and uh… what's her name…?

SM: Patty Duke.

KS: Patty Duke was Helen Keller. And then years later they did a TV movie

where Patty Duke played Annie Sullivan and Melissa Gilbert — Laura Ingalls — played Helen Keller.
SM: I think I saw the Patty Duke one.
KS: The one... well, she's in both.
SM: The Patty Duke as Annie Sullivan. I think, I don't remember. But I do remember—
KS: Do you think Patty Duke was like, "Why can't I get a-fucking-way from this story, man? Like, it's just always fucking Helen Keller."
SM: "I don't even believe it."
KS: "I find this incredible. Dis-credible." Um... yeah, that's what I remember from the movie. What do you remember from the movie?
SM: Well, I remember it seemed to me like they were depicting this idea that it was about Annie reaching out to her, and that Helen Keller *wanted* to learn. That's the way it's depicted, her desire was to learn, to be taught things, to understand the world around her as best she could.
KS: Right. Don't you think that story's ripe for a cinematic retelling? I mean 'cause now Helen Keller's just a buzzword.
SM: Or a joke.
KS: Yeah, or literally a punchline. I mean, how many people, how many kids even know that story?
SM: It's a whole series of jokes.
KS: Yeah, totally. It's like Polack jokes, but all about Helen Keller. And I don't know a single one of 'em right now, but there were a bunch, 'cause when I was growing up, when I was like nine years old, it was naughty and funny to tell a Helen Keller joke.
SM: There's one about her in a well. And her hands turn blue.
KS: What is that?
SM: She gets trapped in a well.
KS: Is it a masturbation story?
SM: No, no, no.
KS: That's where my head goes. They should remake that movie.
SM: They should remake it?
KS: But do you think kids today would care? They'd be like, "Whatever, man. I can see weirder shit on the Internet. Fuck that."
SM: 'Cause that's what it is. It's just something *weird*.
KS: [Laughs.] I mean it's an inspiring story, man. If it's in fact true, and we

don't have any proof that it's not true.
SM: You know what would be more interesting, and definitely up your alley, is if somebody made a comprehensive documentary about what happened.
KS: Absolutely. But how can they do that?
SM: Like, Ken Burns.
KS: Yes, alright, if Ken Burns did it. But even Ken Burns' stuff, there's, I think a lot of extrapolation, I know he uses letters and shit but like, he's not talking to somebody who was there.
SM: "He uses letters and shit…" — these horrible, historical documents.
KS: Totally, but I think with a documentary, you need to talk to the person that was there. Like, you watch *Shoah* and shit like that and people are like, "I know, I was there, it was fucking Hell on Earth," and they'll give you details. It's tougher when somebody's like, "I'm gonna make a Helen Keller documentary, even though I know about Helen Keller, like you, from reading books," or something like that. Do you think they have cylinders of old recordings, talking to Annie Sullivan?
SM: They may. I mean, I would have done it.
KS: Right! Wouldn't you wanna put that woman on fucking tape, and be like… Jesus Christ, they should've made that woman President, 'cause if you can teach that person to communicate, you can unify a nation, lead a nation. But yet, she wasn't.
SM: She wasn't. She wasn't President.
KS: As far as I know, she wasn't President. She might have been the Prime Minister of Canada…
SM: At one time.
KS: We'll have to check with Malcolm. It's a fascinating story to me. Although it shouldn't be because I've heard about it since I was a kid…
SM: But it's only a fascinating story to you because you refuse to actually read it.
KS: That's not true. I'm not saying I wholeheartedly disagree with the story, I'm just… I only posit that maybe the story isn't the story we've been told, just because I have such a difficult time getting my head around it. And again, like, I was talking to somebody about it and they were like, "Hey, man, they can teach gorillas sign language." I'm like, "Yes, but a gorilla can hear you, and a gorilla can see you," they're not teaching sign language to deaf and blind gorillas. You try to touch a deaf and blind gorilla's hand, he will

just punch you, or eat you or something like that. We were talking about *Planet Earth* the other night, the documentary… who knew that chimps ate other chimps? That was fucking mind-bending to me. Like these chimps attacked this other village of chimps, just total aggression, just out of nowhere, like, "We want their fucking tree!"

SM: Totally human behavior.

KS: *Very* human behavior. And beat the shit out of them, and stole one of their young, and *ate* it, like ate this little baby chimp…

SM: [Creepy horrified whisper] "They ate the young."

KS: They did! They ate the young! My head exploded! I always think of chimps as, you know, they hang out, and they fucking ride bikes and smoke cigarettes in the circus. And in the wild, they're always shown to be very loving toward their own kids.

SM: Picking mites off each other.

KS: Totally, chilling out, living a cool chimp life; and then they show these chimps that are like [makes war bugle noise] and they're just attacking other chimps and eating their flesh! Oh, it was mind-bending. That's why you don't want to teach a deaf and blind gorilla sign language. You wind up eaten like that poor little baby chimp.

SM: Here's another thing: I feel like, in the end what they're trying to teach the chimp is some sort of concept of language. It's like, that's the part where I think the person's saying, "They took a chimp, and they taught them, on a rudimentary level, the concept of language. A way to communicate with us." You know, it's still not processing things in the same way. It's not thinking of things in human language. Even the sign language they're teaching them is… they don't understand the word, they're not saying the word in their head. Visually they could show them a phone, and then show them the sign language…

KS: And from there forward…

SM: And then their mind is connecting that that object…

KS: ... feels like this, or "These are the hand gesticulations for that thing."

SM: Yes. "That hand gesticulation describes this thing that they're holding up."

KS: Do you think they understand, does a gorilla understand when you're sitting there going like, "Phone, phone," do they hear the word 'phone' or is it just like the kids in *Peanuts* where the teacher sounds like, "Waw-wa-waw-

waw waww…"
SM: Well, they hear a sound, but they don't hear 'phone' in the way that you and I hear 'phone', and our mind is doing what you say, which is like, "This is the word I know, which is 'phone', and this is a phone, and these are all the phones and there's this kind of phone and there's all these things…" It's like, if I come up to you and I say a letter, if I say something in Mandarin Chinese it's like…
KS: I'm like, "Where'd you learn Mandarin Chinese? When did that happen?"
SM: But you would hear this thing, you would hear me say something that… you would at least, from your experience, be like, "Oh, that's some form of Chinese," maybe, "that's an Asian language."
KS: I'd be like, "That's silly talk." I'd be like, "Snootch to the bootch, Scott." You'd be like, "No, I was speaking Mandarin Chinese."
SM: But I could say 'phone' in Mandarin Chinese and you would just be like, "It's some form of Asian language."
KS: What about your dog, since your dog came from Thailand?
SM: Taiwan.
KS: Taiwan — does the dog understand English? I could be like, "Food!" and the dog's just, "I don't know what the fuck you're talking about."
SM: We're on the fence about that because there's times where … she's a puppy, so she's either just ignoring me, or she's just…
KS: You have to be like, "Yungyung wa" or something and the dog's just like, "Holy shit, finally, you're talking my language."
SM: "It's like home!" But, you know, even a dog is just like, what they respond to is tone of voice. But at the same time, she was there pretty much her whole life right up until May, and you know, obviously somebody was trying to give her commands and training…
KS: "Fuck off!"
SM: Yeah, exactly. So their language is just like… you know, "Sit" and stuff like that, you're kinda starting from scratch.
KS: It's so weird that like, Angelina Jolie is adopting kids from other countries, you're adopting dogs from other countries. It's like you're jockeying for a position with *People*

"I am holding your beating fucking heart, Icelandic-style, bitch!"

magazine, but you don't know how to play the game, 'cause you're like, "I'll get a dog from another country..."
SM: "Yeah, what about that?"
KS: "Maybe that's news."
SM: "What about that, Jolie? I'll get *ten*."
KS: "Anybody can get a kid. Look at this dog. He don't understand a fucking word I'm saying." Do you think dogs understand other dogs, like when they bark at one another, is it just like, "That thing is making a sound at me"? Or are they like, "I know exactly what you're saying"?
SM: "He said 'phone'."
KS: "Elephant."
SM: I think, once again, dogs use tone. It's like, they understand if they're barking and growling a certain way that it's aggressive, or it's non-aggressive, or, you know, whimpering... they have a series of sounds they make, that dogs are able to translate as like, "I'm hurting," or it's being submissive, it's whining, you know... but I don't think they use words.
KS: But they understand their names. Like if you're like, "Scully," Scully looks at you. Even if you don't do it like I did it, in a tone where obviously it's a demanding tone and it demands attention. But I can lay on the bed and Scully's on the other side of the room and I can go [softly] "Scully" and Scully will look up, and know her name; as opposed to Mulder, who knows his name. Mulder not only knows his name, but knows every variation of his name, 'cause we call him Mulder, Mr Mulder Man, I call him the Boodelaire, 'cause we call him the Buddy Man all the time, that's his nickname, so it went from Buddy Man to Boodelaire, and then I call him Captain Boodelaire of the Poodelaire division, and since he fucked Shecky we call her Mrs Boodelaire, and you can tell Mulder doesn't really like that. But he understands every variation of his name. Like, he knows when I say "Shecky," and he knows the difference between me going "Shecky," and he knows when I'm saying "Buddy Man," or "Boodelaire," or "Mulder," he knows all of his different names, he must understand what I'm saying. Different than just like, the tone of my voice. 'Cause I could sit there and be like, "Wiener Schnitzel," and he wouldn't look. Also, we were watching — this was fucked up — recently we were watching *The X-Files*, and somebody said Mulder's name, and the dog fucking looked up at the TV, and I was like, "That's fucking amazing!" I had to rewind and watch him do it four more times. And he

looked at the TV and then he looked at me, and he looked at Jen. 'Cause he was like, "Did somebody just say my name?"

SM: "Do they have food?"

KS: And then I'd rewind it while he was keeping direct eye-contact with me, and rewind it to the part where somebody said, "Mulder," and then he would fucking look! Like he was so fucking perplexed by the whole thing.

SM: I don't know if I would use the term 'understand' — to say that they understand, it's like, they recognize a sound.

KS: I disagree. He has to understand his name.

SM: But he doesn't… like, to me, I don't think a dog understands the concept of name.

KS: Alright, but he understands… well, I disagree, I think they do, because he knows that — all dogs — seem to know, "That is what identifies me. When somebody says 'Mulder,' they're talking to me."

SM: Well, I think they sit there and they go, "Whenever he says that fucking sound, he's looking at me."

KS: What, they've never said "Mulder" from another part of the room? Alright, so what if I'm looking in his general direction but I say, "Shecky," and he knows I'm not talking to him, he doesn't respond to "Shecky".

SM: My point is… my take on it is that it's learned behavior. When you say "Shecky" you *don't* look at him.

KS: But I can look at Mulder and say "Shecky" and he won't come over to me.

SM: But if you *always* looked at him and said "Shecky"… like, to me, you could change his name.

KS: And he would be like, "Alright." Just like we give him nicknames and shit? He's like, "I'm Boodelaire now."

SM: Yeah. Because if…

KS: "Now I'm Shecky, now I'm…"

SM: Because if you get a bunch of wild dogs, it's not like they're sitting in a circle and it's like, "You're Fred. You got spots, we're gonna call you Spots."

KS: "You're Slappy."

SM: "Your name's Slowpoke."

KS: "You're gonna be Dick Chugger."

SM: "You're Shit Eater 'cause… you know who you are."

KS: "'Cause we've seen it." But when it comes to their interaction with humans, they must understand the concept of a name, of a title.

SM: I don't…

KS: You don't buy that?

SM: To me it's more like, what *we* do… I had Wolfie, and so for twelve years somebody says "Wolfie," and stares at him, and then says like, "Come here," he's like…

KS: "Why do they keep saying that word at me, and looking at me?"

SM: When they hear those noises, they can recognize the sounds, but I don't think they ever sit there and go like, "That's my special name."

KS: I think they do!

SM: I don't think they do.

KS: I think they do, and I think when we're not there they sit around going like, "Fuck, where'd they come up with 'Shecky' from? 'Wolfie'? I look like a bear, why not 'Bearie'?"

SM: I don't think they do. 'Cause I think like, the word 'sit' is just… you say it, and then you make them sit. But I'm pretty sure you could say "Fart," and then push the dog's ass down on the ground, and then motion to sitting, and then if you said "Fart" enough, the dog would sit when you said "Fart."

KS: It would be even better if every time you farted, the dog would sit. So, as you fart you have somebody pushing the dog's ass down, and you direct your ass in their general direction so they know it's being indicated towards them, at least in the learning stage, so that every time for the rest of your life…

SM: If somebody farts…

KS: The dog immediately sits down. People are like, "That is one well-behaved dog."

SM: To me, dogs generally, it's all learned behavior. And the smarter they are, the more they process stuff. So Mulder is like, he processes what you're doing, and what you're doing is you're saying, "Your name's Mulder," and so when he hears it on the TV he's like, "Oh, that's that sound." And they're able to distinguish direction, but it's not like they're gonna sit there and go, "You want me to sit and you keep saying "Fart", what's the fuck's the matter with you?"

KS: Right, "Use the right word and I'll do it."

SM: And to me, based on that, then they can't understand the concept of a name.

KS: Do you think Annie Sullivan had to teach Helen Keller the term 'fart'? She had to give her language for everything. So do you think maybe they're sitting there, and they're doing their lessons, and Helen Keller farts, and then Annie Sullivan has to be like, "Fuck, now I've got to teach her what a fucking fart is…"

SM: Possibly.

KS: And she signs it into her hand, like, "Any time a little wind comes out of your hiney, that is a fart."

SM: And then, she could smell, too, she had the power of smell.

KS: She did. Well, I believe she did.

SM: You're not gonna take that away from her.

KS: I didn't attribute any of the olfactory sense to her. Alright, so she smells it and then she signs in her hand — just imagine how long it takes to sign this sentence: "That thing that you're smelling, that odor, that is… we call it a fart, it comes out of your butt, we call it a hiney burp…"

SM: Well, with sign language, it becomes words. Like at first you teach an alphabet — just like with normal kids, it's like you're going to teach an alphabet, and out of that alphabet we create words, and out of those words come sentences. So at a certain point, I don't assume that Annie was doing like… she didn't have to spell out every letter, she could sit there and say, "This is a…," those words, and then say, "Fart." She didn't have to go "T-H-I-S…"

KS: Right. She had like a push or a sign for "The" — for articles. For connecting sentences…

SM: Yes, she taught her an alphabet, and then she taught her words…

KS: Subject predicate breakdown…

SM: Yeah. It wasn't like she was spelling everything… but then when she got to "elephant" or "fart" or "masturbation," all the important words…

KS: That would fascinate me, if there was a comprehensive biography.

SM: The words taught?

KS: Yes, if Annie Sullivan's like, "Before I die, I'm going to pass it on to somebody, these are every word I ever taught Helen Keller, this is historically important, so hold onto this." And they published it, and just seeing words like…

SM: Day 78: 'Fuck'…

KS: Annie was mad at somebody and she was just like, "Fucktard." You know, "I taught her 'fucktard' and then explained that 'fucktard' is somebody you don't like." Just, anything, did she teach her…

SM: … the minutiae of language.

KS: Did she call it "vagina" or did she call it "pussy"? What did she call it?

SM: Vagina, I'm sure.

KS: "Vag," do you think? Or just "cookie"?

SM: Probably just "vagina." Not "vag."

[Pause, as the enormity of this conversation sinks in.]

KS: That's SModcast for this week. I think we've covered a lot of terrain.

SM: We have. But really about one person.

KS: But a fascinating person, man. Fascinating.

From SModcast 19: We Owe It All to Nook-Nook

A Nook-Nook tribute

SM: Here's another ignorant question, did the animals know that what they were doing is procreating, or were they just, "I gotta fucking put this thing in a hole"?

KS: I think it's just heat, it's what they call heat. They're not sitting there going, "Well, we've got to make more of us," they're just sitting there going, "It's that season, I smell pussy, I've got to fuck it." Or if you're a female animal, "It's that season, my pussy is all wide and open, I'm putting out this stench I normally don't, I've gotta have it." There's a physical push, but it's all about keeping the species going.

SM: Exactly, but obviously we as a civilization started out that same way. Just a bunch of people, it's a seasonal schtupp, and they just want to get in and do it. I assume over time that we've developed civilization, and all these other things have come into it, but we were aware that if I fuck, even before they had language, painted on a wall, a cock and a pussy, that equals baby.

KS: Totally. Weeney and puss equals waa-waa. You know what's sad? We weren't good at keeping records back then because we didn't have language skills, pictograms were about it. Of our species, when we finally went from Cro-Mag to—

SM: Mag.

KS: Homo sapiens. Mag, whatever. The unsung hero is the first guy, I'll take

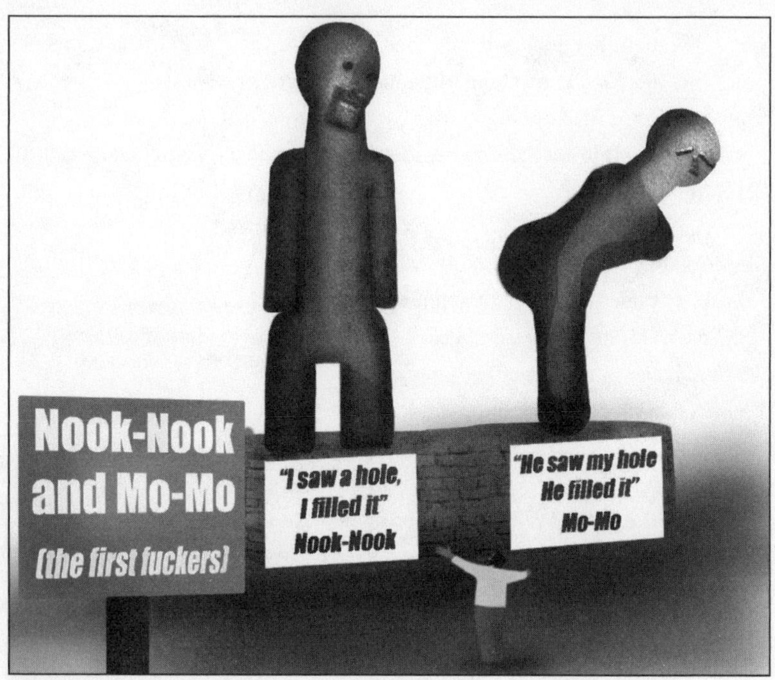

even a Cro-Mag, or even if we were chimps, the first one that said, "I'm going to put that in there." Where's the monument for that? Never mind the Washington Monument, the Lincoln Memorial…

SM: A knuckle-dragger with a boner?

KS: Totally! Give me a big statue for Nook-Nook and Mo-Mo, the first fucking cave people that were like, "We're going to put our dirties at each other and make it come!" *That's* monumental.

From SModcast 21: Little Outhouse On the Prairie
Wiping technique

KS: Welcome to… [Dissolves into coughing fit.]

SM: Welcome to SModcast!

KS: Thanks for the assist, for heaven's sakes. I got lost there in my phlegm. It's the smoker in me coming out, sorry.

SM: Well, I quit.

KS: You don't smoke all the time, though. You're a social smoker, you smoke when you drink. Smoke when the tough kids, when you're leaving the playground, are like, "What? You don't smoke, baby?" And you're like, "Well of course I do!" Let me ask you a question. When you wipe your bung: toilet paper?

SM: Yeah. What's the other option? Your hand?

KS: Well, not all Hindus, but I believe in India they use their hand, in some cultures. But I go for the wet wipes.

SM: Oh, like a moist towelette? A baby wipe?

KS: Yeah, but look, you're diminishing it and me when you call it a baby wipe! A bunch of companies have released them I think, but Continental is the one I use. It's got a little puppy dog on the packaging. Which almost communicates the message, "It's like wiping your ass with a puppy!" But they make a fine product that's targeted at the adult audience — because you're right, primarily people think of moist wipes as baby wipes. But these are flushable, aloe-scented adult wipes. It's important that they're flushable, because once when we were living in Rumson, we were flushing the regular baby wipes, and it backed up our fucking plumbing and it was a mess. But yeah, these things break down. You don't use these at all?

SM: I actually didn't know that they existed.

KS: Now that you know, will you start using them?

SM: No. I mean, why use them?

KS: Because there's a better way out there!

SM: A better way to…

KS: To wipe your ass! And the way that it's meant to be wiped. I don't think we were meant to wipe our ass with dry paper. I think we were meant to wipe it with wet paper. It makes clean up easy, and more hygienic, I think. Think about it. You know how the CD player replaced the cassette player and the cassette player replaced the record player? Why these wet wipes haven't replaced toilet paper is beyond me. This is a huge advent in human technology.

SM: This is like going into space! The moon landing!

KS: Absolutely — John Glenn stepping on the moon… he was the first one, right?

SM: Yeah. Him and Helen Keller.

KS: Right. John Glenn stepping on the moon doesn't hold a fucking candle to the adult wet wipe. They should get rid of toilet paper in general. Rolls should just go away now. Because to me, it's akin to the day they came up with toilet paper. Up until then — this was the outhouse days — they would use the Sears and Roebuck catalog pages. They would use a dry corncob, which I find fucking shocking. Why weren't there more reported cases of anal fissure back in the days of the outhouse?
SM: Well, I don't think they shoved it up their ass. I think they kinda put it between their cheeks.
KS: No, I don't think they shoved it up their ass either, but I don't care how they use it, but have you ever felt a dry corncob?

From SModcast 23: Good Vibrations
Malcolm floods the Rumson house

JS: This is one of my favorite Malcolm stories. When we were in New Jersey, in the Rumson house, he was staying in the basement, and the toilet down there overflowed sewage all over the basement. He's like, "I'm hiring someone to take fingerprints of the toilet *right now*, it's not my fault this time."
KS: To lay the groundwork for this, Malcolm broke a cookie jar I gave to Jen early in our relationship—
JS: Malcolm did acid or X or something and left a fucking faucet on in our house and woke up in a flood… that was a genius move.
KS: When we were shooting *Jay and Silent Bob Strike Back* we were living in this house on a ledge—
JS: Malcolm has lived with us for years at a time…
KS: Malcolm had come home and got very imbibed and turned on a faucet and fell asleep and we woke up to a flooded room. We had to rip up the carpet, pay for that to be done.
JS: In a rental. Eurgh!
KS: In a rental house. So, the toilet — we didn't even really live in that Rumson house for two months, we bought it just before we went to do *Jay and Silent Bob Strike Back* and we came back and we stayed for a longer period than *Jay and Silent Bob Strike Back* and we wound up coming out to

Los Angeles for eleven months, it was only supposed to be four. We came back, we were in the house for two months, and then we wound up moving out.

JS: That was not money well spent.

KS: Well, it's history. That house had a basement that was below the sewage level. Also the house itself had a septic tank, it wasn't working off sewage. So this toilet was below the septic tank level, so it had this sub-pump affair that when you flush it, it didn't work on traditional plumbing, when you flushed the toilet there were grinders in the toilet to grind up poo—

JS: Something ridiculous.

KS: Then it would be sub-pumped up to the main sewage system and then go out.

JS: This isn't important to the story really.

KS: Yes it is, because what happened was that I told him specifically, "Don't use the fucking toilet in the basement." He was staying in the basement, it had a big TV in it.

JS: It was furnished.

KS: It was his own apartment. I said, "Whatever you do, if you've got to shit, come up the fucking stairs."

JS: There's a bathroom right there right at the top of the stairs.

KS: "Don't use that fucking toilet!" and he was like, "I won't." Then fucking the next day he comes up in a panic, "There's poo on the floor and there's water and I swear to god it wasn't me! It's not me." I was, "What the *fuck* dude?!" I went downstairs, and one of the rooms off the basement was a safe room with a lock on it, I had a lot of artwork on the floor and valuables in it, and it was getting dangerously close to going under that door.

JS: And it smelled a fucking fright.

KS: It did. I was screaming at him.

JS: I was screaming too.

KS: He's like, "It wasn't me, I swear to god! I will hire a private detective to dust for prints on the bowl and the poo." He was so defensive about it. Then we had a plumber come out and checking into it, he snaked the upstairs toilets and he found a bunch of baby wipes.

JS: Which I told you not to fucking flush down the toilet.

KS: They were of a non-flushable variety, not the flushable type that I was advocating, but the baby wipes you're not supposed to flush. So I was responsible for that and it kinda leaked out upon us.

JS: For once it turned out well for Malcolm. That's the one and only time.

From SModcast 23: Good Vibrations
Kevin sees Chay's boob and then runs

KS: You've seen Chay's boobs. I've seen one of them.

JS: I know, that was awesome. Totally awesome.

KS: It wasn't awesome for me. That's weird — as much as I like nudity, I don't like the nudity *live in person* of somebody I know. Not even nudity, but just scantily clad. If you're up at the pool and your girlfriends are up there with you in their bikinis, I can't be up there.

JS: He's mortified.

KS: Yeah. It's weird, because you can't *not* look, and it makes you uncomfortable.

JS: I don't mind. You can look.

KS: But I don't want to look.

JS: Do you want to tell the Chay boob story? 'Cause I find it funny. Chay is my best girlfriend.

KS: And she was getting changed in Harley's room and I didn't even know it. And I went in to get Harley. I opened the door and walked in, and she was like mid-shirt coming down or up or whatever, so I saw one of the boobs. So that was really…

JS: And you *fled*.

KS: I was like, "Whoa!" And she was like, "Ahh!" and quickly pulled her shirt down, and I really did have to fucking get out of there.

JS: It was awesome. You ran back to me and you were like, "Oh my god, oh my god, I just saw Chay! Oh my god!" And I'm like, "I'm sure Chay didn't give a shit."

KS: I was unsettled by it. But meanwhile, if you showed me a picture of Chay, naked, I'd look at it. But her being there, live and in person, I was just like, I don't want to see Chay like that.

JS: We have weird lines.

KS: We do. Very liberal in some places, very conservative in others. But that's marriage.

From SModcast 25: Lynching Vixen
Bryan Johnson trying to pep-talk strippers

KS: There was that period when me and Johnson found [the strip club] Strutters, and we went every weekend for a month straight and then got real depressed. It was just like, "These girls don't really like us, they just want our money," then watching other dudes looking at the girls like they really wanted them and shit. I remember looking over and there was a Hindu kid who looked like he was about early twenties. He was there with whom I assumed was his dad, a Hindu gentleman in his fifties. They had all their bills lined up, and the chicks would dance on the pole then they'd fucking slink over. Strutters was a juice bar so they'd be completely fucking naked and the chicks would crawl over on all fours. The dude would hand her the money and lock eyes with her and shit like it was real.
WF: Like it was a tether?
KS: Like a tractor beam pulled them together! He wouldn't take his eyes off her. Then sometimes the chicks would do things where they'd reach their hand round the back of their legs so that their hand is between their legs near the puss and they're pulling the dollar, a dollar no less — I mean, you imagine a little more for a move like that — and pulling it with the person's hand close to them but just letting go before they touch and then backing away a little bit. Or doing the thing where they rub the boob in the face. Watching that just depressed me so much because I was like, "I think this dude really believes he could get this chick. But there's no way on earth this chick would fuck this guy." Then she'd come over to us and Johnson would break into a twenty-minute discussion with them about, "Why are you doing this? What's it feel like?" And the chicks get this look on their face where they're like, "Fuck you! I don't want to be judged, I'm fucking doing this for the money obviously." But they would always sucker Johnson out of a lot of money. I remember we were talking to this one chick and he's like, "How's your night going?" "It's not good, some guy tried to jam his finger in my asshole." And Bryan gave her forty bucks! Then the next time we went back, the same fucking chick said the same thing, and Bryan said, "That happened to you last time." And she had this look on her face of, "Uh? [Pause.] Oh yeah!"
WF: "You're the forty dollar guy!"

KS: Totally, and she remembered that she had run this scam on him once before. Then we just kinda lost interest in going to strip clubs.

From SModcast 26: Beware the Hobo
Bryan Johnson's scorpion story

KS: Tell the fucking spider story. I always call it the spider story but that's not right.
BJ: It's actually the scorpion story. Walter and I had gone to the Woodbridge Center, one of the many trips where I'd gone to the mall with Walter, and for whatever reason, I guess I was eighteen, I wanted to get a small pet scorpion which seemed the most 'metal' pet at the time.
KS: You were quite metal at the time. You were a Yngwie Malmsteen fan...
BJ: … Diamond.
KS: Metal to the point where you had the hair, I'm sure there's a picture of you on the Internet with the hair and shit, I think you might have had the long hair in one of the flicks, I think maybe in *Mallrats*.
BJ: Yeah, *Mallrats* and *Chasing Amy* to a lesser extent.
KS: You were pretty entrenched in metal and the metal scene, in the central Jersey, Monmouth county metal scene.
BJ: Yeah we'd go to Murphy's Law, a local metal club. Ed went a lot too, we were regulars, but I guess what had happened was I bought a scorpion—
KS: To be more 'metal'.
BJ: To be a little bit more metal, and to have a pet that would… I didn't like spiders really, the irony being that you always call it a spider.
KS: I always remember it as 'the spider story' and it's weird because I wasn't even there for it, it happened years before we started hanging out. The retelling of the story always occurs to me as you bought a tarantula or black widow, trying to be as fucking metal as possible.
BJ: I think at the time, I can't say for sure, but that I was really into The Scorpions at the time so that may have played into it.
KS: What a Lloyd.
BJ: That's the cool kids, right?
KS: Lloyd is a very cool term.
BJ: So we went to the mall, spent the day, came home and when Edgar, who's

my father, I rarely call him dad or father—
KS: You call him Edgar to his face?
BJ: Yeah.
KS: I couldn't do that. If I called my father Don he would have kicked me, even later in life.
BJ: Maybe that's why I got kicked, because I got kicked also. Maybe it was the whole first name thing?

Random SModquotes

"Welcome to Russia, where we sew dogs' heads to each other! Come! Fuck a chimp!!"

KS: And you just didn't hear the part about, "Don't call me Edgar!" before the kick came in because the blow was so fucking hard.
BJ: Well I fancied myself as a Greg Brady type, or Mike and Carol.
KS: Also you had the Johnny fucking Bravo pad—
BJ: Yeah, exactly.
KS: You kinda did.
BJ: Yeah, I was a lot like Greg Brady. Except I don't remember his dad kicking him, that's probably in the outtakes. So me and Walter came in and Edgar immediately began questioning me about it because it was in one of those little plastic things, casings around it.
KS: Habitat.
BJ: Yeah, some stony type stuff and then you used to throw in crickets and shit. He started questioning me about it, "What's that, what's that?" "Ah, it's a scorpion. I bought it as a pet." He was, "Don't you owe your mother for the phone bill?" And I did. Looking back, sure I was in the wrong because I was just, "What, am I just supposed to not buy anything for myself?"
KS: But in the moment, metal reared its head...
BJ: The rebellion of metal, there was no other answer at the time. "Go fuck yourself!" So I imagine I had to have set it down, the scorpion, set it down on the table or something because we started going back and forth and all of a sudden he jumps me. He jumps and starts wrestling me, which is not the first, nor the last time we got into a physical altercation. So he starts pushing me and I push him back and then he does this embrace type thing as we're wrestling around and out of the corner of my eye I see Flanagan just jet out the back door. I couldn't see the back door, but I could see him put his hands up and then scurry through our living room and shut the door.
KS: What would have been the move, the preferred move? When Flanagan

jumps in? "I'm working the body!"
BJ: The metal move would have been to throw fucking piano wire around Edgar's neck or something. But I remember the thing that freaked out Walter, right before he left, was as we're wrestling he gets real emotional—
KS: Edgar?
BJ: Yeah, and he goes, "You've got to stop this. I love you Bryan." I was like, "What?"
KS: While he's got you in the fucking Greco-Roman death hold?
BJ: Exactly. It's such mixed messages in my family you know. One in the gulliver and then a kiss on the cheek.

From SModcast 28: Scottacita Wants a Carnita!
Lard conversation

KS: I love a Twinkie. But it took me fifteen years to figure out what the ingredient that they call animal shortening is. That's whipped pig. Whipped fucking leftover shit that they can't sell to eat as a grade A meat. They whip it up, pour a ton of sugar on it and that's what shortening is. It's fat.
SM: It's lard. It's animal fat.
KS: I never knew what lard was, then people were like, "Hey, lard-ass," and I was like, "Yeah!" I didn't know what lard was. If you watch old episodes of *Little Rascals* and every once in a while they try to cook and they put lard on a grill or something like that. Or Alfalfa slicks his hair back with it. I never knew what it was.
SM: I've cooked with lard.
KS: You've cooked with it?
SM: Yeah.
KS: That's just cooking with fat.
SM: Yeah. Sometimes I'll make carnitas, a slow cook pork.
KS: "Carnitas! Scottacita wants a carnita!"
SM: And that's exactly what I say as well whilst I'm cooking it.
KS: I'm gonna put that on your fucking tombstone. "Here lies Scott Mosier," then in quotes, "Scottacita wants a carnita!"
SM: "He wanted something else and he got stuck with this." No, I've used lard because it has lots of flavor. But I wouldn't put it on popcorn.

From SModcast 29: Harry Scotter
Bertie Bott's beans in the ass

[Kevin is asking Scott about the ending of *Harry Potter and The Deathly Hallows*]
KS: Is it a chapter? A where-are-they-now kinda thing?
SM: Yeah, it's a chapter, one scene, that gives you a bunch of information.
KS: What happened to Hermione? I want to see if you can say this without fucking tearing up.
SM: It was just kinda sweet, man. What do you think happened?
KS: What happens to Hermione later on in life, in my version? She fucks a lot, that would be my years-later chapter. "And Hermione fucked a lot. The mudblood that she is, she was taking it from wizards and muggles alike." No, I have no clue what would happen to Hermione. She doesn't die does she?
SM: No.
KS: Do any of the three kids die?
SM: No.
KS: So what happens?
SM: If no one has read it you should put a big warning in, "If you haven't read this yet," even on the thing before you download it.
KS: I said it on the thing.
SM: They all three survive.
KS: Ok. What happens to her years later? I'm only interested in her.
SM: She's married to Ron.
KS: She marries Ron Weasley?
SM: Yes. If you haven't read the second to last book?
KS: Do they finally kiss in *The Half-Blood Prince*?
SM: No, not in that one, in the last one.
KS: In *Deathly Hollows*?
SM: Yes.
KS: They kiss? How is it described, is it sexy or is it more romantic?
SM: It's spontaneous and romantic, it's not really sexy. It's in the midst of a bunch of shit going down. There's not Barry White playing.
KS: Does it get dirty? "And then Ron started slipping some Bertie Bott's beans into her ass"? "And then they all tasted like shit."

KS & SM: [Extended giggling.]
KS: No? There's no magic?
SM: Yeah, J.K. Rowling was like, "I'm going to not only destroy the franchise, but everybody's fond memories of these books by making the last chapter just a filthy descriptive of deviant sex acts."
KS: That's not deviant, that's… what do you call those things?
SM: Anal beads?
KS: Yeah, like anal beads. So it would be like Bertie Bott's beads, you know they all taste different and whatnot, these wind up all tasting like shit because they're coming out her ass.
SM: That's not really magic, you and I could do that!
KS: She administers a fistful of Bertie Bott beans to herself and pinches one out, keeps pinching them out and Ron's eating them like a rabbit. But that didn't happen?
SM: That's not what happened.

From SModcast 30: Smith & Wesson
Tales of Crime and Punishment

[Kevin and Scott are discussing a news story, headlined "Federal Prosecutor Arrested in Child Sex Sting".]
KS: What the fuck man. Bryan Johnson sent me this. Bryan Johnson always sends me horrible fucking news headlines and horrible news. Cringe-inducing shit. I finally had to write him back to be like, "Dude, why can't it ever be like 'This just in — Puppies are cute.'"
SM: "A clown made people happy."
KS: Oh my god, what a horrible story this is. I sat back after I read it and was enraged and disgusted and angry, and just wanted to beat the shit out of the dude. But you have to sit there and admit that at this moment in time, it's a victimless crime. That little girl didn't exist, but in his mind that little girl *did* exist and he traveled to Detroit so he could fuck a five-year-old girl. This is a dude whose job it is to prosecute people for breaking the law, doesn't it just fucking shatter your faith in humanity?
SM: Yeah, it doesn't strengthen it. That goes for the dude who breaks open a vending machine and takes all the money. That's breaking the law too.

Though I don't sit there and go, "Yeah, but dude, you should be put on an island full of fucking people like you, vending machine breakers." But that guy is not only breaking the law—

KS: He's breaking the public's trust.

SM: Yeah, and he's also putting himself into a category where you don't even know how to deal with that person.

KS: I do. You just fucking de-ball them.

SM: Just cut off their nuts.

KS: I wish I was in charge of the justice system. I'll never be, but I do wish it sometimes. You just do horrible things to people, never mind putting them in jail because there are some crimes… and I know some people will be like, "Who made you judge, jury and executioner?"…

SM: I did!

KS: Yeah totally, Scott said, "Kev, do it!" And I was like, "Right on, Scott's the moral authority." I say you take that dude, you don't give him any medication or anything like that, and you shoot him. One in the leg, one in the other leg. One in the arm, one in the other. You let him sit there for a little while in pain. Then you cut his fucking nuts off and show him. Be like, "Here are your nuts you fucking criminal fuck, you horrible human being." Then you're like, "You're free to go." But he is responsible to get himself to medical care, nobody is allowed to help him out and be, "Oh my god, this man is bleeding, he's probably going to die." If he can get himself to the hospital and fix himself up and get himself better, then fine. But that's punishment. You know what he's going to say, he'll be, "I'm operating my own sting operation and I was trying to arrest this woman for offering me her five-year-old kid. So I was playing a role." He's going to find some sick and twisted defense that might actually hold a little fucking water.

SM: I don't know man, I think that dude is in trouble.

KS: I would not be surprised at all if this was the end of the story, or if the next story was — 'Acquitted.'

SM: I don't know, I say that if you follow that story that guy is in trouble. Because who is going to come to his defense?

[Pause.]

KS: Santa?

SM: Santa.

KS: I don't think anybody. Who could defend that? But somebody's job will be to defend that. Some lawyer is going to have to stand there and be like, "Even though I find this reprehensible, I have to defend this dude to the best of my ability and try to get this dude off." I get it. We need the justice system, we need the courts. But some crimes man… if he's dead to rights and he made the trip, that's intent to me, that is a dude that had every intention of fucking a child. Do him wrong. Hurt him.

SM: The only thing that I can see that's wrong with your plan is taking a fucking debauched person and just injuring them and sending them back out in the world.

KS: But I'm saying that you're doing this to him in the middle of the desert, in a little hut. So the nearest hospital is two and half hours away and he doesn't have a car. After you do these things — shoot him and cut his nuts off, then show them to him — then you just leave, "Alright, bye." If he gets himself help — and he's got no cell phone and no way of contacting anyone — then he goes through trial.

SM: "This is your chance to go to trial, now look at your balls!"

KS: "You could go straight to jail, or you could take a shot like this. Deal or no deal?" He's like, "Fuck, no deal!" What a horrible story, man. Even if you're not a parent, that's a horrible story. That to me is up there with the priest molesting kids. Somebody who holds the public trust. You're the guy that keeps the monsters at bay and punishes the monsters and he's one of the worst monsters. So fucking wrong.

SM: If you're going to do your thing, I'm just, "Why not just shoot him?"

KS: I agree. But I said shoot him four times. You shoot a guy once in the head and it's all over. Make him hurt for a while. Make him hurt for the kids he presumably... that he intimated he has hurt in the past.

SM: But the whole idea of torture and that kinda violence, I'm sure you could find some people to do it, but that's a fucked up thing in itself. I think the guy is fucked up.

KS: I know where you can find those people fucking easily. You go to the parents of children who've been murdered in violent crimes and rapes and say, "We would like you to be the person in charge of punishing this man who was going to do it, and probably has done it based on his own testimony, to other kids." Those people would do it in a heartbeat. If my kid was killed and they came in and said, "You want to kill kid-killers for a living? Legally, all legit, and we'll pay you like 50,000 dollars a year?" I'd be

like, "Why ain't I doing it *now*? Can we start *today*?"
SM: I like the idea of shooting somebody once, but the idea of shooting somebody four times and cutting off their balls?
KS: Satisfaction! That would feel so good to me. I say that as a Christian.

From SModcast 31: Loneliness of the Long Distance Mosier
The Jesus list

KS: I was driving over to get weighed, and when you're driving around L.A. on the surface streets, you get to look around because you're not moving a lot. And today was one of those days where it took me an hour and a half to do something that should have taken twenty minutes because I was driving there. But I'm looking at couples, people walking on the street. I find that fascinating, because before those people were walking hand in hand, they didn't know each other, presumably.
SM: In most cases, I'd say.
KS: It's not like they were born and raised together like brother and sister. It's a stranger. And it's natural, but it's also kinda weird when you take a step back and look at it — you spend most of your life fucking total strangers. Putting your dick into people you don't know.
SM: Well, the opposite of that is being an inbred, isn't it?
KS: But that's the thing. I'm not advocating it, but if you think about it, basically everyone in your life — outside, first your parents, and then your brother and sister — are veritable strangers. You can sit there and make the argument that, "Well, you never really know your parents," but your parents are the ultimate non-strangers. They're the ultimate familiars, because the moment you shoot out the fucking puss, it's, "Hey, I know that face." That face feeds you, and these are the people that clothe you, so those are the people you trust, the people that you know. And then if you have siblings, you know them too, because you spend time with them and shit. But everyone else in the world is a stranger. At one point you and I were fucking strangers, and we've known each other for, god — going on twenty years or something like that. But pretty much everyone is a stranger. It just freaks me out sometimes, when I think about it. I'm married. I'm fucking a total stranger! I didn't know this broad. I didn't know her at one point. And I do

now, but still, it's weird. They always tell you, when you're a kid, "Don't talk to strangers." Then you grow up and you fuck strangers! And you do a lot of things with strangers. It's just so weird, and it almost seems like, you know, if you were to script it, you would want to not fuck strangers, you'd want to fuck people you know. But that would mean fucking your parents and your siblings, and that would be wrong. But I guess that's how nature works. We get punished if we fuck our siblings, by having weird-looking kids. You've seen pictures online, or in encyclopedias. Because they indoctrinate you young — "Don't fuck your brother. Don't have sex with family members because your kids might look like *this*." But it's weird that nature pushed us away from fucking the familiar into fucking strangers. And then we become familiar with those people. I'm married to my wife, so we are technically family, but we're not bound by blood. We're bound by a cock.

SM: Bound by cock and a puss. As it should be. Or a cock and an ass.

KS: But they should tell you when you're a kid, "Look, don't talk to some strangers. But you're going to need to talk to some of them, because eventually you're going to want to fuck somebody!"

SM: Don't talk to strangers is sort of an elementary school rule.

KS: My mom *still* stresses that I shouldn't talk to strangers. Even to this day, she's like, "Don't talk to strangers," and I'm like, "Mom, I've got to meet them to cast them in the movie," but she's like, "Just keep casting the same people." That's why I keep casting the same people — my mother! But it's so strange. Who was the first one that figured, "I shouldn't fuck my mother, I should fuck that other cave woman who's not my mother"? Or sister.

SM: Maybe they didn't. Maybe it took generations.

KS: Maybe the neighbor was like, "Hey man, I fucked the broad on the other side of the hill and my kid looks fine. Your kid has nine eyes. Your kid should be consumed and its bones offered up to the sun." But that was nature. Because there's no rulebook. There's no like, "This is how you be a homo sapiens. You don't fuck a relative." You have to figure it out by trial and error.

SM: But people still do it.

KS: Yeah, but now everybody's got enough smarts to figure out it's bad.

SM: But there are still some people who are like, "I don't know, man, she looks good."

KS: Have you ever once looked at your sister in a sexual way?

SM: No.

KS: I have — I've looked at your sister in a sexual way, that's for sure.

SM: I know.

KS: But no, I've never looked at my sister that way either, "I'd like to tap that fucking blood-related ass." And my sister's a good-looking chick. You think that's more to do with society, or like, "Ugh, she irritates me, because I live with her all the time"? Is having a sibling kinda like being married without the sex? You spend an inordinate amount of time with that person, you know all their fucking faults, and they're sure to irritate you — sometimes they hold you down and fart on you and shit like that.

SM: That's not like my marriage.

KS: That's what my marriage is. That's our foreplay. I'm like, come here, and she's like, "Don't!" [makes farting noise]. Then I'm like, "Now you want it, don't you?" And she's, "Christ, no." Do you think you were never attracted to your sister — 'cause your sister is a good-looking woman — because she's your sister, or because, "Ugh, she drives me nuts"? Or was it because your parents were like, "Scott, stop touching your sister?" What was it?

SM: The big question is, is not having sex with your siblings chemical, instinctual? At this point in time it seems more like it's society — you're just told not to do it.

KS: It couldn't be instinctual, because let's say your parents had a kid that they gave up for adoption and never told you about, and you ran into this chick by fucking happenstance and she was hot and good to go and she's like, "I feel oddly attracted to you, like I know you or something..."

SM: "That means we should fuck!"

KS: Yeah, "That means you want it in the butt!" There would be nothing in you saying, "Don't fuck her, she's blood." I don't think it's chemical. It's got to be either societal or the irritation factor. Because there are girls you know in the world that you wouldn't fuck because you just know, "That fucking bitch drives me nuts. I wouldn't fuck her with a stolen dick, no matter what she looks like." And I imagine that would be the case, not just with your sister, but in this case it's your sister.

SM: I would say it has to be a mixture of both. Your initial thing is that it's ingrained in you that you're not supposed to do it. Those are the rules. Although I don't remember — that wasn't a part of sex ed, where they were like, "Oh yeah, and don't fuck your sister."

KS: "Chapter One — stay away from relatives."

SM: I don't remember that. Do you?

KS: That's something you get early on.

SM: But — through osmosis? How do you get it? I don't remember ever directly being told, "Don't fuck that."

KS: That's true. There was never any sit down with my parents and my brother and sisters.

SM: They point to the neighbor's house and say, "Fuck *that*."

KS: Yeah, they point out the window and say, "See them? Fuck them. Not yet — actually, don't fuck them, they irritate us. Fuck someone from across town." Actually, my parents were like, "Don't fuck *anybody*. 'Cause you'll get them pregnant and you'll want to get married too young." And we were Catholic, so there was a lot of, "Only fuck people Jesus says you can fuck."

SM: Where's that list? Can I get the Jesus list?

KS: Yeah — how many people are on it?

SM: That'd be hot, if you're like eighteen or sixteen, you get your Jesus list. Can you imagine, on your sixteenth birthday, and I come over and I'm like, "Who's on your list?"

KS: "Check it out — you!" And you're like, "What?"

> **Random SModquotes**
>
> **"I'm telling you man, I've said it before, I'll say it again — I really am one cock shy in the mouth of being gay."**

SM: "What, I'm gay?"

KS: And you're like, "How does Jesus *know*?" "'Cause he's Jesus." "Want to get it out of the way now?" "I guess!"

SM: Or it's like, you'd be excited by like, "I've got thirty people on my list!"

KS: I've got a rock.

SM: [Laughs.] I've got a melon, a banana…

KS: I think Jesus is fucking with me.

SM: That would be fucked up, if there was just one person on your list.

KS: Wouldn't that be oddly comforting? That would be oddly comforting to me. I'm a monogamist by nature. I'm not one of those dudes that's, "I've got to fuck everything that moves!"

SM: Yeah, but *one*?

KS: One would be enough, dude, as long as she was good at it.

SM: But what happens if you've got one and you fuck the first time and

you're like, "Oh Jesus!"
KS: Yeah — "Oh Jesus, why did you do that to me?" Well, think about your Hindu arranged marriages. Like Mr and Mrs Thapar. They owned the Quick Stop, they had a son named Rajiv. And he got married in a traditional arranged marriage.
SM: Well, I guess if it was a list provided by Jesus Christ himself, that would be proof that he exists. Which, you know, would change my opinion.
KS: I will argue that Jesus existed, there's just no proof that he's the Son of God.
SM: That he did magic. He's not Harry Potter.
KS: But what's tougher to prove, and that people get hung up on, is, was he the Son of God? And you can go vague and say, "We're all children of God." You know, Catholics believe that he is the Son of God. He wasn't fucking God because they were related. They were blood.
SM: But if he could provide the list — and then I guess if that had been happening for centuries, you would be comforted by the idea, based on—
KS: Because Jesus is the ultimate matchmaker? He's like Bob Eubanks on the fucking *Newlywed Game*? "You're making whoopee!" "Oh Jesus, don't say whoopee."

From SModcast 34: Jersey Justice League
An act of tenderness with Walt

KS: We left that party fucking bored, and we said, "Maybe Walt wants to hang out." So we go around the block to Debbie's, where we went from people on a rooftop staring at somebody else's party, to three dudes staring at their friend through a window. And you were in like a dining room area, at the Grassos' house, and it looked like you were doing homework. Was she at college at that point, or was she taking a test to be a teacher or something like that?
WF: Probably, yeah, she was in college.
KS: There was some book work involved, and of course we can't hear anything. And we're just looking at the visual, and we were debating whether we should go up and knock, or if you'd be mad, like, "I'm hanging out with Debbie!" And then out of nowhere, you stand up, and get her to

stand up, and you guys start slow dancing! It was like a box step or something! And it was a weird insight into, like, "I don't know this guy *at all*!"

[Laughter.]

KS: "I've never seen him box step at fucking Fantasy Zone when we're buying comics!" It was a bizarre little insight into your character that I was theretofore unfamiliar with. But I mean it would stand to reason, because you were dating the girl. But I just never — and not that you aren't charismatic, but I'd just never thought, "I wonder what Walt does when we're not around and he's with a girl alone?" Like, I'd just assumed I knew what you did, but it was weird. I think it would have been different if we'd looked through the window and seen you fucking. Then we'd have been like, "Right on, Walt, do it! Walt likes pussy!" but looking through the window and seeing you being fucking tender and box stepping — it was like Tender Walt. It was *so* fucking Tender Walt. Do you remember that? Do you remember that dance, what spurred it?

WF: It probably was just nothing. I don't remember, really. I don't think there was even music playing.

[Laughter.]

KS: And now you've been married about what, ten years?

WF: It's longer than that now.

KS: Would you do something like that in this day and age, where you'd be like, "Come on, get up, let's dance, let's sway and hug." Or is it just like, "Let's go to bed"?

WF: I'm sure we've, ah, box stepped once in a while!

KS: I just remember we were all agog and giggling, until it set in that, "At least Walt has a girlfriend. And something to do on a Friday night."

From SModcast 37: In a Row?
Jennifer Connelly remakes Scott Mosier

KS: I think a lot of people give credit to a lot of old movies because you're supposed to. I don't think people really like them as much as they say. They just announced a remake of *The Day the Earth Stood Still*. Of course online people are like, "This is a fucking outrage! How could they?" But I don't think there are that many hard-core fans of that movie. You give it honor because it's an old movie that was maybe a little bit ahead of its time, and of course it has the very famous image of the big robot coming out that everybody knows. But when was the last time you watched *The Day the Earth Stood Still*? Or have you even seen it?

SM: I watched it a long time ago on TV.

KS: So if somebody said, "Jennifer Connelly is going to be in a remake of *The Day the Earth Stood Still*," do you get mad?

SM: No.

KS: If somebody said, "Jennifer Connelly is going to be in a remake of *Goodfellas*," do you get mad?

SM: I don't think there's a remake that would make me mad.

KS: If somebody said, "Jennifer Connelly is going to be you from now on, remake you"?

SM: She's going to remake me? My life?

KS: Yeah, and you have to stop living in order for her… No, you don't even have to stop living. You're allowed to keep living but she's remaking you. From now on she's going to refer to herself as Scott Mosier.

SM: Like, married to Alex? I can't go home?

KS: She's going to marry Alex. You don't stop existing, your life doesn't stop happening — just like when you remake a movie, the old one doesn't stop.

SM: Is she going to be a lesbian? Or is she going to marry a guy named Alex?

KS: Honestly, I don't have all the particulars, but she has just announced that she is going to remake your life.

SM: I'm all for it.

KS: She wants to create the definitive version of Scott Mosier and Scott Mosier's life.

SM: I would think that is the weirdest idea anyone ever had.

KS: Especially coming from her, she's generally really quiet.

SM: It would be hard for me to be upset because on a certain level I would want to see it, more than anyone else. I would be her captive audience, like, "Nice move."

KS: I can totally see that too.

SM: "I fucked that up."

KS: I would like to witness that life and be like, "Well, having been a fan of the old Scott Mosier and his life, I've got to say this one is kinda like *The Shining*…."

SM: "Has better boobs…"

KS: "… Good book, good movie." Two separate entities. This Scott Mosier, I could fuck if I wanted to, without people being, "Eeuw, you're gay!" or, "You're cheating on your wife with Jennifer Connelly." I'd be like, "No. I cheated on my wife with Scott Mosier, and I knew Scott before Jen." "But not that Scott." "Well, who's to say which is the better Scott?"

SM: I would be all for it. In fact, if she gets a hold of this, I'm encouraging her to become Scott Mosier.

KS: She won an Oscar.

SM: She did.

KS: It would be a bold move for her, because she's done some shit in her life. That would be her being, "The Jennifer Connelly you all know and love from *Career Opportunities* and the *Rocketeer* and *The Hot Spot*, where you saw my boobs, is going to cease to exist. In the new paradigm, I am Scott Mosier."

SM: It would be like live theater, like interactive theater. That's the ultimate acting job. The whole world is your audience, constantly.

KS: Yes, but in order to maintain and become the paradigm of the new Scott Mosier, she has to lead some semblance of your life. She can't go back to birth and do it because she's too old, she's a grown up lady now. But she'll want to be you, so she'll come to me and ask me, "When do we start *Zack and Miri*? Because I'm your producer Scott Mosier." Suddenly she's competing with you!

SM: So I actually come into contact with her constantly?

KS: She just ignores you if you're in the room.

SM: Like I don't exist.

KS: No. She has to treat you like she's a remake. Whenever a director makes a remake they're like, "I like the original, but this is a different spin on it." So she'll say, "Obviously if I'm remaking Scott Mosier's life, I'm something of a fan of the original, but there's room for improvement." So if she sees you, she regards it as more of a nuisance that you exist than anything else. But she wants to be you, so she wants to be my producer.

SM: What would you do?

KS: I'd be like, "Do you have any production experience aside from being in movies?"

SM: She's like, "Yeah, I worked on all your movies."

KS: "No, but you haven't really! Scott did." Then she's like, "I am Scott." And

you're sitting on the couch. I'm like, "Is anyone taping this for YouTube, this is awesome!" What do I do though? Do I hire her or not?
SM: If you hire her then she's affecting my ability to actually pay my bills and stuff.
KS: Let's say that the people that finance it, Harvey Weinstein is like, "I love Scott too, but…"
SM: "I love Jennifer Connelly"
KS: Yeah, "… Jennifer Connelly's got some sweet cans. I'd rather see her in a picture with you than see Mosier in a picture with you. If you don't hire Scott as a producer I don't think I can make this movie." But I'd be, "But I am, Scott is the producer." He's like, "Not that Scott."
SM: "The better Scott. Scott of Earth-Two."
KS: I would definitely say no, but there would be a moment of me going, "This is so fucked up I might have to do it, I might have to just see how it plays out."

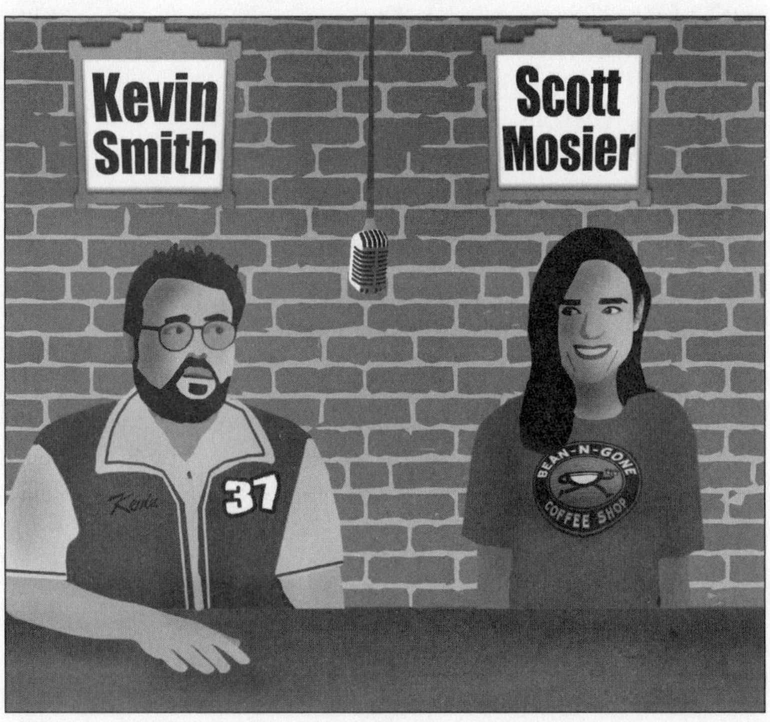

SM: This would be my proposal, because I would be like, "This could amount to the most fascinating experience of all of our collective lives..."

KS: Totally.

SM: "...I would become someone else."

KS: Will you become Jennifer Connelly? Or do you go for somebody else altogether?

SM: So for the movie *Zack and Miri*, she wants to be the producer—

KS: She is the producer, Scott Mosier.

SM: What if I become so-and-so the associate producer?

KS: A whole different being? So you're not a remake, you're a re-imagining?

SM: Yes. I'm a different entity. So I can still participate.

KS: So in movie parlance, you're just a new movie?

SM: Yes.

KS: And you're going to participate as that guy? Do I interview you?

SM: Yeah, we would sit down and I'd be like, "I know my resume sucks..."

KS: "You've done nothing, and as far as I can tell you only came into existence ten minutes ago."

SM: OK, what if I portray myself as a reincarnation of a famous producer?

KS: Like who? Like Saul Zaentz? He's still alive.

SM: I'll be Robert Evans. I will re-imagine myself as Robert Evans.

KS: And Robert Evans wants to produce the movie now?

SM: Yes, I would like to come on as Robert Evans.

KS: Can you tell me stories?

SM: Stories that will fucking make your eyes melt and your ears fall off.

KS: But they've got to be true. If you're becoming Robert Evans, are you doing the same thing that Jennifer Connelly's doing inasmuch as you're just taking over everything that Robert Evans has done and making it your own? So are you telling me Robert Evans stories, from his book *The Kid Stays in the Picture*? Just putting your own spin on it? Or are you just making up stories? Because then that's not Robert Evans.

SM: OK, I wouldn't be Robert Evans. I would go find some obscure producer that nobody has ever heard of and I would become him.

KS: Then you want to work on this movie?

SM: Yeah.

KS: Well you've got to come in on an entry-level salary.

SM: Alright.

KS: I might do that, just to see what would happen.

SM: Well I would hope that actually when I came to you, you'd understand that I'm changing who I am so I can have a job, work on the movie like normal and we can both sit there and be, "That's so fucked up!"

KS: But for the purposes of when I go to Harvey Weinstein and be, "I'm hiring, um, Tarsus Seven as an associate producer," he's like, "Who's that? What's he done?" I'm like, "He's kinda new on the scene."

SM: "He's a robot."

KS: [Laughs] "…very efficient, never needs to sleep, just needs to be plugged in at all times." He's like, "Well, I should meet him." I introduce you as Tarsus Seven and he's like, "Wait a second! That's Scott Mosier." I'm like, "No. That's Scott Mosier!" And Jennifer Connelly has her top off over on the side, reenacting a scene from *The Hot Spot*.

SM: But then she wouldn't be me.

KS: She would be you, but then Scott Mosier's favorite joke is, "Look at me, I'm Jennifer Connelly in *The Hot Spot*!"

SM: Is that what you would tell her?

KS: Yes.

SM: "You didn't know this about him, but now that you're trying to be him, these were his favorite jokes."

KS: We would be so busy being postmodern that there would be no time to make the movie.

From SModcast 38: Leeroy Jenkem!
Defending Kevin's honor

KS: Let's say we went to Disney World and we get onto the boat at the It's a Small World ride, me and you, and there's a line of people behind us, but the boat guy goes, "You can go…"

SM: "That's OK, you guys are famous."

KS: He doesn't even say that, he just doesn't load anybody else, and I go, "Hey, buddy, we can fit more on this boat," and he's like, "No, that's OK." And knowing what that means, that secret message — do you get loud with that guy? You, personally, on my behalf? Are you like, "Fuck you! He's not that fat!" Or do you pull him off to one side — do you say anything? Or do we just talk about it through the whole ride — "You know why they did that, right?"

SM: Well, if we were going to get on It's a Small World at this particular moment, and the story has broken that there's a weight restriction on the fiberglass boats… The Disney guys, some of them are carneys, basically, that can guess weight. [Laughs.]

KS: There it is! It's a theme park, so naturally that goes hand in hand with, like, "Guess your weight, sonny! Come over here and let me guess your weight."

SM: So they're silently guessing people's weights, and they're counting it out, and when it gets to a certain weight, they're moving it forward.

KS: Are you like, "Hey, that's your issue, man, I don't want to get heavy with the guy"? OK, let's take it further — you see me get hurt. When I say, "Hey dude, we've got more room for people on the boat," and he's like, "No, that's OK, your boat has to take off for the happiest cruise that ever sailed, so… you need to go, you need to go *fast*." And I get a little crestfallen because I see what the dude has done is essentially call me fat. *Then* do you get my back? Do you get defensive and be like, "Hey, come here, let me talk to you for a second. That man is a great American hero, alright?" [Laughs.] Do you say anything on my behalf? Or do you just comfort me on the ride?

SM: First of all, I would say before we go on, "Look, there's a chance it's going to be you and me in a boat." [Laughs.]

KS: Would you say that?

SM: Yeah.

KS: Now, do you say that up front, or are you, "Hey, do you remember what we talked about in SModcast, the boat thing?" But secretly meaning, "God, I hope he takes the hint," or do you just flat out put it on Front Street: "Not for nothing, but you might be setting yourself up for heartbreak because you're just fucking fat and they might point you out as fat and not put anybody else on a boat with us. They're going to leave Jen and Alex behind on land because they won't let all four of us in the boat."

SM: Based on *you* deciding to go — you're like, "I want to go on It's a Small World!"

KS: I'm drunk. It's one of the four times a year I get drunk and I'm like, "Hey man! Let's fucking rock Small World and shit! I fucking love Small World!"

SM: Oh, the hell of like, we're all sober…

KS: And I'm drunk!

SM: I would actually try to get us out of the park…

KS: OK, we're both drunk.

SM: Oh, well then I'd be like, "Yeah, alright."

KS: But the good times come to an end when the dude's like, "Alright, this boat needs to take off before you fucking plummet."

SM: If I was drunk enough, I probably wouldn't even understand. I'd be like, "Yeah! Boat! Solooooo!"

KS: What if, after your reverie, after your "Solooooo!" you turn around and go to me and you're like, "Right?" and I'm just [sobs].

SM: I'd be like, "What's your problem? We've got a boat to ourselves!"

KS: Let's play it out. Let me do the guy first.

SM: OK.

KS: "Alright. OK, this boat can go." And then I'm me: [Slurring] "Hey man! Why? What's the — there's plenty of room, man! Put some more motherfuckers on this boat! We can — happiest cruise that ever sailed! Put more people on the boat!" "Uh, no, that's OK."

SM: [Slurring] "Right on, man!" 'Cause I don't like people. I would rather be on the boat by myself.

KS: is that you, though?

SM: Yeah.

KS: Well, stay in the moment.

SM: OK. You're the one that broke it!

KS: Go ahead.

SM: Um.. [Slurs] "Right on, let's go. It's Smaaaaaaaaall World!"

KS: I have been around you drunk, and you would never say, "Right on, let's go!" You don't become like a Red Foxx character! [Laughs.]

SM: Well, I didn't really feel like I was looking back in time when you were pretending you were drunk!

KS: I think we're both playing drunk characters.

SM: OK, I guess I would be like, "Yes! Let's go, let's go."

KS: "Yes, that's what I said, sir." I'm the guy.

SM: "Alright. You don't have to be ho-ostile."

KS: [Laughs.] And now I'm me. [Sobs gently.]

SM: Is the boat moving yet?

KS: Not yet. We're still in dry dock. I'm a dude a few people back: "Hey! Can we fucking speed this up? My kid wants to get on the ride. Why can't we get on that boat? There's seats right there." Now I'm the Disney guy, "Uh, you'll get your own boat, sir" — 'cause they're always polite, "It's coming along presently, don't worry, your boat is on its way." "Why the fuck do they get to go by themselves?" That's the other guy again. "Uh, there's no call for that language, sir, your boat will be — there's one just pulled up." Now I'm me again: [Sobs.]

SM: [Slurs] "Why are you… Why're you cryin?"

KS: "Because I'm fat!"

SM: [Dissolves into laughter.]

KS: "I'm so fucking fat, Scott. It hurts me to know I'm fat."

SM: [Slurs] "Why… why are you saying that now?"

KS: "'Cause the man won't — we're riding alone, [descends into a pathetic squeak] and we did SModcast about it…"

SM: "Yeah, but these are the new retro-fitted boats…"

KS: "I just wish you would defend my honor. Go kick his ass." [Laughs.] So, drunkenly — we're both drunk — I ask you to go kick that dude's ass. And you're DrunkScott.

SM: I'm DrunkScott? I'm not an angry drunk, though.

KS: You're not an angry drunk. You're kinda a loveable drunk. But your boy has come to you and how often have I asked you to kick someone's ass? Never. So obviously it means something to me. And you don't have the presence of mind, the sobriety to go, "Well, he's just talking drunk." You're drunk too, so we're both thinking not very clearly. Obviously, if we're at Disney World and we're going on that stupid-ass ride. So I'm like, "Go kick his ass." What do you do?

SM: Um, I guess if I was drunk, probably what would happen would be I'd try to get off the boat, I'd trip, break my head open and fall in the water.

KS: Ahh — so you fall on the dock and hit your face?

SM: Yeah, I stumble onto the dock.

KS: Dude, what happens when you hit your face?

SM: "Aww, fuckin' god damn it…"

KS: [Slurs] "Hold on, Scott! I'll save you!" And I climb over and kick the dude's ass myself.

SM: OK.

KS: And we both get thrown out of the park.

From SModcast 39: Of Berries and Twigs
Scott Mosier discovers the true nature of Alex Mosier

KS: Would you let your wife videotape you having sex? For like a memento or something?
SM: Yeah.
KS: What if after she did it she was like, "Look, just so you know and in the interests of putting it on Front Street — I'm going to sell this when you're dead. *Scott Mosier Fucks*." Would that bother you? "I've gotta earn!"
SM: The countdown to death part?
KS: Not even that, because you're dead and people are curious — and you're fucking, people are always curious about watching people fuck. "You know him as Snowball, but now watch him as… Low Ball."
SM: It would be really out of character for her.
KS: Well, you're dying, so her head's not in the right space.
SM: But even then, to put pornography up on the Internet for money... I've also got to tell you, I really don't think it's going to be a windfall of cash!
KS: She's like, "Yeah, but every little bit helps. We've got a mortgage to pay, motherfucker, and you're leaving me, so I gotta earn off you still."
SM: Like I said, I don't care.
KS: What if she said, "OK, in the interest of total candor, in order to market it, it's going to be a mockery of you. Like, I'm going to put in Benny Hill type music and sound effects and shit!" And you're being tender in the love making, "Oh baby, I love you so much, we're making love…" And under it she's putting [makes comedy sound effect] and shit like that! At any point, are you like, "Look, please don't do this. Give me my dignity in death!" [Laughs.]
SM: That's like, even more out of character! But I don't know, as soon as I'm dying, I don't really care.
KS: Really? That might bug me.
SM: Once again, I'm more just like, "That's strange. That's odd."
KS: She's like, "This is who I've always been, motherfucker. Welcome to me."
SM: "On the eve of your death, meet the real cookie."
KS: "Couldn't you let me go to my grave assuming I knew the real cookie?"

SM: "Not the fucking exploitative..."

KS: "... mean-spirited, anything for a buck or a laugh cookie Mosier." Would you ever do a porno with your wife? Would you ever shoot it? Have you ever done it?

SM: Nah.

KS: Would you ever do it?

SM: Probably not.

KS: But she's like, "This is what I want for Christmas."

SM: Oh, if she wanted it, sure.

KS: But she's like, "I want to show all my friends, too."

SM: Uh — no.

KS: Really? But she's like, "That's what I want for Christmas too."

SM: "Then you're going to be disappointed!"

KS: For the first Christmas, she says, "All I want is to shoot a porno."

SM: Yeah, fine.

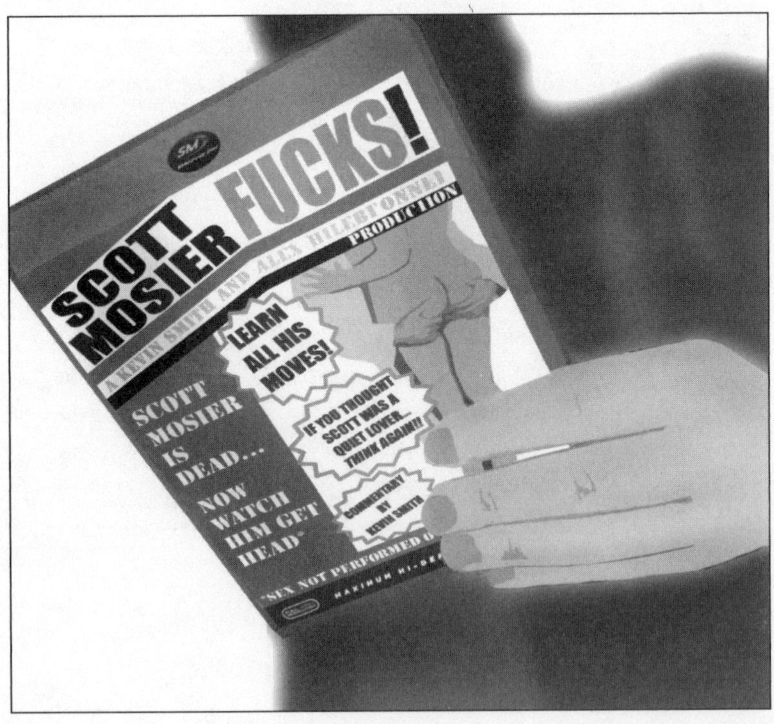

KS: And then the next Christmas she says, "This year I really want to show it to people."
SM: No. Would you?
KS: No. If I had your body though, I probably would. I'd be like, "Yeah, go on man — fucking show that shit. Watch the ladies fall into my web of sexuality!"

From SModcast 40: Ned Smitty
The Ned Smitty routine

SM: [In character as a fictional porn producer] "I want to do a series called *Deli-Porns* and I want you to be the counter-clerk."
KS: I'm the guy working?
SM: Yeah.
KS: But somebody is soliciting me for porn?
SM: Yes. This is the guy that comes in.
KS: You be the guy. I'm Kevin Smith, aged eighteen, working at Krauszer's, [eager 'young' Kevin voice] "Well, I can't wait to see *Batman*." My voice wasn't even that high! I pretty much sounded like I do now, and *Batman* was '89. "Hey can I help you?"
SM: "Yeah, can I have a pack of cigarettes?"
KS: "What kinda cigarettes?"
SM: "I'll have some Kools."
KS: "Kools? Alright. Normally a cigarette associated with the black community but…"
SM: "Well, you know, I'm down."
KS: "You're very white and it just throws me a little bit. Can I make you a sandwich? I make an excellent sandwich."
SM: "Yeah, I'd like to observe you making a sandwich."
KS: "Alright. Why? That's kinda creepy."
KS: "Oh, ok. I don't want to freak you out. So, my name is Ned, Ned Smitty."
KS: "Oh, alright." At this point my hand is on the alarm button.
SM: "I am a porno film producer."
KS: "Get out of here!"
SM: "I am."
KS: "Get the fuck out of here!"

SM: "I'm here in your town visiting my aunty."

KS: "Are you shooting a porno here in Atlantic Highlands?"

SM: "Well, we're not but I will be. I'm here visiting my aunty who's sick, it's OK, she's going to be alright, but I was driving to her house when..." Well, I'm trying to share.

KS: "Right on," I wouldn't say "Right on." Well, "OK."

SM: "I was in here and..."

KS: "This is crazy man! Let me ask you stuff about porn!"

SM: "OK."

KS: "Do they really have sex? They must."

SM: "They do. That's actual sex, that's real penetration."

KS: If I'm eighteen this is '88 or '89. "Is there a lot of AIDs in porn now?"

SM: "No, no no. That's only on the west coast."

KS: "Oh, OK. In west coast porn. Man, I've only seen two porno," at that point I hadn't seen a lot, "I've only seen two porno but I support it. I like the idea."

SM: "It's great, it's fun."

KS: "Wow! I never thought I would meet a porn producer. What do you do?"

SM: "I'm a porn producer."

KS: "Never in a million years thought I'd meet one. And you're shooting one here in Atlantic Highlands?"

SM: "I will be, I've come into your establishment and I am inspired by this location. Nobody has shot a porno in a convenience deli-style store."

KS: "A movie set in a convenience store you say? Hmm. I'll put that idea away for later."

SM: "I mean it will work in a porno."

KS: "It'll never work in a normal movie. Nobody wants to see that."

SM: "Not only am I inspired by the location but you've got a look."

KS: "Really?"

SM: "You have a look."

KS: OK wait, it's '89, so I'm probably buying my clothes at The Oaktree, the urban clothier in the Mall where I got my Silent Bob coat, essentially all the fashions that the people on *The Cosby Show* would wear. If you watch *House Party* they were all wearing clothing that came from The Oaktree. There's a moment in *House Party* where the chick who was on *Martin*, what's her name? That actress who was also in *House Party*, she was in a number of films. *Boomerang*, Eddie Murphy's mouthy neighbor. But she played Kid's love interest. When they have the actual house party at Play's house, her and the other chick are dancing and they all get into a dance-off, as you do. Because that happened at every party I ever went to [not]. She is wearing a vest in that scene that I owned. I owned that mustard vest. I was watching the movie a couple of years back with Johnson and I was like, "I totally fucking had that vest, that same vest." So anyway, I'm dressed in my Oaktree-type gear. White man trying to look like an upscale black man, like a buppie.

SM: Porn, a porn star.

KS: So you like my look?

SM: I like your look.

KS: OK thanks. Now back into the scene. "Hey, thanks man. I shop at the Oaktree."

SM: I'm peeling back my own label: "Oaktree!"

KS: "Get out of town! Isn't it a great store?"

SM: "It's amazing."

KS: "That store will never go out of business!" And it did.

SM: It's capturing the moment.

KS: "But let's be honest, I'm fat and overweight."

SM: "No. Not in porno."

KS: "I've only seen two pornos but I've never seen a dude look like me unless it was Ron Jeremy."

SM: "You strike me that you haven't seen a lot of porn."

KS: "Is this gay porn that you're talking about?"

SM: "No, no, no, no."

KS: "Because I don't go in for that backdoor shenanigans."

SM: "No, this will be you and a woman, you young whippersnapper."

KS: "Wow, OK I'm overwhelmed." OK, taking a break from the scene. Me at age eighteen, no prospects whatsoever. Dropped out of college, was going to Brookdale community college. Didn't know what I wanted to do with my life. Don't think about film for another three years until I'm aged twenty-one. So that's my mindset. Don't like this job, don't like working at all. But "Ooh, I'd like to be in a movie" because I was in the high school productions and stuff. Just never thought about it being a porn movie. So, huge opportunity presenting itself. OK, back into scene. "I've got to tell you, I never thought about this."

SM: "Nobody necessarily thinks about it."
KS: "Can I be frank with you?"
SM: "People fall into this business."
KS: Are there are people in line behind you at this point, at the store? Or is it just slow.
SM: It's slow.
KS: OK, so we can have this conversation. "I've got to be honest. My dick is pretty small."
SM: "You know, I as a porn producer am trying to create a line of real man porns. People don't necessarily want to only watch the perfect male. People want to watch guys like them, the average Joe."
KS: "So a dude like me who gets a hot chick?"
SM: "Yes, that's it!"
KS: "That is a fucking..." OK, out of the scene. That is a brilliant idea. Never mind this *Clerks* nonsense, years ago that's what we should have said.
SM: I could have been Ned, Ned Smitty.
KS: You should have been Ned. But back in film school we should have been, "Hey man, what about a series of porn featuring an average dude with insanely hot chicks?" Because that's what is popular in sit-coms, like when you watch *The King of Queens*, Kevin James, portly actor, and then the chick who plays his wife is thin and cute. That formula happens for *The World According to Jim*, which I don't watch but I've seen posters for it, Jim Belushi is Jim Belushi but he's married to the *Melrose Place* chick in the show. Then there's another one Jamie Gertz is in and she's married to that British dude, he's chunky as well. So obviously, this was an idea ahead of its time in terms of if you had thought about it circa '92...
SM: Our make-believe moment.
KS: We could really have gone down the road of, "Let's make a series of porn with real dudes having sex with hot chicks."
SM: We get porn stars and then we bring in the average guy.
KS: Well, we missed the boat. Anyway, back into the scene. "I don't know what to say, I'm flabbergasted. Would I be the comic relief in this porn? Like the fat loser gets his ass kicked?"
SM: "No, no, no."
KS: "I'm having sex with this woman and then..."
SM: "You're the man pipe. Like a plumber after a storm. You're down there,

you're going to have so much sex."

KS: That's horrible.

SM: I was just trying to go with it. You're eighteen.

KS: "Yeah, right after the storm, Mr Ned!"

SM: I was trying to bring in the… but that happened later.

KS: That happened years later.

SM: I was anticipating it. "You're going to be having sex with two or three girls. No dudes, two or three girls."

KS: "Will there be other dudes in the room?"

SM: "We'll do a three-way! There will not be other dudes in the room."

KS: "Who's shooting it, chicks?"

SM: "Well, there'll be a crew. There'll be a camera guy and stuff like that."

KS: "I'll be embarrassed to have other dudes in the room looking at my dick. It's small."

SM: "It's strange the first time but you've just got to feel it out, get in there."

KS: "Have you had the experience?"

SM: "I've been in there."

KS: "In the ass? Because I've always wanted to try anal."

SM: "We'll have some anal. We'll have the anal scene."

KS: "I've had my finger in girl's asses but I've never had my dick."

SM: "We'll have the anal scene."

KS: I was eighteen, right? I don't know if I'd had any anal by then.

SM: "The way I see it starting is that two hot girls are there, and they're in line. One of them spills her slurpie on the other's top and they take off the top, start making out and then you join in. That's how the movie's going to start, so you're in a three-way."

KS: "Do I have to take my shirt off? Because I don't like to take my shirt off, can I keep a shirt on? Be bottomless? I'm more embarrassed by my gut than my small dick."

SM: "Yeah, sure."

KS: "So I can keep my shirt on?"

SM: "Yes!"

KS: "Mmmm."

SM: "Your shmock."

KS: Oh, I have a vest, an apron?

SM: No, isn't that what they call it?

"When it's soft it won't reach, and when it's hard it won't bend."

KS: Yeah, but I never had to wear that though, I didn't have a uniform. You took me out of the scene…

SM: "Your shirt!"

KS: "OK, I can wear my shirt?"

SM: "Yeah, I want you to be you. But fucking in the store."

KS: "My name, or can I use a porn name?"

SM: "I don't even care what your real name is right now. You think my name is Ned Smitty?"

KS: "Is it?"

SM: "No!"

KS: "Well, what is it if we're being honest with each other? My name is Kev."

SM: "My name is Ted."

KS: "You didn't really stretch with the Ted to Ned thing. You know I never thought this would ever happen to me."

SM: "It will take a couple of days."

KS: "And I get to have real sex?"

SM: "Yeah, you'll make a couple of hundred bucks."

KS: "You're not suckerpunching me here? Like I'm in the midst of fucking a good looking chick and then some dude races in and quick-drops it in my asshole?"

SM: "Yeah, I don't think anyone wants to watch that."

KS: "Well, I don't think anyone wants to watch me fuck hot chicks either."

SM: "You don't know that, are you in the porn business? How old are you, eighteen?"

KS: "Eighteen. You're right, I apologize."

SM: "You tell Ned Smitty — you can barely make a fucking sandwich, and you're telling me what people want to watch in porno?"

KS: "I'll have you know that I can make a hell of a sandwich."

SM: "What are you driving? I'm driving a Porsche."

KS: "Oh, really!?" Because circa '89 that's impressive. "You drive a Porsche?"

SM: "I'm Ned Smitty, porn producer, I'm producing up to fifty, sixty movies a year. I've got my own post-production house. I'm making them."

KS: "What's post-production?" I'm eighteen, I don't know.

SM: "You don't need to know that."

KS: "How am I supposed to be impressed by that if I don't know what it is? Explain post-production to me Ned."

SM: "That's where we finish them."

KS: "Finish what?"

SM: "Most suckers finish their pornos in some other facility. I have my own facility because I have that much money, because I have that much clout."

KS: "OK. I have to tell you man, based on the criteria you've laid out" — I would never use that word at aged eighteen — "it's sounding good to me. I've got nothing going on in my life, Ned. I'll be honest with you."

SM: "I could tell."

KS: "She broke up with me, went to college. I've been dating a series of different girls but nothing that serious. I might be into this."

SM: "This could turn into a career."

KS: "Is there a lot of money in it? How much do I get if I'm going to show my weenie?"

SM: "Ned Smitty's driving a Porsche."

KS: "Yeah, well that's Ned Smitty."

SM: "Ned Smitty started off on camera. I was a construction worker."

KS: "This feels like you're avoiding my question. You're being evasive Ned."

SM: "Are you going to make money?"

KS: "How much will you give me to show my wiener?"

SM: "I told you, the first job you're going to make like four hundred bucks."

KS: "Really?"

SM: "It's your first job. Don't get greedy."

KS: "Yeah, but four hundred? I mean I could steal more than that here at work."

SM: "Yeah but can you steal four hundred dollars whilst fucking multiple hot chicks? Can you do that?"

KS: "Well depends what your definition of hot is, I've had some pretty good looking girls. None in the butt though."

SM: "*Exactly*."

KS: "You're hooking me with that."

SM: "We'll have two anal scenes for you."

KS: "But not *my* anal?"

SM: "Your anus will remain untouched. You and sexy girls."

KS: "I've had a finger in my ass, Ned. To be honest with you. Chicks put it there."

SM: "Well that's alright."

KS: "But I don't want no wiener."

SM: "Well, that's alright."

KS: "I've got nothing against it."

SM: "I have a gay porn division where that happens, but you don't have to."

KS: "Now I see, now I see. Start me with the temptation of the siren song, bring me in with 'Hey, have sex with chicks' and then suddenly I'm blowing some fucking jock."

SM: "No."

KS: Because I just got out of high school I'm still thinking about jocks verses non-jocks. "I don't want to blow some jock, Ned!"

SM: "You're not going to blow some jock. Who said that? I was being upfront with you. You asked me my business. I do produce some gay porn but that's off to the side."

KS: "Really? And those dudes do it in the butt?"

SM: "They do."

KS: "Wow."

SM: "In the butt."

KS: "Wow, I've never known any gay people." I probably did. I did! My brother was gay, but I didn't know it at that point. "I've got to tell you Ned that you're turning me around here. I'm going to give this some serious thought." I would *totally* have given that some serious thought. If aged eighteen some porn producer comes in and sells me like you sold me… with the allure of "post-production"? I would've, because I had nothing going on.

From SModcast 40: Ned Smitty
Kevin finds out he's foppish

KS: I have a fat cock but that sounds sexier than it is. It probably doesn't sound sexy at all. You think you go, "Hey man, I have a fat cock!" and that sounds kinda impressive but I'm talking about, "I've got fat *around* my cock!" The pelvis area, my gut extends below my waistline into the pelvis area. So there's fat around the cock. I remember when I was in high school I was talking to Ernie O'Donnell and this kid Pat Guba, and I was heavy and shit. This was the early days of hip-hop so we were all talking like, "Yo man, I've got a big fucking fat cock."

SM: I missed out!

KS: Ernie reputedly had a big dick. I never saw it, but he always said that his dick was pretty big. But I was saying that, "Well, my dick ain't big, but I've got the weight behind it for the pushing." Pat Goober was like, "That ain't cool!"

[Kevin pauses for an extended laugh, which dissolves into a coughing fit.]

I remember being like, "What do you mean man? That's cool!" and he's like, "No it ain't! You've got fop!" I'm like, "What's fop?" and he goes, "Fat Overweight Penis!" So we run with it, and from that moment forward I'm foppish.

[Kevin continues to fight for breath.]

A conversation that I guarantee you that Pat Goober doesn't remember having, but it made an impression on me, because I was trying to pass off that it was cool. Trying to sell him a, "Hey everybody, get fat! Because you'll have a fat cock!"

[Kevin begins to cry with laughter.]

"That ain't cool!"

SM: [Also helpless by this stage] Man, that is my favorite story *ever.*

From SModcast 42: SMerry Christmas
Scott is told he will raise the second coming of Christ

KS: An angel appeared to you and he looks like me. He's like, "Hey man."

SM: I'm like, "What are you doing?"

KS: "What do you mean, 'What am I doing?'"

SM: How angelic are you? Are you floating? If you're just standing at the foot of my bed in a white robe…

KS: No, I'm dressed like this, but I have a halo.

SM: Like tinfoil?

KS: No, it's hovering.

SM: There would have to be something about you.

KS: I'm the angel Gabriel. You're you. [Yells] "Hey man, wake up!"

SM: "Why are you so aggressive?"

KS: "I'm just happy. I'm here to deliver the good news. The gospel!" Oh wait, Alex has got to sleep through it… it's an angel thing.

SM: "Yeah but I'm half asleep too. You don't have to yell."
KS: "Well, wake up. I've got big news. This is important."
SM: "Alright, I'm right here."
KS: "You know your lady is having a baby right?"
SM: "Yeah?"
KS: "You know that baby is not yours?"
SM: "Er, that's what I hear."
KS: "Who's baby is that?"
SM: "I don't know."
KS: "Take a guess."
SM: "Yours?"
KS: "No man, I'm an angel. We don't have sexual organs. I don't have a dick. It's fucked up, wanna see?"
SM: "No. Erm, I don't know."
KS: "It's God's baby. Did that fucking blow your hair back? It's God's baby in your lady's tummy!"
SM: "It does." At this point isn't that the anti-Christ? Isn't that the second coming?
KS: Well no, there's a difference between those two things. There's an anti-Christ and there's a second coming. So let's say this is the second coming. "Hell shit, yeah! It's the second coming man!"
SM: Yeah, but isn't the second coming like he's coming to bring us peanut butter jelly sandwiches?
KS: Actually the second coming, they say that he returns as a lion, not a lamb. First time he came as a lamb. Which was why he was in the fucking trough in a stable, makes sense. But he says, "When I come back I'm coming back as a lion not a lamb." So actually he wouldn't come back as a baby I don't think, he'd come back as a man. He'd come down as Jesus, as the Jesus we all know from pictures.
SM: He'd just take the elevator down?
KS: No, he wouldn't need an elevator. He's Jesus. But the angel's like, "Yeah, we were going to send him down as a lion not a lamb, but we figured why not make him a lamb again. Worked out so well the first time."
SM: So he's the second lamb?
KS: Yeah, he's the second lamb. The lamb of God. "Your old lady is carrying God and that God-baby is going to grow up to be God-man — not to be

confused with Batman or Superman — but God-man. He will fight his arch-nemesis The Joker. No, the anti-Christ. So you cool with this? I guess we should've asked you before but…"

SM: "Yeah, you're not really giving me a choice."

KS: "Nah, well this is America."

SM: "We didn't want kids. Why didn't you pick someone who wanted children?"

KS: "Because, it makes a bigger profound statement."

SM: "But I didn't want that."

KS: "It's not about what you want, fool! This is about the will of God."

SM: "I don't believe in you."

KS: What the angel? "I'm right here!"

SM: What he's still you?

KS: "Put your hand in my belly."

SM: "I don't want to."

KS: "Do it!"

SM: "In it?"

KS: "Yeah, go ahead, you'll go right through. It's ectoplasm. Kinda like a ghost."

SM: Does it do it?

KS: Yeah, you go right through me.

SM: Oh.

KS: I'm gooey. You come out at the end like Slimer.

SM: How unique.

KS: "Shit yes it's unique! So don't giver her any shit alright?"

SM: "Alright, fine…"

KS: "It wasn't her choice."

SM: "… now that I've touched your ectoplasm."

KS: "But she will be held greatest amongst all women, the greatest mother that ever lived since the first one."

SM: OK, what happens? So we raise it, is there any private or public school funding?"

KS: Hey, you're a producer. Dude, we know how much you make. You're doing alright. Stick that kid in a private school.

SM: Look, I'm just saying the other father could give a little something-something for the effort.

KS: "When you die you're going to go to Heaven."

SM: [Unimpressed noises.]

KS: "What?! You don't want to go to Heaven?"

SM: "I don't know."

KS: "Hey, I live in Heaven. It's awesome! We have cable!"

SM: "What? Fucking people shouting at you?"

KS: "Shit yeah, it's fun!"

SM: "I guess that's OK."

KS: "Heaven's great man. You don't want to go to the other place, I can tell you that much."

SM: "So there *is* another place."

KS: "Oh yeah buddy."

SM: "So the Bible is true."

KS: "Some of it."

SM: "Some of it? You've just said most of it. Heaven and Hell?"

KS: That's not most of it. There's way more in the Bible. You never read the Bible, did you?

SM: No, but I meant the stuff that really…

KS: OK, I'm going to tell you. The Flood? Never happened. All of us spawning from two people? That's just retarded. Stop saying it.

SM: OK, now you're not the angel.

KS: But I am the angel.

SM: But you've changed your whole tone. You used to be like, "Hey man!"

KS: Well just because it makes me mad when you talk about the Bible.

SM: So now you've got fire?

KS: Yeah, I'm on a little bit of a soap-box. "The Flood's not true. Yes, there have been floods but not one with Noah."

SM: "Noah's ark?"

KS: "Not load up two-by-two. Like every being on the planet came from two of everything? That's crazy."

SM: All I'm saying is that—

KS: "You all came from monkeys!"

SM: —you're talking about Heaven and Hell, I'm talking about the shit that counts.

KS: Like what?

SM: The shit that affects you now.

KS: Hit me with something and I'll tell you if it's true or not.

SM: What else is in the Bible that affects you now? The rest of it is history.

KS: Yeah, but some of it ain't right.

SM: I didn't read any of it. Floods and stuff.

KS: Do you know the story of Lot's wife? Sodom and Gomorrah?

SM: I know about Lot's wife and something about salt.

KS: "Sodom and Gomorrah, two cities where lots of sodomy was going on and lots of Gomorrahy was going on. That was the word that we came up with. In Sodom they gave a lot of head, and in Gomorrah they did a lot of butt-fucking. So we thought that sodomy would be the word for head and gomorrahy would be the word for butt-fucking, but you guys just used sodomy for both, which makes no sense to us in Heaven. That's a true story but his wife didn't turn into a pillar of salt. A pillar of paprika."

SM: It was a pillar of paprika?

KS: But they didn't have a word for paprika back then, so now it's just salt.

SM: It's true, but just off. It was just a little wrong. It wasn't a flood, it was really a tsunami, a couple of hundred people died.

KS: "Oh, a couple of hundred thousand people died, but there was no one guy with a boat. There was a lot of people with boats. Once they saw the rains coming they were like, 'Shit, let's build boats.'"

SM: "Was there one guy that pretty much…"

KS: "— one guy who predicted it? Yes. His name was Bob Cummins.

SM: "Bob Cummins?"

KS: "Yeah, but he didn't get any credit. Well, you wouldn't have taken that story seriously if it was Bob Cummins who predicted the flood."

SM: "Why in the world would you come down… I know that you've come to visit me so I'm not mad at my wife—"

KS: "Ease your worried mind, Scott Mosier."

SM: "… why didn't you go talk to the Bible people? Make them get it right? Why tell me? Do I have to write a new Bible? Is that my… I have to correct it?"

KS: "Most people will think you're crazy if you do that. But don't worry about the Bible people, they're going to get theirs. That's what we're waiting for when they die."

SM: "So people will think that I'm crazy for trying to write a new Bible, but people aren't going to think I'm crazy that my wife, who is clearly not a

Random SModquotes

"I'm more inspired by Wayne Gretzky than Jesus, 'cause I got more video on Wayne Gretzky."

virgin, who I have a sexual relationship with, has the second coming of Christ, the second lamb, not lion? People aren't going to think I'm crazy?"

KS: "You're on the same page! People aren't going to think you're crazy about that. First off, don't tell anybody that I told you this."

SM: "So what do I do?"

KS: "This is for you, man. So you don't… Hey man!"

SM: "You can't just start getting loud at me."

KS: "I came down, I just came to tell you this so that you felt OK about it. I don't want you to give your old lady shit because she's got it tough ahead of her. And so do you!"

SM: "But I don't want it."

KS: "Just tell people the kid is yours. Nobody will know. You're married, you're fucking, they'll just assume the kid is yours anyway. Oddly enough the kid is going to look like your buddy, Kevin Smith."

SM: "Everyone will wonder why we chose to have kids after saying we weren't going to have kids."

KS: "Just make something up… 'We love him.'"

SM: "That's not making something up."

KS: "Hey, we watched *Roots* and then wanted a kid after we saw *Roots* again."

SM: That's not good.

KS: OK, give me another movie.

SM: The opening credits of *Garp*?

KS: No, "We watched *Curly Sue* and were like, 'Wouldn't it be great to have a little *Curly Sue*-type kid'?"

SM: "Oh, nobody would believe that. Of course, they'd know her. You guys did write the Bible. You keep coming up with the same thing."

KS: "We were a little drunk. But this is just for you, I don't recommend you tell anybody that."

SM: "So I have to raise him?"

KS: "Yes. Treat him like your own. Raise him as if he's your own. He's kinda yours."

SM: "But then do I have to raise him in the faith? I'm not that person…"

KS: "But now you know that's happening… it's the proof."

SM: I'll probably wake up and be like, "I had the most fucked up dream. I took an Ambien tonight."

KS: "I'm going to leave you two maracas under your pillow, like in that movie *Dogma*. Which you produced! And we all like very much."

SM: "Thanks."

KS: "Lots of butt-sex jokes in that movie. That Jay character is funny."

SM: "Awesome. Why didn't you give him the baby?"

KS: "Because he's fucking retarded, that dude."

SM: "Why didn't you give Kevin Smith the baby?"

KS: "Because he's already got a kid. You know what kinda pressure that it on the older sibling if all of a sudden your younger sibling is God? Did you ever see *Fred Claus*? It's terrible, the movie and being the younger sibling to a larger-than-life figure."

SM: "I've got you."

KS: "You've got a sister?"

SM: "I do."

KS: "There was a period where she had a tough time adjusting to the fact that you were very successful, yes?"

SM: "A little bit, yeah."

KS: "There you go. That's why we chose people who wouldn't have a kid and it would never be a problem."

SM: "No sibling rivalry."

KS: "We've been watching you man! You make sense. Years from now, if there was going to be a history — though there won't be because when your kid grows up he battles the anti-Christ and the world stops being — but if they were going to write books, they'd be writing them about you and your brave choice."

SM: "Do I have to train him to fight the anti-Christ?"

KS: "Yes, do you know judo?"

SM: "I don't know anything, that's why I don't think you should have picked me. You should have picked an Ultimate Fighter or something."

KS: "Just set the kid down with, did you ever see *Every Which Way But Loose*?"

SM: "I did, yeah."

KS: "*Every Which Way But Loose* and *Any Which Way You Can*, just let the kid watch that and see—"

SM: "Just let him absorb."

KS: "— the bareknuckle boxing and shit. Get him a monkey to drive around with. Teach him 'Right Turn Clyde', everything's going to be totally cool. Let the kid watch *The Matrix*."

SM: I really hope this never happens.

KS: "Anyway it's all going to be good, blessed art thou amongst men. When I appeared to your wife I said, 'Blessed art thou amongst women.' Blessed art thou amongst men, you, sir, I would say singular but it's happened before, but you have the *great* honor of being the step-father—"

SM: "Me and Joseph are in the box seats?"

KS: "Totally. He's a saint and so you'll be a saint too. You don't want to go to Hell, trust me."

SM: "OK."

KS: "OK, so we good?"

SM: "Yeah, that's amazing. Thank you!"

KS: "Sweet. Hey I got to take a shit, can I use your bathroom?"

SM: "You don't have organs."

KS: "I know, I was just kidding. Alright, blessed art thou."

SM: "Blessed are the angels who speak loudly."

KS: "That's how we say goodbye in Heaven. 'Blessed art thou!' We don't add shit to the end of it. OK, so blessed art thou."

SM: "Later!"

KS: Whooop! And then he's gone.

From SModcast 45: End of the SMod-fast
How long before a stranded Kevin and Scott would fuck?

KS: If we were in *Lost*, and there was nobody else...

SM: On the show, or if we were actually trapped on the island?

KS: It's like *Lost*, but the plane that went down, we were the only two survivors.

SM: OK, so we're stranded on an island.

KS: We're stranded on an island. That island. But there's only two of us, so the Others don't bother with us, they're not a threat or anything like that.

SM: They just watch, and snicker.

KS: Yeah, they're just like, "Let's watch and see how long it takes for these two to fuck." If we were lost on the desert island, and… how long have they been lost? At least half a year, in TV time?
SM: Something like that, yeah.
KS: Like, in real time, it's been three, four seasons, but I think it's only like…
SM: I thought it was like a hundred and ten days.
KS: Something like that. So… We're on the island with no hope of… we don't know if we're ever gonna get rescued, we don't even have hope like these fuckers, like every once in a while they find a plane or some such shit…
SM: Yeah. What, we never leave the beach?
KS: Yeah, we're always just like, "Let's stay here!" Or you're like, "Let's go hiking!" and I'm like, "Fuck that, let's stay here in case somebody comes. Plus, hiking sucks." So, we're just living on the beach and shit, and maybe every once in a while you go out and run into a polar bear, and you're like, "There's a fucking polar bear on the island!" And I'm like, "I told you you should stay on the beach!"
SM: I don't think I'd be doing recreational things. It would be more like, "I'm gonna go try to get us some food."
KS: I'm like, "Alright, I'm down with that."
SM: If I ended up on an island, I might introduce the idea of like, "I should hike to a vantage point, where we can see most of the island, 'cause maybe there's something, anything on there, as opposed to staying on one beach; two, I would hike into the interior to try to find food. You would have to deal with fish.
KS: Like, catching them?
SM: Yeah, but also eating them.
KS: Yeah, that'd be tough for me. I mean, I guess if you're hungry you'd fucking do it.
SM: We'd have to create fire. There would be a part of me that would be like… I love the idea of us standing around, trying to figure out when we're going to fuck each other.
KS: That's what I'm talking about. How long would it be before we were like, "Alright, we're gonna…" Well, first off, let's take it to the first level. Do you jerk off on the island?
SM: Sure.
KS: Do you do it privately? Do you do it while I'm sleeping?

SM: Uh…

KS: Or are you like, "I'm going on a hike," and it's like a three minute hike and you're like, "I'm back!"

SM: I'm just behind a tree, five feet away, you can see me…

KS: Finding a knot on a fucking palm tree, drilling it… You do jerk off? Do you jerk off in the ocean, underwater, or is that like, salt water on your dick?

SM: Um…. Maybe I would do it there. I don't know where I would do it. I think that there would be… initially, my thing would be food and shelter.

KS: Right.

SM: And I would think I would use masturbation as more of just a…

KS: Tension reliever?

SM: Yeah, like, you know, after a long day. I mean, it's pitch dark, it's not like there's lots of light.

KS: It's true.

SM: I could be in the same room, and you wouldn't see it.

KS: Yeah, I'm like, "What is that noise?" "Nothing. Go back to sleep." "I'm not sleeping." "Just — you didn't hear nothing."

SM: "You don't see nothing, you don't hear nothing."

KS: "Get lost." I'm like, "We *are* lost!"

SM: I'd probably do it in private.

KS: Mmm. How long… how many years do think it's before you're like, "Let's fuck." Or, do you ever get to that point, or is it too weird? You're like, "We're too… I don't want to ruin the friendship."

SM: It would be a strange… I think it would have to be something that you would have to experience. On the outset, I would be like…

KS: "Never!"

SM: Well, it wouldn't occur to me that… like, at this point… I think you would have to go through the experience, because at this point off the top of my head, my initial reaction is that one, I would think about surviving…

KS: Right.

SM: And getting rescued. Not to avoid fucking you.

KS: Right, right. I mean, I'm starting to get a little hurt, my feelings are hurt.

SM: I'm just sending out all these messages, "Please rescue me so we don't have to fuck…"

KS: "I'm within a month of fucking this fat pig and I don't wanna do it. Please, help us get unlost."

SM: I assume that it might be something that might progress over time. It would have to be at that moment… not because I'm so like appalled by the idea of having sex, with you…
KS: Right. Thanks.
SM: But more, um, it would be way down on the list of things. Even if we crashed, in the *Lost* sense, and we were part of a larger group…
KS: Well, there would be broads.
SM: Right, but I also don't know how quickly it would just be like, "Who wants to fuck?"
KS: Oh my god, right away. If I'm not married, and I crash on *Lost*, and there's Jack and all those people are like, "We're building the shelters, we're going to find food," they're taking the lead, I'm like, "Right on. Hey ladies, who wants to fuck me?" I would be thinking about it.
SM: Once again, it would not be my initial… I don't think it would occur to me about sex until I knew that I was like, "I am in a situation where I can survive on a day-to-day basis."
KS: Well, it's like *Lost*, where we find a bunch of food, the Dharma Initiative food…
SM: Fresh water, food and shelter. As long as I was like, "I'm not gonna eat every day but I have a…" there's a method…
KS: You're eating every day, you have like cornflakes and shit, and peanut butter, all that Dharma food.
SM: Oh, we do? Just quickly… we find a hole in the ground…
KS: Totally. The hatch, and, fucking awesome, "Holy shit there's food," but nobody's in the hatch, it's not like we've got to deal with Desmond who's [in Desmond accent] "Alright, brudda, who's gonna fuck me," it's like, we find the hatch and it's, "Holy shit, someone was here before, and there's food." I guess if we found the hatch, and food, we would be less inclined to fuck because we would be like, "Somebody might be watching."
SM: Exactly. There's literally a red tube feed to fucking home and everyone's like, "They're alive… and they're totally gay."
KS: Everyone's taking bets and shit, Vegas odds are up, "How soon before these idiots fuck."
SM: It's like *Porn Survivor.* "We've stranded two men on an island, who think they're alone…"
KS: But it happens in jail, like, dudes go to jail, and you're talking about

dudes who are in jail for like, three years, and they'll still fucking down-low it and shit, and get blown by other dudes, and fuck other dudes... Remember *Midnight Express*, that dude fucking in the shower scene, where they made tender love? Like, I don't know how long he was in jail at that point, but, dudes fuck if they're left to their own devices. 'Cause if you're talking about the two genders, one is more inclined to fuck on a regular basis. I think. And I hope that doesn't sound misogynist, or gender-biased, but I think dudes have a way higher libido than chicks, at least to a certain point, and then chicks kick into their prime or whatever and then their libido goes up or something.

SM: I think... I'm sure that women would all say, if there were two women...

KS: Oh, they would totally fuck. They'd be more inclined to fuck, and eat pussy, than...

SM: Be intimate.

KS: Well, eat pussy. You can call it intimate, I call it eating pussy.

SM: Um, I mean... once again, I couldn't put a time frame on it, but I'm sure that…

KS: Three years?

SM: I'm sure within three years.

KS: *Within* three years? [Pause.] Fag.

SM: [Resigned] I was like, "I know the hook's out there, if I don't bite it it's just gonna keep going on…"

KS: I think that would be strange. I think there would be a lot of jerking off though. 'Cause if you want to talk about it as a tension reliever, what's more tense than like, "We're fucking trapped, man, nobody knows where we are"? I'd be jerking off every hour, I think.

SM: Unless you're going to start eating your semen, you gotta like…

KS: Totally. It's like, we get a fire going, we take that shit, put it in a makeshift coconut pan, and make eggs, kinda. Like, whip it up. Like egg whites.

SM: Um… [long pause]. That means… so we don't have cornflakes, now? We're fucking making cum egg?

KS: Dude, there's a whole closet full of cornflakes. I'm like, "I know, but I want some bukkake eggs!"

From SModcast 46: Mr Deaves Goes to Town
"Where's my shirt?!"

[Kevin and Scott are talking about incest. Again.]

KS: You're married to Alex.

SM: Yeah.

KS: So, I come to you and I'm like, "I don't know why, but I did some digging around…"

SM: "In my family tree? You dirty fuck…"

KS: "Yeah, and I found out that your parents had a child before Kristen, but they gave it up for adoption, because you know, they just weren't ready. That child is Alex." What do you do?

SM: Well, I think we both would be like, "That's kinda weird…"

KS: Really? I don't know, dude, I don't know if she would be like, "That's weird." She loves you.

SM: Well, it's not like I don't love *her*. I think it would be… at that point, it's not an internal thing. It's not like you have a gland, the incest gland, that

goes off, that makes you feel sick when you're sexually attracted to somebody that you're related to. Because otherwise that couple in London would be like, "Oh my god, I got the shits," all the time…
KS: It's the reverse. What they're saying is like, genetic sexual attraction is predicated on meeting someone you haven't known your whole life, having an instant fucking attraction to them, and the reason is because you're genetically connected.
SM: But then, you know, why it's really wrong is a social thing.
KS: Would you get divorced?
SM: Yeah, I can't imagine I could deal with that. I mean, I love her and she loves me…
KS: Would you get divorced, or would you have it annulled? I guess technically you could have it annulled.
SM: I guess you could.
KS: The government would be like, "Let's just all pretend this never happened."
SM: "… and like, eww."
KS: "And we would like to close up this session by saying, eww." You're like, "Yeah, it is, but we didn't know."
SM: "We didn't know. C'mon, eww?"
KS: "Yeah, c'mon, I mean look at her, you'd fuck her, right?"
SM: "Not if she was my sister!"
KS: "Well I didn't know!"
SM: "EWWW! Eww on you!"
KS: That could be a sentence from the court. "Eww on you." They're like, "We can't officially penalise you or put you in jail, but this court declares: Eww on you, Mr Mosier." You're like, "No, don't bang the gavel! Can't I say something first?"
SM: "Goddamnit!"
KS: Would you seek to have it annulled, or would you go through the divorce proceeding?
SM: Um… I think that we would talk about it, and talk about what we wanted to do.
KS: Wouldn't you find it weird to talk to her?
SM: I don't think that part would be weird.
KS: Would you start fighting with her like a sister?

SM: Yeah, like, "Where's my shirt?!"

KS: Was that a fight that you had with your sister?

SM: I don't know, I was just like, what do you fight about… just that accusatory…

KS: [Laughing] "Where's my shirt…!" She's like, "I think we have bigger problems in front of us, Scott!"

SM: "Yeah…"

KS: "Not right now, I don't have a shirt!"

SM: "… after I have a fucking shirt on!"

KS: "You're probably attracted to me! I gotta put a shirt on!"

SM: "You got me walking around without a shirt! That's what started all this!"

KS: Would you…

SM: I wouldn't suddenly be, like…

KS: A dick? Where you're like, "You're not getting half."

SM: No, that wouldn't occur to me.

KS: Well she's your relative, so you'd wanna help her out, I guess.

SM: Well, I mean I would feel like…

KS: More divorces would be friendly if it turned out they were siblings. You're like, "Well, you're my sister, so I don't wanna…"

SM: "… I don't wanna be a dick."

KS: "Yeah, you can have the house."

SM: "What are we gonna do at reunions?" That would be terrible.

KS: Oh, that would be so bad. How mad would you be at your parents?

SM: Um… I mean it would depend, it would have to be like, "Look, now fucking tell me the whole thing. Number one, are there more? 'Cause I don't wanna do this again."

KS: They're like, "Yeah, there are approximately… the final seven have yet to be revealed." It's like *Battlestar Galactica*.

SM: Um, I would wanna know… and I would be mad because I would be like, "Look, if this was a possibility, you coulda thrown it out there." You know, especially 'cause I would have been like, "You knew that Alex was the exact same age of the baby…"

KS: Yeah, but that's a stretch, man. They gave her up for adoption, she changed her name, they didn't follow her.

SM: Yeah, but at least they could have been like, "There's this possibility…"

KS: What, any time you fuck somebody Alex's age, they're gonna be like, "Look, if it's a girl, and she's aged blank..."

SM: Why not? It's the one thing they gotta dissuade me from doing!

KS: Because I'm sure they would think, in a million years that would never happen.

SM: Yeah, but once again, the *one thing* they gotta dissuade me from doing is fucking somebody born that year. That's all. That's *all* they gotta do to make sure they're not gonna create this awful situation.

KS: So, they would be like, "When's her birthday, Scott?"

SM: And I'm like, "Um, May first."

KS: "Oh, Scott, we have to talk..."

SM: I'm like, "Five years after...?" Yeah, I mean that's... I feel like, wouldn't you do that?

KS: Nah.

SM: No?

KS: I'd be like, "Let's see what happens! This could be fucked up!"

SM: "This is better'n blackjack!"

From SModcast 50: Gnome Alone
Kevin and Walt discuss what Mewes would do for a comic

KS: Do you remember the show, we were driving back from New York? It was me...

WF: If you're talking about the Mewes?

KS: Yes.

WF: That wasn't New York.

KS: Where was it?

WF: That was down South, like at Toms River. We went to the most terrible show we ever went to, and there was like, one comic book dealer, and it was Blotchy.

KS: Blotchy, a dude that we saw all the time in our neck of the woods. So we're like, "We're busting this shit exotic, we're going to new places!" And the only fucking comic book dealer was Blotchy.

WF: I know what you're talking about. That was... Like, my jaw hurt for hours later from laughing so much that... I never felt a pain like that.

KS: It was me, you, Johnson, and Mewes. And this was a fourteen-year-old Mewes, who was like, *way* into comics, but didn't *have* any comics. He had some comics…

WF: That we would just give him.

KS: Yes, the real dregs. Like, he had an entire run of *Vigilante*, that you were like, "I hate this book," and gave to him, and it was the best comic in the world. That's one of the things that's always been charming about Mewes — there's no such thing as a bad comic. He's never read a bad comic. It's like, "How was that?," he's like, "Oh, it was awesome." And you're like, "Dude, it was *Richie Rich*," and he's like, "Oh, it was awesome." But even the worst… like the *New Universe* books and shit like that…

WF: He would find something in it that just…

KS: *Sonic Disruptors*, shit like that, he would just be like, "Oh, man that was awesome." And it was just the graphic art somehow appealed to him, or whatever, fantasy, who knows what it was, but he fucking loved it. So we started taking him to the shows and this dude didn't have any fucking money to buy comic books. It was just so weird, 'cause we were all like, late teens, early twenties, hanging out with a fourteen-year-old kid. Driving around, sometimes taking him out of state, taking him weird places… if he'd had conventional parents, they might have been like, "Can we meet your old friends? Are they trying to give you drugs? Do they ever ask you to look at their pee-pees?" It's just such a weird notion, but we *did* hang out with him a lot.

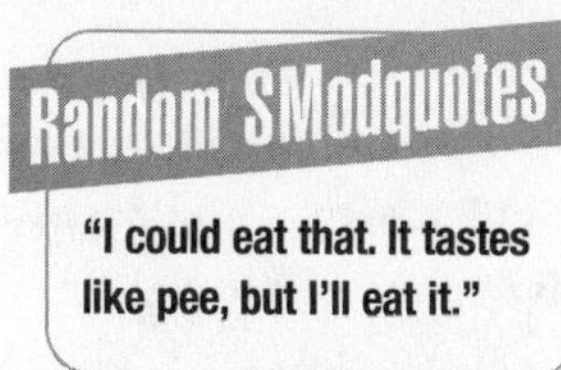

Random SModquotes
"I could eat that. It tastes like pee, but I'll eat it."

WF: Exactly, like if my daughter turns fourteen and she's driving around with twenty-year-olds, *young* twenty-year-olds taking her around, I'd be like, "No, that ain't happening. Something's wrong with them. Normal people don't hang out with fourteen-year-olds."

KS: Yeah, "Why are they doing this? What do they want from you?"

WF: Exactly.

KS: "Have they introduced a video camera yet?" And it was a weird motley crew, too… I was working in convenience stores, you were working at the rec, Johnson was, I think, a two-time college drop-out at that point. Could you imagine, if Mewes had traditional parents it would be like, "OK, so let me understand it… one of these dudes doesn't have a license?" 'Cause how old were you when you finally got your driver's license?

WF: Twenties. I don't even remember.

KS: I would probably call the police. Like, "Officer, I don't know that any crime's been committed, but this is just weird. It's a fishy situation." And oddly enough, it wasn't like we'd go to a comic book show and then we'd go get fucked up and drink beers or anything. None of us drank, none of us did drugs, it was completely fucking innocent…

WF: Innocent in terms of, he made us laugh so we were like, "He's funny! Let's bring him!"

KS: But that day, he made us laugh, but he didn't intentionally make us laugh. The day we came back from that Toms River show, I think I almost got in a fucking car accident 'cause I was laughing so hard. It was the drive from Toms River to Highlands, maybe a forty-five-minute drive. And it was forty-five minutes of the most humiliating beratement, like jovial beratement, that anyone has ever been subjected to. And it started very simply, 'cause we were talking about, you know, Mewes couldn't get books.

WF: But Mewes, I think started it off, like, "Maybe if I sucked his dick he'd give me a comic book." Like, he opened the door, that we just kicked open…

KS: It was, it was the notion of Mewes just going like, "Maybe if I sucked his dick he'd give me a *Vigilante*." And then suddenly we're all like, "Yeah! And *then*...!" And the forty-five-minute ride was just a non-stop series of just… deeds so fucking, so insane…

WF: Heinous.

KS: Heinous, worse than pissing in a little gnome's mouth… of him and these things that Blotchy would do to him, in order to give him a fucking comic book.

WF: Just out of his 50 cent box!

KS: Sucking this dude's cock, sucking the cocks of his friends that weren't even there, him taking a shit in his mouth, just really fucking weird heinous stuff… going home and having to live with him for a week…

WF: Do you remember how we played it up, though? Like as if Blotchy… as we entered the room Blotchy was all sweaty and nervous, waiting for him? Like pacing back and forth like a fucking lion, waiting for Mewes to arrive! 'Cause he had tasted Mewes at previous shows?

And he was just hoping beyond hope that he might appear at this show! And he'd be like, "This show is closed!"

[Prolonged hysterical laughter.]

KS: And it would go on for so long… and he started as a participant, 'cause he instigated it with his comment, and then it would slowly fucking devolve…

WF: He pretended he was sleeping! Like, after we said we were done, he was like, "Oh, I was sleeping, I didn't even hear any of that."

KS: It just went from four people making fun of one guy, to three people making fun of one guy, and the guy we were making fun of checked out twenty minutes prior… And yet another situation where, if he had conventional parents and he went home, and he was like, "These guys were saying that this caged animal of a man with a skin condition was pacing back and forth sweating, waiting to taste me…" Oh my god. He would, he would get kinda… First he would lose interest, it would go from him laughing to him being like, "Huh…"

WF: He would add some jokes to it…

KS: Then Johnson, who was kinda the ring leader — once you opened a door for "What if?," Johnson's the king of "What if?" And Johnson took it to insanely dark places, and we were cackling, and Mewes would go from laughing to like, "Uhuh, huh-huh…" and then just, "Huh." And then suddenly there was no laughter, and then he would sit there reading a comic book, like, giving us more material! We're like, "How much for that fucking page, buddy?" Just laying into him like crazy. And then he would literally close the book and go to sleep against the door, pretend to go to sleep!

WF: I think that's the only time I'd ever seen him do that, because ninety-nine percent of the time, he would go back at you with like, "Well then *you* did this!" but I guess he wasn't feeling well that day, or he just didn't have it in him.

KS: Yeah, he was just like, "I don't know how many different ways you can have me fucking this guy, but it stopped being funny twenty minutes ago." And it was one of the only times I'd ever seen him shut down. And also, put yourself in his position: you're trapped in a fucking car, you can't even be like, "Pull over, let me out," 'cause you're on the fucking parkway somewhere between Toms River and Highlands.

WF: He was that rare fourteen-year-old who had a wit, a humor about him that he could go back at a twenty-year-old, and school him… like, he had enough ammunition most of the time…

KS: To where you're just like, "Yeah, that's funny. Fucking Mewes."

WF: Not this day!

KS: NO. Oh, my god.

WF: I can't remember crying laughing like that since then…

KS: But he did not go to the next show.

WF: No?

KS: No, he took the next show off. He was like, "Yeah, that's alright. You guys are just gonna make fun of me."

From SModcast 52: The (c)Rapture
What if Jesus came back?

KS: What if Jesus came back? Would they believe him, that he was Jesus? Would he have to do some miracles?

SM: Yeah, if he had some powers.

KS: What kind of powers? Lasers-out-of-his-eyes Jesus?

SM: No one wants magic.

KS: Yeah, they don't want the Jesus that's like, "How many loaves of bread do you have? 'Cause now you have ninety!" I'm talking about the Jesus who's like, "I return as a lion, *bitch*, not a lamb." He's got the gas finger like the aliens in *Signs*. He lifts his finger and…

SM: I dunno, that might get some giggles. Then everybody would get a fuckin' baseball bat and a glass of water and Jesus would be dead.

KS: Like, "We saw that movie."

SM: "Yeah, way to fuck up, Jesus." And Jesus' return is over in twenty minutes 'cause somebody doused him with water and fucking beat him to death with a piece of wood.

KS: "Swing away Meryl!"

SM: "It's the Second Coming!... oh it's over."

KS: "Everything's back to normal."

SM: "Is there a Third Coming? Have we read about a Third Coming?"

KS: If there is, show them a better movie, where the aliens are unstoppable. Don't show them a movie where the aliens have a weakness.

SM: Even if he had the power where people throw bombs at him and shoot him and he'd just be like, "Nah."

KS: He's indestructible?

SM: Yeah, that could be a peaceful Jesus, who's just like, "You could do anything you want to me, but the power of love is so strong that you cannot touch me." That would have to make people think.

KS: What, gay Jesus?

SM: Well it's not like Jesus before was out there preaching about—

KS: That's my point, though, he's like, "Look, last time I was gay. This time I'm coming back like a hillbilly. I'm filled with hate. I got a dog, a truck and a shotgun slung under my dash. I'm mad as hell."

SM: That would be effective too. "Is that a 4x4 pick-up?"

KS: "You're damn right it is! I gotta 350 big block under the hood, bitch!" No, if Jesus came back, less love, more like, "Look, I tried love and you fucking nailed me to wood. Now I'm coming back and I'm not gonna shield my glory, I'm not gonna hide my light under a bushel. I am the Son of God…"

SM: "… and I will fuck you up."

KS: "… and if you're Christian or Catholic, I am God himself, because I'm part of the blessed trinity, three people, one God: God the Father, God the Son, God the Holy Spirit. I'm God the Son but that makes me God, period. I am… I am um…" Which is weird, because we believe in monotheism. Most people do. But still, they find a way to sneak it in, like, "Well, there's really three people in one God." So, at that point you're almost like, what, you're back to like, Zeus, Hera and Mars? You know, there's multiple Gods. But anyway, so he comes back and he's like, "I'm powerful! Look at these things I can do!"

SM: What, you mean like he came back and he dropped into the middle of… you know, to fight on behalf of Christianity, and he fucking shot lasers out of his eyes, and destroyed everybody?

KS: Yes.

SM: Do I feel that that would somehow convince people to fear him? To the point of being like, "I will believe in you, 'cause I don't want to be incinerated by the lasers coming out of your eyes."

KS: Yes.

SM: I think that that could convert a lot of people. Way more than door-to-door.

KS: Yeah. What, walking around with a bunch of dudes…

SM: If he showed up to my house… there were some people walking around the neighborhood the other day, with pamphlets, and I don't answer the door, I don't do that.

KS: You're like, "I don't want a *Watchtower*."

SM: If it's a dude that's like, "I'll incinerate you with my laser vision. Let me in your house." You're like, "Alright."

KS: Does he have to be normal size, or can he be like, the size of…

SM and KS simultaneously: Voltron?

KS: So strange that we both went to Voltron as being like — instant tall.

SM: I guess it doesn't really matter. I mean, once he shoots lasers out of his eyes… he could be a midget. I mean, he could literally be like the fucking little alien from *The Flintstones*.

KS: Like The Great Gazoo? [Does the voice] "Hello, Fred!" Yeah, I guess. But I think it would be more impressive if he was like… Like I called you and was like, "Look out your fucking window!" And you did and you saw Jesus traversing the landscape, and he was as tall as a building.

SM: And he was just picking shit up and tossing it.

KS: And you just saw him like [makes laser noise] lasers coming out of his eyes, fucking fire from where the lasers were hitting, smoke…

SM: I would no doubt be frightened.

KS: OK, let's say he was just man-size Jesus. He's no bigger'n you. He's a little guy.

SM: Yeah.

KS: You look at him, you figure you could take him in a bar fight. But he starts zapping motherfuckers with lasers out of his eyes. And he says… alright, let's go one beyond that. He didn't even come to see you. Yet.

SM: Not yet.

KS: First he goes over there, to let's say… not Iraq, but um… Afghanistan.

SM: OK.

KS: He's like, "I'll find… I don't even have to *find* Osama bin Laden, I know where he is, I'm God."

SM: And he'll pay that motherfucker a visit.

KS: Yes, "Ding dong! Guess who's here! It's Jesus, the mighty Jesus!" Let's say he started

"And then I took my shirt off and started playing the saxophone."

taking out the extremist Muslims. Like, Al-Qaeda and the Taliban. People who are the current source of our misery, and fear-mongers. Are you OK with that?

SM: Am I OK with the fact that he's like, killing everybody?

KS: The liquidation of the foreign aggressor, yes.

SM: Just killing everybody isn't necessarily the solution to any problem.

KS: Well, then what is your solution to the Al-Qaeda problem?

SM: SModcast Resolution 402…

KS: Is that what it is?

SM: No, I mean, the big thing is that you have what's happening now, and you have the future, and one of the keys to it is the future, and how do you prevent more people joining. It's like smoking.

KS: By going to war against a country, and lying and saying they have Weapons of Mass Destruction, and killing a lot of families, and orphaning a lot of children. I'm sure that's how it's done.

SM: Exactly. Enraging the locals.

KS: Yes. I'm sure that's how we're doing it. But no, be serious. Jesus comes back…

SM: OK, back to being serious.

KS: … and starts taking out members of Al-Qaeda. Including Osama bin Laden.

SM: There's not much I could do.

KS: But are you for it? I mean, they do a vote, you get a call from Pollster, they're like, "Are you pro-vengeful bloody Jesus, or against vengeful bloody Jesus?"

SM: Um, I'm not pro-vengeful bloody Jesus.

KS: So, you're against him?

SM: Um, I would argue that…

KS: You're like, "Don't tell him, but yes, I'm against him."

SM: "Can I give… my name's Ned. Can I give a false name? Scott Mosier fucking loves him, but uh… I'm his cousin." I would hope that if Jesus came back, almighty powerful, and could do anything he wanted, he would come to a possibly better, more peaceful solution than just eradicating everybody who looked at him cross-eyed.

KS: I disagree, man, I disagree. I think you know, next time, according to the Christian faith, when Jesus is supposed to come back, he's supposed to come back as the lion, not the lamb...

SM: As Voltron.

KS: As Voltron, the Everliving. No, that's Mumm-Ra. He's coming back as Mumm-Ra, the Everliving! Um... When he comes back, it's supposed to be the End of All Things. He comes back as the judge and the jury and the executioner.

SM: Yeah. There's a reason I'm not a Christian.

KS: I know, but that's the fun part of Christianity. All the fucking rules, that are like, "You can't do this, you can't do that..."

SM: It's like, "I'm gonna masturbate, I'm waiting for the end."

KS: Yes, that's the shit that's a pain in the ass. But when you think about the sci-fi aspect to it...

SM: Coming down and laying waste to everybody?

KS: Yes! That'd be awesome!

SM: I've been waiting for this! It's like *Iron Man*!

KS: People have been waiting for hundreds of years, yes, like *Iron Man*!

SM: That's what Mel Gibson should make.

KS: What, the angry Jesus movie? If you made the angry Jesus movie, would people go?

SM: Like, him coming down and just laying waste to everybody?

KS: Yeah, like *Jesus the Avenger*.

SM: I'm sure somebody would go. I mean...

KS: Or you call it, *Holy Christ!* That's the name of the picture, and it's essentially about the end times, but in a way that both Christians and non-Christians can enjoy it. Because Christians can enjoy it like, "This is what was prophesied."

SM: "I always wanted to see it depicted!"

KS: Totally. And non-Christians could be like...

SM: "It's like the *Transformers*!"

KS: "It's fucked up!"

SM: "With more blood!"

KS: "But believable!"... I think that movie would do business. 'Cause you could have all the Christians going, and you could make it bloody, 'cause they went to *The Passion of the Christ* and that was very bloody. And you could have non-Christians going like, "That's so fucked up I have to see it."

SM: I mean you'd have to, you know, spend enough money. It'd have to be like a 250 million dollar movie, your effects have to be through the roof. It can't be like a Corman picture, with fucking guys in rubber suits…

KS: Like a *Godzilla* Jesus.

SM: Exactly. You know, you'd have to spend money.

KS: Would someone finance that picture, you think?

SM: I assume that if you wanted to put together… I don't see as how you couldn't… someone could put together a hundred million bucks, and make *Holy Christ!*

KS: With an exclamation point at the end of it. I would totally see that movie. That'd be a buzz movie, man.

SM: What's the end? Is the end literally just, one guy's like…

KS: No man, the end is we stop him.

SM: Oh yeah, we fight back?

KS: No, we can't do that. If we do that, the Christian audience wouldn't turn out.

SM: They'd be pissed. Everybody's gone? Is that the end, everybody's gone?

KS: Well, it depends what you believe. If you're a pre-Tribulationist, or a post-Tribulationist. Your pre-Tribulationist believes that the Rapture happens in advance of the Tribulation, so the Rapture happens, all the faithful are taken body and soul to Heaven, that's kinda the plot of the *Left Behind* books, and then we endure seven years… those who are left behind on Earth endure seven years of the Tribulation, where essentially it's almost like Hell on Earth. Not like with fires and demons running around, but just… it's ghost town, kinda. And you have, I think, seven more years to be like, "I'm sorry, take me too!" Then the post-Tribulationists believe that we're living…

SM: …in Hell right now.

KS: …we're living in the seven years of Tribulation as we speak, and then it ends with the Rapture, and after that then it's gone, then the Earth is just no more.

SM: How long has the seven years been going on?

KS: A long time! Well, you know, but people Loosey Goosey it, 'cause they're like, "Well, seven biblical years is like thirty man years…"

SM: It's like dog years.

KS: Exactly, you know like "God created the Earth in six days and on the seventh day he rested," then, they say, "Well, but it's not… God's day is much longer than *your* average day. God puts in a…"

SM: A God day.

KS: A God day. Um… so, you could do…

SM: The ending of the movie could either be that you're revealing, in the third act, that we've been in the Tribulation…

KS: Well, it depends. If you're gonna do the movie… if you want him in there as soon as possible, you don't want to bury the lead, you want to do it like *Jaws*, where the first attack happens right up front. Then, you are a pre-Tribulation *Holy Christ!* movie, because Jesus comes, and you could spend an hour and a half, two hours, of just… he picks up motherfuckers and hurls them up to Heaven. So it's kinda terrifying at the same time? And the other people he's just stepping on, and just [makes laser noise] lasering eyes at them, ripping them in two, vivisections…

SM: Yeah.

KS: Um… and then you do that the whole time, and then suddenly he's like, "Later, fuckers!" and takes off, and people who are left behind, like the Kevin Dillon character, is like, "What do we do now?" Credits.

SM: Gotcha.

KS: Because if you were gonna do the other one, then it would be like, he shows up, does his business, and it's done. Well, no, he shows up, does his business… well that would be the one… shit, now I'm getting confused.

SM: If we're in the…

KS: If we're *in* the Tribulation…

SM: Then he doesn't set it into motion, it's already been set into motion.

KS: And then he just comes and kicks ass for two hours, and then credits, and *nobody*'s left at the end.

SM: *That* is a summer movie.

KS: Yeah, but then there's no chance for a sequel.

SM: Yeah, but is there a chance for a sequel in the other one?

KS: You could do a movie where everyone's like, scared he's coming back. They're like, "What if he comes back?"

SM: 'Cause there's people left?

KS: Yeah, there's some people left behind and shit.

SM: During the seven years.

KS: Yeah, I think…

SM: You could do seven sequels. *Year 2*…

KS: … I think maybe the Prince of Darkness takes over the Earth for those seven years, or something. Not Dracula, but Lucifer. So maybe then you get like, *Holy Christ 2… It's the Devil!* As a subtitle. I don't know, I think people would totally go see that movie. I'm not talking about people doing like, just the Rapture as a movie. I'm talking about taking it to a degree where…
SM: A Michael Bay blockbuster Summer Jesus, like… fucking throwing shit, Jesus laying waste.
KS: Yes. And Jesus has more screen time than the Transformers did.
SM: Can you have… I guess you can't be too sexy.
KS: No, you can't do anything sexy. He's Jesus.
SM: He doesn't have to, but there's fucking tons of people, you've gotta have some…
KS: Like a Megan Fox, the chick who was in *Transformers*?
SM: Sure, you could have her.
KS: But you can't have any sex, because then… Let's say it was like Shia LaBeouf and Megan Fox. And they're like, "It's all over, we should fuck anyway." But then you're incurring the wrath of Jesus, who's like, "I said no fucking!"
SM: Well, maybe they're like thinking about it, and then they hear him.
KS: "He's coming!" And he's like, "So am I!" And like, "Don't do it, I mean he's here!"
SM: "If we don't fuck, we'll stay alive longer."
KS: Yes. It would have to be a bunch of people converting…
SM: They're both virgins.
KS: … you know, out of fear.
SM: And then he still doesn't care.
KS: No, he's alright with that. He's like, "Good. It's about time."
SM: So they're trying to curry favor so they can go to Heaven. Is that the plot of the movie?
KS: Yeah…
SM: Well, I mean someone's gotta live.
KS: Yeah…
SM: I mean, be killed in a nice way.
KS: I haven't really fleshed it out yet. I tell you, he's pitching them into the air. Just like the *Hancock* trailer, where he picks up the whale and whips it into the air? Just like that. But he's huge.

SM: But if Jesus comes down and everybody has a bad time, then who's the movie about?

KS: Well, it's like *War of the Worlds*.

SM: Yeah, but *War of the Worlds* is about Tom's family, and trying to stay together and stay alive.

KS: Well, I'm sure we'd have some kinda human element to it. But I'm more interested in the battle scenes. Where the nations of the Earth are like, "We gotta bring him down!" and they're launching nukes at him and he's just eating them. Tanks, stepping on them, huge battle scenes.

SM: I'm on it, but if you're going make it that huge blockbuster thing…

KS: The governments of the Earth are just like…

SM: The United Nations…

KS: Yes, the United Nations are like, "We can't stop Jesus. What should we do?" And then somebody steps up and says, "We have to reach out to the Dark Lord." And so the United Nations, they summon up the Beast, and they're like, "We will sell you our souls to stop this from happening. You have to take on Jesus, and keep Earth alive, and then you will be the King of Earth." And then he's like, "I've been the King of Earth since day one. Don't you people read the Bible? I've been given dominion over…"

SM: "…all you bitches."

KS: Yeah, "Why do think people do naughty things?" Um… but *that*, what a wrinkle that would be! Like, suddenly we're in the United Nations, and they're sacrificing a child… and the floor opens up, and the fucking Beast comes out, the corruption of the Earth… and he's just like, "I got it."

SM: I think you need a rewrite. Fucking Devil comes out of the Earth and goes "I got it"?

KS: That's the dumb version. I'd give them some better dialogue than that. So, your third act finale is a giant Jesus versus a giant Lucifer, depicted in a more crimson way than you've ever seen. First he would be pretty, because he was an angel…

SM: Does anyone at the United Nations go, like, "Why are we assuming that things will be better under Lucifer?"

KS: Because it's the human survival instinct.

SM: To try anything?

KS: Yeah, like, everybody wants to live. What we know is living on the Earth, what we don't know is what happens afterwards.

SM: Sure. Oh, so Lucifer would be like, "I'll keep you here! There'll be more titty bars!"
KS: Yes. They're like, "Look, we want the status quo. Are you happy with the status quo?" And he's like, "Yeah, it's alright." And they're like, "Well, help us then, and we can maintain the status quo." So, you have the United Nations turning on Jesus and God, in an effort to save the Earth. In that instance, who are you rooting for?
SM: ... who am *I* rooting for? I'm not, uh...
KS: I'm torn! I'm sitting here going like, "Wow, what do I want?"
SM: Well, as an agnostic, who has to experience a giant Jesus Christ...
KS: Right away, you're like, "Look, I'm not an agnostic any more. There's proof. And he's huge."
SM: "This sixty-foot Jesus with the lasers for eyes has totally blown my idea that it might not be true."
KS: "I've been going about this all wrong. Thank God I never said I was an atheist."
SM: I'm just like, six of one, half dozen of the other... like, neither of them seem like good people. I mean if Jesus is laying waste on people...
KS: Yes. But that's the plan, in the instance that Jesus came back as a sixty-foot-tall Jesus...
SM: He's gonna kill me!
KS: Yes, but he was like, "I'm God, I created the world, I always had an expiration date in mind, I *said* it in the book. Just 'cause *you* didn't like the book, doesn't mean it ain't right. So I'm not a bad guy. I *told* you what I was gonna do. You've been told, you've been warned, the prophets..."
SM: Yeah, but just because he tells what he's gonna do, doesn't mean that it's a nice thing. Like if I tell you that I'm gonna like, kill all your dogs in a week, it doesn't mean that just because I *warned* you, I'm a good dude.
KS: But that's a weird example. The better example would be... I have a daughter, and I tell my daughter, "Don't hurt Shecky, or else you will be punished." And if she hurt Shecky, then I'm like, "I told you! Now you'll be punished." I'm in charge of her, so I make the rules. In a world where Jesus is revealed to be God, and he's come back and he's pissed, he's saying like, "Hey man, I told you in the book. You guys knew the plan. You are my creation, I can do with you what I damn well please."
SM: Yeah, but that's whimsy.

KS: That's not whimsy! He laid it out in the book, years ago.
SM: What did he lay out? I didn't read the book… but what did he lay out, that he's gonna come back for a reason?
KS: Yes, to end the world.
SM: Why?
KS: Because it's just run its course. That was always the plan, it had a finite existence.
SM: Yeah, but if you tell Harley not to do something to Shecky, and then she does it, obviously… it's not like you're like, "Don't feed Shecky! I'm gonna starve that fucking dog." If you were just like, "Don't kick her," and she kicked her, you're telling her not to do something that most people could agree on as being wrong: she shouldn't kick the dog, she shouldn't hurt the dog.
KS: Yes.
SM: You're telling her not to do it or she'll be punished.
KS: Yes, but we live in a world where I would say the majority would argue with you that most things we do are wrong: sex outside of marriage, titty bars, drinking, drugging, greed, sloth.
SM: They drink in the Bible!
KS: Not a lot. Not, you know…
SM: He turned water into wine!
KS: He did, but what they left out was he's like, "One per customer, please. Only one glass." If you believe in the faith, or any sort of faith, there are always limitations.
SM: Yeah, but my point is, if in the book he literally is just like, "I created it, and at some point I'm just gonna end it," like, not because you guys opened titty bars, not because the cumulative echo of your sins is gonna be so deafening…
KS: "The stink has reached Heaven and I can't take it any more!"
SM: "The Earth is a giant outhouse!"
KS: "This cesspool ends now! I flush it!"
SM: Like, I know there are rules, but does it distinctly say in the Bible, "Listen, if you guys don't fucking keep a lid on this shit, *that* is when I'm gonna come down."
KS: He says I'm coming regardless.
SM: Then I do think it makes him into somebody who's just gonna kill all of

us indiscriminately.

KS: Well, kill, but you live forever, in Paradise. If you're a believer. If you have honored God with your life.

SM: Well that's different. So… Nobody wants to be here.

KS: Yeah. Nobody wants… not in that world, not in that version of Earth. Ain't no more movies. And food is hard to come by.

SM: Even right now, isn't the idea that if you *are* of that mind, then you would hope Jesus comes now. Why wait ten years?

KS: Yeah, there are lots of them who are always like, "He's on his way, and I can't wait!" There are a bunch of people across this great nation of ours…

SM: "Leave a light on!"

KS: Yes, who are *praying* for it, they want the end to come. They hate living in this world 'cause it's so dirty and wrong and sinful and they want to see the end of things, they *want* the Rapture. There's a lot of them out there. A lot of them don't live on the West Coast or the East Coast but in the middle of the country? Heavens, yes.

SM: Well I would argue that if Jesus was, or God, is that intolerant — I don't think it necessarily makes him a good God.

KS: But is he intolerant? If he's like, "Look, I built…" Alright, let's put it like this. You're six years old. You're given a big set of Legos. You build a little Lego world.

SM: Yep.

KS: Well, do you have to leave it up for the rest of your life, or do you eventually put it away? Make another Lego world. Make a Lego moon landing.

SM: Yeah, but if I was able to like, have all my Lego people come to life and be like [little Lego voice] "Hi, it's me!" And I'm just like, "Party's over."

KS: Yeah, but to Him, to God, it's like it's Legos.

SM: Yeah, I understand from his perspective…

KS: He's like, "That ain't living! *This* is living."

SM: But I'm saying from my perspective, as a human being on Earth, I'm not going to be like — and maybe it's crazy, I'm sure everyone would be like, "You can't judge God in the same way that you would judge Man" — but if his actions are to just wipe everybody out, then I can sit there and say, he's a bad dude.

[A dog barks at someone in the background.]

SM: [Laughs] Jesus is here…

KS: Yeah I'm like, "Scott, pipe down." Um… yeah, I guess, but the hardcore Christians would tell you that you're not…

SM: I'm judging him on the standard of…

KS: They'd also just say that you're a lunatic, because they're like, "It's God's world, he can do anything he wants with it. He can end your life like that."

SM: But to me… my argument, and obviously I'm not gonna go and seek out this argument, but the idea that…

KS: That's our third act! He fights Lucifer in the second act, third act we send Scott Mosier to reason with Jesus. "Hey, you're not a good guy."

SM: "I think this is mean."

KS: "If my Legos had come to life…" He's like, "What are you talking about?"

SM: "Just stay with me, just hold on, hold on. So, my Legos come to life and they're like [Lego voice] "Hey, how's it going?," I wouldn't tear down my Legos and put them in a box and suffocate all my Lego people."

KS: But he's like, "Ah, but what if you take that Lego world down, you build a better Lego world. You've learned from that, so now you wanna create a better Lego world."

SM: I would say that, you know, I would try to assist the people, my Lego people, into creating a better version of the world.

KS: And he's like, "I've done that! For fucking 2000 years!"

SM: And I would say like, "OK! Sh sh sh!" I would say, "You know what, dude? Why don't you stick around, and stop presenting us with all these other people who are supposed to be relating this for you. Because they suck."

KS: He's like, "They'll be punished, Scott. Don't think that they're getting away lightly. Anyone who's misinterpreting my message is getting a swift kick in the ass!"

SM: "But why don't you just spend a decade down here?"

KS: "'Cause it stinks! 'Cause I'm God, I don't wanna hang out with a bunch of lowlifes! It'd be like you living in the gutter for ten years — Hey, Scott, go live in the gutter for ten years. How's that feel?"

SM: "Well, if I had lived in the gutter and I could pull a bunch of people out of the gutter by spending that time, then I might do it."

KS: "Well, why haven't you done it yet?" I'm Jesus still. That ain't me. I'm

Jesus. "Why haven't you done it yet? You've been alive thirty-six years, thirty-seven years…" — thirty-seven?

SM: Thirty-seven.

KS: "Thirty-seven years, why haven't you spent ten years in the gutter?"

SM: "I don't know, 'cause we're just having this conversation now."

KS: Scott just threw up the horns for thirty-seven, that was cute. With his tongue out.

SM: Jesus is like, "What are you doing?"

KS: "Thirty-seven, man, didn't you see *Clerks*?"

SM: "You're omnipotent, you see everything."

KS: He's like, "Yeah, that was pretty funny. But back to the point."

SM: "Um… I don't… I mean, this is just coming up right now."

KS: He's like, "Hey, it's coming up just now to *you*. But, it's been laid out, I've sent warnings, there's been a book that you could've read, a *manual*, and you didn't choose to believe in it."

SM: I… I… I…

KS: "The fat one — he's in Heaven already! How 'bout that?"

SM: "OK. Goddamnit."

KS: "No more SModcast. Now it's *Mod*cast…" Nah, I don't know that I would necessarily go to Heaven. But if they were like, "Go argue with Jesus," I would be like, "Fuck, no! I've always been kinda pro-Jesus, and now I'm *really* pro-Jesus!"

SM: If you're saying that he's running around, he's liquefying the planet, I would just be like, "Most likely, I'm gonna be liquefied, so if I could get ten minutes with him…"

KS: "Jesus! Hi, can I…? Down here! Can I get ten minutes of your time, please?"

SM: "Starting now… wait! Waitwaitwait! It's taking too long to come down here — starting now!"

KS: He's like, "Ten of *my* minutes, or your minutes?"

SM: I'm like, "Whatever's longer."

KS: "Alright, you want ten of your minutes."

SM: Uh… Yeah, I'd give it a shot.

KS: Alright, what if that didn't work. And he's just like, "Look, you can't run circles…"

SM: He's just like, miming masturbation the whole time…

KS: Yeah, he's just like [makes whiny noise like a kid doing a retard impression].

SM: I'm like, "Now hold on, Jesus…"

KS: [in same voice] "No you hold on!" You're like, "Man, this is not the ten minutes I was hoping for."

SM: Yeah, "Can we start the ten minutes over, and you maybe act a little more mature? 'Cause this is like, stupid."

KS: [same voice] "I'm being immatuuure… Jerk!" Wow, Jesus is acting like he's putting a retard voice on.

SM: I know, he's fucked up.

KS: Um, let's say it fails. And it will.

SM: It did. I'm saying I would take my shot. Why not?

KS: Because he's like, "Look man, you can't argue logic with me, I created arguments and logic. You can't…"

SM: "I know, but you gotta give me something for the effort."

KS: He's like, "Look, I think it's cute." He pats you on the head, he's like, "Run along, get ready for the fucking oblivion."

SM: "Make my death quick. At least I tried."

KS: He's like, "… Alright, I'll take that into consideration." But then the UN — you know, you have to go back to the UN and they're like, "Did it work?" And you're like, "Not really."

SM: "Well, I have an audio recording. And it went something like this — [whiny retard noise]." They're like, "Who's that?"

KS: "That's Jesus. If you can believe it."

SM: "That was his answer to me, he basically mocked me, it was three minutes, I couldn't even do it for ten minutes."

KS: "He mocked me, he patronized me, and he sent me on my way, he said maybe my death will be quick. I mean, this dude, he ain't having it." And then they're like, "Look, we need to bond you to the fucking Beast from the depths."

SM: What does that mean, they're gonna *sew* me to him?

KS: No, he needs a human host. And so, he's like, "If you like living…"

SM: "If you wanna get back at Jesus for mocking you…"

KS: Yeah, "You think he got a retard voice? Imagine the retard voice that'll come from *you*, when you're filled with the power of Satan. *And*, you get to grow as big as him."

SM: OK. So I can at least look at him eye-to-eye.

KS: So, he needs a human host to bond to, and then you grow into like, a gigantic Scott Mosier with bat wings. You look the same…

SM: I'm orange?

KS: No orange, you don't have to…

SM: Like, my complexion gets a little reddish?

KS: You look exactly the same, except you have bat wings. That's the only personification of Hell that you have… do you do it? They're like, "We've gotta warn you in advance, you will have all the power of Hell at your disposal, *but*… Jesus knows Kung Fu. Do you know Kung Fu?"

SM: Well, I'm like, "I don't know Kung Fu, but does *Lucifer* know Kung Fu?" Like, if Lucifer's just gonna make me tall, and that's it, I'm not gonna fight… If Jesus has lasers for eyes, Kung Fu, and the power of… he's indestructible, I'm not gonna be like, "OK, make me large."

KS: An easy target… They're like, "Satan doesn't know Kung Fu, *but*…

SM: Jujitsu?

KS: He does know old-timey boxing.

SM: He's a pugilist. Bare-knuckle boxing.

KS: Those men with white mustaches and they hold their arms up in front of their faces and fucking box like the boxing robot…

SM: Like, did you ever see *Every Which Way But Loose*?

KS: No, not even that. That's fucking bare-knuckle boxing. They're like, "Look, if you think it's Clint Eastwood boxing, you're really mistaken. This is like Handsome Jim McKennehy-type boxing."

SM: So I'm like in a fucking leotard with the fucking big curly mustache?

KS: Yes.

SM: Some pomade in my hair?

KS: Yes, you'll have bat wings, a pomade 'do, your beard falls away, you'll have a curly mustache, and you'll wear long tights. Not like boxing shorts. And they come up over your… it's like a body suit.

SM: As we already know that Jesus loves to mock people… making me like, an easy target for ridicule? It's like, "Can't I look cool? He'd fall over laughing."

KS: They're like, "No. But the good news is, you're *really* good at it. You've got a devastating… um… "

SM: Jab?

KS: Yes, "You have a devastating jab. So, you know, yes, you'll look..."

SM: Can't Lucifer be like an Ultimate Fighter?

KS: No.

SM: What happened?

KS: He only went so far as old-timey boxing, and then he got interested in other things. Then he was like, "Why am I...? I should learn fucking." Then he got into sex.

SM: Do I have any powers? Does Jesus have powers or is it literally like, fist on fist? If you make it a situation where there'll be a large pugilist from the early teens versus the Almighty, who could literally, if he wanted to, blink you out of existence...

KS: They're like, "It gets a little worse. He's an old-timey *white* boxer." You're like, "Not even a black dude?"

SM: "So I can't even move? I can't bob and weave?"

KS: They're like, "You have fancy dancin' moves. They called you — back in the day, they called you Fancy Dan McConnaughey. Handsome Fancy Jim McConnaughey.

SM: So I'm gonna be merged with an old-time pugilist, and Satan? But I get nothing from Satan, other than size. And bat wings.

KS: Well, yes, the bat wings are cool though.

SM: Gotcha.

KS: 'Cause then everyone knows whose side you're fighting on.

SM: Gotcha. Couldn't I just have a shirt?

KS: No, you're wearing the old-timey boxing thing, it's like a big one-piece.

SM: But the bat wings — can I fly? Can I like, get air?

KS: Ahh... you can get air, but not fly. You could like, jump up, and...

SM: And suspend myself in the air for a few seconds?

KS: Yeah, basically about ten feet off the ground.

SM: But I'm still outmatched, a million to one.

KS: Well, they're like, "The good news is, um... we found Jesus' Kryptonite. We're gonna whip some nails at him."

SM: OK.

KS: "And he don't like that."

SM: "OK."

KS: "So, while you're fighting him, we're down below..." They're like, "It hurts him. It bugs him." You're like, "Well, which is it? Does it hurt him, or does it bug him?" They're like, "We're not quite sure. And in fact..."

Random SModquotes

"Does anybody want a lap dance from me? ... Didn't think so."

SM: "We're working on it right now."

KS: "... this is more theoretical than anything else. Let's say that Jesus'll be like..."

SM: "This is the best our think-tank can come up with. Nails."

KS: "We went to the RAND Corporation and this is what they came up with: pitch some nails at him."

SM: "Are they big nails?"

KS: "No, they're carpet nails. Little ones."

SM: "Oh, God."

KS: "But lots! Lots, you've got the whole world's supply!"

SM: "Who's firing the nails, do I have other people firing the nails?"

KS: "They've got catapults. Old-timey catapults, that they're firing at him. So you've got that. It's more of a distraction than anything else. It doesn't truly weaken him but it's like, you know..."

SM: But still, I'm being sent to my death.

KS: Not necessarily. Like, when you get that big and you go to face down Jesus you're like, "Let's lay some ground rules down. One: we're only gonna fight old-timey."

SM: "You ever seen *Far and Away*?"

KS: Yes, "You gotta fight like Tom Cruise in *Far and Away*." And he's like, "Fine." "You can't use your eye lasers." And he's like, "Alright." "No knives." He's like, "What about broken bottles?"

SM: I'm like, "No."

KS: "Alright."

SM: But, what am I allowed to do?

KS: Fight.

SM: Um... I just still feel like I'm gonna lose.

KS: Somebody's gotta go down swinging, dude, we need a third act for the picture.

SM: I just wanna know, like, if that's it, then...

KS: By the way, this is all still just a movie. You're taking this very seriously.

SM: I know. But in the course of the movie you would have to introduce that there's a chance that the guy could win.

KS: Yes, well you're old-timey Rocky! Like, Rocky was outmatched, but there was still a chance, and he fought a good fight…

SM: But Apollo Creed didn't have fucking lasers coming out of his eyes!

KS: Well he told you he's not gonna use his lasers.

SM: Yeah, but like, before I agree to bond with Satan, so I can have size and wings that don't really help me fly more than a few feet off the ground…

KS: But they look badass! You gotta wear your colors, man, you're representing the team!

SM: I gotcha. So, before I do that, I'm like, do I have any shot? Even give me a million-to-one. Do I got a million-to-one shot to stop him?

KS: Your odds are better than a million-to-one.

SM: OK, well then that's different. Like, the way it was painted to me it was like, I was just gonna die, very large.

KS: Your odds are… you have…

SM: Shit, I'd even take it if it was just like, I'll just get one good swing at him.

KS: You have a one in ten shot at taking him down.

SM: Oh, OK, then yeah, of course.

KS: That's pretty good, right?

SM: I mean, if it was one in a million I'd still do it.

KS: Really?

SM: Yeah, 'cause it's like, if I'm gonna die anyways, and there's a one in a million shot, shit, that one in a million shot's happening. And even, if anything, if I got a coupla good licks in on him, at least…

KS: Which just makes him more mad.

SM: Yeah, that's fine.

KS: He's like, "After you're dead, everyone's gonna pay double."

SM: I'm like, "Alright, but you know, somebody had to… somebody had to stand up and box like a really feeble white guy from 1905."

KS: Do you want old-timey music, or do you want the *Rocky* theme playing for your fight?

SM: It wouldn't be something I would consider at all. You mean in the course of the movie?

KS: Yeah, they're giving you this option…

SM: "What kinda accompaniment do you want?" Um…

KS: They're like, "Look, of course you're gonna lean toward the *Rocky* music…"

SM: Yeah, I don't want a guy on a fucking canned piano… I don't want fucking Scott Joplin…
KS: But, they're like, "But the power of the old-timey boxer is always tied into the plink-plink of the canned piano."
SM: Well if you're telling me it's going to imbue me with more strength, then I guess…
KS: I'm not gonna say it's gonna make you stronger but, in a weird way, when you're fighting, suddenly the old-timey spirit takes over.
SM: Dapper Dan the Fighting Man?
KS: And it helps! You find your groove to it. Plus, Jesus *hates* old-timey music.
SM: Alright. Well, does it enrage him until the point where he's just like…
KS: It enrages him to the point of making a mistake, so it's like you could probably get a rope-a-dope out of it.
SM: He's just like, "Fuck I hate this!" and I hit him, I get a couple of shots in.
KS: Well, he's in the middle of it, he's like, "I'll fucking deck you."
SM: And then he's like, "Where's that coming from?"
KS: Yes, and then turns around to see where the speakers are.
SM: Yeah, so then, there's a guy… you gotta be in the movie too, so you're gonna be in a car, sort of driving around.
KS: I've got these huge speakers on the back of my truck.
SM: You're on the back of a truck, playing a piano.
KS: I can't play. You're dead, if that's the case. I'm terrible.
SM: Yeah, but it's a movie! I'm bonding with… in the context of the movie, we'll have it prerecorded…
KS: So they're like, "Look — in order to help him, you have to bond with the infernal soul of Scott Joplin."
SM: "He's in Hell, man."
KS: I'm like, "Really? Alright. Um… can I play the theme from *The Sting*?"
SM: They're like, "Yeah, of course, to start. You can't just keep playing it."
KS: "You can do kinda a medley, if you will, and a little bit in there." So I have to fuse with the soul of Scott Joplin.
SM: And then you are driving a truck…
KS: I'm like, "Does it make me bigger?" And they're like, "Look, you can't get much bigger," I'm like, "Fuck you, man! I know this is a dire

circumstance, but that's uncalled-for!" Um… so it's just me, I get little bat wings, tiny ones.

SM: An Ebola bat.

KS: An Ebola, yes, yes, bitch. And I'm driving around…

SM: Somebody else is driving.

KS: OK… No, no, I can't play… Oh, but I can play now that I'm filled with the infernal soul of Scott Joplin.

SM: Yes. You're on the back of this, like, pick-up rig, and somebody else is driving it so Jesus can't get a bead on you. Like, every once in a while he shoots a laser like, "I fucking hate that shit!"

KS: And I'm like [sings 'The Entertainer'] "Shit!" Um… yes, so I'm kinda your… I'm not your corner man, because there's no rounds. It's not like you get a break. Once you're in the fight, you're in the fight 'til one of you falls.

SM: But you're helping me out.

KS: Totally! I'm like a gnat around his ear.

SM: It's like Tennessee Ernie Ford in *Mars Attacks!*

KS: What?

SM: You remember, they play that Tennessee Ernie Ford record, where he's like…

KS: Oh, and they're all like, "Aaaaahhh!"

SM: Yeah.

KS: Was it Tennessee Ernie Ford? Or was it um… [sings] "wooo-wooooo-ooooooh…" Slim Whitman?

SM: I thought it was Tennessee Ernie Ford.

KS: I don't remember.

SM: Slim Whitman's like, an actor.

KS: Slim Pickens is an actor.

SM: Slim Pickens is an actor. Slim Whitman. Who's Slim Whitman?

KS: Slim Whitman was the dude that, like [sings again] "wooo-ooooo-ooooo-oooh…" Maybe. I just remember that commercial when I was a kid.

SM: Oh that's uh… I can't remember that guy's name. Anyway, so, you're not killing him, but you're like…

KS: I can't believe you remember *anything* about *Mars Attacks!* … except for that fucking "Ack! Ack! Ack Ack Ack!" which was like, the best part.

SM: So you're just like more… distracting him.

KS: Yes.

SM: Like he can't… like he hates it so much.
KS: Yeah, yeah. It's helping you, because, like I said…
SM: I'm like, "Keep plaaayiiing!"
KS: "I will, Scott! Demon Scott! Jab, motherfucker! Jab!" And at one point, to help you out, I throw a big medicine ball at you, so you can get a quick workout in.
SM: Before I go up there?
KS: No, it's like, after you punch him, and he stumbles backwards, I throw you a medicine ball and you throw it back to me, and that helps keeps you in shape. Old-timey shape.
SM: … and then we keep going. So, OK. Now I feel like at least I have a shot.
KS: Right.
SM: I don't wanna go into the ring if he's just gonna fucking zap me and I'm dead.
KS: And P.S., there ain't no ring. It's downtown Los Angeles.

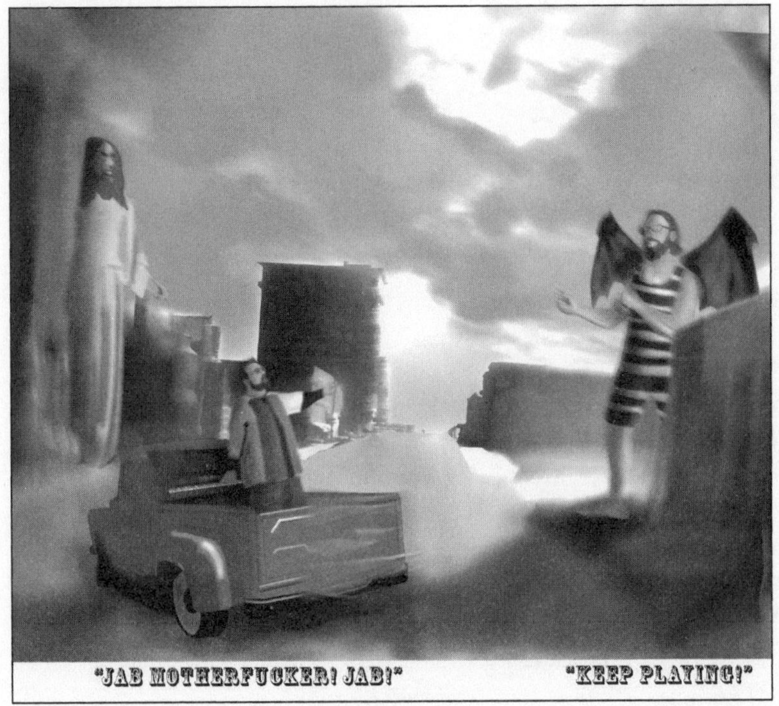

"JAB MOTHERFUCKER! JAB!" "KEEP PLAYING!"

SM: Yeah, yeah yeah. I understand.

KS: There's no escape.

SM: No, it's fucking big giant people fighting in the middle of the city.

KS: Buildings going down…

SM: In a really kinda like… one of them has mastered an Asian martial art, but I am stuck in, you know…

KS: The old-timey shit.

SM: Yeah.

KS: Do you end the movie with the freeze-frame from *Rocky III*, where you're throwing the punch at each other and then it turns into a LeRoy Neiman painting? [sings 'Eye of the Tiger'] Or do you see who wins? 'Cause then, we get a sequel out of it.

SM: Well, somebody's gotta…

KS: I can't believe we've fucking… this coulda been a cool movie, and now it's really bad, but I would like to see this movie.

SM: Where I play a…

KS: Where you're somehow a factor, and I'm a factor. But I think a movie about Jesus coming back and taking over would be, fucking, the tits, man, everyone would go see it. But anyway, back to our movie. Do you see the conclusion?

SM: Well, I think based on the ideas, I think Jesus has to win. I could still exist…

KS: Or, do you not show any winner, and just go with, you know… "To be continued"? Like basically you guys are throwing the punch at each other, you're doing an old-timey jab where your forearm is extending…

SM: He's doing like a round-house kick and I'm like…

KS: Your biceps are in place…

SM: I'm like one of those cheering nuns.

KS: Yes, basically you're a boxing nun. So, you've extended one hand forward like, not quite hitting him yet, and he's coming around with a high kick, like a Jujitsu high kick. And then we freeze-frame, it becomes a LeRoy Neiman painting; you know, with paint splashes…

SM: So then it says "To be continued"?

KS: Yeah, it says "To be continued." Then it's [continues singing 'Eye of the Tiger'].

SM: So then we just come back and like… I mean, the freeze-frame of *Rocky* is more like…

KS: "Hey, who won?"

SM: Yeah, but who won the spar.

KS: Yeah.

SM: Which is more playful. At that point, me and Jesus aren't being playful.

KS: No. But we're taking a good idea, and improving on it. Although that was an *awesome* ending.

SM: It was an awesome ending. But if it was the fight proper, and suddenly in the middle of round ten they just froze and went [sings] "Eye of the tiger…" everybody would be like, "What the fuck?" At least you'd want to know that they tied.

KS: Don't you think that would make people want to come back and see the sequel?

SM: No.

KS: Or would they be like, "This movie went wrong!!"

SM: I wouldn't want to come back in the middle of a fight. It's like, you don't literally want a movie to end in round eight, and then pick up again, a year later, in round nine.

KS: A year, dude. That movie's too big, it would take a couple of years — two years.

SM: Unless you shoot 'em back-to-back, which they do all the time.

KS: That's true, if we were doing like *Lord of the Rings*-style, where we were really banking on the first one working in a big way.

SM: Yeah, we're like, "Holy shit, this did not work out."

KS: Um… I think the freeze-frame ending could work. I think people *would* come see the sequel. I don't think you'd get everyone that came the first time, 'cause they'd be like, "That fucking old-timey boxing shit was gay!"

SM: "Why can't he fight somebody like a Transformer, or robot…?"

KS: And we're like, "How do you know that's not what's gonna happen in the sequel?" Like there are hints of it, we give them a little taste, like… I'm driving around, Scott Joplin on the back of the truck, and you guys are fighting, and the buildings are falling, and one of the buildings blocks our path, so we crash… and right before the freeze-frame of you guys, you see like this mess of me, and the truck, but then all of a sudden there's like, "dzz-dzzz," little electrical shocks around it and you see it start fusing to my body. Then we go to the fucking freeze-frame of you guys, so we give them a little taste that…

SM: That something might happen.

KS: … that all is not lost.

SM: Yeah. That another absurdly stupid series of events…

KS: Even though the deck is stacked against them, all is not lost. Like it could very well be that in the opening of the sequel Jesus fucking, like, finally stops toying with you…

SM: And kills me.

KS: Yeah, just puts you down, and is getting ready for the fucking death-stroke, and all of a sudden like [sings ominous music], like the morphing car Kev…

SM: And then you come and you fight.

KS: And he fucking decks me…

SM: What, you're gonna lose?

KS: Well, you can't tell them what's gonna happen. That's the tease.

SM: That's the bait and hook.

KS: I think it could work. Do you think we've outraged the faithful?

SM: Have we?

KS: No, with that movie. Do you think Christians would be mad? Like, "They've made a mockery of our beliefs."

SM: I think that like, one, you're kinda belittling the beliefs; two, ultimately, the movie becomes about me bonding with Satan, to fight off, you know…

KS: But I would think they'd be into that, 'cause they'd be like, "Look, he's already bonded with Satan."

SM: I have?

KS: Yeah — "He's a sinner, he doesn't believe."

SM: But then they would only enjoy the movie if Jesus won.

KS: But he could win in the sequel.

SM: But you would have to depict Jesus in a way that they would find fitting… you know, they love Jesus a certain way, they don't want—

KS: Alright, here's an ending where maybe both audiences are happy. You nail him to a cross.

SM: Jesus?

KS: Yeah.

SM: I do?

KS: Yes. Christians like that.

SM: Well, they liked it the first time. They don't want the returning Jesus to get nailed to the cross.

KS: That's true, that might not make them happy.

SM: It's just like, "Again?"

KS: We test that version and they're like, "What?! No!"

SM: "Fuck. You."

KS: We're like, "We thought you people liked crucifixes. Tell us what you want."

SM: I assume if I was a believer, I would want Jesus to beat the Satan-infused pugilist, played by me.

KS: Yes, Scott Mosier. Yourself, by the way, you're not even a character.

SM: No, it's me. And then, I assume that after he takes care of everybody he goes back to the Kingdom of Heaven with all the people that have been chosen…

KS: And the world stops.

SM: And the world stops. So that would be the ending they would like. There's a group of people that they would be like, "Hey, that would be us!"

KS: As long as we deliver that in the sequel, everyone's on board, is what you're saying?

SM: I think as long as you end it—

KS: Biblically appropriate.

SM: Yes, a biblically appropriate ending. As opposed to biblically inappropriate…

KS: They're like, "Well, they took a little flight of fancy for a little while, but they eventually got back on message."

SM: "The pugilist thing was actually not any good for anybody, even the non-believers…"

KS: "It's not in the Bible, it should never be in a movie… But, you know, we'll forgive them that little flight of fancy 'cause they eventually gave us the ending we wanted to see, and the evil were punished." So… is that movie art, or commerce?

SM: I think that that movie would fall into its own category.

KS: Of?

SM: Of just like…

KS: Awesomeness?

SM: I mean, could you imagine?

KS: Yes! I've got it half-written already in my head. I'm just waiting to get to my computer.

SM: Imagine it done in a traditional Hollywood way, and that it was going to

be promoted and stuff like that. Name me anything that would be remotely close to it. Name me anything that you would compare it to.
KS: Nothing. Nothing.
SM: The marketers are just like…
KS: "We have no model for this." It captures the imagination of the *Passion of the Christ* audience, *and* the *Terminator* 2 audience. And the Michael Bay audience.
SM: Shit blowing up…
KS: But it could be arty, too.

From SModcast 53: Meat Curtains
The steak tartare story

KS: Will you eat raw beef?
SM: Like tartare?
KS: Yeah.
SM: Sometimes. It's not my favorite.
KS: I was crazy about tartare for a while.
SM: I know, I watched you…
KS: I was like, "What's this?"
SM: "Did you cook that? Fuck that, get out of the way."
KS: "It's *raw meat* with an *egg* mixed in it? A *raw egg*? That's fucked up and wonderful…"
SM: Don't they sear the outside?
KS: And Worcestershire sauce… No.
SM: Oh, it's just flat-out raw.
KS: I was fucking loving steak tartare. Basically, I never really saw it prepared, it just came to me, and it always looked like, "Wow, I'm just eating raw chopped meat." But in France, we were in Paris once — it was me, the kid, the wife, and Byron and Gail, her parents. And I could order a steak tartare — France is the land of steak tartare. So at the hotel, I ordered steak tartare, and I'm always used to getting very small portions, usually done as an appetizer in a restaurant, so I ordered two servings of it. They were like, "Oh, sir, how many people are eating?" I'm like, "Just one!" "Oh." So they show up, and they made it right in front of me, and — I am not exaggerating

— each serving was easily two pounds of meat.

SM: Wow.

KS: Based on my knowledge of buying meat at a grocery store. They put it in a bowl, they put two raw eggs into each bowl — maybe, it was so large, it might have been more than two in that instance. He had like a carton of eggs with him. He came in with, like, two hunks of fucking chopped meat, a carton of eggs… I was just like, "Are you gonna cook it in front of me?" He was like [French accent], "We don't cook it sir, is a beef tartare…"

SM: "Tartare!"

KS: I was like, "I know, I love tartare." And he prepped it in front of me — he put the eggs in it, and then he put some Worcestershire in it, and then, there was one other thing — maybe a little dab of ketchup or something like that. And then they mix it up, and then they're like, "There you go." When they prepare it in front of you, you're just like, "Don't you understand an oven?"

SM: "You want me to pay for this?"

KS: "You're not done."

SM: Yeah.

KS: It'd be like somebody making a Betty Crocker cake without giving it the oven time, they just handed you the fucking mixing bowl and they're like, "Eat it, that's your cake." So, I ate one whole serving, and then I was like, "Well, I've got to eat the other one 'cause it's gonna go bad if I don't, 'cause it's raw meat, it's not refrigerated." We didn't have refrigerators in the room, so I ate the other one. I don't know if it was the sheer volume of raw meat that I ate, or if maybe some of the eggs were rotten eggs, maybe one in the bunch was a rotten egg, but… I got so fucking sick. And I'm used to overeating, so, I've overeaten to the point where I'm like, "Urgh, I think I'm gonna puke," but I never puke. I hadn't puked, at that point, in nineteen years. I hadn't thrown up, didn't remember the feeling of throwing up, nothing like that. Last time I'd thrown up prior to that I was really fucking drunk, I was sixteen and I was like, fucking plastered. You always think about throwing up as a very unpleasant thing, so you don't want to do it, because you know, everything's coming up your oesophagus, pushing up the wrong way, and then you've got a bad acidy taste — bad enough having acid reflux, but like, puking just seems like fucking Hell on Earth.

SM: Puking sucks.

KS: So, I hadn't thrown up in nineteen years. I threw up four times that day, four times, and, I was also, before I threw up, I was just blowing brown piss out of my ass. Thick, puddingy brown piss like... I believe I got some form of food poisoning. I mean, it wasn't obviously E. coli, because I'm still alive. Or maybe it was, do you necessarily die from E. coli each time?

SM: I don't know. I mean, I don't know what it means to have small traces of it or something like that. I mean that's kinda like food poisoning. I had food poisoning once from McDonald's...

KS: What was it from?

SM: Filet-o-Fish.

KS: Well, you don't eat fish from McDonald's. You eat beef.

SM: Yeah. Yeah, I got sick. But I didn't get diarrhea, I fucking threw up.

KS: Well, first I had the diarrhea, and, number one, I'm sitting on a French toilet bowl, and they're so different from an American toilet bowl, just uncomfortable to begin with, and the water — there's only like a fucking spit worth of water in the fucking bowl. And so, I'm filling the bowl...

SM: With the poop.

KS: Yeah, liquidy shit, more than the water.

SM: Yeah.

KS: And then when you flush it — because you can feel it, and it reeks like fuck, 'cause it's not mixing with the water, if you shit in the water it kinda tempers it a little, but... if you shit in a glass of water, which we all do, from time to time, the smell's not nearly as bad as if you shit in a paper towel. It reeks. So this was reeking, and then I'd flush it and there would be fucking spraying shit-water up on my ass, but I was just so sick I didn't care, it was just like [makes squirting diarrhea sound-effect], and when you think you're done, and you're feeling nauseous, and you go to get up and then suddenly you've got to hit the bowl again and you're blowing more muddy piss out your ass... then I started feeling, like, nauseous and I started getting these weird dry-heave-y kinda things, and then I fucking went from the bowl, which, my ass was smeared with liquid shit 'cause I didn't have time to wipe, plus the toilet paper was *really* thin, I just leapt from the bowl straight to the...

SM: Tub?

KS: The tub, and fucking threw up for the first time in nineteen years. And it wasn't that

"I'm the kind of guy you want to cut open like a fucking Tauntaun and sleep inside of!"

unpleasant, the feeling of throwing up. It wasn't like I had feared it would be, for almost twenty years, like, "Oh, I never wanna throw up 'cause it'll be bad." It wasn't that bad, and in fact, I felt a little better afterwards. But I did that three times, and I would — I'm not even exaggerating when I say that I went from the tub to the toilet, to the tub to the toilet, three times within the span of like, four minutes.

SM: It was just, coming out, all…

KS: And it's one of those times when you don't want *anybody* around. It's just like…

SM: This is me at my worst.

KS: Yeah, and it's like… not even me at my worst, my wife has gotten drunk to the point of like, puking and I've held her hair and stuff like that, so that doesn't… it's not, fucking, you know, I'd rather be eating her pussy than watching her puke, but it's not the worst thing in the world. But if you're like, fucking leaning over a tub, vomiting…

SM: With your ass covered in…

KS: With your ass in the air covered in, *smeared* with liquid shit. That's just enough to like… if I was her, and in that room, I'd be like, "I don't think I can ever fuck this guy again without having this image in my head." And you can't like, you know, "My dignity... [vomit sound]." You can't… like, "Throw a towel over my ass." It's just such a fucking…

SM: You just kinda lock yourself in the bathroom.

KS: Oh, I totally did. And then like for twenty-four hours straight, I was in living hell. I was so cold, and fucking… It was bad, man, I really thought I was gonna fucking die. And then like twenty-four hours later suddenly I was OK again. But I never went near fucking steak tartare after that. And I was never quite sure, like I said, if there was a bad egg in there, or whether it's just 'cause I ate four pounds.

From SModcast 54: SModder's Day
Kevin describes to Harley the concept of a mix tape

HS: Remember when we were listening to the radio yesterday and you were talking about tape? And I said, "Well that was ancient history, when nobody had an iPod!"

KS: Yes, I was trying to explain a mix-tape to you, and how people used to make mix-tapes. Like, in high school I used to make a lot of mix-tapes, put a bunch of different songs on and give it to a girl that you were sweet on, or something like that. And you were like, "That's ancient technology!"
HS: That *is* ancient technology! Everybody has iPods now!
KS: Yeah, but back then we didn't have iPods.
HS… or an MP3 player or *something*, not a tape…
KS: But the mix-tape was the forerunner of the iPod, 'cause the iPod, you essentially do the same thing, you can make these wicked mix lists, playlists…
HS: iPods are better.
KS: Hey, much better, I'm not arguing with you, I'm not saying [old man voice] "Things were better then!" I'm just saying I used to have to do it with a tape.
HS: On a tape they don't have really cool games, like 'Vortex', or it shows your name and stuff.
KS: Look, I'm with you. You don't have to sell me, I agree that the iPod is way better…
HS: … or cards, or like poker, or…
KS: I told you, I'm with you! I'm on your side, you don't have to convince me. I was just saying what we used to do, back before the iPod.
HS: That's scary.
KS: Do you look at me like I'm John Adams? You're like, "How could you have ever lived without an iPod, life must have been so boring for you."
HS: No, but it…
KS: "You must have just gotten up, eaten, pooped and slept."
HS: A mix-tape looks so boring!
KS: No, it was a very cool thing. You put together a bunch of songs…
HS: A 'cool' thing?!
KS: Yes. I guarantee you, when you get older, you will put together… versions of a mix-tape. You won't do it on audio cassette, but you'll do it, where you put together a bunch of songs for some boy that you like. [Harley voice] "Oh, Will…"
HS: Hmmm.
KS: "Here is a mix-tape for you, that explains my feelings."
HS: [Aghast] If Will goes on the Internet, and he hears you, you'll be in such big trouble!

KS: I don't think Will's ever gonna hear this. Alright, not Will — that little boy in the movie theater...
HS: [Even more appalled] No!
KS: "Oh, random stranger boy, I put together this collection of songs to tell you how I really feel." I used to not only mix songs, like, we'd put songs together, but I used to put stuff between them, like little comedy bits off comedy albums, and pieces from movies, I used to record stuff off the TV, so there would be a little... a little thing to it. A little pizzazz, if you will.
HS: You mean, old time ancient history, when the dinosaurs were around, mix-tape?
KS: Yes, it was very old-timey. There was Scott Joplin music playing in the background, and we all boxed like boxing nun dolls.
HS: "Oh, random high school girl, I love you, here's a mix-tape."
KS: Are you making fun of me with random high school girl?
HS: "Oh random middle school girl, here's a mix-tape."
KS: That doesn't bother me, I got a girl now, you can't make fun of me.
HS: "Oh, Jennifer..."
KS: Am I supposed to be offended by that? Like am I supposed to get...
HS: Hmmm.
KS: ... like you were? I'm like, "Stop it! Stop saying I love Jennifer!"
HS: Hmmm...
KS: "Oh Will..."
HS: HMMMMM!

From SModcast 56: And Now a Word
Scott's harrowing highway tale/vs. Make-a-Wish

KS: Scott, you went through a harrowing experience, a mere hour ago.
SM: Yeah.
KS: ... Well, help me out dude, build to it. Alright, let me just do it again. Scott, you went through a harrowing experience a mere hour ago.
SM: [Harrowed voice] Yeah.
KS: What happened? You got in a car accident?
SM: Yeah, I got in one of those chain... like a train of fender-benders, a bunch of cars...

KS: A chain reaction?
SM: Yeah.
KS: So what happened? You were on the what?
SM: I was on the 101, and a car up ahead — like, I couldn't even see that far ahead — stopped all of a sudden and then everybody slammed on their brakes and people hit each other, and I kinda tried to swerve out of the way so I wouldn't hit the guy in front of me, but I kinda clipped him on the end of his rear right fender.
KS: Eww. So like you.
SM: I know.
KS: "I met a strange dude and clipped him in the rear."
SM: Yeah, I swerved into his rear. Um, yeah, it was awesome.
KS: That's your approach — you're not direct. You kinda swerve in…
SM: I can't commit to it.
KS: You're like, trying to trick yourself into fucking a dude.
SM: I'm like, "If I swerve, I'm not gay."
KS: So, you hit a dude. And did anyone hit you from behind?
SM: Nope.
KS: You were the last guy in the chain?
SM: I was the last guy, yeah.
KS: Did you ever find out what the first dude stopped for?
SM: No.
KS: What a bitch. It's his fault.
SM: He was running around in a kinda frenzy, and then he kinda like, took off.
KS: Did you do the insurance exchange? Obviously you're unhurt, we should point that out.
SM: Yes, I'm unhurt. No one was hurt.
KS: Nobody was hurt. It was just some damage to the car?
SM: Yeah. Not so much that I couldn't… I can drive it. It's just sort of cosmetic.
KS: What do you drive?
SM: I drive a Ford Escape, which is a hybrid.
KS: A hybrid of some sort.
SM: It's like a small SUV. And he was driving a big pick-up truck.
KS: It's a good thing you're married, 'cause with cosmetic damage on your fucking hybrid SUV, you would never get any pussy. Chicks'd be like, "What

is that? Look at your shitbox."

SM: "You're a fucking loser."

KS: "You are unfuckable."

SM: That's what people were shouting, as they drove by on the freeway.

KS: [Drive-by voice fading away] "You're unfuckablllle…" Um, did you exchange insurance information?

SM: Yeah.

KS: What was the dude that you had to interact with like? Hostile?

SM: He was fine.

KS: He wasn't like…

SM: No. Everyone was very friendly and shit, it was kinda over.

KS: Would've been a better story if you were like, "And then this motherfucker started yelling at me…"

SM: Yeah. But I related the story to you already, and you know it.

KS: I know, I know.

SM: You wanted to lead with it, and I never gave you anything…

KS: I did. I was just…

SM: I don't wanna embellish and make it bigger, 'cause what if they play this in court.

KS: It's like, "Your Honor…"

SM: "Exhibit number one."

KS: "Exhibit A." What would you do if the dude *was* hostile, got up in your grill?

SM: You mean if he was just yelling at me?

KS: Yeah.

SM: If he was just yelling at me, I would just sort of try to deflect it. I wouldn't physically…

KS: In what way? Let's play it out. I'm the guy you hit from behind, you're you.

SM: OK.

KS: … and action. "What the FUCK, buddy?"

SM: "Did you see the guy…"

KS: "All I saw was you in my rear-view mirror, coming up from behind, *swerving* from behind at me!"

SM: "Yeah?"

KS: "Don't you know how to fucking drive, asshole?"

SM: "I do know how to drive, I was trying to avoid you…"

KS: "I don't think so! Jesus Christ, look at this. Look at my car!"

SM: "Look at *my* car. Your car…"

KS: "You look at your fucking car, this is all your fault!"

SM: "Alright."

KS: "Don't alright me!"

SM: "OK."

[Awkward pause.]

KS: "… Fucking say something!"

SM: "I am saying something. I said OK."

KS: [calmer] "I'm just a little hot under the collar."

SM: "I know. Nobody wanted this."

KS: "I… this car is my life."

SM: "I, I… you know, I can tell, that you're really connected to your car."

KS: "I just wish you hadn't hit me."

SM: "I do too."

KS: "Why'd you hit me?" You know how some people like, work themselves back up into a lather? [Angry again] "Why'd you hit me?"

SM: "I was trying to avoid you, the guy two cars in front stopped for some reason."

KS: "Oh, so it's someone else's… Always someone else's fault, isn't it? Fucking typical, SEP, Somebody's Else's Problem, well this is your fucking problem, buddy!"

SM: "Like I said… I uh…"

KS: "You wanna fight?"

SM: "Not really."

KS: "Are you a smart guy?"

SM: "No."

KS: "So you're a dumbass."

SM: "Sure."

KS: "You must be, 'cause you hit my… I'm gonna put your fucking teeth down your throat."

SM: "Why?"

[Kevin breaks down laughing.]

KS: That ain't him, that was me. OK, now I'm him again: "Why?!"

SM: "Yeah, why?"

KS: "Look what you did to my car! You hit me! You hit me."

SM: "I understand that I clipped your car."

KS: "This ain't a clip. You call it a clip."

SM: "It's a minor dent in your car."

KS: "How 'bout I clip you in your fucking eye?"

SM: "I mean, I don't want you to…"

KS: "Let me punch you in the face, I'll feel better."

SM: "No."

KS: "Chest?"

SM: "No."

KS: "Arm, really hard?"

SM: "No, it's not gonna make you feel better."

KS: "It might."

SM: "No."

KS: "I'm very… aggressive."

SM: "It won't."

KS: "My adrenaline's flowing, I gotta hit something."

SM: "Then you should… you know, hit my car, go punch my car."

KS: "You hit my car, that's why I wanna hit you."

SM: "I know, but you…"

KS: "Just let me punch you."

SM: "No."

KS: "Why not?"

SM: "Because… it's not gonna make either of us feel better."

KS: "I won't do your face, I'll leave the face. Let me just give you one body punch."

SM: "No."

KS: "Who are you, fucking Houdini? You can't get hit?"

SM: "Hey, if… I'll make you a deal."

KS: "Alright."

SM: "If you wanna hit me…"

KS: "You know what? Fuck your deal!… Alright, go ahead, make a deal."

SM: "If you wanna hit me, then pay for all the repairs on my car."

KS: "*You* hit *me*!"

SM: "I'm just saying, that you know…"

KS: "I'm oughta hit you for saying that! Now I owe you two hits!"

SM: "OK."

KS: "Where do you want 'em, motherfucker?"

SM: "I don't want any hits."

KS: "I'm winding up, I'm gonna throw a haymaker!"

SM: "If you hit…"

KS: "You know what a haymaker is?"

SM: "Yeah, it's like a big wild punch."

KS: "It is… don't laugh at me! It's a *huge* wild punch!"

SM: "No, I understand that."

KS: "I'm gonna windmill at you!"

SM: "I'm not… I'm not really interested in fighting."

KS: "I can fight!"

SM: "I, I… you seem very…"

KS: "I'm willing to fight!"

SM: "… an excellent pugilist. Way to go."

KS: "Pu… pugilist? I'm just gonna, I will, I'm gonna fucking *kill* you."
SM: "That's not gonna help you win your insurance claim."
KS: "Don't you get all Zen and calm on me. I want you just as angry as I am."
SM: "I'm not, I'm trying to help you out with, like… this is not gonna help your insurance claim."
KS: "Help me out, let me punch you in the arm, once, one punch in the arm."
SM: "This is not gonna help this situation, if you decide to hit me."
KS: "I don't even know why I'm asking, I should just punch you in the fucking face."
SM: "Because you know that you're not supposed to, that's why you're, you know…" So that would be my initial line of defense…
KS: "Who are you talking to?"
SM: "I'm talking to Kevin Smith."
KS: "Who's that?"
SM: "Sorry."
KS: "We're on the fucking 101, I don't see any Kevin Smith! It's just you and me, buddy!"
SM: "I know. And the cop that's coming."
KS: Oh, there's a cop coming?
SM: Yeah.
KS: Woahh… alright. "You're lucky the cop's coming!"
SM: "Yeah, I know. I'm a lucky dog."
KS: … and scene. So… you wouldn't fight the dude? Not fight him, but you wouldn't…? I would take a shot in the arm, if he was that mad.
SM: If he just wanted to punch me?
KS: Yeah, punch you once in the arm, like punch buggy-style.
SM: No.
KS: Not at all?
SM: No. I mean I wouldn't try to be like, "Well I'm gonna try to fucking hit him first." I mean obviously, during that altercation I would be kinda ready.
KS: Right. Especially if the dude was that fucking in your face.
SM: Yeah. I guess I would be prepared to get into a physical altercation, and I guess if somebody else told me, "Just throw the first punch, so you don't lose," but at that point, my mind would be like, "You know what? We're in this situation, and I'm only gonna make it worse for me if I fucking punch

this guy in the head."

KS: At least your approach, you offered soothing, calm tones… I would probably inflame the situation because he'd be like, "Where'd you go?" and I'd be on the ground, wrapped up in the fetal position, rocking back and forth on the 101. And he might start kicking me out of frustration. I don't know if I could handle that kind of confrontation.

SM: I don't think he would kick you. He would be like, "What the fuck?"

KS: All the passersby, going at five miles an hour, like…

SM: That would sort of disable him.

KS: You think it might jar him? What if I started speaking in tongues? If I was like [speaks in tongues]… If I started speaking in a dead tongue…

SM: I think if you're weird enough, people would just kinda back away.

KS: You don't think it makes them want to punch you more?

SM: Like you said, it's adrenaline, and you're gonna kick into some whole other thing, you're gonna be like, "What the fuck's wrong with this guy?" Really, to me, those people, if they're in that situation, it's just like they're *looking* for that thing where it's like, "Fuck you!"

KS: Yeah. They just want… "Light the fuse, bitch!"

SM: They want you to match their energy and start an altercation, so if you go at them with the same energy, you're giving them it right back. If I was in that situation, somebody else might just punch me in the head. And I'm like, "Why?"

KS: Now, today, you were at fault?

SM: I'm pretty sure… my insurance company's probably… [realization dawns] ah, I don't think I should talk about it any more.

KS: Alright, *hypothetically* speaking, if there is a pile-up, like somebody stops short…

SM: You're supposed to be able to stop.

KS: So whoever hits you from behind is at fault?

SM: Whoever hit you, yeah.

KS: So if that dude hit somebody else, then he'd be having a fight with the other person, being in *his* grill.

SM: Yes.

KS: But you didn't do much damage to his car.

SM: No.

KS: Um… what if you had?

SM: Done a lot of damage?

KS: Yeah, like a serious amount of damage. And he was claiming whiplash.

SM: Well if he claims whiplash, generally what happens is, they'll call an ambulance. If you're in an accident and you grab your neck, they're bringing an ambulance.

KS: Really?

SM: Yep. There's nothing you can do about it.

KS: Would you get in trouble for that kinda thing?

SM: Do I, or does the person who says…?

KS: You. The guy who hit the dude who gets the whiplash. Like, they can sue you, right?

SM: Yes. Well, they can sue the insurance company for…

KS: They can't sue you personally? What if he was just like, "Hey! You're that dude from SModcast, you must have money. I hear thinkgeek.com sponsors your show now, you must have money coming out your ass!"

SM: You mean like, a civil suit?

KS: Yeah! Somebody once told me that anybody can sue anybody in this country.

SM: I doubt that… basically it all just goes through the insurance companies.

KS: And that would make your insurance rate in turn go up?

SM: Yes.

KS: What if it was a lot of damage, dude was claiming whiplash, you were looking at a bunch of fucking huge insurance premiums, maybe a court case based on his whiplash, and the dude was like… alright, go back into the scene. I'm the dude. I'm not as hostile this time. You're you, I'm the dude who got hit. You rear-ended me completely. I had a cat in the backseat, and the cat's dead — there was a cat carrier and the cat's dead — and I'm claiming whiplash, and my car looks like shit. Your car looks fine, for some reason. His car is just totaled from the rear.

SM: So I've done a ton of damage. Gotcha.

KS: Yes. And you're looking at a lot of bills.

SM: OK.

KS: I'm the guy.

SM: Where are we?

KS: We're not on the 101, there aren't a lot of witnesses.

SM: Oh, OK.

KS: We're on a side street.

SM: OK.

KS: "Look, this is gonna cost you a lot of money."

SM: "Are you sure you're hurt?"

KS: "Yes, I'm sure I'm hurt! My lash has been whipped! My neck hurts!"

SM: Well, if you're just like… if you're acting like that, then you're generally acting like you're not hurt. That's not how people act when they're hurt.

KS: No, he's sitting on the curb, holding his neck while he says it, rocking back and forth, [whiny pained voice] "This is gonna cost you a lot of money, man…"

SM: Um…

KS: "What have you got to say for yourself?"

SM: "I don't have anything to say. That's not a question."

KS: "Do you have a cigarette?"

SM: "No. That's a question. No I do not have a cigarette, I don't smoke."

KS: "I could use a cigarette, my neck hurts so much. Tell you what — give me a hand job and I'll call it even."

SM: "Um… no."

KS: "Why not? I'm hurt!"

SM: "Because that's not…"

KS: Hold on — what if the dude was dying? You put him through his windshield.

SM: He's in a bloody mess?

KS: He's laying on the fucking curb, and there's no one around, for fucking miles, no passerby or anything.

SM: So we're out in the country?

KS: Yeah, or just on a side street where there's no…

SM: We're out in the country.

KS: Alright, you're in the country.

SM: We've gotta be on a road where it's like, there's no way for me to—

KS: There's no signal, you got no signal on your cell phone.

SM: Yeah.

KS: And he's like, "I'm dying, man!" He's dying. He looks bad.

SM: OK.

KS: From the shoulders up…

SM: So it's not like he has a little cut on his head, and he like, pulls his pants down…

KS: No. No, from the shoulders up you're looking at some serious fucking, hardcore damage. And he's like, "I'm dying… I'm dying…"

SM: Like he's trapped in his car?

KS: No, no he went through the windshield, he's on the curb. He hit the curb, and it fucking tore open the back of his scalp, so if you turned him over you'd see bone, a lot of blood and shit, but he's still somewhat conscious. It's like — remember the dude that got trapped between the rail and the train, and he was alive, but like, the moment they moved the train he was gonna die? Like it kinda cauterized the wound?

SM: You know, I'm kinda upset already at this point. And now we're going into the hand job scene…

KS: Well, not yet. Hold on. So he's fucking… somehow he's alive, but it's tenuous at best. His grip on life is fading fast.

SM: OK.

KS: And he's like, [weak, pained voice] "Ahh… my wife and kids… why'd you do this to my wife and kids?" What do you say? Let's just do the scene. "My wife and kids… I'm so hurt… why are you laughing at me?"

SM: I can't, I can't do this scene. I don't have any jokes for this scene, where it's like there's a guy dying in the middle of the road, supposedly my fault… I would be trying to help him.

KS: Alright, so you would be trying to like, what? Give him CPR? What do you do?

SM: Well, I mean you have to assess the injuries.

KS: [Back to weak voice]: "Put a coat under my head…"

SM: I mean, I would do that, if he wants a coat under his head. I was also trying to assess where he's injured, and trying to stop him from bleeding.

KS: "Who are you, George Clooney? You're not a doctor… Are you a doctor?"

SM: Why is this guy like, such a…

KS: Why is he what?

SM: I mean he's just kinda weird.

KS: He's fucking dying, dude!

SM: I know, but it's not like he's trying to stay alive.

KS: Sure he is!

SM: No he's not!

KS: He's trying to maintain consciousness. You know, he's fucking… he's fading fast.
SM: I would say you'd focus on your… it's not like he's really focused on the problem.
KS: He's just been fucking put through a windshield, landed fucking face first and back of the head on the curb, opened up his scalp and shit, he's… he doesn't know what he's saying at this point.
SM: I would be trying to say, "Let me help you, what do we do?" I wouldn't say what do we do… "Let me help you, let me try to tend your wounds."
KS: And he says, "You wanna help me? Gimme a hand job, before I die. I'm gonna die. I'm dying here."
SM: I would be like, "Well, I don't think you're… you're gonna be fine…"
KS: "I'm gonna die, all I'm asking is for a hand job…"
SM: "You're gonna be fine."
KS: "… just… touch it."
SM: "I think it's more important that I tend to your wounds than I tend to your…"
KS: "You're not a doctor! Tend to my sexual need..."
SM: "I'm not that either, so… if you're so concerned with having a professional dude tend to you…"
KS: "We're in the middle of the country, it's a rural road, nobody can see, just… jerk me off until I die…"
SM: "You seem fine to me, the way you're talking."
KS: "Look at me! I'm dying. It hurts! There's blood everywhere, I can feel the blood rushing out of my body."
SM: "I think we should focus on staying alive."
KS: "I just wanna die… I just wanna die cumming. It's always been my dream. Just do this for me. And karmically we'll be even."
SM: "No."
KS: Really?! You don't fucking jerk the dude off?
SM: No.
KS: Why not?
SM: Because I would try to keep him alive!
KS: "This will keep me alive, this will give me

Random SModquotes

"If you're too old to believe in Santa, you can't believe in magic... or Jesus."

the will to live…"

SM: "Nah, you can't keep changing your story." No, I would try to make sure the person…

KS: Would you give any dying man a hand job if they requested it?

SM: Like, somebody who was in the hospital…?

KS: Not your dad. My first instinct is like, "Your dad's dying, would you give him a hand job?" That's just weird. But yeah, some dude… you get a call from the Make-a-Wish Foundation, and they're like, "We got a kid who's a huge Scott Mosier fan…"

SM: No.

KS: "… please come see the kid…" and you get there and the kid's like, "I've always wanted a hand job from you."

SM: First of all, this is illegal.

KS: I don't think a hand job's illegal, he's not paying you money for it.

SM: If I fucking like, give a little kid a hand job?

KS: He's eighteen, he's legit.

SM: Um… no!

KS: No?

SM: Fuck, no.

KS: But he's dying!

SM: I understand that. We're all dying technically.

KS: But this dude's fucking closer to the end.

SM: I know, and that's a bummer, but like… go to Disneyland.

KS: He's like, "I can't make it to Disneyland."

SM: "Fuck, I'll get you… have a three-way with some fucking hookers, I'll pay for it. I'm not giving you a hand job."

KS: "It's always been you, Scott Mosier."

SM: "Well, that's just weird."

KS: "Well it's weird that I have to die so young, unfulfilled."

SM: "I know, it sucks."

KS: "Just give me half a hand job, I'll finish the rest."

SM: "No. No way."

KS: "Will you watch me jerk off?"

SM: "No!"

KS: "What?!" You wouldn't watch a fucking dying kid jerk off?

SM: Would you?

KS: If that was his last request, and he was just like, "Just watch me jerk off," I'd be like, "Alright… I guess." I would totally have something to talk about on SModcast. I'd be like, "Does this make me gay?"
SM: I'd be like, "Um… I don't think it makes you gay." No, I wouldn't do it.
KS: I think it'd be tough to not honor the dying request of somebody.
SM: I mean my thing is, I feel that like… if I… I'm imposing my own ideas on death. If I was dying I wouldn't go out of my way to make somebody incredibly uncomfortable in order to make myself happy, so in return, if I was in that situation, I would just say, "Look, I understand that you're dying and I think that sucks, and there are many things I would do to try to make you feel happy, but those two things are not on the list."
KS: I can't believe you wouldn't watch. That's so harmless.
SM: Um… I don't think it's… I mean I have no interest in watching somebody jerk off.
KS: I know, but this is a special circumstance. This is a kid's dying wish, an eighteen-year-old's dying wish. Who's a big fan of you.
SM: You cannot sit there and say that it would not be the most bizarre and strange thing ever. And therefore…
KS: It might be very strange and very bizarre, but it's just like, that's death. Death is strange and bizarre.
SM: No it's not! Death is not strange and bizarre at all!
KS: In this instance, it is.
SM: The one thing in this world that's not strange and bizarre is death. Death is like, it happens to everybody. So it's not strange, nor is it bizarre. It's absolutely the norm.
KS: But it's this person's last gasp. You're not a religious person, you don't believe in the afterlife. You believe, what? You go in a box, and it's done.
SM: Yeah.
KS: There's no… you're not a ghost, you're not like [spooky ghost noise] "Whooo-ooooh."
SM: Generally no, I don't believe in—
KS: So that's it, this kid's last request before he shuffles loose the mortal coil, is… Look, I think it's a little weird, but I understand you don't want to jerk off a dying eighteen-year-old guy. But him saying, "Just watch me jerk off," I don't think that's tough to honor.
SM: I mean… no, I would not do it.

KS: He's not like, "Catch it in your mouth," he's just like, "Just watch."

SM: No. Because in the end…

KS: You're a fucking hate-tank, dude…

SM: No way. In that moment, you're dying, and you could do anything you want… Yes, it's me being judgmental because I'm sitting there going like, "That's just… no, I'm not gonna watch you jerk off. Like, I understand you're dying. And dying's not fun, but everybody dies." It's not like he's the one guy who's gonna die on Earth.

KS: No, but he's also not like, the first in a line of hundreds that are going to ask you to do this.

SM: No, exactly. And for all of you out there that are thinking about it…

KS: He's cut down in the prime of his life, dude.

SM: I understand, I'm not saying that it's not sad.

KS: Don't you have any heart?

SM: I do! But that to me is like… delivering that to him is like…

KS: It's fulfilling his last wish, his dying wish.

SM: I mean, psychologically he's doing it for reasons of… fetish? Or…

KS: Yes. It's always been his fucking dream to have you watch him jerk off.

SM: I just wouldn't do it.

KS: He's like, "I just want you to see how good I am at it. You need proof, you can't take my word for it. You gotta see it."

SM: "I don't… I'm totally fine with… I'm sure the quality of your masturbation is, you know, top of the line."

KS: "Here, let me show you."

SM: "No."

KS: He starts lifting up his hospital gown…

SM: I wouldn't do it.

KS: Where are you at this point?

SM: I'm in the hallway!

KS: No way, because the fucking Make-a-Wish people are looking through the little slot in the door…

SM: How did the Make-a-Wish people get me there?

KS: … and you just hear 'click' — they locked you in, and they turn their back on the door, so you're trapped in the room with this guy…

SM: So now the situation is that I have no choice.

KS: I guess you could be in the room and like, shut your eyes and sing

yourself a lullaby or something…
SM: I would not shut my eyes, if there was a dude in the room fucking jerking off. If I've gotten into that weird, bizarre thing…
KS: You know what, he's not a threat, he poses no threat.
SM: He could do like a *Silence of the Lambs* and get it in his hand and chuck it at me.
KS: Like Miggs?
SM: Yeah. He could Miggs me right in the fucking head.
KS: "Miggs me…" So… they lock you in…
SM: Awesome. How did they lure me in there?
KS: They said the kid's dying request is to meet you.
SM: No, but I wouldn't fly up there.
KS: They flew you out.
SM: To meet me?
KS: I've done that, I've went and met people who are on death's door and shit like that. And nobody's ever asked me that but, you know, somebody asks and it's tough to be like, "I'm not gonna…" I mean, luckily this case was in Los Angeles, the one that I went to, so it was a drive. But this kid's in Los Angeles too, he lives two blocks from you.
SM: It really doesn't matter. Proximity.
KS: I'm just saying that's how they got you there. Played on your sympathies.
SM: I just have to go in there and be like…
KS: Yeah, and chit-chat with him for an hour and shit like that…
SM: So then I'd go. And then they lock me in?
KS: Yeah, when you make for the door, they quickly click the door shut, they lock it shut, and then they… you know, in a hospital room door there's a little window? They turn around so their backs are against the window. Are you pounding on the door?
SM: I wouldn't go out of my way to get out of there.
KS: No? And you're on the third floor of the hospital, so the window's not an option.
SM: I'm not fucking *scared* to be in there, it's not like I'm fucking like, petrified of it.
KS: And he's like, "Look. Just look. Look at it." [Makes disturbingly realistic masturbating noise…] The room's all quiet and you just hear [noise again] "Look at it…" [again] "Scott…"

SM: I mean at that point I would look at it, and I would be like, "Alright." But then I would get to the point where I would be pretty mad with Make-a-Wish.

KS: OK, that's fine, I'm not saying…

SM: I'd be known as fucking Hitler, 'cause I'd sue Make-a-Wish and be like, "Here's my wish."

KS: Alright, so you'd give him a cursory glance.

SM: I mean, I would…

KS: He's like, "I'm coming, please watch."

SM: "Ah, there you go. There it is. There's your cum. Way to go."

KS: "Can you hand me a rag?"

SM: "No."

KS: "OK I'm done."

SM: "OK."

KS: "It was excellent meeting you."

SM: "It was uh… you know."

KS: "I'm sorry, I realize this might have made you a little uncomfortable."

SM: "Well… it has."

KS: "Say something nice to me before you leave."

SM: "Um… you have a very nice voice."

KS: "Thank you. You can go now, I'm tired."

SM: "'Kay."

KS: And so they open the door, the two Make-a-Wish dudes. What's the first thing you say to them?

SM: I don't know, I guess I would be like, "What the fuck's the matter with you guys?"

KS: "Look, we didn't know he was gonna do that."

SM: "Yeah, you did."

KS: "Honest to god, we had no idea."

SM: "Yeah, yeah yeah."

KS: "We didn't know he was gonna do that!"

SM: "Why would you lock me in?"

KS: "Well…"

SM: "Did you lock me in because you thought I was trying to run away from him talking to me?"

KS: "Here's the thing. We didn't know he was gonna do that, *at all*. He just said he wanted to meet you. I swear we didn't. But you know, we couldn't help but overhear the conversation…"

SM: "But in the moment you decided it would be better to lock me in there."

KS: "Yes. Yes…"

SM: "Well that was probably a very bad decision on your part."

KS: "… to maintain the integrity of Make-a-Wish."

SM: "I would argue that locking somebody in a room with somebody who wants to masturbate in front of them is not maintaining the integrity of Make-a-Wish."

KS: "Look, we have to honor *his* wish, not yours. I know your wish was to get out of that room…"

SM: "I'm sure that the bylines of your organization do not…"

KS: "What was the harm? Why'd you have to act like such a sissy?"

SM: "Why don't *you* go in there and watch him masturbate?"

KS: "He didn't want… look, if the kid had of said that to me, I woulda done it. I appreciate what Make-a-Wish stands for. You clearly don't."

SM: "Then you're obviously a better person than I am."

KS: "There's a dying eighteen-year-old boy and you just can't give him this one thing?"

SM: "Yeah… no."

KS: "Well, you did it anyway, 'cause we locked you in."

SM: "I know."

KS: "So we're even."

SM: "Thank you. What a great moment. I'll continue to make wishes."

KS: Would you ever uh… [Kevin's dog approaches]: oh, come on, fuck off. Go go go.

SM: Would I do it again? Would I be jerked again?

KS: Yes. Would you ever partake in Make-a-Wish again?

SM: I doubt I would sue them, but I would definitely be like, if they called me again, "Are you high?"

KS: Alright. Hold on. This is Make-a-Wish calling you again. You're you, I'm the Make-a-Wish Foundation.

SM: Alright, I'm at home.

KS: "Hi, is Scott Mosier there?"

SM: "Uh, yes he is."

KS: "Is this Scott?"

SM: "Yes it is."

KS: "Hey, Scott. This is Doug Thompson."

SM: "From the Make-a-Wish?" Click.

KS: Brrringg…

SM: "Hello?"

KS: "Uh, Scott, I think we got…"

SM: Click!

KS: And then an hour later you hear [knocks].

SM: [Makes footsteps noise]

KS: Was that you going to the door?

SM: Yeah. What the fuck? Didn't you ever listen to fucking 1920s radio? It's like *The Shadow*.

KS: I thought you were padding away quietly, you're like, "I don't wanna answer it!" But you don't know it's him yet.

SM: No, I don't.

KS: It might not be him, I don't want to ruin it.

SM: If it's the same guy, the way my house is laid out, I could see.

KS: Alright, let's do it! [knocks]

SM: "Hey, honey, I got the door!" [Footsteps… "Crsh"]

KS: What was that? Did you shoot him?

SM: I don't know, like Coke opening. I was trying to do a door. Alright, 'click'.

KS: "Hey, Mr Mosier. It's me, Doug Thompson."

SM: "Yeah, I know."

KS: "We got disconnected twice on the phone."

SM: "No, I hung up on you."

KS: "OK, fair enough. Look, I understand you may not be the biggest fan of Make-a-Wish."

SM: "You don't understand."

KS: "No, I get it."

SM: "No, 'cause if you understood you wouldn't have called me, nor come by here."

KS: "And believe me, the last thing in the world I'd ever want to do is call you."

SM: "That's not true."

KS: "Well, alright, it's not the last thing. One of the thousand last things I'd ever want to do is have to call on you again, but there's a little six-year-old girl who…"

SM: "I know what your organization does, so I know why you're here."

KS: "… six-year-old girl, she's dying of a horrible disease, she's got like a week left, she's a huge fan of yours, has all your lines from the movies memorized and whatnot. Listens to SModcast…"

SM: "And she's six years old? Why is she watching the movies?"

KS: "Because, you know, she was dying, her parents… Look, I can't judge how parents raise their children. For whatever reason she's a fan of you, six-year-old girl, she lives very close…"

SM: "I can't do it, because I don't believe you."

KS: "Here's a picture of her." And he pulls out a picture…

SM: "I mean, the fact you got a picture of a kid…"

KS: "But this kid…"

SM: "I understand that, but I don't believe you."

KS: "Mr Mosier, I awfully appreciate you being angry with me."

SM: "I'll more likely convert to whatever religious person comes to my door than actually…"

KS: "Mr Mosier, I appreciate your feelings on the matter, but…"

SM: "No you don't."

KS: "I completely do."

SM: "No, you don't."

KS: "I *do*…"

SM: "'Cause you wouldn't be here."

KS: "I feel bad. I don't wanna be here! But this six-year-old girl…"

SM: "You don't feel bad."

KS: "… just wants to spend an hour with you in her hospital room."

SM: "No."

KS: "It's not the same hospital."

SM: "No, man! And you know what? If you want to go to her and tell her why not, then you tell her that it's your fault."

KS: "How am I going to say that to a six-year-old girl?"

SM: "Well, that's part of… you have to say you couldn't fulfill her wish, because of how you guys conducted yourselves."

KS: "Because you're a big meanie?"

SM: "No, because you guys are… because *you* guys are big meanies."

KS: "But she's gonna say, 'Why am I being penalized?' She might not say penalized, but she'll… she won't understand why she's being punished for something she didn't do. Mr Mosier, please have a heart. I will never bother you again."

SM: "I don't believe you. I'll take nothing that you say at face value."

KS: [Laughs.] "I'm just giggling at the irony of the situation. I just never met a man who was scared of a six-year-old dying little girl before."

SM: "I'm not scared of a six-year-old dying little girl."

KS: "I think you might be a little chicken."

SM: "No."

KS: "Little bit?"

SM: "No."

KS: [Makes chicken noise.]

SM: "What am I afraid of?"

KS: [Continues to make chicken noise.]

SM: I just shut the door. [Slam.]

KS: And I'm him outside the door: "You're a fucking chicken! You're a chicken! I'm gonna tell all your neighbors you're a goddamn chicken! This son of a bitch in this house right here…" This is me talking through the door…

SM: I understand. I'm in the moment.

KS: "This son of a bitch who lives here has no heart! He doesn't want to visit a dying six-year-old!"

SM: [Makes phone keypad noise.]

KS: "What was that? He doesn't want to visit a dying six-year-old kid!"

SM: "Hello, operator, yes. I have a disturbance… I have a disturbed human being on my front porch."

KS: "I'm not…! You're disturbed! What kinda hate-tank doesn't want to visit a six-year-old dying girl!"

SM: I'm in the other room, you can't hear me.

KS: I'm just yelling… I can hear you, the window's open.

SM: "Yes. He won't leave."

KS: "I've half a mind to climb inside that open window..."

SM: "He won't leave."

KS: "… and beat the shit out of you!"

SM: "Now he's threatening violence. He's threatening to trespass, and…"

KS: "Go ahead, call the cops! Tell them why I'm upset, go ahead, big man! Tell him the story. I'll tell him!"

SM: "Alright, I'll see you soon."

KS: And then the cops show up.

SM: The cops show up.

KS: Woo! Woo! Woo! [siren noise] Um... you be the cop.

SM: [Clears throat] "Um, sir?"

KS: [Sotto voce] "Do we have a problem here?"

SM: [Gravelly monotone] "Do we have a problem here?"

KS: No, I was feeding you the line.

SM: Oh, OK. I'm the cop? Yeah, I just said it!

KS: No, he wouldn't say it like [mimics Scott] "Do we have a problem here?"

SM: "Uh... Do we have a problem here, sir?"

KS: "Yeah, we have a *big* problem officer, that son of a bitch in the house right over, behind me, who probably called you..."

SM: "Sir, you're going to have to bring your tone down."

KS: "OK, I'll use my inside voice. [Quieter, calmer] That son of a bitch, in the house behind me... I work for the Make-a-Wish Foundation, you're familiar with our work?"

SM: "I understand."

KS: "Dying children, last wishes...?"

SM: "Yes."

KS: "Little six-year-old girl... stricken by a horrible disease..."

SM: "Yes."

KS: "Her dying wish is to meet him. He's refusing."

SM: "I understand that sir, but that's not illegal."

KS: "I understand it's not illegal, but officer, you've got to feel where I'm coming from here."

SM: "I understand that but it's my job to uphold the law, and you are trespassing, and you are disturbing the peace."

KS: "Well, officer, there ought to be a law that..."

SM: "Sir, I'm going to have to ask you to leave.

KS: "... show some heart..."

SM: "Sir, this is..."

KS: "Sir, I have no problem leaving, but I just need you to understand..."

SM: "Sir, I'm going to have to ask you to leave *now*."

KS: Alright, I'm walking up the driveway. I'm across the street. "Can you hear me from here, officer? I'm OK to be here, across the street."
SM: "Um…"
KS: "There's no injunction against me, no court order to tell me I can't be here, this is a public street."
SM: "You're causing a public disturbance and I'm going to have to ask you to leave."
KS: "There's nobody around, officer."
SM: "Um… you're going to have to leave."
KS: "Do I go to tell the world, the *LA Times*, that the LAPD can't stand Make-a-Wish Foundation, don't want to see a little six-year-old girl get her dying wish?"
SM: "We don't have anything to do with that, sir, but you're not allowed to trespass…"
KS: "You represent the LAPD."
SM: "I represent the Los Angeles Police Department, yes."
KS: "And you're not helping me?"
SM: "I can't help you, sir, that is not my…"
KS: "I want you to go in there and drag that guy out in cuffs. This little girl, she's right down the street at the hospital, officer. It'll take him ten minutes."
SM: "Sir, I'm not going to sacrifice my career…"
KS: "Why not? I'm sure you can get a movie deal out of this. You'll be a hero cop. They'll write about you. They'll write editorials about you."
SM: "I don't think…"
KS: "You know who that son of a bitch in that house is?"
SM: "Um, no I don't know who that son of a bitch in that house is."
KS: "Scott Mosier."
SM: "… OK."
KS: "Well?"
SM: "Well, what does that mean to me?"
KS: "It's just, I'm saying, he could spare ten minutes for a dying girl."
SM: "That's fine, and he'll be held up in the court of public opinion, but he's not going to be held in the court of law, because he's not breaking the law."
KS: "Well, can I get your information so that I can have a journalist contact you for a statement…"
SM: "No."

[Barking in the background.]

KS: "What is that? Who said that?"

SM: "Sir, are you hearing voices in your head?"

KS: "Yes, the voice that tells me that I should give a dying girl her last wish. It's a voice we should all have, officer."

SM: "Well does she have a number two person?"

KS: "She didn't, strangely."

SM: "Well maybe you should enquire as to whether there was somebody else, like a number two. A runner-up."

KS: "Fuck you." And he leaves… Wow that's harsh, dude. So just because of the other incident, you wouldn't go visit a dying six-year-old?

SM: Well let me put it this way. If we go back to reality — if that happened, they contacted me, I would say to them, "Allow me to contact the parents directly, and talk to them and meet." And then I would be like, "But if any of you are within fucking five feet of me, or anywhere near that place, I'm just gonna leave."

KS: Fair enough. Fair enough. And so then you contact the parents…

SM: And then I have to watch them masturbate.

KS: No, nothing like that. Contact the parents, and they're like, "Look, I'm so glad you called us. We can't explain why she loves you so much but she does; I'm sorry about your problems with Make-a-Wish, that sounds horrible, but would you please come and see little Melissa Sue."

SM: "Yeah."

KS: "OK." And then you get there…

SM: Yeah.

KS: … and you get into the room, the parents are there, and the little girl in bed…

[Kevin giggles gleefully throughout this set-up…]

SM: And obviously, I've made a mistake.

KS: And then all of a sudden you hear 'click'. What do you say when you hear the click?

SM: Well first off, I would stand in the doorway, having learned my lesson.

KS: No, but they're… I mean clearly there's no threat anywhere. No Make-a-Wish guys, the kid doesn't wanna jerk off in front of you…

SM: OK, so I go in the room and I hear a click. What do I do?

KS: Yes. What's your first reaction?

SM: Well I'd try to go open the door.
KS: You can't.
SM: Because it's locked?
KS: 'Cause it's locked, and the father's standing in front of the door and he pulls out a large knife.
SM: OK.
KS: And he's like, "Our little girl's dying wish is... TO WATCH YOU DIE!" [Kevin loses it.]
SM: Um... I guess my immediate reaction would be that uh...
KS: [Struggling to keep giggling under control] You're like, "Why does this keep happening to me?"
SM: Yeah. Um... obviously I would feel like I should've... that I was right.
KS: "I knew it!"
SM: Obviously, I guess I would try to assess my situation, and whether I could escape, alive.
KS: The wife pulls out a knife as well. They both have knives and the dying little girl's holding a knife as well.
SM: Am I afraid of her?
KS: She wants to strike the killing blow.
SM: OK. Um... I would, uh...
KS: Wouldn't it be worth it though, for a dying six-year-old girl? Like, you'd get a sense of justice, because you know your killer is going to be dead soon.
SM: No! Fuck that, are you crazy? Not at all.
KS: I know. I'm asking the dude who wouldn't watch the dying guy masturbate.
SM: Well fuck that! I mean would you fucking like, go to your death?
KS: No. I agree with you.
SM: Like, once again I think that the request level of... I mean at a certain point, yes, people are dying, and it's unfortunate they're dying early. But there does have to be... I think there is a line that you cross.
KS: Do you think they have parameters? They must have parameters, at Make-a-Wish.
SM: I guarantee you there's nothing sexual in their charter.
KS: Really? I think that's a shame, I think if like... you know, it's always like, "I wanna go to Disneyland!" The shit that they kinda put out there... "I wanna meet Michael J. Fox," whatever...

SM: But some things are just like, you don't need Make-a-Wish if you want to meet Michael J. Fox. You want a hooker? Your parents can go get you a hooker.
KS: But they're broke! They're like, "Make-a-Wish will pay for it."
SM: Yeah, but they won't do that.
KS: That's a shame, man. 'Cause then it's false advertising. They're not truly… you're making a wish, but they're not getting it granted.
SM: But I think that their job is to grant wishes that would otherwise seem impossible to achieve. Like, if the kid was just like, "I want to go to the Dairy Queen," it'd be like, "Well, just fucking take your kid to the Dairy Queen."
KS: They're like, "Aim higher."
SM: "We're not really set up to take someone to Dairy Queen."
KS: "Hey, do you want a celebrity to take you to Dairy Queen?" They're like, "No. I just want a Dilly Bar."
SM: "What the fuck?"
KS: "Will somebody fucking take me to Dairy Queen? I'm dying!"
SM: "I don't feel well, and I want to get a Dilly." Yeah, I mean I think otherwise, if you were a parent then I'd think it would fall on you. And even if you don't have a lot of money, then to me… everything that you've been taunting me with for the last thirty-something minutes about how they're dying…
KS: I don't know if it's taunting.
SM: Well, you know, you're telling me I have no heart. Whether *you* are, or fucking Darren from the Make-a-Wish, or Darryl… I think then it would be their — the parents' — job… If you had a boy that was eighteen years old, or anyways, if you had…
KS: Hey, man if I had a fifteen-year-old dying son, and he was like, "I want pussy," I'd be like, "Right on. I'm gonna set that up for you."
SM: Yeah.
KS: Even if he was twelve. The kid's dying, I'm gonna go out of my way to give him…
SM: Well, if he's twelve he's like, "I don't want pussy."
KS: He wants cock?
SM: No, he doesn't want either.
KS: Then what are we talking about? Why am I talking?
SM: No, he wants Dairy Queen. What, you're going to ignore your kid who's

dying?

KS: Yeah, I'm like, "I don't want to know from that kid unless he's got a fucked-up last wish."

SM: "That's really depressing. You're bringing me down, man."

KS: I would happily bring him to Dairy Queen, that would not be a problem for me at all. I'd buy him a Dairy Queen franchise.

SM: Would there be a line?

KS: A line? Yeah, if the kid was like, "I want you to die in front of me," or "Kill Mom," that would be my line.

SM: Or kill anybody.

KS: Yeah.

SM: You wouldn't even bring in a vagrant and have him killed?

KS: Yeah, if he was just like, "I want you… to stab a homeless man in the heart… I want you to kill a hobo for me." I'd be like, "OK but I probably can't do it here, 'cause we don't want any evidence. I'm gonna go down to the train yard…"

SM: "I'm not a fucking idiot. Don't try to fake it."

KS: "I don't think you're an idiot."

SM: "Don't try to fake it."

KS: "I won't try to fake it, I'm gonna go to the train yard…"

SM: "If you fake it, you break it…"

KS: "I won't. Daddy's gonna kill a hobo for you. Daddy's gonna kill you a hobo, and he's gonna bring you back the heart. You know what, I'll bring back the head." No, not the head, 'cause…

SM: "I wanna see it."

KS: "I can't do it here in the house. I might get busted, and then…"

SM: "Take me to the train yard."

KS: "You're too sick to go to the train yard."

SM: "What am I gonna do, die?"

KS: "Well, you got me there. I don't want you dying at the scene of the crime…"

SM: "Take me to the train yard."

KS: "… I don't want you dying at the scene… "

SM: "Train yard. Take."

KS: "Why you talking like an idiot all of a sudden?"

SM: "Just… why do you say that?"

KS: "Because, you're eighteen!"

SM: I thought I was fifteen. Or twelve.

KS: Alright, you're twelve. "I don't know any twelve-year-old who talks like that."

SM: "I'm dying. Are you dying?"

KS: "Yeah! Scott Mosier once said that we're all dying."

SM: "Are you dying more quickly, like now?"

KS: "Did you ever see the way your dad eats? And conducts his affairs?"

SM: "Are you judging me?"

KS: "I'm not judging you."

SM: "You are too."

KS: "I would never judge the way you're dying."

SM: "You're mocking my death."

KS: "I'm gonna go kill a hobo and bring the heart back to you."

SM: "It's gonna be a beef heart. I don't believe you."

KS: "Well, a human body is made up of beef."

SM: "You're going to lie to me."

KS: "I wouldn't… I… just stay here."

SM: "Liar."

KS: "Man… how 'bout a hooker?"

SM: "No."

KS: "Why not? Sex is better than watching someone die…"

SM: "Kill a hooker?"

KS: "Why do you want to see someone die? What happened to you?"

SM: "… Don't know."

KS: "Are you sure I'm your father?"

SM: "Yes."

KS: "I want to study your scalp, see if there's any 666 marks on there…"

[Scott makes freaky demon noise…]

KS: "Oh my god! It's the Hell-spawn! For years we've been housing the Hell-spawn!" Is he really dying, the Hell-spawn? Or is he playing at it? Trying to get me to kill someone?

SM: He's pretending.

KS: Get out of here. It was a test?

"Your trenchant fucking mouth I can get past, because the smell of your cock is intoxicating."

SM: It was a test.
KS: A fucking twelve-year test?
SM: Yeah.
KS: Did I pass?
SM: Well he woulda… "You're a pussy."
KS: That's it? That's as bad as it gets?
SM: Yeah. Then he spontaneously combusts.

From SModcast 57: Terrorist Pizza
Gordo, the righteously indignant Canadian

SM: The whole pizza thing never happened in Canada [i.e. making crank calls to have pizzas sent to people who hadn't ordered them]. I was in Canada in high school, so…
KS: Not even Canadian pizza?
SM: That was a *shameful* thing to do.
KS: People felt very guilty about it?
SM: Yeah.
KS: "Don't do that, it's not Canadian, eh."
SM: "You sent a pizza to 'em, eh? He didn't order it!"
KS: Is that the dude who's like, afterwards, enraged that he partook?
SM: No, that's just somebody that… "That was the point…"
KS: "It was fucking good, eh? It was fun! It was good times!"
SM: "It's just good times, it was good clean fun!"
KS: "No it wasn't. He didn't want those pizzas, eh? He didn't want 'em!"
SM: "Those are gonna go to waste! There's people in parts of the country, who fucking really need that pizza!"
KS: "You're ruining it for everybody. I don't care! It ends now! You're acting like you're in the fucking States, eh?! It ain't right. You people have no fucking heart. That ain't hockey."
SM: "This is fucking Canada!"
KS: [Penitent] "He's got a point, eh? It is Canada."
SM: "Aw, fuck…"
KS: "I don't know what we were thinking." "You all were in Hollywood!" They're like, "What?" "Yeah! That's a Hollywood thing to do!"

SM: "Down in Hollywood, all the pizza goes to the wrong houses!"

KS: "That shit don't roll in Alberta!"

SM: "You can't do that shit in Richmond, Burnaby!"... That's all it takes, is some fucking Canadian names...

KS: "That may be a South Kitsilano type of behaviour, but it don't roll here!"

SM: "There's a few in South Kitsilano, but there, you know, they've been handled. They've been taken care of."

KS: "It's just not patriotic!"

SM: "There's gonna be fucking anarchy up here."

KS: "This is how it starts! This is how the Holocaust started, eh? Hitler and his buddies in a beer hall, sending pizzas to some Jews, they thought it was funny, and then what? Ovens. And not pizza ovens!"

SM: "I gotta take a stand! I gotta take this to the Parliament!"

KS: I like the angry Canadian. I like the Canadian with the righteous indignation.

SM: Yeah. They're there.

KS: I like your Canadian with the righteous indignation. That's my favourite Canadian.

SM: They're out there.

KS: Let's do... alright, you're that guy, you're Gordo.

SM: I'm Gordo.

KS: The righteously indignant Canadian.

SM: OK.

KS: And I'm a... I'm me, visiting.

SM: OK.

KS: And he's some dude, I was hanging out with some other dude and he was there too.

SM: OK.

KS: And I'm trying to get into some shenanigans.

SM: So there's three people?

KS: Yeah, but we don't have to worry about the other guy. Basically it's us. Well that dude, the dude that I was hanging out with, he went home early, and awkwardly left me with this dude...

SM: With Gordo.

KS: Yes, with Gordo. And for some reason, in this alternate reality, I'm not like, "Well, bye. I'm going back to the hotel." I'm hanging out with Gordo.

SM: OK.

KS: "Hey man, um…"

SM: "Yeah?"

KS: "You wanna go to the peelers?"

[Scott adopts a strong Canadian accent.]

SM: "The peelers?!"

KS: It starts already. This guy's got a hair-trigger. "Yeah, the peelers, man. You wanna go to?" We're in Toronto. "You wanna go to The Brass Rail, see some peelers?"

SM: "The peelers? The Brass Rail, huh?"

KS: "Yeah. You know, over…"

SM: "You know how many of those young girls are underage?"

KS: "No…!"

SM: "They've had problems growing up! You're gonna exploit their problems, and go in there for money, and for, touching nipples and stuff?"

KS: "Well, I wouldn't do that. I wouldn't touch their nipples, it just… you don't like…?"

SM: "Ogle their nipples, and their private parts, and things like that, to make yourself all… all… all big and horny and, you know, wanting to go to the bathroom, and then you put things in the stalls?"

KS: "You sound like you've had a lot of experience."

SM: "I've heard about these things. My friend is a bouncer at The Brass Rail, he tells me about Americans and their, you know, their hygiene."

KS: "Look, Americans… here's the thing…"

SM: "There's American sperm all over that place. Yankee sperm up and down the walls, eh?"

KS: "Is there really?"

SM: "Yeah. You get one of those lights, and you shine it and it's just red, white and blue sperm all over!"

KS: "A UV light?"

SM: "Yeah! You calling me, just 'cause I don't know the fucking name to everything, I'm a fucking dumbass?"

KS: "Alright, calm down. Let's talk about…"

SM: "*You* calm down!"

KS: "I'm not that excited. But look, I don't know you from Adam, I don't know why we're hanging out, but you seem a little…"

SM: "You don't want to hang out, I see."

KS: "No, I, I…"

SM: "Just 'cause Pat's gone. Just 'cause Pat had to run home, to be with his family, good wholesome stuff, and then he leaves me with you and you're just like, 'Hey Gordo, he doesn't care, he has no morals, he'll go to the peelers with me!'"

KS: "I didn't make that judgement on you, it's just, we're in Toronto, and…"

SM: "And what? That's all it is, [the accent begins to wobble] is titty bars and donuts?!"

KS: "Why do you sound Irish all of a sudden?"

SM: "Why are you… you're on my ass…?"

KS: "'Cause you…

SM: "Eh?"

KS: "Oh, there you go."

SM: [Sounding even more Irish] "Well, I got a little bit of Irish in me."

KS: "I see I got your Irish up. Here's the thing, in the States, you have a strip club…"

SM: "Here comes another lecture from an American, 'In the States…'"

KS: "Alright, elsewhere…"

SM: "No, bring it!"

KS: "OK, in the States, down South…"

SM: "I understand that's your only frame of reference. What happens in the *States*."

KS: "No, I'm fairly Canadian, in terms of… I'm not from Canada, but I'm open to all things Canadian. I've had many Canadian experiences, Gordo."

SM: "Tell me a little, tell me your story, eh? Come on."

KS: "I went to school at the Vancouver Film School. So I was in Vancouver."

SM: "Yeah?"

KS: "And I've been to Toronto quite a bit, and I've… you know what, fuck you Gordo, I've been to Calgary, I've…"

SM: "Wait a second, eh!"

KS: "Yeah?"

SM: "Did you just say 'Fuck you'?"

KS: "Yeah, I did."

SM: "Well I, you know… That's not any kinda language to call me, to say 'Fuck you' to Gordo, your pal, who you're hanging out with, you know…'cause I'll go home, I'll go home and leave you alone, eh? I didn't want to come out here, Pat called me and said there's this sorry guy from America, we'll go out and show him a good time, some fun, have a few… Mooseheads…"

KS: "Yeah, and fucking what happened there? Where'd Pat go?"

SM: "Pat had to go home, eh? 'Cause Pat's wife has…"

KS: "Well dude I understand you have a good time as a couple of twofers, Labatt Blue, or something, but like…"

SM: "You don't like the Blue, eh?"

KS: "Well no, the Blue's fine, I'm not really a beer drinker. Bartles and Jaymes, have you heard of them? Wine cooler? That's more my… I like that. Got any weed?"

SM: "That's not… I don't smoke weed."

KS: "Wow, really? You're a pretty strait-laced Canadian."

SM: "I live a clean, good life."

KS: "Like Lance Armstrong?"

SM: "I don't know who you're talking about, eh? Terry Fox."

KS: Nice pull. "Terry Fox, OK. You don't think Terry Fox ever went to the peelers? Peeled off his leg and went to the peelers?"

SM: "You're talking about Terry Fox!"

KS: "I know."

SM: "Eh?!"

KS: "Statue of him at BC Place, outside the, you know, where the lions play…"

SM: "Do you hold nothing sacred in America, eh? You just make fun of everything, everything's fodder."

KS: "Yeah, well, we're just joking around…"

SM: "Fodder Bob! I'm making jokes about everybody! I'll take your national heroes and I'll drop my poop on them!"

KS: "Would you say…"

SM: "You're pooping on a hero!"

KS: "Would you say that Terry Fox is truly a hero?"

SM: "You've pooped on Ghandi, and all these other…"

KS: "Ghandi's not Canadian!"

SM: "Well, international heroes! You poop on it all!"

KS: "I don't think I've said word one about Ghandi all night."

SM: "I wouldn't be surprised if you haven't ragged on every goddamn national hero in the world."
KS: "All I'm saying is, I know a lot about Canada, for a guy who's not from Canada. I have a lot of respect for Canadiana. But I'm just saying, in the States — don't let that ruffle your feathers, I'm just making a…"
SM: "NO, NO I'M ALRIGHT! I'm alright!"
KS: "Alright, in the States, you have a strip club, where you can drink alcohol but they don't take all their clothes off, or you have a juice bar, where you don't drink alcohol and they *do* take *all* their clothes off. The Brass Rail, you can actually get drunk, and the women take all their clothes off. We don't really have that down South."
SM: "Yeah …"
KS: "That's why I think a lot of Americans are interested in going to the peelers up here. Particularly The Brass Rail. Canadian women are pretty, you know."
SM: "I know, but they're not, you know, eh, it's not like they're just little pieces of meat, flashing around…"
KS: "You don't want me objectifying them."
SM: "Yeah, eh? That's somebody's Mom! Sister! Cousin!"
KS: "Alright, wow, you're really…"
SM: "That's one of my *actual* fucking cousins."
KS: "You got a cousin that works there?
SM: "Yeah, eh?"
KS: "Is that why you don't wanna go? You could just say that."
SM: "No, I… you know, it's like, because that's wrong. It's wrong!"
KS: "To want to go?"
SM: "It's wrong to, to, to…sh!"
KS: "I didn't say anything."
SM: "Just, hold on! Don't speak, in your American stuff, eh? When I'm like, bringing it, to you."
KS: "Setting me Canadian."
SM: "Yeah! So just sit down!"
KS: "OK."
SM: "I think that you know, you come up, and you find these Canadian girls, and you ogle them and you stare at them and you spray your…"
KS: "But that's what you do to peelers, you ogle, you're there to look."

SM: “But you’re not Canadian.”
KS: “Oh, so only Canadians should go?”
SM: “I, I… you know, I have certain ideas about…”
KS: “You’re Canadian. So I’ll be your guest.”
SM: “Yeah, but I think that all the naked Canadian women should be only for Canadians, eh. Canada for Canada!”
KS: “Uh… Alright.”
SM: “My bumper sticker says ‘Canada for Canadians’.”
KS: “I got a bumper sticker that says, ‘Canada: Red, White but never Blue, eh?’ ’Cause the flag is red and white? Do you ever listen to SModcast, I talked about it once, a long time ago…”
SM: “You think you’re a funny guy, eh?”
KS: “Not really…”
SM: “You think you’re like, clever…”
KS: “You don’t think that’s a clever bumper sticker?”

SM: "That's what Pat said about you."

KS: "Pat said that I was…?"

SM: "Pat said that you're real happy with yourself."

KS: "Pat said that about me?"

SM: "Yeah."

KS: "Well, he's a motherfucker, isn't he."

SM: "Pat's one of the best guys I ever met, eh?!"

KS: "Well, he ain't that great, he left us here to fight."

SM: "Pat had to go… how many fucking times I got to tell you, eh? Pat had to go home and take care of his wife."

KS: "That's fine."

SM: "She's got a thyroid issue."

KS: "Really?"

SM: "Oh, you find that funny?"

KS: "No, I just…"

SM: "A little giggle, off the thyroid? You think everybody's ailments are funny do you, eh?"

KS: "Not at all, dude. I'm with you, that's sad. That's a bad thing."

SM: "That was so insincere. That was crap."

KS: "You know what, alright."

SM: "Hey, Mister, that's crap."

KS: "Alright, alright, dude. Let's not go to the peelers. Um… do you wanna look at some online porn together? American porn? Would that be OK?"

SM: "That's the weirdest thing anyone's ever asked me to do. I'm not doing that, eh? I'm not gonna…"

KS: "Well, you won't let me look at naked Canadian women."

SM: "Well can you not think of anything else to do, eh?"

KS: "Not really, dude."

SM: "… that doesn't need a naked person around you?"

KS: "Not really. I'm just… I'm here in Canada, I'm feeling a little crazy…"

SM: "We've got hockey games, we've got…"

KS: "Not now, it's off season, dude."

SM: "There's always a hockey game."

KS: "Yeah, but I don't wanna go see some Junior League hockey shit."

SM: "Those are the future stars of, of tomorrow, eh? You think Wayne Gretzky was born at twenty-five years old? No, he was a little man! He was a little hockey man, playing, eh?"

KS: "I've seen the A&E biography, I'm familiar…"

SM: "That's one of the genius forms, and you're just pissing all over it."

KS: "Dude, I love hockey. I love it. I respect the game. It's the only sport I like."

SM: "You talk a big game, eh, but I just think that you…"

KS: "I betcha I know more in hockey than you do!"

SM: "Now you're throwing down, eh?"

KS: "Fuck yeah, I'm throwing down! You ready Gordo, are you ready for the hockey challenge?"

SM: "Are you out of your mind? Bring it!"

KS: "Who won last year's Stanley Cup?"

SM: "… This year, that just happened?"

KS: "Last year."

SM: "Last year?"

KS: "This year's too easy."

SM: [still in Gordo voice] Well I can't, like, do that, 'cause I'm not Gordo!

KS: "What do you mean, Gordo?"

SM: I'm not Gordo, I don't know.

KS: "Gordo, I'm starting to suspect you're not truly Canadian!"

SM: [in Scott's voice] I only *play* a Canadian.

KS: Here's a way out of that one — you go: "It wasn't a Canadian team, so why do I give a fuck?"

SM: "If it ain't Canada in the finals, we don't even air it up here, eh?"

KS: "That's bullshit, Gordo."

SM: "Fuck you, were you ever here?"

KS: "I've been here for the play-offs…"

SM: "We just satellite that down there, eh, to make some money…"

KS: "No, but I mean I've been in Canada, while the play-offs are going on, between two American teams… You got nothing to say now, right?"

SM: I don't know, that was… [Disconsolate] I'm a terrible Canadian. That half of me.

KS: I guess it *would* be weird if I was like, "Let's look at online porn together."

SM: I was like, "Whether I'm an indignant Canadian, or me right now…"

KS: "Either way, that's bugging me."

From SModcast 57: Terrorist Pizza
Kevin explores the world while high

KS: Did I talk about this? I got stoned, fairly recently. I spent all last week in getting stoned.
SM: You've brought up being stoned, I don't know if it was in reference to a while ago.
KS: Four-day weekend, all I did was get stoned.
SM: The July Fourth weekend.
KS: Yes.
SM: Celebrating our country's birthday. Baked off your butt.
KS: I was like, "We're free!" [inhale] "Ohhh, I'm real free." I can't... you know what, I tried to use a fucking bong, couldn't handle it.
SM: What about a vaporizer?
KS: What do you mean, put it into a vaporizer? Like, mix it into some Vicks Vaporub and rub it on my chest?
SM: No, you can buy it... is it a vaporizer? Yeah, it's like a vaporizer, you can go to a head shop and you buy it and it's basically, like it steams you.
KS: It does all the work for you?
SM: Yeah.
KS: Man, that's really lazy.
SM: Well, what I understand is that it's for people — I mean, you probably won't feel this way, 'cause it's for people who don't like to smoke.
KS: Right.
SM: So it takes out the smoking element of it.
KS: And just gives you the herb.
SM: And, I thought that it was like — I know very little about it, but it, you know, it preserves the THC? Is that what it is?
KS: I believe it's called THC. I've heard that term before.
SM: I've heard that it's a good way to get your THC, pure.
KS: Pure.
SM: Or something like that.
KS: Um... that's what I did for July...
SM: Every day?
KS: Every day but one. Byron and Gail took Harley to Big Bear, so it was just me and Schwalbach, and I don't know why but one night, the first night they

were gone, like July third or something like that, somebody gave me a bunch of pot and I was like, "I'm gonna roll it and smoke it like a cigarette."

SM: Like a pot cigarette.

KS: I did, I was like, "I'm gonna have one of those marijuana cigarettes I hear so much about." And I'd been on the [slimming] shakes, I've lost thirty pounds on the shakes so far, with so much more to go… but I'd been on it for a month, so I was like, "You know what? I know if I smoke this, I'm gonna wanna eat, and fuck. I'm gonna get the job done on both departments." So, we wound up going out. This was such a weird experience.

SM: To go out stoned, in the world?

KS: Yes. I don't do that, I know it sounds like… I just don't smoke pot a lot. Like, previously maybe once or twice a year, if that. Lately, more than that. But not like… although that was fucking four days in a row, but not like…

SM: You don't wake 'n' bake.

KS: No. Although that sounds not a bad idea. So… I got stoned, and she had a few drinks, and normally if she has a few drinks I'm always, I don't drink, so I'm fucking, Morgan Freeman and shit, *Driving Miss Daisy*. But I was like, "Man, we should go out and eat. Where do you wanna eat?" And she was like, "I don't know. Wherever you want, it's your choice, you haven't eaten in a month." I was like, "Yeah, sure haven't." And then we settled on this restaurant called Simon LA, which is at the Sofitel Hotel across from Beverly Centre.

SM: Uh-huh?

KS: They got this dessert platter…

SM: Oh, OK.

KS: It's like, cotton candy, cookies…

SM: I went there. For Shay's birthday.

KS: Yeah, for Shay's birthday. Cotton candy, cookies… They got like, caramel corn, it's like this carnival fucking platter, there's a lot of it. And you wash it down with a fucking milkshake… pretty damn awesome. So I was like, "Fuck, I'm baked, that's what I want." And so she was like, "Well, call a cab," and it was such a foreign notion to me.

SM: To like, call for transportation?

KS: Yeah, like even when I lived in New York for a brief time I never really… like, "Let's get a cab."

SM: That's very responsible.

KS: Well, there was no choice, if we wanted to go out, it was either that or order off yummy.com, and have them deliver food, but I felt like, "Let's go out."

SM: You wanted to go to a restaurant, yeah.

KS: So we took a cab, and just gorged, man. I don't know which I like more, when I'm stoned — fucking or eating. Eating is just an endless succession... I could see, if I was really baked, and given a room full of food... I might be, you know how they're like, "A dog won't stop eating," if you keep feeding a dog, its stomach will explode? Same fucking thing.

SM: Or a horse. I think horses are that way too.

KS: Maybe. Um... I don't know, maybe it wasn't a dog. But, it was just constant, like, I don't even know if we had conversation, 'cause I was just lifting things to my mouth. It was just so fucking *fantastic*. And then the next day, I didn't eat, but then at night, I got stoned again, I was like, "Let's go back!"

SM: Nice.

KS: Did it again.

SM: Return?

KS: Totally. You know they're like, "You can never do the same thing twice and have the same experience" — bullshit. It was awesome. Just as awesome the second time. Then on Saturday, we went to Elizabeth Banks' barbecue, and I didn't get high. I probably should have, I would have been a lot more fucking social, and shit. Like, we came home after the first night at Simon, the first night I got stoned, and there was two dudes, our gay-bors — like, the two dudes who are gay, and are our neighbors.

SM: You just outed them.

KS: Yeah, totally. You know those guys, they live across the street, and they were putting their garbage out and it was like, "Hey man, how are *you*?!" — that was me, and they were like, "What the fuck?" And we just sparked up conversation with them, and it turned out they'd been living there for three years, I never knew it, I'd never really seen them before... And they started talking about — like, it was the kinda conversation that, if I was not stoned, it wouldn't have even happened. I would have gotten out of my car, maybe nodded, and just immediately dashed into the house. But we're just sitting there in the street, chit-chatting, like it's the fucking Fifties and shit and we're in the suburbs... And they're talking about... like, I was like, "Man," 'cause they had one of those dumpster bins, 'cause I guess they're doing some work on the house, and they were apologizing for that, and we were like, "Oh, don't worry about it." And they had a porta-potty 'cause usually when people have work on their house done they put a porta-potty, and we were like, "Oh, years back, when we had to redo our whole house after the flood, we had one in front of our house, don't worry. It's awesome. Where can we get one?" — you know, joking around and shit. [Scott laughs]. I didn't even know that was that funny. And it probably wasn't. But they started talking about like, "Yeah, we redid our kitchen," and I was… it's so funny 'cause when you're — I don't know if it's the same for everybody else — when I'm stoned, there's still a cognizant part of me that's listening to the stoned part of me.

SM: You're like, standing outside of yourself. Straight Kev's like, "What are you doing?"

KS: Yeah, it's like, "Why are you saying these things?" But still, is entertained by it, so internally I'm kinda entertained as well? And I was just like, "Getouttahere, you redid your kitchen, how was *that*?!" [Laughs] Like, never in a million years, dude… If I had made it that far, straight, in a conversation with those cats…

SM: You'd be like, "Right on!"

KS: "Well, good night."

SM: "I gotta, you know, the house is… calling…"

KS: "You know, we live there, so we're gonna go in it." Um… and then it led to them like — something that I would never do straight, the dude was just like, "Well…" — 'cause we were talking about their kitchen for what felt like five minutes…

SM: With so much excitement.

KS: …and, yes, and I was so fucking feverish about his description of his kitchen…

SM: That they invited you to see it?

KS: Yeah, he was like, "Would you like to see it?" And I was like, "Fuck, yes! I would *love* to see that!" And went into their house, and there was the cognizant part of me, was just like, "This could end *so* badly." Like, this could end like, you walk in the door and they could hit you over the head, and you fucking wake up roped to the ceiling and shit, and they're burning us with cigarette lighters and… just horrible…

SM: After three years of living there, they're like, "Finally our plan comes to fruition!"

KS: Totally. "You know, we normally don't hunt our human prey this close to home, but, fuck it, who's gonna miss them," or whatever. But they didn't do that, and then they showed us their kitchen.

SM: They did what they said, they showed us the kitchen.

KS: And the cherry wood counters... and Jen had had a bunch of drinks, so... she was just like, she was also — when she drinks, she's very like, "Oh my god! How are *you*?" Very social and engaging and shit. Way more so than usual. And so she's like, "*Oh*, what *is* that? The counters are *cherry wood*?!" And like, even stoned, I had to stop and be like, "You don't give a fuck. Like, what do you know from cherry wood?"

SM: You mean inside, to yourself?

KS: Yeah, inside. That would have been tremendous, they're like, "You seemed real nice in the street."

SM: "He was so excited about the kitchen, now he's fucking yelling at his wife."

KS: "He's turning on his wife? We should get him out of here." But, she was just like, "Is that cherry wood?" and I was like, "I think it *is* cherry wood! Isn't that great?!" Like, everything was just real special and great. So that was very strange and uncharacteristic. If I'd gotten stoned just before I went to Banks' party probably I would have been way more gregarious. 'Cause we saw the dude who was in *Weeds*, who plays Andy, the uncle?

SM: Yeah.

KS: If I was stoned I would have been like, "You fucking *rock* on *Weeds*, man! Let's talk! For a while!"

SM: "I rock on weed too! Like, I am right now!"

KS: "You're in *Weeds*, I'm on weed, right now!" Um... we saw a dude who was on that show *Tell Me You Love Me*. He was there — he plays one of the guys in the couple, and if I was stoned I would have been like, "Did you really fuck on that show? 'Cause it really looks... like, I've seen your dick! I saw that chick give you a hand job! And then, it came!"

SM: "Show me your dick, I want to confirm that that's your dick."

KS: Yeah, "Let me see. Did you really cum? I gotta look at the dick. I'm not gay, but I just wanna look at it. You don't have to show everyone, come to the bathroom with me."

SM: "Is that made of flesh?"

KS: "Let me touch it. It could be rubber, like the one on the show." Um… I just would have been a lot more social, instead I just wound up talking to you the whole time.

SM: Exactly. Because neither of us were stoned.

KS: No, we were sober and just like, "Man, why do we leave the house." It's not like it wasn't a nice party, but I'm just not… like, it's so weird to sit there in an environment like that, and you see people chit-chatting and whatnot, and I'm sure most of them know one another, but I'm just like, "How come I'm not that guy?" That just wants to go over and join in the convo.

SM: I don't know. I even had a couple of drinks before… not before I got there, but when I was there, and it's still not enough social lubricant to get me to walk up to a group of people and be like, "Hey, how d'you guys know Liz?"

KS: See, but that is an intro.

SM: I know, I know the intro.

KS: I don't even know the intro.

SM: I don't have the sack to walk up there.

KS: Even if I had the technology, like, if I was given that line…

SM: *The Six-Million-Dollar Social Man?*

KS: Yeah, I don't think I could do it, I don't think I could walk up and be like, "How do you guys know Liz?"

SM: I couldn't either.

KS: 'Cause if someone did that to me I'd be like, "Fuck off!" I don't know what I'd say. I'm sure I'd be like, "Oh, we made…"

SM: I would answer the question.

KS: I'd be like, you know, "We made a movie together and whatnot…" But I'd peter out, like that, it's like [increasingly mumbled] "Oh, we made a movie together and whatnot." Which sends a clear signal…

SM: As opposed to being like, "How do *you* know Liz?"

KS: Yeah, I'm not inviting a fucking return question from you, 'cause I don't care. But I

"I mean, if a bear could drive a car.... and, I'm not even sure what question I'm answering anymore..."

think if I was stoned I would have totally fucking… If I was stoned, and you were like [whispers] "Here's the opening line" — you know what, let's do it.
SM: OK.
KS: Alright, I'm stoned. You're you. We're at Banks' party. [Stoned voice] "I don't know… I don't know… this party seems long. Does it seem long? How long have I been here?"
SM: "Uh, you've been here fifteen minutes."
KS: "Fift…? Feels a lot longer, man."
SM: "Yeah. You've only been here a few minutes."
KS: "You know why?"
SM: "I don't know why."
KS: "'Cause I'm baked, niggah! I'm fucked up!"
SM: "Yeah."
KS: "No, I'm not really. But I am stoned, Scott."
SM: "Yeah, I can tell."
KS: "I wanna talk to people! Don't you? I mean, I like talking to you but don't you wanna talk to… who are these people? What are their little stories?"
SM: "Uh… I don't know, I'm not stoned, so I'm…"
KS: "But you're drinking."
SM: "… I'm socially awkward.
KS: "Are you judging me?"
SM: "No, not at all."
KS: I would never get hostile like that, that would never happen. OK…
SM: "You should *go* talk to them."
KS: "How do I do it, Scott?"
SM: "You just, you know, you just go up to them and say, 'Hey,' you know, 'how do you guys know Liz?'"
KS: [Exhales] "Alright. You wanna come?"
SM: "Not really."
KS: "But you want me to go? Why don't you wanna talk to me any more?"
SM: "I… well, *you* wanted to go."
KS: "I just think we're missing out. There's so many people we could be talking to here."
SM: "Alright, I'll go with you, so…"
KS: "Alright, but what's the line? What's the line? What's the line?"

SM: "Um, 'How do you know Liz?' 'How did you come to know Liz?'"

KS: "You said that already."

SM: "I did say that already."

KS: "But, how long ago did you say it? Felt like a long time since we had that part of the conversation."

SM: "It was thirty seconds ago."

KS: "Wow. Alright, let's do it."

SM: "OK, but you're the front man."

KS: "I'm the front man." Alright, now you be the guy that I'm talking to.

SM: OK.

KS: "HEY MAN how do *you* know Liz?!!"

SM: "… Hi."

[Laughter]

KS: Hold on, let me use my inside voice. [More soberly]: "Hey man, I'm Kevin, how do you know Liz?"

SM: "I… went to school with Liz."

KS: "Yeah, man? Get the fuck out of here, what was she like?"

SM: "She was…"

KS: "You're a Masshole? You're from Massachusetts?"

SM: "I am from Massachusetts. I… don't know the 'Masshole', first time I've heard that."

KS: "Really? You can't be from Massachusetts and never heard the term 'Masshole'."

SM: "Um… I…"

KS: "Isn't this a great party?"

SM: "Yeah, I'm having a really good time."

KS: "How do you know Liz?"

SM: "I… like I said before, I went to school with her."

KS: "Yeah?"

SM: "Yeah, I went to college with her. How do *you* know Liz?"

KS: "I made… we made… we made a movie together."

SM: "Yeah?"

KS: "Yeah. It's pretty funny. She's awesome in it."

SM: "Awesome."

KS: "She's an awesome actress."

SM: "That's great. She *is* an awesome actress."

KS: "Was she an awesome actress in high school? Was it high school you said, or was it college?"
SM: "It was college, it was college."
KS: "College."
SM: "Yes."
KS: "Right on."
SM: "After high school."
KS: "Did you pledge?"
SM: "No, I didn't pledge."
KS: "The allegiance? 'Nanu Nanu'?"
SM: "Um, yes... I don't know what 'Nanu Nanu' means, but..."
KS: "What if... Have I, am I bugging you?"
SM: "Not at all."
KS: "I feel like I've been talking to you for a long time." That's what happens to me when I'm high. Everything seems like it's been going on for a long time. "Have I been talking to you for a long time?"
SM: "No, no, it just started, really."
KS: "Fucking hungry."
SM: "Yeah? There's tacos..."
KS: "No, they're gone." They were gone when we got there.
SM: OK. I think the actual parts were available...
KS: "I wish there was some taco meat. I'd just eat the meat, man."
SM: "There is..." Well, there was taco meat.
KS: They left it?
SM: Yeah.
KS: I didn't want it. See, that's the thing, if I was high, I would have eaten, around them. I would have pulled up a chair, gotten one of those big serving tongs, and just started shoveling taco meat in my mouth.
SM: "Is this weird, if I do this? Is everybody done? 'Cause I'm..."
KS: "Who wants some of this? You guys all hate it, right? Isn't taco meat great? It's so... meaty. You! Youyouyou. Have some of this. *Have* some. Alright. More for me!" Alright, so back to the dude. "How do you know Liz? College. You said college."
SM: "College, yes."
KS: "Did you... did you fuck her?"
SM: "No, I did not. I didn't. I was friends with her *and* Max, her husband."

KS: "Her husband."
SM: "Yes."
KS: "Did he fuck her?"
SM: "I think he did."
KS: "Let me ask you this… What's your name?"
SM: "My name is… Bill."
KS: "Bill. Wow, I've never, I don't know many Bills."
SM: "I mean, it's pretty common."
KS: "Bill. Bill."
SM: "Yeah."
KS: "Do you think…"
SM: "Yeah, Kev. Kevin."
KS: "Bill."
SM: "Kevin."
KS: "Bill."
SM: "Kevin."
KS: "Bi-illl."
SM: "Keviiin."
KS: "Bill, do you think — on the down-low — do you think they fucked before the party? Or do you think there was too much party pressure? Do you think they fuck a lot?"
SM: "Uh, I, I uh… I don't know."
KS: "But you're friends with them, you've known them since college. Did they fuck a lot in college?"
SM: "Um… I mean, not abnormally so, I mean not, I don't believe any more or less than anybody else."
KS: "Well, let's define 'more or less'. I gotta compare it to my fucking."
SM: "I, I, I don't know."
KS: "What's a lot, Bill?"
SM: "I don't know, like…"
KS: "How… Bill? May I call you Bill?"
SM: "If you can."
KS: "Willy-Bill."
SM: "… yes, call me Bill."
KS: "You got a girlfriend? Or a boyfriend? I don't want to presuppose."
SM: "I have a girlfriend. I'm engaged."

KS: "You're engaged?"

SM: "I am."

KS: "Oh, man, marriage rocks. Well, you know what, marriage…"

SM: "I'm not there yet, I don't know."

KS: "… marriage to my wife rocks. I can't say, speak for your fiancée. But you can't marry my wife, Bill."

SM: "I can't, I know, Kevin."

KS: "Fuck you."

SM: "OK."

KS: "Listen, Bill… The… How much do you fuck your fiancée, if you don't mind me asking. Do you mind?

SM: "I… you know…"

KS: "I won't tell nobody."

SM: "I wasn't necessarily prepared for this conversation, but I guess I could, you know."

KS: "I got a little stoned before I got here Bill, I'll be honest with you. I'm not normally this guy."

SM: "I'm sensing that, but uh… it's OK. It's alright. It's a holiday."

KS: "How often do you fuck?"

SM: "Um, you know… I try to, once a day."

KS: "Really? You're fucking once a day?"

SM: "Sure."

KS: "You're a fucking stud, Bill. Where's your… is your lady here?"

SM: "Well, I said I *try* to once a day."

KS: "Oh, yeah? What does that mean?"

SM: "I mean, you know, it's the idea to maintain…"

KS: "You don't force yourself on her, do you, Bill?"

SM: "No, no, nothing like that, nothing like that."

KS: "I won't stand for that."

SM: "Put your collar down."

KS: "OK. You saw it going up, bro."

SM: "I saw it, I saw that. I don't wanna get, you know, I don't want to start some shit with a man on reefer."

KS: "Alright, well, that's what you want, that's how often you *want* to fuck. How often do you wind up fucking?"

SM: "You know, like three or four times a week."

KS: "Get the fuck out of here. That's a lot, Bill."

SM: "Really? What about you?"

KS: "You know… twice a week, maybe, if I'm lucky."

SM: "Yeah."

KS: "Yeah, but sometimes, she's on her period right now…"

SM: "Yeah, but we're newlyweds…"

KS: "I thought you were engaged…"

SM: "I mean we're engaged, so we're…"

KS: "You're fucking with me now, aren't you, Bill?"

SM: "I… a little bit, Kevin."

KS: "Ah, fucking Bill, don't fuck with me like that."

SM: "Fucking with your stoned mind."

KS: "College Bill and shit."

SM: "Yeah. Not any more. I'm out of college."

KS: "Are you?"

SM: "Yes, a while ago."

KS: "What'd you major in, Bill?"

SM: "I majored in…"

KS: "Am I annoying, Bill? Is this bugging you?"

SM: "No, no, no."

KS: "I feel like… we're friends."

SM: "I… I feel that way too. I feel like I've known you for… hours."

KS: "It feels like we've been talking a long time. Have we been talking a long time?"

SM: "Um, yeah. Quite a while."

KS: "You want to stop?"

SM: "Um, you know, it's totally up to you."

KS: "You want a drink? You want me to get you a drink?"

SM: "Um, no no no, I'm fine, I've still got a drink here."

KS: "So what, so… does she fuck good?"

SM: "Now, you know, I don't know if we need to talk about that."

KS: "She must fuck good if you wanna marry her."

SM: "Well yeah, I mean, amongst other things."

KS: "Bill, that's the secret to marriage. Just 'cause, there'll be days where she's a real bitch. You know what Bill, she may even be a cunt, but…"

SM: "Well… uhuh-huh, huh."

KS: [Laughs] I like Bill. I like Bill's 'huh-huh, huh.' Um… "You know what, pardon my French, but there are days where you're like, 'She bugging me.' But… but, a lot of people say love is what does it for marriage."

SM: "Yeah, a strong bond of love."

KS: "People… you fall in and out of love all the time, Bill. Love ain't enough."

SM: "OK."

KS: "Sometimes, love just ain't enough. Like the song said. 'Cause you, 'cause love, whatever… right…?"

SM: "Is that a song?"

KS: "No, but it could be. You play music?"

SM: "No, not at all."

KS: "'Cause I could write the lyrics, if you want."

SM: "Um, I don't have any musical talents whatsoever, so…"

KS: "Me neither man, it's fucked up. Wish I did…"

SM: "Lots of regrets."

KS: "Wish I could play piano. Don't you wish you could play piano, Bill?"

SM: "Um yeah, I would, you know… sure."

KS: "Um… Bill, do I look like I g…" [collapses in laughter]. Hold on. "Bill, do I look like I gained weight, to you?"

SM: "Since I met you?"

KS: "Yeah. No, just in general."

SM: "Um… in, uh, I mean… From the time I've known you, um, you… you know, not at all."

KS: "How long have we known each other?"

SM: "Um, you know, I guess it's been… eighteen to twenty minutes."

KS: "Did you ever see… I make movies, did you ever see the movies we made?"

SM: "You know, I haven't. I am sorry to say I haven't. I um, I rarely get to…"

KS: Jen! …I'm just kidding. "It's cool. It don't matter. I just, I was just gonna say if you look at me in the first movie and now, you would see that I gained a lot of weight, and I was wondering if you'd noticed it."

SM: "Oh, so you're in the movies?"

KS: "Yeah, sometimes I'm in them."

SM: "Oh, OK."

KS: "But fuck that."

SM: "OK."

KS: "Does your lady do anal?"
SM: "I don't uh… huh, huh. Kevin. Um, you know, I feel like, maybe after we've known each other for a few hours, I'll feel more comfortable..."
KS: "I'll take that as a yes, sir. As a yes."
SM: "I don't know why you would, but…"
KS: "You like the ass?"
SM: "Like I said…"
KS: "Do you like it stinky Bill?"
SM: "Now… now, huh huh, now we've really steered into a weird direction."
KS: "It's cool, we're all here."
SM: "Yeah, but we're not all here to talk about anal sex. I came here, you know, it's more casual…"
KS: "Alright, alright, you're harshing my buzz."
SM: "Well…"
KS: "I don't wanna… I kinda got a mellow on. Alright, maybe that's… maybe I went too far."
SM: "I mean, you did a little bit. I don't wanna… we just met, and… I'm a private person, Kevin."
KS: "Yeah, but you know… anal ain't private."
SM: "I'd say that it is, probably, pretty private."
KS: "You… you use your privates, Bill, in anal, you put it in the butt."
SM: "That's true. You really aren't getting the fact that I don't want to talk about it."
KS: "It's just that… it's just… I'm not even like saying, you gotta do it."
SM: "OK. Thank you for that."
KS: "But it's a nice option, there, sometimes."
SM: "Yeah, yeah yeah."
KS: "But… you think… you think Liz and Max do anal?"
SM: "You know, I… you know I, like I said, I…"
KS: "You've known them since college."
SM: "… I'm growing steadily uncomfortable…"
KS: "Who do you know better, her or him?"
SM: "I kinda knew them both, they were always kinda around, and you know…"
KS: "So Max was never like, 'Hey man, I fucking rocked that ass the other night'?"

SM: "You know I don't, uh, you know I… this is becoming inappropriate."
KS: "Really? How old are you man?"
SM: "I, you know, I am…"
KS: "You're a real fuck, Bill, you know that?"
SM: "OK, now, I…"
[They break down laughing.]
KS: No, finish, that was going somewhere good. "You're a real fuck, Bill, you know that?"
SM: [Angry] "OK, now that's not called for."
KS: "No, but it's not called for to make me feel fucking bad about… I'm just trying to have a conversation."
SM: "Look, Mr Wake 'n' Bake, stoned…"
KS: "I'm not…"
SM: "Coming up, cornering me, you don't understand…"
KS: "You're Mr 'I Fuck My Lady All the Time' — hey everybody, this dude fucks his lady once a day, he says."
SM: "Everybody has moved away from us, we're like, all alone…"
KS: "Well, maybe we should bring them back so they can fucking judge you."
SM: "They don't… You were making everybody uncomfortable."
KS: "No I'm not. Shut up."
SM: "You're making a spectacle of yourself."
KS: "Shut the fuck up, man."
SM: "You, are a…"
KS: "I'm not a fighter, Bill, but I'm gonna fight you."
SM: "… you are a belligerent…"
KS: "Let's *wrestle*, Bill."
SM: "… and angry human being."
KS: "I'm not, but I was just, you're making me feel bad when you're like, fucking 'Don't try all that anal fucking talk, buh buh buh.' Come on man, we're just fucking… You know what man, let's just bring it down. Let's bring it back to the beginning of our relationship. [Quietly] Do you think they do anal?"
[Sound of running footsteps.]
KS: "Bill, where you going?" They were on a

Random SModquotes

"Laughter through tears is my favorite emotion!"

lawn, I don't know that you would necessarily be able to hear those footsteps.

SM: There was cement.

KS: Yeah, but in my version, they were on a lawn.

SM: Oh, you're on a lawn.

KS: That would've been probably very bad for everybody at the party, but I would have enjoyed that.

SM: I mean, if I had been standing behind you, the whole time you were talking to Bill…

KS: You would have loved it, you would have been like, "That was the best party ever."

SM: Yes.

KS: "This is the greatest moment of my life."

SM: I would have enjoyed it.

KS: Um… so, I wasn't stoned for the party. And then the next night… I think…

SM: Sunday.

KS: Sunday. I don't know if I got stoned on… yeah, during the day, early. I didn't wake 'n' bake, but I figure around noon I got stoned and we watched movies and shit. And we went out to eat — where did we go? We went to a different place. I forget. But… but anyway, the whole reason I brought that up was, last time I got stoned, we tried to watch a movie. Tried to watch *Blue City*, with um, Judd Nelson…

SM: Oh, and Ally Sheedy.

KS: Ally Sheedy.

SM: *Blue City*?

KS: *Blue City*. I think it's called *Blue City*. It's about Miami. It's not *Miami Blues*, 'cause that's the one with Alec Baldwin, and it's not *Blue Steel*, that's the one with Jamie Lee Curtis, I think it's *Blue City*.

SM: I know what it is. I saw that in the theater.

KS: Get the fuck out of here.

SM: I did.

KS: I've never seen that movie. And I had the DVD, and so I was fucking stoned, and I was like, "Let's watch something we never watched before." Which was stupid, we should have watched something that we were familiar with, and a comedy at that. So we're watching *Blue City* and I'm *really*

fucking stoned, and I think she was… she'd smoked a little bit, but she also had a few drinks. And the whole time, I was just sitting there going like — it started about ten, fifteen minutes in — I'm like, "What's going on?" I was like, "Is it me, or is this movie just really hard to follow? I feel like I'm being defeated by the plot, who is that guy? Why is Judd Nelson talking to him? Is that *his* dad? Who died? Is Ally Sheedy even in this movie?" I just couldn't… *Blue City* flat out defeated me, in the first fifteen, twenty minutes.
SM: Beat you down.
KS: I was so *lost*, dude, it was like watching a Jodorowsky film or something like that. I was just like, "What the fuck's going on?" It was like, it went from being like a mid-to-late Eighties actioner, to being some early Atom Egoyan movie, where I'm like, "I have no clue what's happening in this movie." So…
SM: I can't help you, 'cause…
KS: You don't remember it?
SM: I don't remember it.
KS: Honestly, I should… the next day I was like, "Should we try to watch it?" And she was like, "We shouldn't have tried to watch it last night."
SM: "The first time." I don't remember being mesmerized by it.
KS: Well, I will always remember it 'cause I was so confused, and lost, and just like, "This is the most intricately plotted film ever made, I don't know what's going on."
SM: Do you still want to watch it?
KS: No, 'cause I know if I watch the movie it'll be a total come-down, it'll just be like, "Oh my god, how did this movie beat me? In the first twenty minutes?" I think I would be fucking very disappointed. But my memory of it was just like, "Wow, how complex."
SM: Yeah.
KS: But… That'll happen when you're stoned, I guess.
SM: Yep.
KS: I like it, I'm kinda a late in life stoner. I'm a little more open to it. Not that I was ever closed to it, I was just always doing shit.
SM: Do you feel like you could… like, there's people that I know who like, work, and…
KS: Oh, there are people that fucking, yeah, who do it every day.
SM: Oh, yeah yeah yeah.
KS: I don't think I could do it every day, 'cause it's just, it always feels like a

vacation to me. A true vacation, which for me, is very good, 'cause I have a very hard time vacating. So, it was kinda cool, because I really felt like, "Man, I'm really getting away from it all. By laying in the same spot I always lay in, but high while I'm doing it."
SM: "I'm going on a cannabis journey."
KS: "A cannabis Chautauqua."

From SModcast 59: Frosh Meat
Initiation and night baseball

KS: Explain the initiation concept. We touched on it in *Clerks II* a bit. Is it more urban legend than anything else?
WF: I think that's a legend. I never heard of anybody who really had to do it.
KS: It was usually for freshmen. And — what class would do it, any upper classman or seniors?
WF: Seniors.
BJ: I thought the seniors did it to the freshmen…
KS: So as seniors, did you guys ever do it?
WF: Never.
BJ: No, it didn't even occur to me.
KS: What were the initiation samples?
WF: That the seniors would shove a pickle up your butt, and make you walk across a baseball field, and if it fell out of your butt, you had to take a bite out of it.
BJ: And then stick it back in and keep walking until you made it there.
WF: I don't know if I ever got that far before I…
KS: What, they did it to you?
WF: No, I mean in terms of when I was listening to the story… the horror on my face when I was in eighth grade, when I heard that that might happen.
BJ: "It dropped out at 42."
KS: I heard a variation on that was, they would take you to a dock, put a pickle up your ass, push you off the dock, and if the pickle came out of your ass in the water they wouldn't let you back up until you bit it.
BJ: So, there was some sort of physical activity that went along with the

pickle in the ass.

KS: You had to save your life, *and* maintain a pickle in your ass at the same time.

WF: That'd be some sort of law broken right there, right? With the pickle?

BJ: I would assume so. I think it's commonly referred to as rape.

KS: I think it would have to be. Or at the very least sexual harassment, but probably rape.

WF: You put the pickle in yourself, though. They make you put it in.

KS: Still, it's like… that would be like if you force somebody to fuck themselves with a bottle. It's still, you may not be hands-on, but…

BJ: It's coercion. "My hands are clean, man! This kid fucking stuck a pickle up his own ass!"

KS: "Smell my hand. Do you smell pickle?"

WF: That was a stressful summer, though.

KS: Getting ready for it?

WF: Yeah, 'cause you didn't know if it was true or not.

KS: Were you loosening up your asshole, and shit? Putting a fucking shoe-spreader in there? "I gotta get this shit as tight as possible…" I would go the other way, I'd be like, "Well if I gotta take a whole fucking pickle I gotta get used to it, so I can get it in there pretty quick…"

WF: You spent the whole summer with a pickle in your cavity?

BJ: Getting limber?

KS: Take a shoe-spreader, fucking keep turning it, and shit like that… Because I wouldn't want to be sitting there fumbling with a pickle, you know, trying to get it into my ass for twenty minutes…

BJ: "Sorry, guys, just… give me a minute…"

KS: "I'm almost there! Hold on!"

WF: Wouldn't you try to fake putting it in, and just put it between your thighs and just squeeze it?

KS: You've given it some thought. You were frightened about it! You were like, "I think I can get away with just the fucking cheek-squeeze."

BJ: They're fucking seniors, dude, they…

WF: They ain't gonna do it in fucking broad daylight, you know, it's gonna be done at night, no one's gonna be able to see unless they're a fucking inch away from your fucking asshole, so you just put it in there, and fucking squeeze your thighs together!

BJ: But the people that are doing it, right, let's assume that these seniors are jamming pickles in freshmen's asses... Is it because it happened to them?
KS: Yeah.
BJ: So this has happened to them.
KS: Yeah. That's the way I always heard it, like, every senior class did it to the freshman class, so that meant... I mean, it started somewhere, it's not a chicken or an egg thing, like, somebody was first and they got to bypass it. Unless they were like, "Let's test it out on each other first."
BJ: Yeah, like the mechanics of it had to have been tested at some point, so...
KS: If you were in charge of the initiation, you're not gonna be outwitted by a freshman who's just gonna squeeze it between their legs.
BJ: Come on, now.
WF: Come on, you've seen a million movies haven't you?
BJ: I would be like a proctologist...
KS: Totally, I'd be like, "You hold one cheek, you hold the other cheek..."
BJ: I've got a Maglite between my teeth...
KS: That's why I... it wouldn't be a night thing, too, I'd do it in broad daylight or a very brightly lit spot.
BJ: A fucking prison intake would be fucking more gentle than the way I'd be treating Walt if I was initiating him.
KS: "This is the largest gherkin I can find." Um... why the bite, you think? Which is worse, the fucking pickle into the ass, or having to bite the pickle that's been in the ass? Going ass to mouth with the pickle.
WF: Um... I don't know if either's worse than the other...
KS: One's gotta be worse than the other.
WF: I guess the bite.
KS: The bite is worse than fucking taking the pickle?
WF: I don't know... They're both *horrific*.
BJ: Let's put it into context; like, let's say you're with your fucking lady and she's got a slim little pickle, and she's sucking you off and fucking you with the pickle in your ass, fucking hitting all the right places, it's not nearly as bad as...
KS: This is part of the initiation?
BJ: You know, that's not as bad as...
KS: This is the summer before? You're like, "Look, you gotta help me out, help me get ready. So we're gonna introduce a pickle into the boudoir."

BJ: "I got something for the mix..." Not nearly as bad as if somebody's forcing a pickle into your ass, but I think I agree with Walt that it's the added humiliation of, OK it's in your ass, if that was all it was, OK. But now it falls out — OK, you've got a little bit of relief. They're like, "Motherfucker, pick that up, bite it..." — and I'm not even a big fan of pickles — "...stick it back in there."

KS: So not only is it a pickle that's been in your ass, it's a pickle that's hit the ground as well. So it's a dirty, assy pickle.

WF: Oh, believe me. Fucking dirt, and fucking grass, have nothing on...

KS: You're like, "Can I wash the shit end off? I'll eat the dirt and grass, but, I really don't want to taste the poop."

BJ: Now, if you have to reinsert it, do you use the bitten end, or do you flip it around?

WF: The bitten end.

KS: So they would make you take the bitten end?

WF: Yeah.

BJ: Oh, that was a fact?

WF: That was a fact.

KS: But at that point, you've already accepted a pickle, so you're kinda loosed-up already.

WF: No. You're so fucking in shock. You're all tight and constricted.

KS: You're body goes right back to like [makes a contracting sound].

WF: Yeah.

KS: Fucking super-tight?

BJ: You've regained your elasticity.

WF: Who the fuck could even do that? Like, you know it's happened, somewhere across the country. That happened at some point, some year. Who are the fucking people that fucking carry that shit out?

KS: It's so homoerotic. 'Cause, think about it, you can't be like, "We're gonna turn around, and you're gonna put that pickle in your ass, and we're not gonna look 'cause we don't wanna see your fucking stinky asshole. That's gay. But tell us if it falls out, 'cause then we have a part too."

BJ: Yeah, like do they walk alongside you?

KS: Mm-hm. And they have to be watching.

WF: They had their fucking... what's that beer that... what was that big beer?

BJ: Budweiser?

WF: Yeah, they got their Buds, and they're like…

KS: Only the most famous beer in the world, you're like, "What is that beer called?"

WF: … and they're all having a great time while you're walking, there's no one really paying attention to what's going on. That's why I think you could.

BJ: You could have gotten away with it?

WF: You could have put it between your thighs. And then let it drop…

KS: I think it's funny that you're under the impression they're drunk. I think they're stone-cold sober when it's going on.

WF: What do you think?

BJ: I think… I would lean towards drunk.

KS: Really?

WF: I think some of them… Not all of them are fucking cold-hearted fucking SS fucking seniors. Some of 'em *gotta* get drunk to pull this off.

BJ: He-wolves.

KS: He-wolf of the SS. That dude is stone-cold sober, everyone else is drunk, and he's fucking… everyone else has half-closed eyes and they're swaying, this dude is laser-sharp, man. It's like, he took a full dose of Ritalin, he has *all* your attention. "Now put ze pickle in ze ass…"

BJ: That's a senior you don't wanna come across. "Goddamnit…"

KS: Um… when did you feel safe, finally? How deep into the school year?

BJ: When we threw our caps in the air. "Fuck all y'aall!!!"

KS: That's why Walt's like, "I was so glad when I graduated. 'Cause I knew there was no threat of taking a pickle!"

BJ: Twenty years later, you might run into a senior…"

KS: Some dude coming into the store, he's like, "You're Walter Flanagan, aren't you?" You're checking him out, you're like, "Yeah," and he's like, "I never got you for initiation!"

BJ: "What's with those pickles?"

WF: "What are you doing with those pickles?"

KS: "Wait, I can give you a discount! We can work a deal!"

BJ: "No tax!"

WF: Wasn't there a time, a set date in between… like an expiration? Like if you didn't get the freshman by a certain…

KS: There was a window?

WF: Yeah, you couldn't do it.

BJ: I mean, I know that's the way a lot of initiations are supposed to work.

WF: They caught you outside after dark, it could happen. I didn't go out that whole summer.

BJ: I agree with him, because I remember…

KS: Just the fucking look on your face, even now — "If they caught you outside, after dark, *they could do it.* It could happen at any fucking time."

WF: You got your Daisy Dukes on, out on the baseball field…

BJ: Playing some night baseball…

KS: Cruising the baseball fields…

WF: "Didn't we get this guy already? Twice?"

BJ: "Fucking funny mustache…"

KS: "No, that was my cousin. But I'm ready to take mine, 'cause, you know, I wanna be a freshman…" Daisy Dukes… Like, "There's that dude with the high-ridin' shorts. Cut-offs."

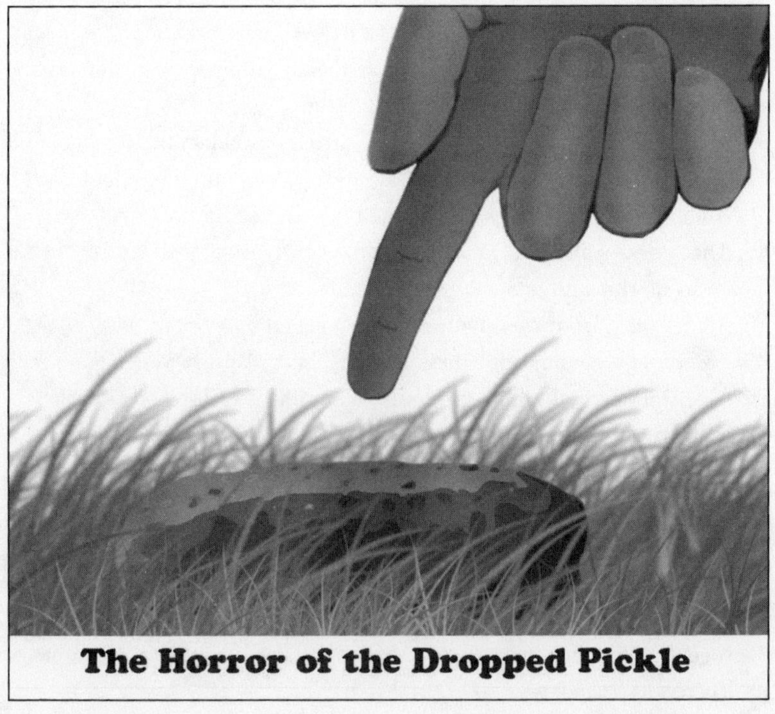

The Horror of the Dropped Pickle

BJ: My parents saw me twice that whole summer, I never came home.
KS: "Bryan's spending an awful lot of time up at the field."
BJ: I stayed back three times in a row on purpose.
KS: "Oh, no, they might get me again! A second bite of the pickle, boys!"
WF: You killed that fucking initiation.
KS: They're like, "This used to be fun, when kids hated it!"

From SModcast 60: The Clone War
Pillow Babies and Stalin's ape-man army

KS: Before SModcast we were talking about the concept of Pillow Babies. What is that?
BJ: A Pillow Baby is, and I don't have the exact science so I might be wrong on this so don't take it as fact, but I believe that they do something to a pituitary gland to stop a kid from growing, so they stay really fucking small and manageable. They call them Pillow Babies. In fact the other day I was trying to convince my nephew that he was a Pillow Baby. He was like, "I am not, look how tall I am!" I also tell him that he is a primordial dwarf.
KS: Wait, they intentionally… what do they do?
BJ: Somehow they stop production in the pituitary gland with some chemical.
KS: On purpose?
BJ: On purpose. So that the kids don't grow large, so that way as the parents get older they'll be manageable, they'll be real small. I'm not talking twelve inches but like little kids.
WF: They remain ten-year-old size.
KS: Why would one do that though?
WF: Because they can't care for an adult. It's very frowned upon in society.
KS: Gee, I wonder why. It sounds horrific. Wait, a parent intentionally decides?
WF: The kids don't have a clue though.
BJ: It's not normal kids.
KS: Oh, I thought this was some new elective procedure where it's like, "You can stop your child at three feet high!"
BJ: I want to do it and create an army of midgets.
KS: So it's like if you've got a severely autistic child or something like that, a headbanger?

WF: Yeah, you have to change it and feed it.

KS: Oh well, this would be the opposite of that.

WF: You can't care for that one once they get really big you can't lift them out of bed and everything because you're getting older, you're in your sixties or seventies.

KS: You can go through this procedure and have them frozen in time kinda?

WF: Yeah.

KS: That sounds heinous.

WF: Why does it sound heinous?

KS: I don't know, it just sounds weird.

BJ: It would have when you thought it was normal kids.

KS: But still, even non-normal kids, or kids with issues, it just sounds like monkeying with nature in a weird way. It's also kinda frightening. Could they just do it to anybody?

WF: Yeah, it could work on anybody.

KS: Could they do it to me, right now?

WF: No, you're not going to grow any more.

KS: Oh, that's it?

WF: They stop your puberty too.

KS: You don't get a period or anything? Secondary sex characteristics?

BJ: No fucking hair.

WF: No hair, nothing.

KS: Really? And why Pillow Baby?

WF: Don't you always shave?

BJ: Yeah I shave my nuts, as we're doing SModcast.

KS: So why do they call them Pillow Babies?

BJ: I guess it's because they're really small.

WF: Because they fit on a pillow.

KS: What, are they like Tom Thumb?

BJ: I don't think that technically they fit on a pillow but it's just saying that they stay really small.

KS: Wow, but how do you know? Maybe the kid would grow out of whatever it is.

WF: It's only for very severe cases.

BJ: Yeah, they're pretty sure.

WF: I'm sure most doctors won't do it. You've got to go to a handful who will.

KS: Really, I'd have to assume it can't be a common practice.

BJ: There was a case not too long ago.

WF: But can you imagine if someone did it to a normal person? I wonder what they would look like at forty. They would still look like a ten year old.

KS: Like Gary Coleman.

BJ: Webster.

KS: Webster!

WF: Do you think that's what happened?

KS: Yeah, they were like, "Let's Pillow Baby this motherfucker!" Nah, but maybe that's what the issue there was, some kind of pituitary problem. Is that what's responsible for the growth of your body?

BJ: Yeah.

KS: Your pituitary gland? You're a grown up Pillow Baby.

WF: Yeah. When I got my license that was a part of the Pillow Baby thing, I was trying to act out as a Pillow Baby.

KS: Most people when they get their license, they get a learners permit at sixteen, seventeen get the license. How old were you when you finally got your license?

WF: Thirty.

KS: Shut the fuck up!

BJ: It wasn't that far off, it was twenty-one or twenty-two, something like that.

KS: He is a theoretical Pillow Baby. His pituitary gland was fine but you just acted like it wasn't.

BJ: He was one of the first, a failed experiment.

WF: Hey, did you ever hear about how Stalin was trying to create an army of human monkeys?

KS: No.

WF: Saw it on *Monster Quest* the other night, it was fucking riveting.

KS: What was it?

WF: He had gotten these scientists that had women lined up…

KS: Mating with apes?

WF: Mating with apes.

KS: Ape embryos?

WF: Yeah, it was fucking nuts.

KS: He wanted to create an ape army?

WF: Yeah.

BJ: And the women were…?

WF: The women were broken and they were shunned by society, they had nothing left, they were willing to take the money to do it.

KS: Whoa.

BJ: I'm seriously about to go fuck an ape because you just described me.

WF: Well, they never look for males to impregnate female apes though. They never brought up the subject of a male doing it to a female.

KS: They were hoping to crossbreed simians and humans. It didn't work though?

WF: Well, they say that it might have worked.

KS: Really?

WF: Yeah, and that one might have gotten away and it still lives in Siberia, a couple of them and there are sightings to this day.

BJ: A Sasquatch kinda thing.

KS: Get out of here.

WF: It was really good.

KS: I don't think I've heard of that.

WF: Just type in Stalin monkey soldiers…

KS: …Pillow Babies…

BJ: …porn!

[All three laugh for quite a long time.]

WF: If they could have secured the music for that [makes the hunting horn sound from the 'human hunt' scene in *Planet of the Apes*], and used it for this documentary it would have been so perfect. Can you imagine being on the battlefield and seeing a bunch of uniformed apes come at you during World War Two?

KS: Man sized?

WF: Man sized.

KS: Who run with their arms as well?

WF: Yeah.

KS: So they're propelling themselves with their upper body. So it would be like fighting an army of the beast?

BJ: So basically he wants their physical attributes with a human's intelligence, that's what he was trying to do.
KS: He wanted gorilla grunts.
WF: He wanted something he could control but wouldn't be like, "I want to go home." He wanted to just feed it and send it out to kill.
KS: I'd say there is something morally wrong about that.
WF: Oh definitely.

From SModcast 60: The Clone War
Cloning debate and Walt's loneliness

KS: Are you pro-cloning?
WF: Am I pro-cloning? I'm not against it.
KS: You're all for it?
WF: I don't really have a real stance on it. Why were some people against it?
KS: Because they say it's playing god.
WF: Because you're trying to create a master race, the perfect human?
KS: No. Basically if you trace it back to the stem cell argument, theoretically stem cells could cure a lot of ills such as Parkinson's disease and stuff like that.
WF: You're trying to build a clone of yourself to harvest the parts?
KS: The fear is that people are against stem cell research and cloning because they feel that ultimately down the road they'll be creating human beings just for their parts.
BJ: Can't they just create the parts as opposed to creating a person?
WF: I've seen a mouse with an ear on its back.
BJ: Yeah, I saw that.
KS: That was just so fucking out of nowhere, "I've seen a mouse with an ear on its back."
WF: This was to take the ear off, to surgically remove it and then put it on a person's head.
KS: A human?
WF: Yeah.
KS: The idea would be let's say your kidneys go, then you would have a clone.

WF: But where is that clone stored?

KS: Well that's the thing.

BJ: Do you clone a whole person or can you just clone the kidney?

KS: I don't think you can just clone the kidneys. I think in order to create functioning kidneys you have to create a human being.

WF: I would say I am against that, unless my fucking kidneys go tomorrow and I'd be like, "Yeah!"

KS: "Where are all the clones? Send in the clones!"

WF: As soon as I need something.

BJ: A fucking rat with a kidney on its back!

KS: Would you have an issue with that, would you have a hard time knowing…

WF: That you're creating things…

KS: That something else had to die so that you could live? Another human being.

BJ: Do they become sentient?

WF: Or were they just in a tube?

KS: Of course they're sentient, they're human beings.

WF: Then as soon as I need it they're going to cut it up?

KS: Yes.

WF: No, I couldn't do that, that wouldn't be right. No one's saying that's what they want to do.

KS: But that is the fear, that if you start down that road… why go into the field of cloning unless you were doing it with the purpose of…

WF: Because you can clone perfect specimens.

BJ: Chicks!

KS: With boobs… The people who are against cloning are like, "Look, if you're just creating clones to create more human beings, well, we can do that naturally."

WF: What about people who can't have children?

KS: You can adopt.

WF: That's not that easy.

KS: No, but once you kick open that door…

WF: But cloning is so easy!

KS: "I was doing some light cloning myself earlier today!" I think it's once you kick open the door, how far down that road can you possibly travel?

WF: Are you against it?

KS: I don't know, I'm not sure.

WF: Yeah, I'm not sure either.

KS: Ultimately I don't know, it's easy to say from this position, but it's not like I want to live forever.

WF: If you could live a really good life forever, it would be a different story.

KS: Nah, it just kinda seems more of the same after a certain point.

WF: Oh come on!

BJ: That was ten years ago.

WF: If you could live the state of your life right now, the same quality of life you have right now, you wouldn't want to do it forever?

KS: But my whole body is breaking down, I'm constantly decaying.

WF: But it's going to stop.

KS: You're going to freeze me in time?

WF: There's going to be something to stop it.

KS: Are you saying they can freeze me in time right now, I'd always look the same, I'll never age more than thirty-seven?

WF: Nothing else goes.

KS: And I could live for how long?

WF: Unless you get into a car accident or some sort of…

KS: Unnatural…?

WF: Yeah, so disease is not going to affect you.

KS: And I'm not aging?

WF: You're not aging any more.

KS: But what is my life expectancy at that point?

WF: They're not sure but it could be up to… [authoritatively] five thousand years.

[Kevin and Bryan laugh.]

BJ: That was awesome!

KS: I was expecting about two hundred but you're like, "They're not sure but it could be up to five thousand years." Alright, so here's my first question: are you guys cloned?

WF: We're probably not in the program that you're in. You've probably got the gusto to get that shit, you've got the juice to get the program.

KS: Why does anyone want me to live for five thousand years?

WF: They like *Clerks*.

KS: OK, I gotta keep making SModcast so I'll need the entire SModcast crew to go through this process. I wouldn't want to live that long without my friends.
WF: Well, there's a drug out there that people can take and do it, but there are also the ramifications now.
KS: Overpopulation.
WF: Everyone's living and no one is dying off.
KS: Then we've got to go to the moon, or Mars.
WF: And we've got to choose who deserves it, who has to go and who gets to stay by what you bring to the game.
KS: Oh really?
BJ: What does SModcast bring to the game?
KS: We're off the clones now?
WF: We're off the clones. It's what you bring to the table is the basis of what you're judged upon to see if you stay on or go.
KS: Yeah but people might get tired of my shit after a certain point, where they're like, "You know what? This other guy is funnier."
WF: But you still have enough juice.
KS: Yeah, "Dane Cook has a bigger following than you."
WF: It's five thousand years, you don't know what you're producing. You might be producing the fucking *Citizen Kane* of comedy.
KS: Can you imagine doing an interview? "Well four thousand years ago when I did *Clerks*, I don't know if you've ever seen that, that was a while ago, it was..."
BJ: "It was four hundred generations ago."
KS: "... it was forty centuries ago when I made *Clerks* I remember thinking..."
BJ: "What was the budget on that?"
KS: And I ring up the fucking Scott clone. Scott's just a head in a jar floating. I don't think I would want to live five hundred years let alone a thousand. Then you're fucking Connor MacLeod and shit.
WF: Who's that?
KS: *Highlander* bitch!
WF: But he was alone though.
KS: And you're watching your wife get old and die.
WF: No, no, no. Everyone around you is staying the same. Everybody stays

the same age as they took the drug.

KS: So everyone in the world is suddenly frozen?

WF: If they're under twenty most will wait until they're in their twenties. Everybody who is over thirty will take it as soon as possible.

KS: Can I get a drug to reverse me?

WF: No. You take it or you put a gun in your mouth if you don't like the way it goes.

KS: These are rather harsh choices.

BJ: That or get yourself into a car accident.

KS: No, I don't think I'd want to live that long.

WF: You?

BJ: Five thousand years?

KS: Five thousand years, the exact same life you're living now.

WF: You could change things.

KS: But then you're saying that if I don't keep doing what I do, then suddenly my value isn't as high and they can decide to kick me off the island.

BJ: That's non-stop pressure for five thousand years!

KS: Totally!

WF: So what!

KS: You've got to keep producing, if you stop producing, you die.

WF: Do you know how many people would be under you just in terms of looking at today's society and what it has to offer? How many people, like bums and people that don't have jobs and stuff…

BJ: Whoa! Watch your mouth!

WF: … who bring nothing of value to society. But a filmmaker with your body of work…?

KS: I'm not fucking Spielberg dude. I can see these fucking people being like, "Spielberg, we want him to live for five thousand years, but the guy who did fucking *Clerks*? I don't know…"

WF: But you have a big enough fan base that there is no way that they would allow the guy who made *Clerks* to be fucking executed.

BJ: They'll take to the streets!

KS: Now it's execution!?

WF: Well, you've got to get rid of them somehow!

KS: Well I would imagine that they just stop giving you the drug. So you just start aging. But you're saying it's like *Logan's Run*?

WF: Yeah, it's like *Logan's Run*.

KS: Oh my god!

BJ: What was *Logan's Run*, was it thirty?

KS: No twenty-one, wasn't it?

WF: Yeah, it was thirty I think.

BJ: In the original movie or TV series or whatever I think it was thirty.

WF: Or, they just outlaw having children.

KS: To keep down the population?

WF: Yeah.

KS: But isn't that the point of living, to procreate? It's in our DNA, our genetics.

WF: Now the point is to stay alive.

KS: Well, that's kinda the point anyway, I can't see the difference.

WF: Now you're only thinking about yourself.

KS: But life doesn't change that much because one of the points of life is to stay alive, survival, the survival instinct. Now the survival instinct goes away?

WF: The people who refuse to take the drug are allowed to procreate.

KS: How does that affect me?

WF: Because they are going to die. If you want to have a child then you can't…

KS: So it's a choice between selfishness or community, because having a child is keeping the species going or in some way a selfless act because you're bringing another life into the world.

WF: Which in turn will take your place in line at some point.

BJ: Then that motherfucker will take the drug I bet.

KS: Well, that's the case now. I've got a kid and that kid will eventually take my place one day.

WF: No, you already had a kid. It's not a grandfather clause.

KS: You're talking about from this point on if you take the drug then you can't have any more kids?

WF: Yes.

KS: Well, we haven't had any more kids since that first one.

WF: But anyone who takes the drug, let's say you never had kids, then you can never have kids.

KS: Am I worried about other examples or mine specifically? You certainly have a lot of rules in place for it, this wonderful drug. No, I wouldn't want to live for five thousand years.

WF: Wow, I would.

KS: Would you really?

WF: Yeah.

KS: You just want to see the aliens, that's it.

WF: No, no, no. I just would not want to die.

KS: Really? Well, I mean I'd be hard pressed to say that I *want* to die.

WF: But it sounds like you do!

KS: "Is there a drug where I can just instantly die?" "Yeah, that's not special." No, but that's the natural course of life, eventually all good things come to an end.

WF: But if there was a way for it not to come to an end then I would be for it.

KS: Even if it meant, let's take it back to the clones, at the expense of another living human being? Just because it's a clone doesn't mean it's not human.

WF: No, I agree. Probably not. I wouldn't want to destroy another creature just so I can stay on Earth.

KS: Even though they're cloning it from you? They're taking some of your cells and DNA and whipping it up. But the thing is that they become self-aware.

WF: Yeah, you can't cross that line.

BJ: What if it was like a baboon?

WF: Hell yeah.

BJ: Would you take its heart?

WF: Yeah, I'd take its heart.

KS: What if it was a sentient baboon that could speak?

BJ: He was one of those Stalin monkeys.

WF: Did he have a name?

KS: He had a name for you, he called you his 'Other.' "Is my Other coming today? To visit?"

WF: Then you can't kill that creature.

KS: "It's like a Pillow Baby, you can't kill that creature."

BJ: It's one of those Stalin apes and he fucking knows it.

KS: If you had a clone would you choose to hang out with it?

WF: Oh yeah, that would be the best. That would be awesome. I've always thought about that.

KS: Hang out with the clone?

WF: Yeah, remember when we used to play hockey, I used to wish that we had clones of myself so that we always had enough guys to play because I know there is never a day when I would not want to play.

Random SModquotes

"The fat people are taking over, we're after your pizza."

KS: Then didn't your knee start hurting you at some point? Didn't you fuck up your knee?

WF: Yeah.

KS: So you could be like, "Give me your knee, clone!" And he's like, "OK, Other. Other Walt."

WF: Well if he's my clone and I'm hanging out with him then we're friends. We would have a fucking good time.

BJ: What'd you do?

WF: Whatever I'd want to do.

KS: What if you're clone was like, "Can you jerk me off?"

WF: That would not happen.

KS: Why not? You're jerking yourself off.

WF: But I know as me, that I would never ask that question of myself.

KS: But the clones become self-aware.

WF: Why would the clone need me to jerk him off?

KS: Because he's bonded to you, he feels a strong bond to you.

WF: My clone is gay?

KS: He came from you, he's like, "It's not a gay thing…"

WF: It's not like that…

KS: "… I'm not interested in other guys, just you."

WF: … he's his own person he goes and lives in his own place now.

BJ: He has his own house? So you go and pick up all your clones?

WF: It's like *Multiplicity*. When we were growing up, if I had clones of myself growing up.

BJ: But now? Now they have their own place?

WF: Yeah, they get to live their own lives. Get somebody else to jerk them off, get a girl to jerk them off.

KS: But he can't because he's drawn to you, because he came from your genetic material. He's you.

WF: So what? What does that have to do with anything?

KS: He's like, "Look I can't explain it, but you're the only one I'm interested in having jerk me off."

WF: Then you gotta die!

BJ: That's a little harsh. "Give me that fucking knee!"

WF: Nah, that would not happen. A clone of me, that thinks like me and acts like me, would never ask that question, or even want it.

KS: But that's the question of cloning though. When do they become individuals as opposed to just a copy of you?

WF: I think immediately — they can't be exact, not your memories…

BJ: Your experiences form you.

WF: They have their own experiences, but they're preordained to like things that I like, but they don't share my memories so they would just go out and do their own thing.

KS: But this one is not, this one is…

WF: Why? Is this the weirdo fucking clone? He's the perv clone?

BJ: It's a misfiring synapse or something, some electrical short in his brain.

KS: You paid for a lesser clone.

WF: "Get one of the other clones to jerk you off."

KS: How many clones do you have?

WF: Four.

KS: What if you found out they were all having sex with each other?

WF: That would be weird.

BJ: Or your clone raped you. "Oh, No! No!"

KS: "I'm changing my stance on cloning."

BJ: "I just wanted to play hockey, go to the comic store."

KS: "Now you're playing cockey Other, cockey!"

BJ: "This isn't something I would do."

KS: Would you let one of the clones have sex with your wife?

WF: No.

KS: Why? It's you.

WF: It's not me though, it doesn't have any of my memories, any of my feelings. It's not me, it just looks like me and has the same interests.

KS: You be you, and I'll be the Walt clone.

BJ: He's cock-blocking himself, man.

KS: Let's have a conversation, you be you and I'll be the Walt clone. "Me want Debbie."

WF: What, is he retarded?

KS: He's not retarded, he's just like Bizarro. "Goodbye," that's him coming up to you, "Goodbye."

WF: "Hello."

KS: "Me want Debbie."

WF: "You can't have her."

KS: [Roars] "Me want Debbie!" He just gets retard strong and starts throwing you across the room, throwing you into the walls and shit. You're like, "Why did I do this again? Oh, yeah, I wanted to play hockey." "Me want Debbie."

WF: "It is time for you, clone, to go out and find yourself your own Debbie."

KS: "Why?"

WF: "Because you are an individual, you are a person."

KS: "Me you."

WF: This is fucking ridiculous.

BJ: "I'm stuck with this stupid fucking clone, everybody else's clone fucking acts normal and shit."

KS: "Me you Walt."

WF: "You are not me."

KS: "Me you!"

WF: "OK, you're me."

KS: "Me want Debbie."

WF: "You can have her."

KS: "Now? Where Deb? Where Deb Walt? Me put peepee in peepee Walt."

WF: If you browbeat me constantly like this I probably would just give in.

KS: Browbeat? It's only the second time he's asked and you're like, "Ah, I'm tired of this guy."

WF: So you wouldn't want clones of yourself?

KS: I don't think so.

WF: One?

KS: Nah.

WF: To do the shit you don't want to do?

KS: Like what? I barely do the shit that I don't want to do. Writing? I like that. Autographing shit? Nah, I don't mind that.

WF: Send them to Florida.

KS: Yeah, I'll be like, "I'm going to send you down to Uncle Don and you're

going to sign stuff." "Me no go."
BJ: Fucking clone-gate, all the fans find out that the clones signed the shit...
KS: I'm like, "Technically I did sign it, he's my clone." Nah I wouldn't want another me.
WF: But it's not like you own it, it goes out and does its own thing. It's not like fucking Bizarro, it's like you. It has its own thoughts and constantly you're back and forth cracking each other up.
KS: But what if he's a more gifted filmmaker than I am? People are like, "We like the fucking copy better than the real thing. This dude's got talent." I'm like, "Come here clone…"
BJ: That's why you're not living five thousand years.
WF: "Make a deal."
KS: "What kind of deal?"
WF: "Let me put my name on the project."
KS: "Me no lie. That me work."
BJ: Your clone doesn't have the same name?
WF: I don't think the clone should have the same name, it's its own individual now. I think you're thinking more that he's a slave or something.
KS: Well yeah, that was the idea because he's been grown to replace your body parts.
WF: No, when I said I wanted a clone I said I just wanted to hang out with them.
KS: It sounds like you just want a brother.
WF: Yeah.
BJ: I don't understand because the only reason I would have a clone would be to give me hand jobs. Fuck the cooties and shit.
KS: Non-gay hand jobs.
BJ: That doesn't make me gay. Well he's gay, I'm not.
KS: You're like, "I'm going to put it in your poo-poo, it's not gay because you're me." "No? Yes! We're having some clone-sex." I don't know, I don't think I'd want a clone of me. I think it would be a weird world.
WF: No, you don't connect to anything else like your clone though. I mean you guys have the greatest times. That's what I would think.
KS: You have this image of a clone in your head that's like the ultimate best friend.
WF: Yeah, and that would fucking make me laugh no matter how fucking

sad I am.

KS: But isn't that what Bryan does?

WF: Not all the time. He does not want to do what I want to do all the time.

KS: Like what?

BJ: Two-for-two at the fucking movies though.

WF: OK. But you know what I mean though.

BJ: I've been to see *Hulk* and fucking *Hellboy* with this guy.

KS: No clone would do that.

WF: But there are certain things that you just have that little special bond like twins with your clone.

BJ: So the clone wants to go to all different Wal-Marts in one day?

WF: It wants to do exactly the same things that I want to do, finds the same things funny that I think are funny, it is just the best time when the clone is around. Busting each other up, it's just wonderful.

BJ: It's a non-stop party.

KS: I think they should put you in front of the American Medical Association as the argument for clones. You're like, "Look, if we can all have a clone of ourselves it would be our best friend!" But what about the ramifications of creating life and taking life from that life, just to support your own life — the moral ambiguities — "I just want someone to make me laugh." He's like, "Get the fucking comedy channel dude." That would never occur to me, "My clone would be my best friend."

BJ: He's an individual but he does sound very demanding of his time.

KS: Totally. "I'm not fucking here to amuse you!"

WF: We would need our own space without a doubt.

KS: It sounds like he would need a lot more of his own space, because he's always in demand.

BJ: He's like, "Dude, back the fuck up."

KS: "Fuck, that's my Other again. Must want me to give him a fucking chuckle, he's feeling blue... Hello, Walt!"

WF: He's having just as good a time as I am.

KS: Really? But if he's his own individual maybe he doesn't have the same sense of humor.

WF: Well I'm going on the assumption that he does. Or else he's no good to me.

KS: "You're dead to me clone." He's like, "Thank god!"

WF: But he does his own thing, I do mine. He's got his family, I've got mine.

BJ: Where the fuck is his family, he's a clone?

WF: Why can't he marry somebody?

BJ: So he's going to marry a real person?

WF: He is a real person.

BJ: Is he going to marry a non-clone?

WF: Yes. You could if you were a clone.

KS: No, the government puts laws into place.

WF: People are saying, not just in our fantasy here, but that if a clone really did grow there would be nothing wrong with it, nothing dangerous for it to mate with a 'normal' human being.

KS: I don't think so, but just as there is no danger to homosexuality but the government put laws in place against it, governments are afraid of clone-sex.

BJ: Afraid of clone-love.

KS: And once again, it's just selfish self-interest. Like they're, "If they start fucking the clones then there is less pussy for us. So let's make it illegal for normies to fuck clones."

WF: Let's make it illegal?

KS: Yes.

WF: But you do know that the clones would be the fucking hottest of the hot. People would be cloning hot chicks to fuck.

KS: Well, you can't.

WF: Because there's a law in place now? What's the point? If you're going to clone why not clone the hottest of the hot?

BJ: Didn't you say earlier on that you can't stand the hottest of the hot?

WF: If you have the ability to make a clone then…

KS: Yeah, but you can only make a clone out of your own genetic material. You can't be like, "I want to make a Cindy Crawford clone." No. Cindy Crawford might sell you her genetic material for like a hundred million dollars.

WF: Somebody would buy it. But again, it's not your slave though, so I guess it wouldn't work. You couldn't force the clone to do what you wanted just because you paid a hundred million for the genetic material.

KS: You've created another Cindy Crawford who also won't fuck you. You're like, "But I paid for your creation!" She's like, "Later, loser." "Why Crawford go?" "Shut up!" I don't know, I don't think I want my own clone. You?

BJ: Nah. I wouldn't want to hang out with him all the time. It would be so bothersome.

WF: Really, why?

BJ: I would just be annoyed.

WF: It's got the same exact razor wit, you guys are just going back and forth, it'd be like the best time.

KS: But then that would be like having a conversation with yourself, making yourself laugh all the time. But I don't need a clone for that. I could just amuse myself.

WF: But you have no idea what he is going to say.

KS: If we have a similar sense of humor then we're pretty much beating each other to the punch on jokes and shit. We're always doing it in unison. Like, "Right! You owe me a beer, psych!" "What beer?" I don't know if clones would turn out that way. I think that's the question. If they start developing their own personality then maybe it's completely different to you. Maybe he's the anti-Walt. He's like, "I want to go eat at a vegetarian restaurant. I would like to go see *The Notebook*, comic books are for children, hockey is nothing but boxing on skates and it's a very brutal sport, I'd rather watch cricket."

WF: That's the chance I took.

BJ: Well, something has to be done with him there. He needs to be taken care of.

WF: He lives his own life.

BJ: So you just turn your back on him?

KS: But you've got to pay for his life.

WF: Why? He's an adult, he can go get a job.

KS: OK, so let's say he comes out as an adult, they flat out clone you so when they roll him out of the tube he looks exactly like you. He's got no skills whatsoever.

WF: Neither did I.

KS: But you're way ahead of the curve. You've lived forty years of life. This dude comes out like a fucking idiot man-child.

WF: Oh, he'd have to go to school and everything?

KS: Yeah, he's got to be educated.

WF: I thought he knew what I knew?

KS: You said no, you said he doesn't have your memories.

WF: Well then nobody would ever want to clone anybody as nobody would want to deal with the fact.

KS: That's the thing, you've got this picture in your mind where you're like, "We're going to be the best of buddies," and then he comes out and just wails. It's like having a full-grown Pillow Baby.

WF: To get real serious though, you could clone lost loved ones. Who would want to do that?

KS: Who might also come out like, [wails] because they don't have the memories.

BJ: I can tell you one person who would want to do that.

WF: But you would want to invest the time and effort to school them.

KS: But how much time would it take to re-train that clone to be a facsimile of the lost love? The only thing they would share in common is the looks.

WF: But they're going to have the same traits though. If we're going to be on my theory that we're going to be best friends with my clone, they're going to share the same traits as the person that you were cloned from. So it's a good chance, not a hundred percent, but there is a good chance that they are going to have the same personality.

KS: But what if that clone is attracted to someone else, not attracted to you?

WF: I didn't say it was a loved one.

KS: You're taking about a grandparent or some such thing? Why would you want to clone an old person?

BJ: They die two days after you clone them.

KS: "Why did you bring me into this world? Only for me to decay and die."

WF: It could be any part of your family.

KS: Like a lost pet?

WF: I'm talking about human.

KS: Like what? Give me an example.

WF: A child.

KS: OK, let's say you're a couple and your kid got hit by a car, aged nine. You can create an exact duplicate of that kid aged nine. The question is would I want to do that? No. Because it's not the kid any more.

WF: I know but I think some people might want to do that, they might disagree with that and jump at the chance to have their child back again.

KS: But they can have a new child.

WF: Some people can't.

KS: But you're not getting that child back again. You're getting a clone.

WF: But in your state of despair…

BJ: They wouldn't even have the memories.

KS: It's coming out like a blank slate.

WF: But I still think the fact that it looks the same…

KS: Then you're showing him books like, "This is your Other. We loved him and he was into baseball and Hot Wheels…"

WF: "So much that we had you too."

KS: No. "We loved him so much that we took you from his genetic material."

WF: "Because we couldn't bear to live without him."

KS: That kid is going to grow up fucked up! Because everyone else around him is a product of love, or at least sex.

WF: So is he!

KS: Not really.

WF: He's a product of even more…

KS: No, he's a product of sorrow and desperation.

WF: But there is no more sorrow once he's there though. It's even better and more love because they realize he was gone and now he's back.

KS: They would never treat him with more love.

WF: You're crazy.

KS: Because they would always view him as, "Well, it's not really him."

BJ: Eventually he would know that he was different and that everyone knew he was different.

WF: How would everybody know?

KS: You can't keep something like that secret. All of a sudden your kid is dead and then all of a sudden you have another kid who shows up.

WF: You start a new life in a new town.

KS: Well then, you're not telling the kid that he's a clone.

WF: You could, or you might not want to. It's entirely up to the couple's choice. What would be the benefits to tell him, what would be the disadvantages to tell him?

KS: If you were going to do it I'd say never tell.

WF: Never tell?

KS: You would have to do the move away option first. You cannot give out that information.

WF: If my mom told me that I was a clone…

KS: And she told you the whole story?

WF: … yeah, she told me the whole story, that, “I loved you so much that I couldn’t bear to live life without you.”
KS: But she didn’t love you. She loved the original.
WF: But it’s me.
KS: But it’s not you.
WF: It’s a part of me. It was a part of that kid who just grew up.
KS: It was some cells, you were some cells from that.
WF: I would not feel like, “Oh my god! I’m not real.” I wouldn’t feel that way.
KS: You would. You would have to.
WF: I don’t think I would.
KS: A human being is more than just flesh and bone, it’s soul, heart. Thought, feeling.
WF: But I think that everything that I lived up to this point is no less real.
KS: You would have no problem whatsoever, if you found this out on Sunday then Monday would be… You don’t think that fucks with people’s heads?
WF: If my mom told me I was adopted I wouldn’t feel devastated by that.
KS: But it would fuck with your head a little bit.
WF: I don’t think it would. That person is still a hundred percent my mom.
KS: Still, you’d wonder who it was that didn’t want me. What was the circumstance?
WF: I know I would never actively pursue looking for my real mother.
KS: Really?
WF: Because I know who my real mother is.
KS: But what if one day you get the information your real mother is a billionaire?
BJ: Cindy Crawford. Do you think you could get her genetic material for free?
WF: The money wouldn’t change anything.
KS: I think finding out you were a clone would really sincerely fuck with your head.
WF: I think it really would fuck with some people’s head, you’re right without a doubt. Some clones couldn’t handle the truth.
KS: Totally. That’s when they go retard.
WF: I don’t know why though.
KS: Right now we live in a world where everybody has the same shot.

Everybody's standard.

WF: If you come out of a vagina does that make you more real than somebody who came out of a dish?

KS: The thought process is yes, because that person who comes out of a vagina has many years of experience, learning, growth, intellectualizing, to get to that point.

WF: Let's say the baby died a couple of days after birth and they cloned it. It would virtually be the same thing wouldn't it?

KS: That's a little easier to swallow than cloning a nine-year-old boy. Because that nine-year-old boy would suddenly become self-aware, instantly when they pull him out of the fucking tube that they grew him in.

BJ: But his brain is that of an infant.

WF: They'd probably opt to grow him as a baby and know that he'll grow eventually in nine years to look just like the child you just lost.

KS: That's a different story, that's the same as having another kid if you were growing it from an infant. But I think that if I was that clone and they said, "We had a son who looked like you, he was hit by a car and we cloned you from his material. So technically, you're still our son but we replaced him with you. But you're him." That would fuck with my head. I'd be like, "You guys were trying to console one another and just fucking made me from scratch."

WF: But it wouldn't take away any of the love that they had for you though. They wouldn't take away any of the memories or how they raised you or anything.

KS: Yeah, but it would still be like, "I was brought into this world as a band-aid for some emotional hurt, emotional devastation."

WF: Yeah, but you could have been brought into the world under the natural way too though.

KS: But I think I would be thrown by that. "So basically…

WF: I can see how some would.

KS: … you created me because you were broken-hearted. I was born out of your broken heart."

WF: If you had a loving, healthy childhood, were raised that way and everything was fine and then you found that out and that still fucked with your head, I would have to wonder why. Nothing would change, other than the fact that you were taken from someone else's cells rather than from an egg and sperm.

KS: I think it would still fuck with me.

WF: I can see why it would.

KS: It wouldn't fuck with you at all?

WF: No. I'd like to say it wouldn't, hopefully it wouldn't.

KS: OK. I'm you and you're your mom telling me that I'm a clone. Go ahead.

BJ: Bizarro?

WF: "Kevin."

KS: I'm Walt.

WF: You're Walt?

KS: I'm Walt, and you're Walt's mom.

WF: "You were hit by a car."

KS: "Who was hit by a car?"

WF: "You were, well the person you came from."

KS: "I don't remember being hit by a car. What do you mean the person I came from? Dad got hit by a car?"

WF: Is cloning known?

KS: I don't know, is it? It's even worse if cloning is known and this kid his whole life is like [teasing], "You're a fucking clone buddy!" Then one day is fucking told that *he's* a clone?

WF: That's why you probably wouldn't tell him that you were a clone. You'd wait until he was an adult. Don't tell a child that he's a clone.

KS: I think it's devastating whenever you find out.

BJ: "You're a clone!"

WF: Why?

KS: Because you're not like everyone else.

WF: You're not real.

KS: Yeah, you're synthesized.

WF: So you're against cloning.

KS: I'm not against it. I certainly wouldn't replace a dead child with a clone.

WF: So for what purpose can you ever see…

BJ: Fucking hand jobs! I said that a full half hour ago!!

WF: Is there any reason ever to clone?

KS: No, so I don't think there is a reason to clone.

WF: So you're against cloning?

KS: I'm not against it but I just can't think of any good reason to do it for me personally, but I'm not against it.

WF: You're not for and you're not against it, you're indifferent.

KS: I'm kinda indifferent on it. In real life. I would say I am more indifferent than anything else. Because you can't harvest them for body parts, that just feels immoral. There seems no point in making synthetic people.

WF: But I told you a good reason: to replace a loved one.

KS: That doesn't seem a good reason, you can have a child.

BJ: The way of the world is that you have to start over, that's how it happens.

WF: Your wife?

KS: My wife dies? I would not want to clone her.

WF: Some people would though.

KS: But why? It would never be… OK, so your wife dies and you're like, "I want to clone my wife," and they hand you an infant? Then you're like, "Is this legal?"

WF: All I'm saying is that there's a way you can bring them back.

KS: A full grown adult copy? So they grow an adult clone, they come out of the tube.

WF: And they are not [wails], they don't have the same memories but they're coherent and you can find love again.

KS: That's impossible. They would have to be educated.

BJ: What do you mean, "Find love again"?

KS: Taught how to write.

WF: They bring them up to speed like *Clockwork Orange*.

KS: That clone is its own individual, so there's a good chance she may not fall in love with me again.

WF: But you tell her the story.

KS: She'd be like, "I think it's really creepy that you did this." I'm like, "Don't you judge me."

WF: It could be really romantic too, "You love me so much."

KS: But I think the clone would be like, "You didn't love me, you loved who I came from."

WF: You're finding ways to be against it.

KS: But you keep saying, "I loved you so much," but that is not you any more. That's not the person you loved, that's just a clone, something taken from that person's genetic material and grown in a lab, that may look identical but that's about it.

BJ: What if he clones his wife, she doesn't fall in love with you and then is out there banging other dudes?

KS: Oh my god! Totally!

WF: OK, but there's also a chance that it could be the storybook…

BJ: The storybook clone?

WF: The storybook clone that does fall back in love with you, and you go on and live your lives and have a happy ending.

KS: But in the world you're picturing then there is never any heartbreak because let's say it's a different situation, the person didn't die, let's say your wife left you. You're like, "I want her to love me again. I'm going to take some of her genetic material and create another version of her, and that one will love me and not leave me."

BJ: Does making clones cost like, three dollars?

KS: It sounds really inexpensive. I think you're ruling out everything that goes into making a human being, it's not as simple as…

WF: I'm romanticized cloning?

BJ: The best friend scenario?

KS: That was said with such wide-eyed childlike faith, like, "We would be best friends, bestest of friends."

BJ: And it came down on me in the fucking process.

KS: Totally.

BJ: "You don't like to do everything that I like to do!"

KS: "Bryan's not good enough. I need a mini-me."

WF: Hey, vice versa, you do things that I don't want to do.

KS: Yeah but he's not clone-hunting like you are.

WF: But I'm saying if I had a clone my clone would never say something to me, and vice versa, "You want to do this?" and we would never be like, "No." Because we both know what we want to do. We would never ask each other something that we didn't want to do.

BJ: Gotcha.

WF: I might not be able to do it because of other…

BJ: Previous engagements?

WF: Yeah.

KS: I don't know if it would work that way.

WF: [Wistful] In my fantasy it would.

> **Random SModquotes**
>
> **"Would you rather get bitten by a great white shark or lose your life in a thread on the Internet?"**

KS: That's like saying you have a child and saying, "That kid's always going to do what I want to do, just because I created that kid, it came from me."
WF: I'm sure some people think that way.
KS: Yeah but we know that's not the case. Same with clones.
WF: It's a rude awakening.
KS: Yeah, the moment your clone becomes self-aware.
WF: Sure. But when I thought about it I assumed that it would always be grand times.
KS: Not the Clone Wars?
WF: No, there would be no wars. Only good times.
KS: That never occurred to me. You're a glass half-full kind of guy! I think you revealed yourself to be a romanticist and an optimist. But I don't know if it's romantic. In your view of the world, anyone is easily replaceable.
WF: In my view of the world I would want it that way.
KS: But that is just not the way it works. You can't really appreciate somebody if you know you can replace them instantly with another version of themselves.
WF: True. But I would want to be able to.
KS: Even though it is no longer that person?
WF: But I would try to convince myself it was.
KS: But the clone the whole time is like, "You're out of your fucking mind! I'm sucking so many cocks it's incredible, when are you gonna get it? My breath tastes like fucking sperm dude, I don't want you."
WF: I guess that would seal it.
KS: "Say something to make me laugh."
WF: I would hope at that point that the clone would see things my way and things would go the way I envisioned them.
KS: And you've totally ruled out the dark clone, the clone which is just like, "I want to be you, and I can't as long as you're here but if I get rid of you then I become you." Like the servant is now the master.
WF: He was never your servant.
KS: It's like Lucifer. "I refuse to believe that…" Well, I guess it's not like Lucifer. But he's like, "I'm not a copy. I cannot live as a copy. I want to live as the original so you have to die. One of us has to die."
BJ: So Walt is on the run?
KS: *Walt's Run*.

WF: Why don't they just move to another state?

BJ: Because the clone wants to fuck him!

KS: Who?

WF: The clone. Just move to another state and take up my identity, I don't care.

KS: "Because it will always sicken me to know that you are out there."

BJ: "Grossing me out."

KS: "I can't live in this world knowing that you're out there."

WF: That would suck.

BJ: You fucked up!

KS: You're like, "I just wanted to play some hockey. Now I'm on the run from a killer clone, a killer clone from outer space." I think it is a cautionary tale, sir. I think you need to give cloning a re-think.

WF: I was just saying that back when I was younger I always wondered about how cool it would be to have an exact replica of myself.

KS: You needed to buy one of those My Buddy dolls.

BJ: "My Buddy. My Buddy, wherever I go he goes too."

KS: You described the commercial perfectly. Like, "We would always be having good times."

WF: I always found it odd that Ed and Danny always used to fight that way. They're so close in age they should have just been best friends.

KS: It's a crapshoot, it's just personality.

WF: But I always wondered why.

KS: Well it's the old adage of you can pick your friends but you can't pick your family. You gravitate towards the people that you have similarities to. It sounds frighteningly though that you're looking for even more than what you've found out there. It seems that you're satisfied with your friends to a point, but you're like, "They're not quite there yet. There are aspects of their personality which I like, but they don't meet me all the way. I'm tired of meeting them half way, I want my friends to meet me all the way."

BJ: "This ain't sick. I want to do what I want to do."

KS: "On call. I'm having a bad day. Make me laugh."

WF: But we would just have so much fun hanging out together that we would never feel like I was imposing on him though.

KS: The clone?

WF: We would get video games. We would play each other at video games.

KS: He's like, "I'm tired of these video games. Don't you want to think Walt? The unexamined life is not worth living."

WF: We would think.

KS: He's like, "Alright, let's get existentialist. I'm not real, am I Walt?"

WF: "You're so wrong."

KS: "No, because I just came from your genetic material, but I'm not your child. It's not your genetic material mixed with someone else's genetic material. I'm just some cells that were scraped off you. I have no place, I didn't come from the same place as everyone else. I have no parents. Who are my parents Walt?"

WF: Why couldn't my mom be his parent?

KS: "Because she's not my parent, Walt. She didn't give birth to me."

WF: You're stuck in that birth thing.

KS: "It's easy for you because you're a normie."

WF: OK, I'll be the clone.

KS: "But we know that's not true Walt."

WF: "Why?"

KS: "Because you came first and I came from your genetic material."

WF: "I lied to you, you're really the real Walt. I'm the clone."

KS: This is where the clone goes dark clone. "For all this time you've been lying to me!"

WF: "Yeah, I'm the clone."

KS: "Well, I have to eradicate the clone! It was fine when the relationship was vice versa."

WF: Would we have papers to identify who was real and who was the clone? None of us would really know.

KS: He's like, "Well considering I just came online yesterday I'm pretty sure that I'm the clone."

WF: "Clone is just a word, you're a human being."

KS: "I was taken from a human being and grown, but I don't know that technically I'm a human being like everybody else."

WF: "You feel? Do you love? Do you hate?"

KS: "Right now I hate a lot."

WF: "Do you love though too?"

KS: "I'm not sure."

WF: "You're lying. You could meet somebody, we could double date. You can have a family. We can go to fucking amusement parks. It would be awesome."

KS: "My Other is so lonely!"

BJ: And he's like, "I'm not hanging out with that clone who always asks if he can have sex with me."

WF: He has married, he has his own family.

KS: When did this happen? When did the marriage and the family happen? I thought you two were spending all your waking moments together.

WF: Yeah, but I said I thought about this when I was younger though.

KS: So how old were you?

WF: Twelve.

KS: So at twelve one day your parents bring home clone Walt, C.W. they call him, C-Dub. He's like, "What does C-Dub mean?" You're like, "Clone Walt," he's like, "Why?"

WF: "You're a clone." I don't think you guys see the beauty of it all.

KS: I think you have just as high a chance that you and your clone would get along like Danny and Ed got along in high school.

WF: Have you ever known brothers to get along splendidly?

KS: I get along with my brother.

WF: Where you guys want to hang out all the time?

KS: I would if he lived around here, I'd hang out with my brother.

WF: Constantly?

KS: I don't hang out with anyone constantly, except Jen.

WF: I'd want to hang out with my clone constantly. Like do things, not 24-7, but like, "Hey man, let's go grab dinner with the family, let's go to the movies, all of us."

KS: I think the clone would grow apart from you because there would be a natural development of just like, "Look, I've got to go be my own man. I'm fucking tired of just eating chicken tenders, going to see movies I don't want to see…"

WF: But he wants to see those movies.

KS: But if he's his own individual then maybe his own tastes differ from yours. He's like, "I want to see a foreign film."

WF: Maybe he'd force himself to get different interests just so he could be his own person.

KS: Yeah but then find out that he liked them and be like, "Oh shit, this is who I am! I'm separating myself from you." I would imagine that sooner or later he would try to distance himself from you to stand as his own individual. Because you guys were in high school together, "What's up C-Dub the human Xerox?" He's like, "I fucking hate this school. Everyone knows I'm a clone."

WF: Nobody would say that though.

KS: Why? He'd be treated like a freak.

WF: No way.

KS: The only clone in school?

WF: Did anyone treat anyone with special needs like a freak at school?

KS: Yes, behind their backs, all the time.

WF: No they didn't.

KS: Yes, they did, absolutely.

BJ: To their faces! You saying that outreach class didn't get teased?

KS: They got teased all the time for being in that class.

WF: They're not as special as a clone, they were just out and out dopey.

KS: Kids are fucking cruel man.

WF: Don't you think it would be more like, "That's amazing!"

KS: Some would, but some would be like, "Fuck that clone!"

WF: "You fuck with my clone you're fucking with the real fucking deal too."

KS: "I'd kick both of your asses!"

WF: That ain't going to happen. Two clones?

KS: The other clone is a pacifist. I don't know who I'm rooting for in this fight. I think the clone would take a lot of fucking stick.

WF: So you wouldn't want a twin then either?

KS: Different.

WF: But would you want a twin?

KS: That wouldn't bother me.

WF: Really? Twin?

BJ: Nah. There's only one me.

WF: Really? Selfish? You want yourself to yourself?

KS: I think twins don't get a world of shit in high school. But I think a clone would.

WF: But what if we lied and said we were twins? That moved to live with my aunt.

KS: But then your clone wouldn't be a fucking celebrity.

WF: No, he'd be treated normal wouldn't he?

KS: So it would just be your twin? Are far as everyone at school is concerned?

WF: Yeah, in the eyes of the world. We lie.

KS: Here's the thing. In the school records someone is going to know that that is a clone.

WF: Why?

KS: Shit like that somehow goes in the records. If it's in the records then…

WF: But no one's going to believe that.

KS: Still, rumor is enough. Like, "My mom works in the office and she says your brother's a fucking clone! Is that true?"

WF: Let's say there really was a clone, would you hold it against the clone?

KS: No, but I'm also not the kind of guy that would bully someone in school. But there were bullies.

WF: But you wouldn't get bullied just because…

KS: You are creating this idyllic paradise where you and your fucking clone skip hand in hand through fucking fields, it's like you kids are growing up in the 1920s. An idyllic paradise where someone who is different from everybody else is treated either equally or better! I mean go ask a fucking black kid in an all white school if they feel like a celebrity…

WF: But why? He doesn't look different from everybody else. Why would they treat him differently?

KS: I doesn't matter, because he's different. Like the fucking dude who's a nerd in school.

WF: How are they going to know? We're not going to tell anyone that he was a clone.

KS: Because I said, it gets out man.

WF: OK, one of us is a clone. Figure out which one.

KS: Still. It's going to get out.

BJ: They'll ostracize them.

WF: We've got each other!

KS: He's like, "I'm *tired* of you. You're so needy!"

WF: "How can you be tired of me?"

BJ: "You're the clone and that means that I can fuck around with other people."

KS: "I'm pretty sure you're the fucking clone. You're so goddamn needy."

WF: Why would he get tired of me though?
KS: I think he would resent you. Because, "I'm getting ostracized in school because of you and you're a goddamn clone!" "Well guess what? I'm the normie and you're the goddamn clone! Try that on." And he's like [wails].
WF: We could do shit though, we could fuck up peoples' heads as clones.
KS: I think all you two would have would be each other because you'd be fucking known as the school freaks. Like a new kid comes to school and is like, "Oh, who are those twins?" "They're not twins. One of them is a fucking clone." "Get the fuck out of here, that is so weird!"
BJ: "They won't tell us which one."
KS: "And all they do is hang out with each other and laugh at each other's jokes."
WF: But when we get out of fucking petty high school and we're out in the real world…
KS: "They fucking hold hands!"
BJ: "All the time."
WF: We'd go to each other's jobs, like, "I don't want to go to work today, do you want to go in for me?"
KS: So two people are living off one income?
WF: No, we both have our own jobs but "I want to change it up today, you work…"
BJ: "We buy one pair of shoes."
WF: No, like I work at the community centre and he works at Home Depot. I'm like, "Hey man, I want to change it up. I don't feel like going to work today. You want to switch jobs today?"
KS: "I hate kids, I don't want to work the rec."
WF: But in this world it's like, "Yes, let's just fucking change it up a little."
KS: He's like, "I'm not in high school any more, dude. I'm tired of this."
BJ: "Let go of my hand."
KS: "You are so clingy."
WF: I mean, we're young, we're dating. "Hey man, you want to go out with Mary-Lou tonight and I'll go out with fucking Susie?"
KS: And he's like, "I *love* Susie you fucking idiot."
BJ: "You want to fuck her, is that what this is? Because I'm never going to trust you again."
KS: "You want to fuck Susie do you? … Mom!"

WF: It's more likely at a young age like that that we'd be up for that kinda shenanigans.
KS: I don't know man, you might be possessive of your girlfriends.
BJ: Fuck that, he'd be possessive of his clone!
KS: "Where are you going?" "I'm going out with Susie." "No you're not! Come in here and make me laugh! I'm feeling blue."
WF: We would have times.
KS: Yeah, sounds like a lot of bad times! Lots of coming to blows times where the dude is like, "I'm pretty sure you're the clone."
BJ: It's the kind of thing that ends up in a 911 call. "What's the emergency?" "There's a dead clone on my floor."
KS: It was the clone that killed you and he takes your identity and they can't prosecute because there's no law against clone killing. So he becomes you and he lies to your family the whole time. He's just like, "I'm Walt. That clone went crazy on me."

WF: [Deflated] That horror story, I never envisioned it going that way.
KS: I know exactly how you envisioned it. I've heard it a few times now. It's very sweet, very uncharacteristic of you, I think maybe that's what's been missing your whole life. Now it's come to the fucking fore, where it's like, "Everything would be different if I just had a buddy." I want a picture of a young Walt just so we can make a little video and lay under it, [sings] "I'm all alone in the world, where is someone to click to my clack..."

From SModcast 61: "Bridge Beach!"
The infamous Bridge Beach story

KS: Have you ever been in a sexual situation where you were not the aggressor? Where you felt victimised a little bit?
WF: No.
KS: There's never been any sex where you're like, "I don't want this."
WF: No.
KS: Never once?
WF: Never once.
KS: You?
BJ: Uh... not that I can recall. I mean, there are times where like...
KS: Where like, you hated yourself for doing it?
BJ: Yeah, sometimes.
KS: Where you had a little fight with yourself, where there's a little angel and devil on your shoulder?
BJ: The only reason I hated myself afterwards is if the person annoyed the shit out of me afterwards, you know? Um, never though, where it's been somebody that was gross, and I'm like, "Ugh, why would I do that?" 'Cause usually I would just, trumpet back to you, or...
KS: You're like, "I'm gonna make out from this story, one, I'm gonna cum, two, I'm gonna tell people about it."
WF: What about Bridge Beach?
BJ: Oh, yeah... I don't regret that.
KS: What was Bridge Beach?
WF: Oh, this is the Hall of Fame, of uh...
KS: I don't think I know this story.

WF: You know it.

BJ: We were in our… probably early twenties, right, at that point? And we used to hang around the Devaneys' house. We used to go down to their house all the time, with a couple of other people that would drop by, Brian Hartsgrove… And we would get beer and drink. What was that famous beer again? Oh yeah, Budweiser. Um… and there was one night, it was kinda a party actually. Some sort of party, maybe a birthday or some shit, but there were more than the average number of people there, and next door to the Devaneys', was… she was old, I can't remember her name… but she was like well into her sixties. And I guess her granddaughter came down. She was there for the summer. And she wasn't like, super-young, but she was maybe seventeen? Sixteen, seventeen, something like that?

KS: And you're how old at this point?

BJ: I was like, twenty. Maybe nineteen.

KS: So you're going through psychological counselling for drinking? This is after fucking Pam and Edgar went and yelled at Jesse Strickland?

BJ: I think it was actually prior to that, but uh… anyway, so the girl comes over, and I'm really drunk, right?

WF: I don't know about that.

BJ: That I was really drunk?

WF: I don't know about that.

BJ: I'm not trying to put it off, I woulda done it anyway. I would do it now.

WF: I am not sure that you were drunk.

BJ: I was pretty drunk. I remember being pretty drunk. But at any rate, let's, for the sake of argument…

WF: You were stone-cold sober.

BJ: … I was buzzed. Um… and I started making out with the girl, who was no less impaired than Geri Jewell. She had, like, CP [Cerebral Palsy]… but, like Hartsgrove, she had those… you know, she couldn't walk correctly, but she had the Geri Jewell sideways-talking, and head bobbing and shit. And uh… So we were making out…

KS: Oh, no.

BJ: For a good part of the night…

KS: Oh, no.

BJ: And at a certain point, Donna Devaney, you know, John and Kevin's mother, is just like, "Bryan, what are you doing? She's *retarded*!"

KS: Oh, no!

BJ: Hartsgrove goes, "She has the same thing I do, I'm not retarded!"

KS: Do you think she would have objected if Hartsgrove and her were hooking up?

BJ: I guess not, no. I guess I was seen as taking advantage.

WF: Who's Geri Jewell?

BJ: Geri Jewell is like, you remember on *Facts of Life*?

WF: Oh, yeah…

KS: She was Blair's CP cousin, who'd make jokes about being Palsy.

BJ: She was also on *Deadwood*.

KS: That's right, she was on *Deadwood*.

BJ: Yeah… so we made out for the better part of the night…

KS: How did that start?

BJ: I don't know, that I don't remember.

WF: I just remember like, being there, and then one minute they're talking, and I turn around and he is like, *full mouth* on this girl that… I didn't know what she had, but that she was definitely…

BJ: There was an apple core at her feet.

WF: … a special ed person. And it was just so startling, it was startling to say the least.

BJ: But the Bridge Beach thing was… was I life guarding at that point? I think I must have been. I worked for the town as a life guard. So I guess I was life guarding…

KS: So you were at the beach that was right next to Careless Navigator?

BJ: Right, right.

WF: The next day, he was scheduled.

BJ: The next guard scheduled to be there. So I told her to meet me there. And it was a real like, "Parting is such sweet sorrow," like, "Come to the Bridge Beach!" She was like, "I'm gonna be there!" I guess she got in trouble, 'cause she never did show up, I think she got in trouble for making out with me.

WF: Bryan was screaming as we're leaving, "Bridge Beach! Bridge BEEAACH!"

BJ: She broke my heart, though, she never did show up.

KS: So the woman with CP came to her senses the next morning, and was like, "I can do better than that guy."

BJ: Yeah, if you were to ask her is there anyone you've ever regretted…

KS: She's like, "There was this one retarded guy in Highlands." "I'm not retarded!"
BJ: I remember Hartsgrove stayed over that night, and the front door was locked, I had to crawl through the bathroom window, fucking cut the shit out of my leg, fucked it up real bad… it was worth it though. Other than that, yeah it's mostly like, "I wish I hadn't done that because now this person is gonna keep wanting to talk to me."
KS: Like metal lady?
BJ: No, she wasn't a ho, metal lady. She was a tough fucking nut to crack, that woman. She was… for all her metal…
KS: She didn't surrender to the ways of metal completely.
BJ: She did not, she did not.
KS: She only flirted with metal.
BJ: Little bit of… it was a lot of, like, feeling up and that sort of stuff. A B-J after fucking… so much work, that it was…
KS: A lot of talking into, like, "C'mon…"
BJ: A lot of begging. A lot of offering payment.
KS: "Please… I'm making out with CP chicks…"
BJ: "I'm over here, in the meantime, floating in a sea of fucking sub-intelligent fucks. Sitting alone at the Bridge Beach."
KS: "I got stood up at Bridge Beach."
WF: "Bridge Beeeach!"
KS: "By who? You'll never believe."
BJ: "You're gonna feel sorry for me, you're gonna at least let me fucking go over the bra on this one."
KS: Such a haunting image: "BRIDGE BEEEACH!"
WF: You turn the corner, they can still hear it.
BJ: You imagine it's a movie, the next shot is me waking up, with a fucking face full of dogshit, and like, "Bridge Beach" is echoing…
KS: I mean, it's just like the story sounds like it's gonna end with "and I didn't go to Bridge Beach. I wasn't gonna go to Bridge Beach."
BJ: But it literally ends… "Where the fuck is she?"
KS: … I just think it's funny that you're like, "She must have gotten in trouble."
BJ: I'm pretty sure she did.
KS: As opposed to, she just thought it over and was like, "Fuck this."

BJ: She got to make out with a normie, why the fuck would she not come back for more of that magic?
WF: No, I gotta agree with him, the way that she was like, hanging on him most of the night, that we left, there was no doubt that she was forcibly kept away from that beach.

From SModcast 62: The Human Quilt
Confronting the Foreigner dude in the cereal aisle

KS: You're the lead singer of Foreigner, and…
SM: Mr Foreigner.
KS: Yeah, the Foreigner himself. Fuzzy Foreigner. And you were just in the grocery store.
SM: OK. I am? Or I'm leaving?
KS: You are.
SM: I'm in.
KS: Yeah, you're in the cereal aisle. And you're British, 'cause I think Foreigner's a British band, no?
SM: I don't know.
KS: Let's pretend that it is.
SM: OK. "Roight."
KS: OK, there you go. I so like it when you rock the accent. And you're so fucking overwhelmed by the amount of different cereal that we have in the food store, compared to a British supermarket.
SM: Gotcha. Even though I've probably lived here for twenty years…
KS: It still confounds you, whenever you encounter it.
SM: Usually someone goes and buys my cereal, maybe it's the first time I'm like [British accent] "I'm gonna get that meself. I'm gonna get some cereal."
KS: OK, that dude is in the cereal aisle, and while he's looking around trying to make his decision he sings:
SM: [Sings] "Feels like the first…" I don't think they're British.
KS: I think they are British, because British people don't really sing with an accent. No, you can sing it like the way you hear the song,

Random SModquotes
"Watch your daddy hit a stranger."

because even if he's British he wouldn't sing it like [sings mimicking Scott's cockney accent]. It's not like Dick Van Dyke.

SM: I just woke up, so maybe he does.

KS: Yeah, that's true. He hasn't poshed it up yet, he's just going real cockney. OK, so you're singing it to yourself and I'm a dude who's in the supermarket aisle, who a) hears that, and b) recognizes you. And c), approaches you about it.

SM: OK. "There's so many cereals… [sings]."

[Kevin lights up]

KS: You can smoke in this supermarket.

SM: [Continues to sing Foreigner song.]

KS: "Hey, man, that's kinda fucking gauche, no?"

SM: "What?"

KS: "Well you're the Foreigner dude, aren'tcha?"

SM: "Well, yeah. I am the Foreigner dude."

KS: "OK; you can't sing your own song in public."

SM: "Why not?"

KS: "'Cause it's gauche!"

SM: "It's a good song!"

KS: "Number one… look, I'm not gonna argue with you, I like that song."

SM: "First of all, I was singing to meself."

KS: "Well, not if I'm hearing you, *mate*."

SM: "Well, 'cause you're right up on me, aren't you? You're right next to me. I can feel your sweat…"

KS: "Well now I am, because you were being *bloody irritating*. Yeah, I know you're British."

SM: "See, I'm proud of what I do and I'm singing it. You're obviously not, you obviously hate your job. You obviously don't like your job."

KS: "What does my job have to do with it? Alright, so I'm an accountant, so if I'm standing over here trying to pick out fucking Pop Tarts and I start doing number crunching out loud?"

SM: "Have you seen all the cereals there are in America? I'm quite… it's quite magnificent, and you don't seem to know how amazing it is that you have so much selection — hold on a minute, you've chosen to come into my space, you're gonna get mad about me..."

KS: "I'm pretty sure Foreigner has… even though they may be British-born,

I think they moved over here a long time ago, during their success in the eighties, no?"

SM: "Oh, what so it's like, it's all over, the Queen and all that, I just let go of all that just 'cause I'm like, 'We're here now'…"

KS: I'm just saying, you haven't encountered a fucking food store, a cereal aisle in all this time?"

SM: "I've been busy, you know, touring…"

KS: "You haven't been busy in fucking fifteen years, let's be honest."

SM: "How do you know, when do you get out of the house?"

KS: "Back in the day I was a Foreigner guy, and when was the last time you guys…"

SM: "So why are you doing this?"

KS: "What do you mean, why am I doing what?"

SM: "It's like, 'Back in the day, I used to…' [adopts throaty British-person-doing-American-accent voice] 'Back in the day, I used to like Foreigner.' Well, you know what? I'm like, Foreigner's still there, we're still rockin'."

KS: "Well you haven't released a new album in a while, that's what I'm getting at."

SM: "How do you know?"

KS: "You certainly haven't had a hit single."

SM: "And what, that's what it's all about? That's why I did it? 'Cause music is about *music*."

KS: "Come on, you used to fill arenas, you know what I'm talking about."

SM: "And that was just, that was what happened. And now it's changed, now it's like, we're filling other places… and we're doing well, but like… it's for the music, brother."

KS: "Where you playing? And why do you sound like the guy from *Lost* all of a sudden? Calling me brudda. Are you really British? Is Foreigner a British band?"

SM: "Of course. Um…"

KS: "Look, just don't sing your songs out loud in public."

SM: "Why?"

KS: "It's just… it's just not right."

SM: "Don't you ever write numbers in your 'ead? Like, sitting there and you're picking out like, a piece of meat for the evening, you know the roast that you're gonna buy, and then you're like, 'Oh, fuck it's tax season,' it's

April, and you've got shit in your head and you're like, 'Oh, I've got to figure out those write-offs,' and then you're there, and you're like counting them out in your head, and then like, what? I'm sposed to be like, 'Hey, fucker, don't bring your shit to the grocery store, you and your numbers and all the rest of the stuff…' This is my job! I'm allowed to sing me song. Have you ever written a song, you fucking twat?"

KS: "No, I haven't…"

SM: "Have you done anything?"

KS: "You're being unnecessarily harsh, man…"

SM: [Really getting into this now] "I'm coming back at you, I was trying to pick out some cereal, I haven't had my coffee, if you can't tell. I'm just singing 'cause I'm like, so surprised — I mean there's so much cereal here!"

KS: I'm delighted that you, like, picked the ball up and ran with it, you're committed! OK, um… "Look, alright, I realize perhaps I shouldn't have said anything in the first place. But look, I'm not saying it 'cause I don't like you. I'm saying it because, you know… for your own benefit. You don't want to be singing songs, your own songs, and being recognized in a fucking food store. It's kinda gauche, kinda tacky, it's the kinda thing that winds up in the rags, like *Us* weekly, like 'Overheard'…"

SM: "If someone wants to write an article about me, saying like, "He loves his music so much, he sings it to himself," go right on. Go call someone right now, I'd love to see that. Let people know I love me music. Sometimes I sing The Beatles, you know…"

KS: "Alright, well that would make more sense to me."

SM: "But I like my own fucking songs. Just 'cause you do something you don't like…"

KS: "Look, I never said I was unhappy as an accountant."

SM: "But you obviously don't have enough pride in your work that you want to like, bring it out into the world and lay it on for people."

KS: "No, I'm just maybe not as fucking… you know, egocentric as to start singing my own fucking songs in public; or in my case, crunching my numbers in public. That'd be like me going up to the fucking register when I check out, and like adding shit up in my head before the register does it…"

SM: "Well, maybe *do* do that."

KS: "… and shouting, you know, '28.12… watch, watch. Yeah, I'm a fucking accountant bitch, what up, that's how I knew that.'"

SM: "How do I know you don't do that?"

KS: "I'm here to tell you right now, Mick, that I don't do that," (I think his name's Mick) "… that I don't do that, and I would never do that. I think that's really unfair to do that to somebody else. That puts her in a very awkward position where she's looking at me like, 'I don't know what to say…'"

SM: "I didn't confront you with me song…"

KS: "… 'I feel I should say *something*, what if I get fired...'"

SM: "I didn't like, grab you by the lapels and like, say, "ey, 'ey, like…'"

KS: "I'm sharing the same space with you, I'm within five fucking feet of you, and I've got to hear you sing that song? It makes me sad. 'Cause I look over…"

SM: "You hate the song?"

KS: "No, I like the song, as a matter of fact. And I wanna look over and be like, 'Right on, fucking Foreigner,' and it *is* the Foreigner guy, and that…"

SM: "And that's not better? It's not better than the milkman singing it?"

KS: "No, it's not better. You know what, circa 1986, '87, yeah, it'd be better, but *now*, in 2000-fucking-8 dude? It ain't better, it's sad."

SM: "So a little distance and suddenly I'm like, an arsehole, eh?"

KS: "Well, now, 'cause I'm filled with a sense of sadness, 'cause I'm like, 'Fuck, they used to be on top, what happened?' And then you have to sympathize…"

SM: Life's happened. Everything goes through cycles."

KS: "I'm sorry for your troubles, but I don't want to be brought in on your troubles and your own personal Hell."

SM: "Then you can go piss off."

KS: "Yeah, well I can't piss off if you're singing the song…"

SM: "You can piss off!"

KS: "… capturing my attention and I look over and it's you. And then I'm involved, I'm emotionally involved!"

SM: "You know I've sang songs in other aisles in this store, and I've had… you know, people are quite tickled by it! They're like, "Ey, it's Mick, and he's singing his song! What a lovely chap!'"

KS: "Come on, who was the last person that recognized you in the United States?"

SM: "Well, you did."

KS: "Besides me."

SM: "Lots of people. If you fucking can, why not other people? Why not your neighbor? Why not…"

KS: "'Cause I keep a special place in my head for useless, stupid trivia. And you just happen to be one of those pieces of…"

SM: "You're not a nice man. From what I know about you. You came in here with a chip on your shoulder…"

KS: "All I know is, I was a fan. Up until about five minutes ago."

SM: "I don't care now, I'm glad you're not. Go fucking burn your records now, you fucking flaming prick."

KS: "Well no, it's not so simple as, I'm just simply not a fan. Now I'm gonna start *campaigning against* Foreigner. That's what you've done to me. You have turned me from a fan…"

SM: "I don't know how far you'll get with that."

KS: "I might get very far."

SM: "How far?"

KS: "Well the Internet's a big place. And sarcasm and cynicism is always fun, and catches people's attention. I'm gonna campaign against you and your stupid fucking band that I used to like five minutes ago, and I'm gonna bring down the wrath of people. People are just gonna be like, 'You're right, they do suck,' or 'Come on, they've always sucked. They sucked back in the 80s, they were sell-outs.'"

SM: "Go right ahead, I stand behind…"

KS: "… 'I Don't Want to Live Without You.'"

SM: "I stand behind me music…"

KS: "…[sings 'I Don't Want to Live Without You'] … you know, that was fucking laughable. You guys used to rock, back in the day, man! And then, fucking that album? Where you had like, five singles and shit, you rocked the charts? You sold out! You don't think I'm gonna get people to rally behind my cause, even thirty years after your popularity has waned?"

SM: "I'd say that anyone who's decided to rethink their thoughts on Foreigner, it's already happened. So I think you're a little late."

KS: I just can't believe how fucking far this has gone, you're still fucking rocking that voice, it's awesome. Um…

SM: "I think you're a little late, to go out there and be like, ''Ey everyone, let's rethink Foreigner.' You know…"

KS: "Nonono, I think people online particularly, where people seem to have a lot of free time, are happy to retro-actively fucking campaign against a band that hasn't been popular in near three decades."
SM: "I would say people'll be like, ''Ey, why you picking on them? Why pick on them?' Why not go pick on... you know... go pick on The Rolling Stones, or..."
KS: "I would agree, that you will have a few defenders. But I guarantee you, more people will come out of the woodwork to say nasty things than nice things. And I'm gonna send you that link."
SM: "I remember me old mate, from back in the day said..."
KS: "Which mate is this?"
SM: "I forget his name, it was, back in you know, 1982, and he was a publicist, and he was quite a good chap, and he said, 'All publicity's good publicity.' It was someone who said that, and so you go on out there, and you type away with your little accountant fingers, that do nothing for the world..."
KS: "'All publicity is good publicity?' How 'bout when I start telling the world that you're a fucking pederast, how 'bout that? Is that the kinda publicity you want? Stop singing your fucking songs in public."
SM: "You go right ahead, and I'll sue you for defamation of character."
KS: "How you gonna sue me? Dude, I leave this grocery store, you don't know me. I know you, you don't know me, OK? Remember that."
SM: "I'll track you down."
KS: "You're not gonna track me down. I'm an anonymous fucking accountant. You will never find me. And I will anonymously post on the Internet that you're a fucking pederast."
SM: "I'm part of the entertainment industry, we've got people..."
KS: "... I will destroy you and Foreigner."
SM: "We'll find you."
KS: "'America for Americans, no Foreigners,' that's gonna be the tagline of my website."
SM: "You're an angry little man. You're an angry little man!"
KS: "You could have just simply stopped singing, took the heartfelt advice, but no, no it had to be a big fucking issue, and then you try to make me feel worse, when I already feel bad from fucking looking over and seeing the fucking dude from Foreigner, singing his own song out loud, near three

decades after the apex of its popularity."
SM: "I was singing it to meself, and I'll keep doing that."
KS: "Obviously you're not singing it to yourself, fucking, *mate*, because I..."
SM: "You are literally like a fucking coat, it was like you were so close to me I'm like, wearing you like a coat! If you would just piss off..."
KS: "Alright, these aisles are at least five people deep."
SM: "You're obviously the one who's in like, bathrooms, tapping your feet under the stall door..."
KS: "Oh, now I'm gay?"
SM: "Yeah! You're gay."
KS: "You know what? Maybe I am."
SM: "If anything I know, you're gay. Deal with that."
KS: "Well OK, well fucking fine. So I'm gonna go on the Internet and talk about how you're a pederast, a self-loathing pederast who also hates homosexuals."
SM: "Why are you doing this to me?"
KS: "You know, I don't know man... I'm just..."
SM: "Why you doing it to me? Don't you remember? Didn't you ever hear one of me toons in the car, you're driving in the car, the wind's in your hair, and you know... maybe you just had a spliff and you're with your lady, like, what up?"
KS: "No, nothing like that. But I remember being in high school and being in love with a girl when that song was playing [sings] I wanna know what love is... Sing it with me now!"
SM: "Well I'm not gonna do it, 'cause you fucking yelled at me the last time I did it. That's entrapment, prick."
KS: "Alright, well played. Alright, you saw my snare. But it was half-snare, and it was half-true. I was kinda into the idea."
SM: "I'm sure you want to know where love is, 'cause no one'd love you, you fucking prick."
KS: "The song, *Mick*, is I wanna know *what* love is, not *where* it is. I know where the love is. And in this aisle of this grocery store, there's none for you."
SM: "I'm sure you wanna know *what* it is, too, 'cause I'm sure your mother didn't love you."
KS: "Why would you say something as asinine as that? You don't know me, or my mother. My mother was a beautiful woman."
SM: "I know your type."
KS: "You want to hear about my mother? My mother raised me and my

brothers, my two brothers and my three sisters by herself, after my old man left for booze."

SM: "I didn't say your mum wasn't nice, I just said your mum didn't like you."

KS: "She knew what love and sacrifice was, and she instilled that love in me. *And* that sense of sacrifice and duty. Now you, you're a musician, c'mon dude, you're a rock'n'roller, if that — I'd say you're more a soft rocker — but you don't know from responsibility, you don't know from pain or hardship."

SM: "How do you know that?"

KS: "… and you don't even know love, because all you know is fandom, and people liking your songs, but you'll never know if someone truly loves you for you."

SM: "I would now."

KS: "How? Why, because you haven't been on the charts in thirty years?"

SM: "Well, from what you pointed out earlier, yeah. I ain't got a hit single. I'm down here, in the fucking cereal aisle, Safeway, trying to figure out whether I want granola or, you know, something with more sugar in it. But I gotta watch me weight, I'm still up on stage ain't I?"

KS: "Yeah, but if you take the suggested serving size on the side panel of the box of Trix, it's like 180 calories max, dude. So you get your nice taste, your burst of sugar, but it's also got vitamins and minerals…"

SM: "I don't need your advice. I don't need advice from…"

KS: "Then don't solicit it, when you were like, "'Ey, I don't know whether I want granola or something with less sugar in it…"

SM: "It was a rhetorical question! I was talking to meself, I wasn't asking you, you bloody stump!"

KS: "This has gotta be the most attention you've received in years. That's why it's going on so long, I'm sitting here going 'Why the fuck hasn't this idiot walked away yet?' This has gotta be the most attention you've received in years."

SM: "Not at all."

KS: "No?"

SM: "You obviously don't know… Foreigner, we've touched people. Have you ever touched somebody? Have you ever touched someone's soul with your music?"

KS: "I've written a poem."

SM: "Yeah? Where? Where is it?"

KS: "What do you mean, where?"

SM: "Let me read it!"

KS: "I don't carry it around, and if I did, I wouldn't be like you, where I'm like, 'Ooh, I'm in a public space, I might as well play, please love me, love me.' I keep that shit to myself."

SM: "Because it's crap."

KS: "Ah, maybe it is, maybe it's not, it's very subjective."

SM: "No it's not."

KS: "A lot of your songs are crap! Someone loved my poem once."

SM: "Who?"

KS: "A woman."

SM: "A woman named what?"

KS: "A woman named Maria loved my poem, and loved me."

SM: "Because you wrote it for her. What choice did you give her? What's she spposed to do, use it as a diaper?"

KS: "Yeah, well she could just as easily be like, 'Look, this isn't my thing, I think your stanzas are off, I'd prefer something written in the iambic pentameter,' she could have said any number of things, but she didn't…"

SM: "Yeah, but why would she want the bother, she's like, 'I want this guy to get off me…'"

KS: "Oh, she didn't want me off her, Mick. She wanted me on and in her, all night long, all the time."

SM: [Back as Scott for a second] … I'm like, *sweating* now.

KS: [Laughs]. Hold on, we gotta put a cap on that. "Hey, you're not even really Mick the dude from Foreigner, are you?"

SM: "No."

KS: "Alright. Bye…." And scene!

SM: That was like, thirty minutes!

KS: That was good dude, you were on fire. I was engaged man, I was in it…

SM: You're like, "Now I don't feel like I need to meet that guy."

KS: No, not at all!

SM: Or you'd be let down by it. First of all he'd be like, "I'm not from Britain. I'm from Detroit."

KS: He's like, "a) I'm not British, and b) I would never sing my song to myself in a food store, or any public place." He's like, "Look, I get paid to sing, why the fuck would I do it for free?" I'd be like, "Right on, man. You've got a plan."

[The publishers would like to make it absolutely clear that neither Scott nor Kevin intend any offence to the real Mick Jones of Foreigner. Or Mick Jones of The Clash for that matter.]

From SModcast 63: SMod-Kushed

Hitler's dog engineering program and the Nazi stink

KS: Look at this fucking dog [Shecky].

SM: I'm scared of that fucking thing.

KS: I like this dog a lot. I like to get stoned and interact with this dog. 'Cause she's just so strange-looking.

SM: You should get really stoned, and then you could do a SMod…

KS: With Shecky?

SM: A Sh-mod.

KS: I remember one night, I got stoned with Schwalbach, early on. Early on into my recent romance… with weed. I would like, pick this dog up and hold it up, and we just started laughing. And the dog had this — not hurt look, but just like, "I don't understand. What did I do?"

SM: "Why did I suddenly become a joke to you?"

KS: But it was just looking at her — she's so weird. It's so weird that nature makes a dog like this. Stretched-out…

SM: *Did* nature make a dog like that?

KS: Yeah, I don't think this is… I don't think a dachshund is created. I mean they do like, hybrid dogs now and shit, but…

SM: I thought that they were, a little bit.

KS: Were they? In what way?

SM: I don't know, I thought that weird long spine… I don't know.

KS: How would they accomplish that, though? It's not a mix of two breeds.

SM: I don't know.

KS: I think that's what a dachshund naturally looks like, or is meant to look like. I don't think she was engineered. I resent you fucking saying that my dog was clinically engineered.

SM: Well somebody's going to email in and either say that I'm right, or you're wrong.

KS: Well I mean, it depends I guess what your definition of the term 'bred' is.

SM: I do know that you've got to watch as they get older, like back problems and shit like that.

KS: She'll get some sway back going? She's kinda shapely though. [Shecky yaps] Oh, shut the fuck up, I'm paying you a fucking compliment! Please don't make Daddy mad. But man, she's a fucking thing of joy forever. Just to look at her, just to pet her, she has a good feel to her, 'cause her hair's all short.

SM: You should drop some E, and then it would feel awwwesome.

KS: I don't think I can take that fucking trip.

SM: Why not E?

KS: Why weed and not E? Weed is natural, comes right out of the earth. E is manufactured in a lab.

SM: Like your dog?

KS: My dog is a naturally occurring individual!

SM: Alright, alright alright!

KS: This is a naturally occurring species and breed, I think. Because a dachshund been around since at least 19…

SM: It was Nazis created them…

KS: Yeah, they had their pictures of Hitler with a dachshund, so he's been around since at least that era, let's say '35 to '45. They weren't genetically engineering fucking dogs…

SM: By Nazis.

KS: Well, they were doing shit. You think that's where the fucking dachshund came from?

SM: I don't know!

KS: It's a Nazi dog?

SM: I don't know.

KS: It was their first stab at like, gene splicing? And genetic fucking, toying with…

SM: "Let's make a wiener dog."

KS: "Let's make zat, is funny, to laugh at, ja?"

SM: "Ve must entertain ourselves."

KS: "It needs to be long, ze Führer loves long things, he thinks it's funny…"

SM: "Look at ze Führer, he loves the dog! Ve have succeeded!... He's so happy!"

KS: "It has put a schmile on his face!"

SM: "It is so rare to see him so happy…"

KS: [Creepy German voice, as if talking to a child] "Guten tag, Führer, guten tag! I see you're very happy wiz your leetle dog, no? Yes, yes, I know you like the dog. Very good, thank you, sir…" My take was that that was one of the people that genetically engineered the dog, and that's how they get away with talking that way to Hitler. Hitler's not like, "Why are you creeping me out, like, 'Guten tag…'?"

SM: "Hello…ja…"

KS: They can do it 'cause they created the dog, so like, they're "Ve know how much you like the dog!"

SM: Well, in my imagination, he's such a complete fucking maniac, and this dog has made him smile, and these people are like…

KS: "Make more!"

SM: "Make more! Vy is zere only vun?"

KS: "Vun? Vun is funny, but many, wooh! Gott in Himmel!"

SM: "A room full of these little wiener dogs! I might die laughing!"

KS: "Schnitzel vith a head! Is vat ve shall call this dog, no?" "We were

thinking dachshund." "OK." What is it? 'Dachshund' translated means 'badger hound'.

SM: Oh, really?

KS: Yeah, because that's what they went after, they ferret out things in the earth. That's why you get me with the whole breeding thing…

SM: Like, I just wondered if they were bred to be of a certain size and type to get into the badger holes.

KS: But bred from what? Other dachshunds?

SM: I don't know. They're Nazis, they did all kinds of fucked-up shit.

KS: But not even a mad Nazi scientist could create a dachshund from, fucking… a collie and a cow. Or a collie and a worm. They're like, "Ve want it to be a dog, but it needs to be kinda long."

SM: But your idea, what you're saying is there has to be some naturally occurring dog that has an extra-long kinda wiener-shaped body.

KS: Yeah! I mean, this happened. This just happened in nature, man. It wasn't somebody going, "Let's build a better dog," it was just…

SM: A ferret and a…

KS: … how like, there's a rose, there's a tulip, there's a fucking collie, there's a dachshund. They can't all be… they all have to be naturally occurring, until you get into breeding, cross-breeding. But this is not cross-bred from anything. What's it look like?

SM: I don't know, man. I don't know. I'm just, throwing out Nazis…

KS: You're like, "You're being hostile, and I want you to stop."

SM: Yeah.

KS: But they're identified with the Germans.

SM: Yeah.

KS: So their popularity waned for a while, after World War Two.

SM: "Are you sure you don't want a…"

KS: [German accent]: "He's funny, no?" "… No, it fucking calls to mind vivid…"

SM: That same scientist came to America…

KS: He's moved to America, and he's hawking them on the curb.

SM: "You like it, you want ze little dog?"

KS: "Zis is a wiener dog! Do you like? Look at ze wiener dog, he's a funny dog… Vould you like a wiener dog?"

SM: "No!"

KS: "No! You fuckin' Nazi!" "Oh, I vas just defending the wiener dog… und he hit me vit a can."
SM: More likely he's in fucking South America.
KS: Yeah, hiding out… or he's been hired by the American government to work on the rocket program.
SM: No, they're more like, "We… we want our own dog. We saw the wiener dog, and we would like our own… we'd like you to breed us our own dog."
KS: Yeah, "Can you breed us something funny to laugh at? But just one, for here around the office, and shit like that." "I could help put the man into schpace…" "No you can't, just you keep making… you're the funny dog guy, everyone knows that."
SM: Yeah, "Don't think that you can do anything else."
KS: I like the fucking geneticist who's hawking it on the corner and shit. And he gets chased around, touting it around…
SM: "See ze puppies, see ze little puppies grow up. You, little boy, do you want…?"
KS: "Look at it, look at it, and laaaugh…"
SM: Trying to relive past glories.
KS: "Let it transport you to a time when dogs were schweet and funny. Look at him, he's a cartoon, no? He is to be laughed at and enjoyed, and loved! [growing tearful] Like the Führer… guten tag…" Um… but that dude couldn't find anybody to purchase his wares for a while. And then fucking like, one day somebody's like, "Hey man…" with enough distance…
SM: The Nazi stink came off of them.
KS: Dachshunds really did beat the Nazi stink. Like, the name Adolf didn't, you can't name your kid Adolf without people being like [gasps]. I mean, it's cursing your child, essentially. Somebody needs to be ballsy, have a kid, name it Adolf, and that kid fucking creates the cure for cancer, so we win the name back.
SM: That's a gamble.
KS: Yeah, it really is.
SM: Just like, "I mean, I put a lot on you…"
KS: "You have to cure cancer, 'cause I named you Adolf."
SM: "I know you wanna go into hotel management, but… you're really gonna have to…"
KS: "Look, I'm well aware that your IQ is not very high, I know you failed

even the standard tests…"

SM: "I know we're climbing a steep hill."

KS: "… and you identified red as black, and you called yellow 'banana', so clearly…"

SM: "I know I didn't make it easy on you by calling you what I called you."

KS: "I'm saying, as stupid as you are, you really need to pull this off for me, 'cause…"

SM: "… I don't wanna look stupid."

KS: "I mean, I named you Adolf for a reason, you're really not taking us there."

SM: "I might have to disown you."

KS: Yeah, "This is kinda embarrassing… Christ, if you're not gonna do anything special and I'm stuck with a kid named Adolf…"

SM: "Idiot, named Adolf?"

KS: "I mean, you were supposed to change things!"

SM: "You're like a miracle baby."

KS: "You were the one, Neo, but fucking god, you are dumber than a box of rocks, so…"

SM: "You were on the news! On KTLA! They did a little story!"

KS: "You remember? As a child, I sat you on KTLA and said, 'This child will cure cancer. Why? 'Cause his name is Adolf.' And people went [gasp], but I was like, 'No, we're taking it back,' and now, I realize that I might have been premature in my expectations."

SM: "You can't get a stockroom job at Target, man."

KS: "You're an embarrassment, you set me back… you were all I had going for me, you were my only shot."

SM: "You were my shot at greatness, and now…"

KS: But that's what a dachshund is, a dachshund is like… think about it. It was a dog identified with the Nazis, maybe not so much as German shepherds… but they fucking came back too!

SM: Yeah!

KS: Think about it, German shepherds *and* dachshunds…

SM: I mean, I don't remember them sending dachshunds into the Krakow ghetto…

Random SModquotes

"But if she asked me to fuck her on her deathbed, I'd say no, cause that's gross."

KS: Like, "We're invading the ghetto! Send in the dachshunds!" "Yap yap yapyapyap yap yaap! Yaap! Yaap!"
SM: "OK, wait a second."
KS: I would be like, "Look, maybe we should be alarmed, but I think we might be OK! They're sending in little dogs!"
SM: Um, yeah… I think the German shepherds were more used…
KS: Certainly more prominent, but dachshunds were like, Hitler's favorite dog, or he was photographed with dogs…
SM: 'Cause he thought they were fucking funny.
KS: Yeah, he's like, "Zis is hysterical. It looks like a cock-dog, right? Goebbels, isn't zat hysterical? Look at ze cock-dog!" "It's very funny, Führer." "Thanks." But anyway, those two breeds shook the stink of Nazi off them.
SM: They did.
KS: Think about it!
SM: They're dogs, though.
KS: The name Adolf hasn't, *Germany* hasn't... to this day, you know, people are still fucking sensitive about Germans…
SM: But nobody *blames* the dogs.
KS: … but oddly enough, a German shepherd and a dachshund, nobody goes like, "Fucking Nazi dog." You don't get persecuted for having one of these dogs.
SM: Because nobody looks at the dogs and goes like, "They made choices to be Nazis."
KS: Yeah, but I mean, it's *their* breed, it's their dog, it's the dog of fucking Germania.
SM: I think the history of German shepherds goes far beyond the reach of the Nazis…
KS: Then why call them German shepherds?
SM: … and I'm sure there were German shepherds in fucking America by that point.
KS: You think so?
SM: Yeah, they were all over the place.
KS: We're so stupid, we have Wikipedia at our fingertips, but you know what, it would just take too long…
SM: It's more fun to do it in complete ignorance.
KS: I'm saying German shepherds existed only in Germany and that's it, and

then they got out. A few good ones got out in the middle of fucking World War Two…

SM: World War Two, you thought that *that* was when they…?

KS: Yeah, there were a bunch of good German shepherds that were like, "We like Jews, we think people should live in peace," got on a boat and got to America, and that's why we have German shepherds here. They're the good ones.

SM: That's not my uh…

KS: Not your understanding?

SM: I mean, my vote's gonna be that it was probably a German breed originally, but I'm sure it moved all over the place.

KS: Yeah, I'm sure it moved all over… Oh, but you're saying pre-World War Two.

SM: Pre-World War Two. Yeah.

KS: It's a good thing they didn't rename it 'Nazi shepherd'.

SM: Yeah, exactly.

KS: And in Germany, do they call it a German shepherd, or do they call it…

SM: Shepherd.

KS: Just 'shepherd'?

SM: I mean, why wouldn't you?

KS: 'Cause we call American cheese 'American cheese'.

SM: I don't. Do you?

KS: Yeah, of course!

SM: What's American cheese?

KS: It's like, a Kraft single.

SM: Oh. That's a Kraft single.

KS: Well, I would never call it a Kraft single, it'd be like…

SM: I thought you were the fucking band-aid guy, what happened to you?

KS: Well, I'm buying it, I'm buying the named brand, I'm not saying "go buy a processed cheese food product," I'm saying "Go get some American cheese," but I just assume that people know I mean Kraft singles.

SM: See, I wouldn't know that.

KS: Really? I would never call it Kraft singles, though.

SM: But what you're asking for are like, cheese squares.

KS: But you can also get it at the deli, American cheese. It's its own brand. And what I'm saying is, I still call it American cheese. I think in Germany, they call German shepherds 'German shepherds'.

SM: I don't know…

KS: 'Deutsch…' what is it? 'Hund'. 'Deutschhund'.

SM: 'Deutschhund'?

KS: 'German' — 'Deutsch'; 'German' — 'Deutschland', Germany? So 'Deutsch' — 'German'… and 'shepherd', 'dog', 'hund', 'hound'. 'Hund'. Like 'dachshund' is…

SM: But they must have a word for 'shepherd'.

KS: Um… I'm gonna say no. Because I don't know it.

SM: You're officially voting that down?

KS: Yeah. In fact if they had one, it's now the word for 'dog'.

SM: You're just like, "'Shepherd' is a German word, it means 'shepherd.'"

KS: Yeah, I say it's 'Deutschhund'. And… still, I mean, you've gotta have a tremendous publicist to fucking shake the Nazi stink.

SM: I just don't think that, like… I feel that…

KS: I identify those two breeds with death and chaos, and fucking despotism, but still, I love 'em. I mean, I'm not a big German shepherd fan but I love this dachshund, love it. Even though I'm like, "It's kinda a Nazi dog."

SM: I don't know, it never occurs to me, this sort of Nazi connection.

KS: Really?

SM: No.

KS: But it's got like, such a German name. And whenever they depict a wiener dog in cartoons, if they have him speak and not just be there for fucking shits and giggles, to laugh at — which is disrespectful — they give him a fucking accent. He's always like, "Gott in Himmel!" Except in *Toy Story*, where he sounded like…

SM: Jim Varney.

KS: Yeah, Jim Varney. You know what, I don't even know how right I am about that whole German accent for dachshunds in cartoons. 'Cause now I think about it, I don't think I've ever heard a dachshund speak in a cartoon. They always show 'em like, there's a chase happening…

SM: … and they go around a corner…

KS: … and then one of them gets past and then, like a stop box comes up and he walks across and then this dude can't pursue his prey because this fucking dachshund's like, forty feet long.

SM: They're just an obstruction.

KS: Yeah, they're played for laughs. They're like the fat guy of the dog comedy world.

SM: Maybe that's why you felt bad…

KS: That's why I bond to it, I'm like, "I feel your pain. We're both jokes, you and I." She's like, "Speak for yourself, man!"

SM: "I'm fucking right on."

KS: "I'm brand-new to this world, I'm gonna do things!"

SM: "What's a Nazi? Why do you keep calling me a Nazi? I don't even know what that is."

From SModcast 64: Farewell and Adieu
Scott's shark tale

[Scott is talking about surfing in Kauai.]

SM: So we're in this position and guys with outrigger canoes will paddle out and take waves in. So this guy in an outrigger went by us on the far left and was heading towards shore, so he's between us and the beach. Then he goes, "Whoa!" He says something, like, "Shark!" or "Whoa!"

KS: Any of those things is bad.

SM: There wasn't really anyone else out there, but the guy I was with pointed, so between us and the beach and past the outrigger, maybe fifty or sixty yards away, there's a fin.

KS: Breaking the surface?

SM: Yes.

KS: Like, in a movie? How big is the fin?

SM: It was big. Big enough for me to be like, "Holy shit!"

KS: "How ironic. I'm the one that's going to die at a shark's mouth."

SM: I was like, "Whoa!" But I was more like, "Oh OK, there's a shark," but I didn't really amp up until I looked over at Massiah [Scott's surfing instructor] and he was like, "Get your hands out of the water."

KS: Oh my god. Did they give you a knife to carry at a point like that? Because I think they should equip you with a knife for that moment where they're like, "Oh, there's a shark." That way you could choose to take your own life rather than be killed by the shark. Because if someone was like, "Whoa!" and I looked over and saw a fin I'd be like, "Well, Massiah, it's been great," and then I'd cut my own damned throat.

SM: Like, "What are you doing?"

KS: "We've got to save ourselves from the shark."

SM: "We're going to report the weirdest shark attack ever. A man slit his throat…"

KS: "This dude attacked himself and then the shark ate what was left. It was crazy."

SM: "He fed himself to the sharks."

KS: "He was so terrified of the sharks that he cut his own throat, rolled off the fucking board into the drink, many sharks came…"

SM: "Due to all the blood."

KS: "I escaped barely and it was the strangest thing I've ever seen."

SM: "That man was Kevin Smith."

KS: "Yeah, that guy! Did you ever see *Clerks*? It was crazy, he had a lot to live for."

SM: "I kept a piece of him."

KS: "I've got the inside of his thigh chub that floated to the surface and I threw it on my board to bring it back with me."

SM: So we see it and he's like, "Keep your hands out of the water."

KS: [Shudders] Right then and there I would have just died from a heart attack, fright, anything. Just hearing those words.

SM: I wasn't thinking at that point about the SModcast. When I got to the beach, I thought about it. So I look at him, he goes, "Get your hands out of the water, and just look for it." Because it was moving around and then it kinda went under. He doesn't look comfortable.

KS: If he was like, "It's a fucking shark, don't sweat it man."

SM: Like, "It's Kauai. Aloha…"

KS: "It's a hammerhead or a basking, the fucking pussies of sharks. You could beat this shark up." But he wasn't like that, he was like, "Get your fucking hands out of the water!"

SM: I was taking precautions and he was doing the same thing so I was definitely, "This is not necessarily the best situation to be in."

KS: I would be crying right now. I'd be like, "I'm sorry Massiah, I'm sorry but I'm so scared." I'd literally be in tears.

SM: He was fifteen feet away from me, so we were not right next to each other.

KS: Oh my god. So you're literally going to die alone. It's not even like the shark attacks your board and you can grab on to Massiah.

SM: "Just one hug before I die!"

KS: "If I'm going to die you're dying too Massiah!"

SM: The other thing that happened to me was that I feel like the guy in the outrigger is doubling back.

KS: He's like, "I'm going to watch a shark eat this fucking newbie."

SM: He had his fucking cell phone out and was going to YouTube it. "I'm going to put this on ChewTube!"

SM: Then the fin comes back up out of the water and it's headed kinda towards him, my instructor.

KS: At which point I'm like, I feel bad for the instructor but happy that he's going towards that dude.

SM: It's going out towards the ocean and it's kinda heading towards him. He's like, "Holy shit, it's coming right at me."

KS: OK, when your surf instructor says that out loud, at this point you're like, "I regret all of this. I never should have come out here."

SM: In the moment it was freaky but I don't know if it's survival instinct or something, where I was like, "I have to stay calm because freaking out is not going to do anything..."

KS: You are far more level-headed than me, sir. I would be like, "Now is the time on Sprockets when we panic. Now we give it all up, now we show who we really are. To this one dude."

SM: It was definitely headed towards him. He wasn't, "Oh my god, it's headed towards me," he was calmly observing the fact that it was headed in his direction.

KS: Like Spock? Like [calmly], "Wow, the shark is coming."

SM: No. It was like, "Whoa, this is happening." The shark is heading towards him, goes under and ultimately passes by him on his left.

KS: Now, when you see the fin do you see the tail-piece as well?

SM: I only ever saw the fin. I never really got a clear look at it. I only ever saw the fin.

KS: So it could have been like the two kids in *Jaws* who were like, "He made me do it!"...

SM: It definitely wasn't that. Because he saw it. So he is on his board. It passes by him off towards the left, farther away from me. It's weird because I remember looking around in the water and thinking, "Wow, if this thing swims right up to me that's going to be fucking weird."

KS: You were like Michael in *Jaws*, remember when he was out in the pond and he fucking freezes and the shark goes by him and the dude is like, "You guys need help over there?" and all that's left of him is a fucking leg. You see the leg hit the bottom. Did you freeze or no?

SM: No, I was watching what was going on and trying to be observant and it was definitely suddenly your balance was going, "Whoa, this is pretty precarious, this is not the way you're supposed to sit on a board."

KS: At that point you're like, "Wow, this is bad."

SM: It ultimately passed us by. At that point Massiah just said he saw it and he thought it was a ten-foot tiger.

KS: Jesus! Man-eater.

SM: Yeah. So what happens is that the shark is either underwater…

KS: [Genuine fear] I'm ready to wet myself and I wasn't even there. I'm sitting in the safety of my fucking dining room.

SM: So you can't see the fin any more. Supposedly, based on its trajectory, it's headed back out into the deep water.

KS: Because they never turn around?!

SM: Yeah. Well, because I haven't had my hands in the water I'm drifting inland, into the middle of the bay, into the deep water. The coral is to my left and I'm off the coral plain. I'm over the deep water.

KS: You are the fucking broad on the *Jaws* poster, this motherfucker could be straight up at you like on the poster.

SM: Massiah is like, [calmly] "Dude, get out of the deep water."

KS: Oh my god! Did he say it just like that or was it a little bit more urgent?

SM: It was more just like, "Yeah, you probably want to get out of the deep water." So I'm like, "Well you told me not to put my hands in the water!" and he's like, "Just start paddling with your right hand."

KS: He's like, "You're going to die if you don't do what I tell you to do." You're like, "I did what you told me to do, Massiah!"

SM: Messiah. It's me surfing with the messiah.

KS: "I knew I shouldn't have surfed with you Christ! Do something about it!" And he's like, "Well, I can multiply loaves of bread?"

SM: "Turn the fucking water to wine!"

KS: "Yeah, yeah. Kill the shark! Make him a bunch of little fish instead, do something magical."

SM: "Turn him into a porpoise!"

KS: "If I get killed, raise me from the dead Jesus."

SM: "I'll be fine, I'll paddle...

KS: "I won't tell nobody."

SM: So I start paddling. He says, "Paddle with your right arm," so I'm paddling with my right arm. I'm not getting anywhere so he's like, "Let's lay back on the boards and paddle in." So we lay back down and he's, "Don't put your hands all the way in the water." When you're paddling you're lying on your stomach...

KS: And you're doggy paddling, you're swimming. He's looking for more of a doggy paddle.

SM: He's like, "Use more of your wrist and paddle in."

KS: This is going to take like an hour to get back to shore.

SM: The bummer is that it's completely flat, there's no waves. Otherwise if the waves were there we could just have paddled and then the waves would have picked us up and we'd probably make better progress.

KS: The whole time you're doing this, for all you know, there's a shark just hovering under you?

SM: Once you get over the coral, no. Because you can see the bottom.

KS: How long does it take you to get to the coral?

SM: It didn't take me that long to get back to it. I was like five or ten feet away from it. I was just kinda drifting. So I paddled into the coral then started heading back to the beach.

KS: And dove in head first?

SM: Slashed my throat on the coral?

KS: "You'll never get me!"

SM: So we paddled back in and I don't know how far we were from the beach when he was like, "We're fine." But paddling back in, it was running through my head that, "OK, nobody said to me, now that we're paddling we're fine, so now we're paddling back in to get the fuck out of the water there is that underlying sense that something still might happen." So we get all the way to the shore, news has traveled back to the beach that there was a shark sighting, so we've got the boards on our heads and we're walking back, we're getting to the parking lot and I see Alex. She is terrified, she watched the shark and she is terrified that I'm doing this at all and did not want me to be out there. In my head I'm going, "I don't want her to freak out if I say it."

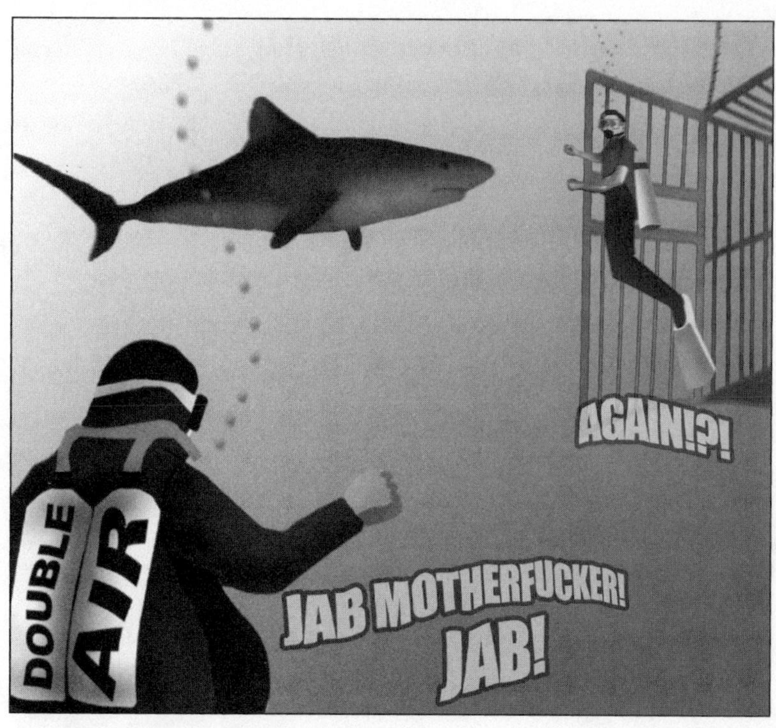

KS: You and I are so different. I'd be screaming it from the middle of the ocean, "Jen there's fucking Jaws out here! Come get me! Swim out here and distract the shark so I can make it to land!"

SM: So then as we're walking up, I'm walking next to Massiah, and a guy in a truck was like, "What was it? What did you see?" Massiah was like, "It was a ten-foot tiger." I can't hide it now, Alex is in the midst of all this stuff. My favorite part of the whole story is we're walking back to the showers and there's the guy who's told it was a ten-foot Tiger, and he's like, "Well, you don't have to worry about being faster than a shark, you've just got to be faster than your buddy."

KS: Get out of here! Really?

SM: Yeah.

KS: So it's mercenary on the high seas?

SM: The guy told it as a joke but I was like, "I'm the buddy."

KS: You were like, "You were faster than me."

SM: "You would have been faster than me."

KS: "Would you have let me die Messiah?" He's like, "If you keep calling me that yeah I'm going to let you fucking die, that's irritating." That is so fucking horrible on so many levels. So at that point you've reached land and you're like, "I'm never doing that again," or are you, "Right on, I survived a shark attack, kinda"?
SM: I would have gone out the next day, I was going to but the surf was too low.
KS: You deserve to get eaten by a fucking shark! You've been in the ocean many times in your life. When you enter into the ocean you enter into the food chain, presumably. You've been in a cage with sharks but you've never entered the water knowing that you were part of the food chain.
SM: When you go to a shark cage you are going to see sharks. I didn't go surfing to go, "Hey man, I want to spot a shark!" As soon as I got out of the water I was like, I've got a firsthand story of something that will horrify you to your core.
KS: I don't know what horrifies me more. All of that is terrifying. There's not one part of that story where I'm like, "Wow, that sounds fun!" It just all sounds terrifying. Then I get angry. Because you're like, "Yeah, I'd do it again…" I'm like, "*Why?!* You looked death in the fin!"

From SModcast 64: Farewell and Adieu
The brain transplant

[Kevin is talking about the questions he'd been asked at a recent Q&A event.]
KS: This was hands down the weirdest, most out-there question of the night.
SM: Of the night?
KS: Maybe of all time. Hands down. I'm going to give them the tops.
SM: The most fucked up question that has ever been asked!
KS: OK, here we go. But I'm going to pose it to you, not as it was posed to me. But you'll see how easy it is… Just change one name. Alex, your wife, gets into a horrendous car accident where she is completely trashed and mutilated. They save her brain. They put her brain into the body of an eight-year-old girl.
SM: OK.
KS: So I'm like, "I don't like where this is going." Then the dude goes, "And

I pose it to you, do you fuck her, the eight-year-old version of your wife?" Or not even the eight-year-old version of your wife, the eight-year-old body with your wife's brain in it.

SM: No way!

KS: Right! It's just like insane pedophilia.

SM: It's like a multi-choice question. It's like first, in my imaginary question, I'm going to kill your wife.

KS: I'm going to demolish your wife.

SM: Then I'm going to take her from her car accident, in an ambulance, to a fucking hospital, where they are going to remove her brain without your permission.

KS: Squeeze it into the cranium of an eight-year-old.

SM: Who obviously unwillingly…

KS: Well, maybe she died moments before. Let's skip beyond all of that. They've sat you down and been like, "Look, it was bad. She died."

SM: "I got drunk. I did this weird thing."

KS: No, it was a car accident.

SM: "The only body that was available was an eight-year-old girl."

KS: Yes.

SM: "Your wife is alive. She has cognitive…"

KS: "She doesn't look like your wife. She looks like an eight-year-old girl. But if you have a conversation with her she has all your wife's memories."

SM: "The pair of you getting married."

KS: "For all intents and purposes, if she doesn't look in a mirror, she is Alex. But really, she is Katy."

SM: The first thing that popped into my head was, what do the parents of this little girl think?

KS: The parents of the little girl were like, "She died some kinda brain death on the table or something like that. Well, if it can help someone else…" They signed her over to fucking medical science. So they are like that.

SM: So they are in the room going, "Hi."

KS: "Hey, you have our daughter now." And you're like, "Excuse me?"

SM: "Why did you do this? Didn't it occur to you to just bury her?"

KS: "We think you guys should get re-married and we want to be at the ceremony."

SM: "Can we go? Can we give her away?"

KS: "We'll pay for the wedding because it's traditional for the parents of the daughter to pay for the wedding." And you're like, "Are they talking to me?" So they explain to you, and after a weird period of adjustment you take Alex home.
SM: It's all happened, everybody is fine with it.
KS: Yes, the only one who is left to be fine with it is you.
SM: It's just like, "Welcome to the family."
KS: She talks to you. She's like, "I know this is a little weird but this is me, it's Alex. I love you. I remember the time you went surfing, I was so scared for you."
SM: "I'm still, 'Don't go in the water.'"
KS: "That doesn't change just because I'm now an eight-year-old. I still believe you shouldn't go in the water. As you can see life is precious, because I died but I'm alive because of this eight-year-old's body."
SM: "Well, so…"
KS: And you have to take her home because she's your wife.
SM: I don't want to deal with that.
KS: First you have the initial reaction of, "This is too fucked up for me to deal with, I've got to go think about it." She's like, "No you won't Scott. We're married!"
SM: That would be her reaction. My reaction would be, if it was Alex and she was literally, after the thirty minutes of, "What did we do on our honeymoon?"...
KS: You quiz her and she's got it all. She can describe your asshole in detail. You're like, "That must be my wife." You're like, "I never showed you my asshole."
SM: "You're not my wife!"
KS: She's like, "No no no. I looked when you were sleeping. And here are pictures to prove it." And there are pictures of you sleeping and she's pulling your cheeks open and taking pictures of your asshole. There's one where she gets her face right close to it. You're like, "Wow, I had no idea that Alex was so creepy."
SM: Either that or she took them for an eight-year-old girl and sent them to her.
KS: This may be the biggest ruse ever played.
SM: So I get through the process of being like, "OK, I believe everybody." Is

this out in public? Am I on *Extra* and shit?

KS: Do you not want it to be? What makes it easier for you?

SM: It doesn't necessarily make it easier because you're still faced with the same problem…

KS: Nobody knows.

SM: The guy's question is, literally, does she say "I'm your wife" and then I fuck her? Which to me is no way.

KS: It's not that quick. We're leading up to it. First you've got to accept her in your life as, "This is my wife now."

SM: OK, so I do that, but my problem with the public is how do you deal with public scrutiny?

KS: The public don't have to know. Just your friends will know.

SM: It'd come out. Who doesn't sit there and go…

KS: "It's top secret, government experiment. It's never going to come out. And if it does get out, we'll kill people."

SM: What do you want me to do? How do you want me to proceed forward?

KS: They're like, "Be married, be as you were."

SM: But how do I go out in public with an eight-year-old girl?

KS: Say she's your daughter. OK, they say, "Mosier, let's be honest, don't go out in public with this girl. Ninety-nine percent of people won't say or look at you any differently as long as you're not jamming your tongue down her throat."

SM: What about school?

KS: She goes to school. She does it all over again. I was like right on, I want to fucking bone up on geography.

SM: "I could fucking ace this shit."

KS: She's like, "Hey, they just jumped me ahead like five grades! It's amazing!"

SM: "It's weird. Your head is abnormally big. You're a fucking brainiac."

KS: "That'll fucking change." But it's your wife. She talks to you like she's your wife. Shared memories, little jokes, she's cooking.

SM: Cooking? On a stool?

KS: She has a little foot-ladder to get to the stove. But you guys are together for about a month and finally you're like, "It's weird but whatever." Then she's just like, "Fuck me stupid."

SM: I'm like, "No."

KS: You couldn't do it. There is no way! Under no conditions in this lifetime or any other do I fuck somebody who is eight years old, nine, ten, eleven, twelve.
SM: Everything up until that point you're being challenged mentally.
KS: You have to re-adjust.
SM: You have to re-adjust to everything, change your mental perception. "This is Alex," OK I can do that stuff. At that moment you're saying it becomes completely physical.
KS: Yes, and she wants it to become physical. Because it's Alex's brain inside this eight-year-old's body.
SM: But the idea is that I'm supposed to lust after an eight-year-old girl and I'm like, "No fucking way."
KS: But she's like, "Just close your eyes. I'll talk so dirty to you."
SM: I'm like, "No fucking way."
KS: She's like, "How about just eat me out? How about just pull your cock out and I'll diddle myself looking at your dick?"
SM: No!
KS: Nothing?
SM: No. It would be way too fucked up! It would be too fucked up.
KS: A more fucked up P.S. to the story was that the dude had kids. I was like, "Dude, you realize you're standing up here championing pedophilia?" And he's, "But it's your wife!" But I'm, "It's stopped being your wife from the moment it's an eight-year-old, dude." Even if I could go back in time I wouldn't fuck an eight-year-old version of my wife. Let alone some strange little eight-year-old with my wife's brain.
SM: If you brought an eight-year-old in here right now, which we're not going to do, physically I'm not into it at all.
KS: Nah, an eight-year-old is an eight-year-old.
SM: No fucking way.
KS: I thought that was such a bizarre fucking question.
SM: And the audience?
KS: The audience thought it was hysterical but they also found it kinda 'eurgh!' It definitely pushed the edge of the envelope, that's for damn sure. But it was a fascinating question, which I only thought more of the further I got from the Q&A. I'm on a plane flying to Austin and I'm like, "Wow man, that was fucked up."

SM: That is a fucked up question.

KS: I stopped then and there in the moment and was like, "I would never fuck an eight-year-old, never fuck a child." Then as I'm flying I'm going, "Oh, it's my wife though and she's telling me that she wants me to fuck her. But she's still in the body of an eight-year-old. Which would go against everything that my wife ever stood for in life."

SM: But then the question becomes, you're committed to it.

KS: I'm telling my wife, "Look, we have to wait."

SM: How long, how long do you wait?

KS: Well, if there's grass on the field play ball — maybe. She's like, "What!? You say that?"

SM: It's pussy hair.

KS: "Yeah, if you've got hair on the puss then we can talk about it. But not right now. For the next five years let's just be father daughter or something like that. We'll hang out and chit-chat, but I'm sorry I can't do this."

SM: Even at sixteen there's that element of…

KS: She's, "Why don't I just give you a blow job Scott?"

SM: No fucking way.

KS: "Look at yourself, you're an eight-year-old girl. A strange eight-year-old girl."

SM: "Go do your homework!"

KS: Oh, it's horrible dude. What if at that point they come to her and say, "Are you getting sad?"

SM: "Yeah, I don't know how to read and I'm getting lost."

KS: "What does it say on it, how many numbers?" If they came to you though and said, "We can do this. Your wife is either dead or we can put her brain into the body of an eight-year-old. Would you be OK with that?" They're not even introducing the questions of, "And you will of course be expected to fuck her."

SM: They are not going, "As soon as the surgery is over…"

KS: "You're going to use the Vaseline and get in there." But they're giving you the option, you can save her life or you can let her die. She's a brain in a jar at this point.

SM: She's not alive.

KS: Just a brain, the body is gone.

SM: I love my wife but that to me is just…

KS: What if they were like, "The brain is screaming! The brain wants to live!"
SM: Can I hear it?
KS: Yes. They bring you over and hook up an attachment and it's going, "Help me!"
SM: Is the guy a ventriloquist?
KS: No, it's clearly Alex. "It's me Alex Mosier, help me Scott! Put me in another body!"
SM: Well, why wouldn't I do it then? I just assume that if I ask her the question when I go home after this, "If you get into a horrible car accident…" which my wife hates when you bring up any kind of make-believe scenario that's…
KS: Death involved?
SM: Yeah. Or god forbid if you're like, "What if we got divorced?" She's like, "No, take it back. Say it doesn't happen." Our little scenarios don't really happen in our house.
KS: I've got one of those too. I can't fuck around with my wife. "Imagine if…" She's just like, "Stop it right there. Save it for your little fucking gay show." She doesn't say that, but she doesn't play like that.
SM: My wife would do it if it is something not involved with people being injured.
KS: Wait, we'll leave Alex out of it, *I* get injured in a car accident and they come to you.
SM: They're going to put your brain in the body of a little girl? Oh yes! I'm like, "Yes, absolutely!"
KS: "A thousand times yes!"
SM: I'm like, "That sounds like the best idea ever."
KS: Do I go about my life?
SM: Fuck yes!
KS: Do I direct?
SM: You'd be back out on the stage immediately. That would be fucking magic!
KS: I'd be like, "Do I have a story for you people!"
SM: Ever see an eight-year-old girl say, "Cunt!"
KS: "How about this: cocksucker! How about fucktard! How about, wait, there's this one story about how I was fucking my wife…" People are like, "This is *insane*."

SM: Oh my god, it would be amazing!
KS: I'd be more famous than Dakota Fanning as a little child.
SM: You'd be more famous than anybody.
KS: I might be the most famous person on the planet.
SM: You'd become more famous than anybody, the most famous person on the planet.
KS: They would be, "Through the years of human existence…"
SM: Think of the DVD sales, "Let's go back, I haven't heard of him."
KS: "…there have been great minds, huge personalities, Abraham Lincoln, George Washington…"
SM: Seabiscuit.
KS: "Seabiscuit the horse. Mahatma Ghandi. Jesus Christ. Now Kevin Smith, the eight-year-old girl, who we all knew from his movies, who after a tragic accident his brain was implanted in an eight-year-old girl." I would make *Time* Man of the Year, hands down.
SM: Man of the Year, and it's a picture of a little girl.
KS: Totally, people are like, "I don't get it," and then they open it up. Then they're like, "This is fucked up!"
SM: And if it happened today you would almost be Harley's age. You would be younger?
KS: Totally, I'd be younger if I was an eight-year-old girl, as Harley is nine. She wouldn't like that though. She doesn't want any siblings. She's always like, "Don't have any kids." She doesn't want a brother or sister.
SM: Wow. So that would be a problem.
KS: She would probably try and kill me in my sleep.

From SModcast 65: Captain Kev and Mister Scott
Harley turns to Satan

KS: If my kid comes to me and she's like, "I'm hanging out with Goths and Satanists," I'm like, "OK, look. Hang out with the Goths, don't hang out with the fucking Satanists. They just believe different things than we do. At least *these* Satanists."
SM: See, those are the kinda Satanists where as a parent you have to be like, "Well, how am I supposed to be like, 'Oh, they're good Satanists'? You can

go to jail. They do things that are illegal, and therefore you're going to go to jail."
KS: Yes and No. Anton LaVey, who established the Church of Satan and wrote *The Satanic Bible* — remember, he had fucking Sammy Davis Jr in the Church of Satan at one point? Sammy Davis Jr isn't joining anything if anybody's getting killed.
SM: My point is that if Harley came to you and says that…
KS: I start investigating Satanism in a big, bad way. I start reading everything I can on it.
SM: But would you be comfortable if she's like, "Do you want to meet my Satan-father?"
KS: She has a Satan-father? "How long have you been hanging out with these people?"
SM: "A couple of months."
KS: "And you've adopted one of them as your dad?"
SM: "That's what happens — you get a Satan-father. And a mother. I'm young, I'm a Satan child."
KS: "Is it like having a godfather but different?"
SM: "Yes."
KS: "Are they looking out for your interests or their own interests?"
SM: "They look after me."
KS: "That's not what I asked, Harley. I asked—" [Laughs.] At this point, I'm like, "Get in your fucking room! You idiot! Dummy! Oh my god, I can't believe I raised such a fucking little retard. Get in the room! Jen!"
SM: She's just staring at you.
KS: Yeah, she's just, "You don't want to make me go to my room, father."
SM: "Do you want to meet Satan, father?"
KS: "My Satan-father will rescue me and you will die!" Like, "What? I just said go to your room! Look, it's cool. You wanna hang out in the living room, it's fine."
SM: "It's alright. You want some money?"
KS: Yeah. "Here's some bucks, go have a good time with your devil buddies." [Laughs.] I would, dude — I'd get so scared. I would not fuck around with that, man. I'd go to Jen and be like, "We have to move. Without the kid. We have to leave the kid in this house. Abandon everything. She's on a path now, and I don't want to be near that path. We've got to save ourselves, because I

predict our deaths at her hands. We've got to leave her." "She's thirteen!" "I don't care. The house is — they can turn it into a fucking devil synagogue for all I care. Just bring the TV."

SM: That would be weird.

KS: That would be a nightmare, sir. But Anton LaVey — those cats weren't Satan worshippers. They didn't believe in God, and they were like, all the power is within you. That church was about self-fulfillment, self-actualization, in a weird way. I'm not saying I'm all for it, but Anton LaVey wasn't like, "Let's hold a fucking sacrificial orgy where someone will get killed."

SM: But if she came to you and was able to say, "No, no, no, no..."

KS: "Everything you know about Satan is wrong, *Dad*!"

SM: "Yeah, *Dad*, once again your head's in your ass!"

KS: I'm like, "Alright, I know a thing about a thing or two, I have access to the Internet!" And she's like, "This isn't the kinda shit you find on the

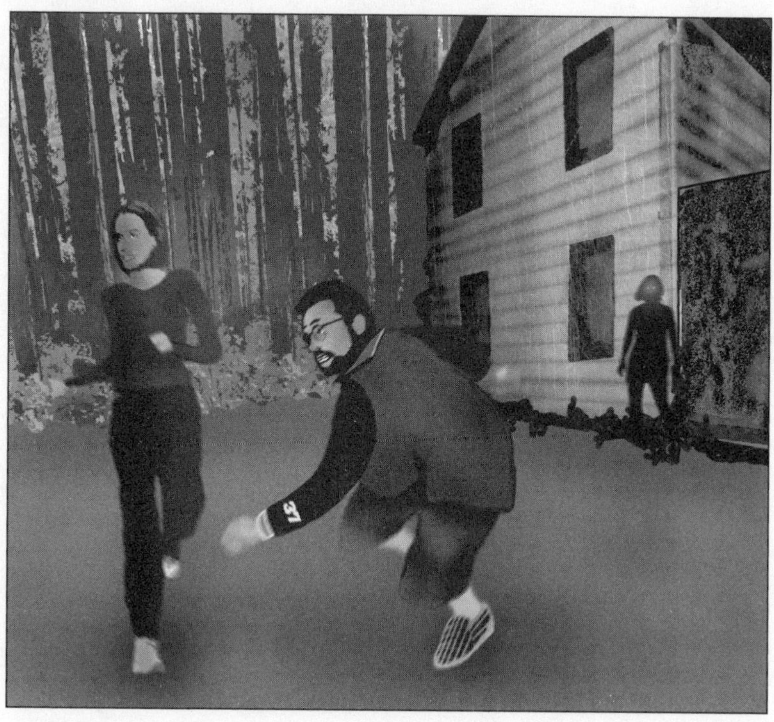

Internet *Dad*! This is real!"
SM: "It's real life! You've got to go out and find it!"
KS: "We killed a drifter," and I say, "What?!" And she's like, "And then I found a twenty dollar bill. Satan pays!" "Man, I'll just *give* you twenty dollars. Stop killing people!"

From SModcast 66: Sleipnir the Conqueror
Origins of Santa Claus and Satan Claus

KS: South Pole? Antarctica is what, top of the world or bottom of the world?
SM: I thought Antarctica is the bottom.
KS: What's the top? Don't you feel stupid at moments like this? Where you're like, "I've been around for thirty-eight fucking years and it's only now occurred to me to ask, 'What's the top of the world?'"
SM: I know that… it's the North Pole. There's the Antarctic and Arctic Sea, but I don't think it's called the Arctic. Now you've got to look it up. Just look at a globe.
KS: I don't have one here.
SM: You've got the Internet. Type in 'globe', 'map of world'.
KS: "Antarctic is the world's southernmost continent," you were right, "overlying the South Pole. It is situated in the southern hemisphere almost entirely south of the Antarctic circle." But it doesn't tell you, "Its opposite, the Joker to its Batman, is…"
SM: I think it says nemesis!
KS: "These two hate each other."
SM: "These two giant ice formations will fight each other in the future." There's the North Pole. It might be called the Arctic.
KS: I'm putting up North Pole.
SM: There's the Arctic Sea. Maybe Antarctic is the opposite of the Arctic?
KS: Hey man, "While the South Pole lies on a continental land mass, the North Pole is located in the middle of the Arctic Ocean, amidst waters that are almost permanently covered with constantly shifting sea-ice. This makes it impossible to construct a permanent station at the North Pole, unlike the South Pole." Wow, that is fascinating. Fuck SModcast, let's just read Wikipedia out loud for the next hour. You mean to tell me though that all

this time that we've been telling kids that Santa lives at the North Pole and all they would have to do is go on the Internet and see "Nothing can live at the North Pole because there's constantly shifting sea-ice..."?

SM: "Santa can't live on a shifting land mass," I mean, he is a magical creature.

KS: Who is?

SM: If you believe in Santa Claus and some kid goes, "There's shifting land masses," I'd be like, "Of course he lives on a shifting land mass, he's fucking Santa Claus."

KS: But at the same time that has never been included in any of the songs, the TV specials. You never heard [sings] "And Santa on his shifting land mass putting together toys for all the girls and boys." There is nothing included in the lore.

SM: That is true.

KS: I've never seen a Rankin/Bass special where the little puppets are like, "Whoa! We're moving again everybody, because as you all know..."

SM: "Everybody buckle up!"

KS: "... the North Pole is a constantly shifting land mass." That would be more credible. If I was a kid and I saw that I'd be like, "Wow, it must be true! Why would they include that in the story if not?"

SM: Why not just make it at the South Pole?

KS: Because nothing good comes from the south, everyone knows that. Santa the racist and stuff, or Santa's just like, "Oh, I've got toys for girls and boys but, you know, are they white?"

SM: "I've got two lists!"

KS: I don't know why they went for the North Pole.

SM: Well, it's northern.

KS: Maybe that's why. When they created Santa, had those dudes raced to the poles yet? Who were the dudes that raced to the poles? Cook and Perry? Is that them? Should I look it up? That's the problem with a little bit of education. Wikipedia is, "There is nothing for Cook and Perry."

SM: I think that the mythology, the folklore surrounding Santa Claus or St Nicolas, would pre-date people going to the North Pole.

KS: But I bet you the North Pole thing came way later. The whole notion of Father Christmas and shit, they never gave him a place to live. Until some fucking kid was like, "Where does he live?" And they're like, "Fuck! Where

will the kid never go? The North Pole!"
SM: I would argue that if you were creating that mythology wouldn't you be like, "No one is ever going to go there, we'll never get there."
KS: At that point? I guess.
SM: "Just say North Pole."
KS: You might as well say, "Santa lives on the Moon."
SM: Who are Cook and Perry? The least famous...
KS: Was that not their names? No dude, I'm right. OK, I entered 'race for the poles'. I got an IMDB hit, I saw a name.
SM: Matthew Perry?
KS: Fredrick Albert Cook. Let's look up this motherfucker. It says Fredrick Albert Cook was an American explorer and physician noted for his claim for having reached the North Pole in April 1908, a year before Robert Peary. It's Peary not Perry, I was right! But I entered Cook and Perry.
SM: You should say, "First man at North Pole."
KS: He was the first guy to get to the North Pole. There were these two dudes, I don't know the full story but I imagine it goes something like this, two dudes in a bar bet, "I'm going to get to the fucking North Pole" and Peary is like, "The fuck you are." Then it happened.
SM: Then they went out after it. But 1908. There was Santa Claus before 1908.
KS: There would have to be, let's look up Santa Claus.
SM: But I would argue that the North Pole was maybe thrown out there as, "No one will ever go out there," or "Who the fuck wants to go there?"
KS: "One legend associated with Santa says that he lives in the far north in a land of perpetual snow. The American version of Santa Claus lives at the North Pole. While Father Christmas is said to reside in Lapland." Lapland? Santa lives in a fucking strip club? He's like, "I enjoy free buffet and fake grinding sex." "Other details include, he is married, lives with Mrs Claus, he makes a list of children throughout the world..." all the shit we know.
SM: Where's Lapland? Norway?
KS: I don't know but I'm going to click on it. "Lapland province is in Finland. Or Lapland, Sweden. The name is not in official use." Maybe they had to change it because they were like, maybe for the Brits it was Lapland, Sweden, and so many people were like, "I can go to Lapland, Sweden!" Finally Sweden was like, "We're changing the fucking name because we're

tired of this tourism, we don't want your money." I want to see if they come up with when they decided it was the North Pole. Who created that?
SM: They say it was American. Maybe it was Cook?
KS: You think so? "I've been there!"
SM: "I was there! And there was this dude making toys."
KS: And nobody was interested, "Who gives a fuck! You're wasting time…"
SM: "It's ice, it's a shifting land mass!"
KS: "Yeah, everyone knows it's just on bed of shifting sea-ice." Then he was, "Fuck, I'm losing them."
SM: "I should have gone south!"
KS: "You know who I saw there? Santa Claus!" They're like, "What!? Really?" People got interested again so he's like, "Yeah, yeah, Santa Claus was up there. It was amazing."
SM: "He's got a really nice house."
KS: "He's got a wife and he's got help and he makes toys and he keeps a list," maybe this dude came up with it. "Influence of Germanic paganism and folklore. Santa taking lives. Numerous parallels have been drawn between Santa Claus and the figure of Odin, a major god to the Germanic peoples prior to the Christianization. Since many of these elements are unrelated to Christianity there are theories regarding the pagan origins of various customs of the holiday stemming from areas with a Germanic people Christianized but retaining elements of their indigenous traditions surviving in various forms into modern depictions of Santa Claus. Odin was sometimes recorded at the native Germanic holiday of Yule as leading a great hunting party through the sky." This sounds so stupid. "Two books from Iceland, the Poetic Edda compiled in the thirteenth century from earlier sources and the Prose Edda written in the thirteenth century by Snorri Sturluson" — what a great name! "What's up Snorri?" — "... described Odin as riding an eight-legged horse named Sleipnir, that could leap great distances, giving rising to the comparisons to Santa's reindeer. Further, Odin was referred to by many in Skaldic poetry, some of which describe his appearance or functions, these include…" — a bunch of words I can't fucking say, but they mean long-beard, or Yule-figure — "… according to Phyllis Siefker, children would place their boots filled with" — this is so weird — "carrots, straw or sugar near the chimney for Odin's flying horse Sleipnir to eat. Odin would then reward those children for their kindness by

replacing Sleipnir's food with gifts or candy. This practice survives in Germany, Norway and the Netherlands after the adoption of Christianity and became associated with St Nicolas as a result of the process of Christianization and can still be seen in the modern practice of hanging stockings at the chimney in some new homes." Wow.

SM: I didn't know that about stockings.

KS: That is amazing man, how shit changes. In Dutch he's called Sinter Claus.

SM: Wow, that sounds dirty.

KS: Doesn't it.

SM: "I am Sinner Claus!"

KS: "Sinner Claus wants to see your wee-wee and then I'll give you a toy!" In Dutch-lands Santa is a frightening figure who scars children for life.

SM: "He's a pedophile."

KS: "Originating from pre-Christian Alpine traditions and influenced by later Christianization, the Krampus is represented as a companion of St Nicolas. Traditionally young men dress up as the Krampus in the first two weeks of December, particularly on the evening of December 5th and roam the streets frightening children with rusty chains and belts."

SM: Awesome! That all sounds way more interesting.

KS: Now it's become sanitized.

SM: Commercialized.

KS: Cleaned up and stuff.

SM: He loves you but, in a world of the current climate of the United States of America why aren't more Christians, based on that information, *not* allowing their kids to believe in Santa Claus at all?

KS: What do you mean?

SM: Based on the fact that its origins are a…

KS: Christian nature? Oh you mean Christian kids?

SM: ... the origins of Santa Claus are Odin, a Norse god.

KS: But it's well documented, all the Christians did was co-opt the pagan holidays. Easter, we say that it's when Christ comes back from the dead, represents the spring solstice, it existed long before, where people get together all naked and dance and pray for good crops and then fuck each other.

SM: Sure but my point is that the Santa Claus thing, you're laying that on top of Jesus' birthday.

KS: Yeah, well I could never quite get the combination between the two but it has to do with St Nicolas. They took their St Nicolas story and it became Santa Claus.

SM: Got weaved in with the boot of Odin with the carrots and the straw.

KS: That's so weird. Can you imagine? We're like, "Kids, get your boots out, put some carrots in them because Sleipnir is coming." I'd be like, "Holy shit, do we have a gun? If Sleipnir comes in this house let's kill it!"

SM: "He has a mutant horse with eight legs!"

KS: But they're like, "Yeah, but if you try to kill Sleipnir, well, Odin One-Eye will come after you!" I'm like, "He's got one eye!"

SM: "I'm going to slap you fuck!"

KS: I'd just hide to the left. "In British colonies of North America and later the United States, British and Dutch versions of the gift-giver merged further. For example, in Washington Irving's *History of New York*, 1809, Sinter Claus was Americanized into Santa Claus, but lost his bishop's apparel," he used to be dressed as a bishop, "and was at first pictured as a thick-bellied Dutch sailor with a pipe and a green winter coat." So Sinter Claus became Santa Claus, who was like Pop-Eye looking for pussy.

SM: A sailor on shore leave!

KS: "I'll give you a toy if you give me some pussy!" "Irving's book was a lampoon of the Dutch culture of New York and much of this portrait is his joking invention. Modern ideas of Santa Claus seemingly became canon after the publication of the poem *A Visit from St Nicolas*, better known today as *The Night Before Christmas* in the Troy, New York, *Sentinel* on December 23rd 1823, anonymously." Somebody just wrote it and put it in there, never took credit for it. "The poem was later attributed to Clement Clarke Moore" — I've never heard that, did you ever know that the author of *The Night Before Christmas* was Clement Clarke Moore?

SM: No.

KS: Never heard of that before. "In this poem, Santa is established as a heavy-set man with eight reindeer who are named for the first time" — that's where all the names came from — "one of the first artists to define Santa Claus's modern image was Thomas Nast, American cartoonist in the 19th century. In 1863 a picture of Santa illustrated by Nast appeared in *Harper's Weekly*." This is so strange. They just made it up! There is no truth to this whatsoever. They made this shit up! You get older and somebody is like, "There's no Santa" and you're like, "Oh alright, I get it," but if you trace the origin it makes you feel even more stupid. I can't believe I ever believed any of this. I can't believe this caught on. If someone wrote an article in the paper it would be like we built an annual holiday around the fucking *Family Circus*, where it's like 'I don't know day', like whenever the mom is like, "Who did this?" and the little girl is "I don't know" and they draw a little ghost who is named I Don't Know. That would be like if I Don't Know had her own holiday. "I Don't Know is the day every year where children can get up to mischief and blame it on their invisible sibling, who might have died in childbirth, we don't know, and in order to stop the ghost of I Don't Know from possessing them they have to put caramels and butterscotches in the cat-litter box."

SM: But you would also have to attach it to some real holiday, like Columbus Day or something.

KS: We'd co-opt Columbus Day? We'd be like, "Back in the day this used to be Columbus Day but now it's I Don't Know day."

SM: The ghost of I Don't Know was on the fucking ship with Columbus and was trying to do something…

KS: It's really, really strange that it caught on.

SM: Did it really shock you that it caught on in a world of all the things that have caught on? If you look at all the things that end up catching on, you look at all the different religions out there, and all the current modern religions, isn't it the same thing?

KS: I don't know man. Cite a modern religion.

SM: Scientology.

KS: Well, that's just very strange that *that* caught on, considering its origins coming from a sci-fi writer.

SM: But the idea that you create something that people, by believing in…

KS: Gives them comfort, gives them joy, takes their minds off…

SM: Exactly. As a kid, that there's a guy who lives in the North Pole and mostly I think it's kids who are like, "OK, so I get presents from Mom and Dad, and aunty blah blah blah, but then I make out because there's this other dude who I don't know and I don't get to hang out with and I don't have to go to their house…"

KS: "Once a year he gives me stuff, this shit he made for free, for nothing!"

SM: "And, if I ask him…" What happens too is that your parents play into

it, by laying it out that the best shit comes from Santa.
KS: Which is so strange. As a parent…
SM: I want to take credit. Not Santa!
KS: Yes!
SM: "I wanted to give you a bike, Santa wanted to give you a book on…"
KS: "Santa gave you socks. Dad and Mom got you a bike! I'm saying it's nice that Santa gave you socks but which do you want more!?"
SM: Everyone needs socks. "Who's better? Socky Claus?"
KS: It is very strange though that every parent goes along with it and it's this thing where you are divesting yourself of credit and potential affection. It would be like your kid coming up to you and being like, "Are you my father?" and I'm like, "No. Odin One-Eye is your father!" For the first ten years of their life, or let's say that kids make it to six years old, "Odin One-Eye came here on Sleipnir the eight-legged horse who ate our food, fucked your mom, and I was forced to watch. But he comes once a year and gives you toys to make up for it. But it hurts me in my heart because I didn't want that, I wanted fidelity from my marriage but what are you going to do? It's Odin One-Eye."
SM: That's how kids are made. "And that's how children are made, forced sex from a Norse god…"
KS: "… who has a very threatening beast who is keeping your father at bay. I had a shovel in my hand but I got to be honest with you, Sleipnir I'm not taking him, he's got eight legs. It's like fighting an octopus on land… you don't know where he's going to hit you." I was cruising around the channels the other day and I saw a special on *Search for the Giant Squid* and I had to fucking stop.
SM: Humboldt Squid?
KS: Yeah. But it wasn't nearly as cool as I thought it was going to be. It was big, and if I was in the water and I saw it I'd be, "Aaarrggh!" But I hear 'giant squid' and I want to see something that's going to take the *Nautilus* down.
SM: Or a ship, or a dingy.
KS: Anything, anything that would be threatening to me on a boat. Everything in the sea is threatening to me, so they could be like, "It's a giant squid," or, "It's a one inch squid," and I'd be like, "Holy shit get me out of here!"
SM: "That one inch squid is going to drill a hole in the dingy!"
KS: "He's going to attack my dingy? Really?"

SM: "He's going to climb up my ass and eat my brain!"

KS: "The little squid burrows through your cock, up to your brain and takes over like Starro, on the inside." But on a boat nothing feels that threatening, except like…

SM: A whale maybe.

KS: But it would have to be a whale who is like…

SM: Moby Dick? Who has a personality?

KS: Totally, who gets angry, has feelings. Most sea animals are just like, the hunt for food.

SM: "Eat."

KS: "I sleep sometimes, I fuck, make other things." But it's never like, "I'm mad as hell and I'm taking down a boat!"

SM: "This time it's personal!"

KS: That's why when I stop on the fucking squid thing I want to see a squid that is climbing a building in New York.

SM: A pissed off squid.

KS: "He's mad, look at that beak! He could fit five grown men in his beak and eat them at once!" But they didn't have that.

SM: Do you think a channel could exist of just like completely fabricated shit that's more interesting than real life?

KS: I would have it locked permanently on my television.

SM: Completely false.

KS: "What created the Chicago fire? Well, that was the giant flying squid, Sleipnir, Odin sent down, he was angry with Chicago and so Sleipnir came, attached himself to the Sears Tower" — which didn't even exist then — "and started shooting fire from his angry beak and incinerated the town!" I would be like, "Holy Shit! Scott, do you know what caused the Chicago fire?" I would watch that channel all the time. I would cite it as a credible source.

SM: What would you call it?

KS: BN, Bullshit Network. You couldn't call it that because then people would be like, "I'm not watching the Bullshit Network." Let's call it CBT, Could Be True.

SM: I think you have to deliver it as fact.

KS: Totally.

SM: Like the History Channel.

KS: Like the fuckers who get up and say, "Dinosaurs existed five thousand

years ago," you've got to be that sure about it.
SM: All of your shows have basically got to be completely manufactured, with maybe partial basis in reality. I think people are ready for that.

Random SModquotes

"I don't think having savings necessarily makes me cheap."

KS: Like *The Lost Legend of Hitler Claus*?
SM: Exactly.
KS: "He comes once a year and kills all non-gentiles. Leaves gifts for all the little gentile, the shitzen and goy little girls."
SM: "It didn't really last that long."
KS: "Yeah, it lasted for about two, maybe eight years."
SM: "It didn't even last a decade. It originated in a very small region of Germany."
KS: "Nobody ever got killed but there were some crimes where some children were heard to have beat up Jewish children in preparation for Hitler Claus."
SM: "Killer Hitler decided he didn't want Santa Claus any more, he wanted to change it so that he was the person."
KS: OK, I am Goebbels and you're Hitler. It's 1939, because they were still winning the war at that point.
SM: I'm doing well.
KS: Yeah, you're doing fucking well, you're on top of shit, on top of the world. We sit down to discuss further global domination. "Herr Hitler."
SM: "Si."
KS: Si?! You're doing Hitler when he's in Buenos Aires hiding after the war. "Der Führer?"
SM: "Yes. Da."
KS: [Attempts German accent] "We have discussed at great length…" — that ain't no fucking German accent! I'm trying to get my German accent down. "We have discussed at great length with the cabinet unt…" — we should just do it in a British accent because every movie about Germans is done in a British accent. "Führer?"
SM: Are we switching?
KS: Now we're British Nazis, but we're Hitler and Goebbels. "Führer?" [Switching to British accents.]
SM: "Yes."
KS: "In discussing it further with the cabinet, we've decided to capture the

minds and hearts of children across the world."

SM: "I like children. You've got to get the kids, it's what I've been saying, 'Get the kids.'"

KS: "Get them whilst they're young. In order to…"

SM: "Spit it out Goebbels. Time is Deutschmarks."

KS: "I feel you. You are known as something of a harsh figure. Children are frightened of you because they hear about the things you've done. You're a world conqueror. So, in order to soften your image, what we propose to do is get rid of the legend of St Nicolas, the Germanic St Nicolas and the American Santa Claus, Father Christmas, and create, if I may say this…"

SM: "Are we going to kill him? We'll slaughter him! Like in the squares."

KS: "You mean in the backstory?"

SM: "Like I murder him in bed while he is sleeping."

KS: "Well perhaps that would be viewed as cowardly, Führer."

SM: "Alright, well I don't actually have to fight him."

KS: "Perhaps it is in self-defense, your eminence?"

SM: [Becoming increasingly Cockney] "Right, he comes to me house and he comes in, I'm like, 'Hey, what are you doing here?'"

KS: Hitler as an Eastender!

SM: "'What are you doing?' and then one in the neck, alright?"

KS: You can't see but Scott is holding up his right hand and poking the air for "One in the neck"!

SM: "One in the neck! One in the stomach!"

KS: "Well, of course. Because he is a fat man and fat men deserve punishment. He hasn't taken care of himself in the grand tradition of the Germanic people. Why do we have this for a role model for children? He is a fat man who gives them things and his genealogy is questionable. So kill the fat man, Hitler."

SM: "So I kill him? I give him one, I put him down."

KS: "Perhaps we could even weave in that maybe he was Jewish?"

SM: "Oh! Right, right."

KS: "Then you have the moral high ground for killing the Santa Jew. You kill the Santa Jew, you become, not the Santa Jew of course, because who would ever want that? You become Hitler Claus! Once a year…"

SM: "Hitler Claus?"

KS: "Yes, the Hitler Claus. Once a year you go around and you do what Santa did but it's you, not Santa. It's not a fictional character, it's you doing fictional things."

SM: "Can we give them, instead of like trains and stuff, my book? Autographed copy of me book?"

KS: "Yes, but in order to win the hearts and minds of a child I don't think you want to hand them a very heavy tome with lots of words they don't know yet, concepts they can't quite process."

SM: "Perhaps we grab someone and we'll do like a picture book of it, so it is my book."

KS: "Drawings you mean?"

SM: "Here we open the page and a little thing pops out and says, 'Hey it's me!'"

KS: "A pop-up version of *Mein Kampf*?"

SM: "Yeah."

KS: "I think we're getting close, sir. But I don't think that that will excuse the murder of such a beloved children's figure as Santa Claus. You need to give them toys, Führer."

SM: "Like little guns?"

KS: "For the boys, perhaps a Luger? Good boys get Lugers."

SM: "Bad boys get?"

KS: "Death?"

SM: "Death."

KS: "Good girls get?"

SM: "Lugers."

KS: "Yes, well." Whatever, it's 1939. "We will give them spoons for cooking in the kitchen." I don't even know, what was the German position on women? Were they prized or, "Hey man, stay home while we go fucking fight the Jewish menace"? Every time I see a movie on Nazis there's a chick in there.

SM: I don't think they were fighting in the trenches but they might have had them in the service.

KS: Do you think they had any top women officials? No. That movie about Hitler, *The Rise of Evil*, there were chicks but they were all married to high-level Nazis. But then there was also *She Wolf of the SS*, that movie, but I don't know if that was based on anything. So maybe there were no chicks in Hitler's cabinet or in Hitler's vision of a government, of the Third Reich,

women had a place that — let's check it out. 'Female Nazis' is what I am entering. Hey, there's a Wikipedia page for it... oh, it's lists of names.

SM: Even the women had to join the party and be a Nazi.

KS: There's a shit ton of names here. "National Socialist German Workers Party, Nazi party, female guards in Nazi concentration camps."

SM: There you go.

KS: "Of the 55,000 guards that served in the Nazi concentration camps, about 3,700 were women. In 1942 the first female guards arrived at Auschwitz and Majdanek, from Ravensbrück." Germans have such scary words. There's a lot of harsh k's and s's and w's.

SM: "Let's just go on vacation."

KS: "Zwe should not zgo to Zwravensbrook! I tell you that much! Zvery Zvery frightening!" "The year after the Nazis began conscripting women because of a guard shortage."

SM: I don't want to speak well of Nazis but I don't think I ever heard of them

being, "We think less of women, we treat them badly, we think women are nothing."
KS: But I'm sure it was a patriarchal society.
SM: Yeah, it's a man's army.
KS: According to that movie he had problems with chicks. He was not like the dude that was like, "Let me put it in your puss and we do it."
SM: He was not a ladies' man.
KS: Apparently he was a shit-eater, he liked to do stuff like that. Surprisingly, Hitler was not a normal guy. But apparently he had sexual problems. Some people have even theorized that he might have been gay. Which is not a sexual problem, but for a guy like Hitler who presented himself as the ultimate male…
SM: He was conflicted. His conflict with coming out of the closet.
KS: See, if Hitler could just have eaten a little cock then none of that would have happened.
SM: That would have changed it all?
KS: Totally. He could be in the beer hall and instead of whipping people up into a frenzy against the Jews…
SM: Some guy is like, "Suck my dick!" And he's like, "OK!"
KS: Instead of going to a beer hall if he'd gone to a bear bar instead…
SM: A gay bear hall?
KS: A bear hall! They were like, "What are you, an otter or a cub, Hitler?"
SM: "Whatever!"
KS: "I have a sloppy party bottom! I come to offer you an orifice for all of your cocks!"
SM: "Just spray it on me!"

From SModcast 69: The Talking Cure, Pt. 2
Rate Your Libido* or *Watch My Dumbass FUCK!!!

KS: I wouldn't go so far as to say that I'm a dog, but I'm pretty houndy at my wife when it comes to fucking. In all the years I've known you, you've always been very like, "Oh, sex. Sex is just one of those things. It's natural, like the mountains. And I like to see the outdoors."
SM: I have a healthy libido.
KS: I'm not fucking, accusing your libido — like, "Wow, you've got the libido

of a fucking seventy-year-old gay man who's fucked and eaten a lot of cock and eaten a lot of ass and he's done with it"!

SM: [Laughs.] I'd just say I have a healthy one, but I definitely would not match you in a game show.

KS: No.

SM: *Rate Your Libido!*

KS: Who do you think people would want to watch fuck more, me or you? I think me, just because it's more visually interesting.

SM: I think people with this show would probably say they want to watch *us* fuck! That would be the tape…

KS: Yeah, no doubt. But not even this show, we're like, in the real world, let's say there's a game show, *Watch My Dumb Ass Fuck!* That's the title of it. It's very popular. Two contestants go on and basically they've created this kinda technology where they wear goggles, and the goggles can sense where their eyes are looking. Left at one set, or right, where there's another set. And there's two couples fucking simultaneously — not each other. And the audience, wearing these goggles, looks left or right. So at the end, we get a tabulation of who they wanted to watch fuck more — i.e., who were they looking at more?

SM: You and I are holding hands…

KS: I'm like, "Let's do this together, are you ready?" And people are like, "I don't know what to do, they're holding hands and fucking! I have to watch them both! I'm learning a lesson!" It's like a *Peanuts* special.

SM: I meant at the end, when they announce the winner.

KS: Oh. I thought you meant during the fucking. Like, to rebel against the show and all it means, we pushed our beds together.

SM: "They have to watch us both!"

KS: Yeah! And behind the scenes, the fucking showrunners are like, "They can't do that!" And like the guy who's the real owner of the network would stop by on that one day, and would be like, "I think we should let the boys do what they want to do, don't you?" And that other guy's like, "I quit!" "You're fired, Bill!" And then it's... It's a happy ending, dude! That's an Act Three, right there! And then we fuck.

SM: Not each other.

KS: We fuck other chicks, holding hands. And then they can't pick a winner. We both win!

SM: Yeah. We won't let this divide our friendship!

KS: But in the real world — let's say that's not real. Which it's not. In the real world the show is…

SM: [Laughs.] In the *real* world.

KS: The show is unrig-able. We start pushing our beds together, and they're like, "What, are you fucking high? Haven't you ever seen the show? It's only the most popular show in America for like, sixteen years."

SM: "Don't be assholes!"

KS: Yeah, "Stop it." I think they wind up looking at me more, not because it's so arousing, but it's like, "Oh, look at that fucking flab roll! Look at it fly! It's going to kill her, it's going to hit her in the nose!" I think people would look at me more. I know I would look at me more. If I was like, not me, I would be like, "Look at that. How did he let himself get like that? Why would she fuck that fat fuck? Why can't I fuck her?! Let me on this show! Oh, he sickens me but I can't look away." It's the way people used to think about Howard Stern and shit, on the radio. If you like him, you listen to him for an hour, if you hate him, you listen to him for two hours.

SM: You may be right. I would watch you, but that would be because I would have no interest in watching myself.

KS: Really? After all this time you really wouldn't want to watch yourself fuck? I personally do not, but mine is more aesthetic. I love watching people fuck, dude. Last month, two months, all that time getting high — I've been looking at a lot of fucking porn. And not even jerking off to it, that's the weird thing. I'm just interested in the human condition, and now there's a *proliferation* online of just voyeuristic stuff. Couples taking pictures of each other and putting them online, or they break up and one of them puts them online. There's so much of it, dude…

From SModcast 69: Talking Cure, Pt. 2
BOOBERTY!

SM: That's always my first memory of when I talk about the boner, from when I was a really young kid…

KS: Is that book? [*What's Happening to Me?*]

SM: Yeah, was that. And then there's boobs, and then there's lots of stuff. It shows all the parts, and stuff.

KS: I think it was a good idea for them to team up… the print was a little larger than usual, too.
SM: The print's larger, everyone's round, and rolling around, and there's some making love.
KS: Yeah.
SM: There's some love-making, in the first one. They're like rolling around, you see his ass…
KS: Yeah. They get intimate in that book.
SM: Yeah, and then you see the sperm swimming up the canal.
[Phone rings in the background.]
KS: Hold on…
SM: [Whispers, in Kevin's absence] The *vaginal* canal.
KS: [Returned] Yeah, I have very specific memories of that book. I have a fondness for it, it was a good book. Don't remember the title.
SM: *Where Did I Come From?*
KS: You think so?
SM: I'm positive, I remember like, *Where Did I Come From?* was the first one, which was all about like, sperm and babies and the love-making, and then *What's Happening to Me?* is all about boobs and boners.
KS: Puberty? Boobs and boners stage.
SM: That'd be awesome, if every time… well, that's what it's called now.
KS: Booberty? "Hey, I see your daughter's entered booberty!" "Shut the fuck up!"
SM: "That's fucked up!"
KS: "That's my daughter, man! You were there when she was born!" "All I know is, my head got all turned around when I entered booberty!"
SM: Will it catch on?
KS: That's your neighbor's loud daughter. Overtly sexual and loud daughter that you really don't like to encounter at parties.
SM: "How did you handle booberty? I'm finding it quite exciting."
KS: "Look at how big my boobs got during booberty!" "Yeah, those are uh…"
SM: "Yeah, I don't, uh…"
KS: "So how, how's your… your dad is a good guy. Friend of mine. Neighbors. I remember when you weren't in the…"
SM: "I'm growing hair in places, that I didn't have before!"
KS: "Yeah? Yeah, that'll happen to a woman. A young lady."

SM: "Am I a woman now?"

KS: "Um… I think that's really a question for your mom. Probably."

SM: "I'm asking you."

KS: "Um… I'd say, you know, there's grass on the field, play ball." [Breaks down laughing] Um…. BOOBERTY!

SM: Booberty.

KS: That's a great word.

SM: Somebody should do a book.

KS: That's a fucking fun word. Why don't we do the book, dude?

SM: *Booberty*?

KS: We can do the twenty-first century version of that book! *Booberty!*

SM: "Teaching young girls to grow"?

KS: Holy shit! Dude, that's a good idea! That is a good idea! That book sold like crazy. I've got a moderately good sense of humor, you draw really well, together we know a thing or two about how a boob works, a wiener, during… or better yet, we just go look at that book, see everything they did…

SM: And kinda copy it?

KS: And copy it, kinda. That's the American way! "What did they do that worked? Let me do it, but let me improve it." And our improvement will be that the title's better: *Booberty*.

SM: Yeah, for the now.

KS: "From the people that brought you *Zack & Miri Make a Porno… Booberty!*"

SM: *Booberty!*

KS: I'm gonna file for copyright on that shit when we get done with this. "Booberty, bitch!" … Like, "Hello, Mr Smith."

SM: "Is it you again?"

KS: "What is it this time, 'pussy-troll' again?"

SM: "'Boob', and 'puberty'!"

KS: "Why would I do 'pussy-troll' again? I did it once, you dumbass."

SM: "You don't have to copyright things twice, asshole."

KS: "Here's the new one. Get ready. Grab your socks and hose and pull…"

SM: "You know 'boobs'?"

KS: "And you know 'puberty'… 'BOOBERTY!'"

SM: It's like, "Booberty." "No, you gotta say it like this: BOOBERTY!"

KS: We could do that book, dude. We can make that book.

SM: Do you think that parents would…

KS: I don't think it matters. I just think it's clever.

SM: Booberty.

KS: You're going after... you know what? That audience has now been defined. It's the *tween* audience.

SM: The tweens.

KS: That's who that book's for. That book is for my kid, next year, 'til... you know, when she's well into booberty.

SM: It's for girls, though.

KS: Yeah, well.

SM: 'Cause no boy is gonna be like...

KS: Yeah, but boys are gonna be into it 'cause it's got 'boob' in the title.

SM: "It's about boobs! ... and puberty... So it's called *Booberty*..."

KS: "Aw, it's about *puberty*?"

SM: "Yeah, but it's about *boobs* first! Yeah, the boobs come first!"

KS: "Boobs, chapter one!"

SM: "It's not *pubes*..."

KS: "It's... just buy it. It's got 'boobs' in the title."

From SModcast 69: Talking Cure, Pt. 2
Hero, question mark?

SM: Do you suck a dick if you're... Let's say you're at a bank.

KS: Mm-hm?

SM: Crazy guy comes in. He doesn't shoot anybody, if you're gonna suck it.

KS: Look — let me tell you right now. I'm at a bank? I start sucking everybody's dick, just in case one of them's the crazy guy, to prevent anything bad from happening to me and mine.

SM: "Get off me, sir."

KS: I'm like, "No, you might be crazy... "

SM: "It's a million in one chance, but..."

KS: No, go ahead — so I'm in a bank...

SM: You're in a bank, and basically somebody comes in with a gun. And he's just like, "I'm gonna kill all you motherfuckers unless... *you* suck my dick. Right here."

"Fuck the breeders, I'm talking about the sphincter."

KS: How many people?

SM: There's twenty.

KS: Any of them very pretty women?

SM: Uh… you know, on average there's probably one or two.

KS: Is my wife present?

SM: No.

KS: So she's not in danger.

SM: You have no personal…

KS: No personal gain?

SM: You have no personal attachment to anybody in there.

KS: Wait, wait wait. Step back. The offer is *what?* This is intriguing…

SM: You are in a bank. You don't know anybody…

KS: I know, get me to the point where he's like, "You're gonna… or…"

SM: "I'm gonna kill everybody in here…"

KS: "Including me?" [Prompts]: "No."

SM: "No."

KS: OK, *that's* when it gets interesting.

SM: He's like, "I'm gonna kill everybody but you, unless you suck my dick."

KS: Uh… "Query?"

SM: "Yes, you have the floor. Recognized."

KS: "When you say 'everybody', do you mean everybody in the room? Everybody in the world?"

SM: "I'm gonna kill everyone in this room."

KS: "In this room. Everyone that you can see, and I can see? Or people that work downstairs, upstairs perhaps?"

SM: "I'm gonna kill whoever I can, that's not you."

KS: "OK."

SM: "In this building."

KS: "Good day to be me, then, right?"

SM: "Yes."

KS: "Right on. Thanks. Well, I'll be seeing you."

SM: "No, you can't go. You gotta watch."

KS: "Oh. Alright, well I guess I'm prepared. I get to live though, right?"

SM: "You get to live, you get to walk out."

KS: "No trick, you're don't pull something out of your back pocket, this ain't… you're not the Devil are you?"

SM: "No, nonono."

KS: "Alright. Well, let's get this moving, I got shit to do."

SM: You're gonna let him shoot everybody?

KS: You never gave me another option.

SM: … No, or you suck his dick.

KS: "*What?* This is new!" This is the first time you ever…

SM: OK.

KS: "I suck whose dick?"

SM: "You suck my… OK, listen."

KS: "Yes?"

SM: "Just sit down."

KS: "Yes?"

SM: "I'm gonna kill everybody in here…"

KS: "Such, such a bad idea."

SM: "… except for you."

KS: "Ooh!"

SM: "But, if you suck my dick right now, in front of everybody, everybody walks out of here. You suck my dick, everyone lives; you don't suck my dick, *you* live but everyone else dies, in the building."

KS: "Hmm." I mean, I'm not even thinking about it, I'm like, I'll suck his dick, to save that many lives… Can I throw out some concessions, though?

SM: To the guy with the gun?

KS: Yes.

SM: Um… you can try.

KS: "Can we just make sure the cameras in the bank are off?"

SM: "No."

KS: "You didn't want to think about it?"

SM: "No."

KS: "Why?"

SM: "Because, it's not about making it more comfortable for you."

KS: "I mean, you're getting head from me, I would think…"

SM: "I know, but I'm gonna like… you know… Is that enough to have me sentence all these people to death, that there's gonna be some grainy black and white fucking cameras?"

KS: "Hold on, you're the crazy one, buddy!"

SM: "I know, but I just think that you're fucking with me now. Like, why tempt fate? I gave you an out, to save all these people. And now you're worried about some fucking 20mm lens seeing you suck my dick on YouTube?"

KS: "I think it's a fair question. You could just say no, and we'll move on."

SM: "I did, and you fucking kept going. You remember?"

KS: "OK, well my bad…"

SM: "We can rewind the tape, if you want."

KS: "OK, I started this, I'm now putting an end to it. OK."

SM: "Any other concessions?"

KS: "I mean… one time only, right?"

SM: "Yeah."

KS: "What happens to you when this is all over?"

SM: "I feel good about getting head, and I'm going home."

KS: "Alright, but you don't ever cross my path again?"

SM: "I don't know. I mean, you know… I go to the grocery store, I get gas, I can't say that we're not gonna… I'm not gonna seek you out."

KS: "Look…"

SM: "Unless you're good."

KS: "… one last time. I'm gonna do this. Um… You or nobody else is gonna kill me afterwards? This isn't a trick?"

SM: "No. Why would I execute…?"

KS: "Just simply 'no' would suffice."

SM: "No, you're gonna live."

KS: "OK. Alright, well let's go." I'd do it. Totally. Save that many people? It's so weird because every fucking TV News station's gonna have the heroic footage of my fucking like, slow, awkward…

SM: "Hero, question mark?"

KS: "Question mark"!

SM: It's just so awkward… like, the press conference…

KS: I'm like, "Well, that's not fair! I'm not saying *call* me a hero, but don't *question* whether you should call me a hero!"

SM: "I didn't *ask* to suck his dick!"

KS: And it's like, really bad ceiling-mounted camera footage, so it's not way close. And it's just this shot, just in shot, of me, and this dude's sitting back on a stair or something like that, and I'm fucking hunched over him, and you just hear [makes rhythmic blow job noise]. And through some fucking Freedom of Information Act, they get that clip out there to the News agencies, and they're like, "We're gonna run this footage, unedited, if you have small children we recommend you have them leave the room." And then they cut to it, and it's just [extended rhythmic blow job noise].

SM: "... UUuhh!"

KS: Not even, dude! It's like, I'm not good at it, so the dude's going for a long time, and the News shows always run it uncut... so it's like, a fucking twenty-six-minute blow job and shit...

SM: Just imagine, like they did a press conference. It's like, "Uh...."

KS: About minute fourteen, during the clip, since there's like, *nothing*...

SM: People start to leave?

KS: [Laughs] No, no... I'm like, "Since there's no fear that we're gonna be trampling over any dialogue," 'cause I remember the footage, and, I just continue blowing him for the next fourteen minutes without... nobody says *anything*, it's deathly, unnervingly quiet.

SM: "Right here, I feel like I really hit my stride..."

KS: "But uh, do we have any other questions from the floor?" And they're like, "Um... why did you ask that they turn the cameras off? Is it for the obvious reason, that we're watching here?" And I say, "Well, that, and for what's about to happen next." And then you just see me in that overhead shot, reach back down my pants, I pull my pants down over my ass, and... I start fingering my asshole.

[Kevin laughs hysterically for a full eleven seconds.]

Oh, I feel a little dizzy...

SM: That would be fucked up. If suddenly, it was like you lose sense of place and you just start playing with yourself...

KS: "I understand why this is generally a news-worthy item, but for the sake of the quote-unquote 'hero's' dignity, could you have cut the last fourteen minutes out?"

SM: "I was just trying to get something out of it."

KS: They're like, "Being that you're in a bank, you grab a roll of quarters and start fucking yourself in the ass with the quarters, is it safe to say that this wasn't a very heroic... that you did in fact enjoy it?" And I'm like, "Well, do they necessarily have to be mutually exclusive?"

SM: "I don't feel that..."

KS: "Look, sometimes, a good is also a bad."

SM: "Well, in the end, I think it's safe to say that the people are alive, whether

I was playing with my bunghole or not, whether I decided to give a little something back to myself…" You saved everybody. Doesn't matter. What would it matter, if you started playing with your asshole? I mean, it would be the most fucked-up thing in the world…

KS: And every time they showed it, they had to air it un-fucking-cut. And it was just like…

SM: Everyone's like, "Oh, here it comes."

KS: All you hear is: [blow job noise, interspersed with farting, anal insertion noise…]

SM: That would be hard to live down.

KS: When the News reports run, they don't air that shit uncut. But they do run a few seconds of what is very clearly me blowing a dude, from overhead.

SM: Yeah, there would probably be a blur around the genital area.

KS: Yes, why they'd show it at all is beyond me, but they wouldn't show fucking twenty-six minutes of it. But then Geraldo Rivera, two months later, is doing a fucking special report, inside probe, you know… 'The Bank Hold-Up…'

SM: 'The Bank Dick.'

KS: '… the True Story.' And *they* run the uncut monitor footage. And it turned out to be *the* highest rated program that's ever been on television. Like, whatever *M*A*S*H*'s final episode was, plus the fifty best Super Bowls ever played… They probably haven't played fifty Super Bowls yet…

SM: No.

KS: Not at all. The ten best Super Bowls ever played. Like, those ratings. Essentially, ninety-six percent of the world…

SM: Is watching. In China, they're like, "Ohh, my god. Is he touching himself?"

KS: Yeah. Can I ever go outside again?

SM: See, actually, to me what makes it interesting is the idea of doing something completely heroic, that people just laughed at.

KS: They're disdainful, they're just like…

SM: Even if you don't play with your own asshole.

KS: Like, somebody… after the dude leaves and shit, and as the cops are arriving, and I speak to some of the hostages. And a few of them are like, "I'm so glad you saved my life, but you're going to Hell for what you just did." I'm like, "*What?*"

SM: Or some people are like, "Hey! You know… thanks. Thanks."

KS: "You're not good at it, and you got fat."

SM: "That took long. That took too long."

KS: "There were many times he could've killed us. Why couldn't you have blown him quicker?"

SM: "He might've killed us 'cause you suck at it." It'd be like that weird thing of like, you would always have that… anywhere you went, even if you walked in a room, there'd be four people like, awkwardly clapping [claps sarcastically]. "Here he is, today's hero!"

KS: It was so watched that discounting kindergarten classrooms, if you walked into any room…

SM: It was just like, the moon landings.

KS: …eighty percent of the people recognized you.

SM: It would be hard. 'Cause you would always go down, as the guy who went down.

KS: 'Cause there's footage of you in interview too. But also they'd bought footage from one of the hostages who had a cellphone camera, and was shooting it all at a different angle of you, that he intended to put up on YouTube, but then, somebody bought the footage instead. So they had somewhat close-ups.

SM: 'Cause you gotta figure the adrenaline of the moment would make you do it. You're like, "I gotta do this, I gotta save everybody." And then a year later, you're just like… "Oh, man."

KS: Where you've become the biggest fucking punch line on the planet. Maybe bigger than OJ Simpson.

SM: Yeah. 'Cause if you'd tackled the dude, removed his gun and saved the day…

KS: Everyone's just like, "You fucking hero!"

SM: "Way to go!" They'd give you the keys to the city…

KS: But you didn't have any choice. You weren't like, "Gimme that!" [makes dick chomping noise]. He made you do it.

SM: What, like you run at him, "I'll save us!"

KS: The dude's like, "Hey, HEY!" Puts one in your fucking scalp.

SM: Guy pulls out a gun and you just run at him and start trying to unbuckle his pants. Everyone's like, "What the fuck was that?"

KS: Like, you get two feet toward him, get thrown back four feet from the

fucking gunshot, everyone's like, "Holy shit! Oh my god!"
SM: Everyone's like, "What were you doing?" You're like, "I was just… trying… to suck… his dick…"
KS: "Ohhh… thank god it was just… a shoulder shot… I was *trying* to suck the man's *dick* to save our *lives*, if you *must* know! If you couldn't figure it out, stupid! Ooh, push on this…" I think head is always the easiest way to solve any fucking issue. All for it.
SM: That's what we should do. The UN should just be a bunch of rooms where like, "Ecuador, you gotta go suck… somebody else's dick…"
KS: I don't think it works on global politics… I think it's more, if I ever encounter trouble, I know I'll be able to handle it.
SM: Offer head?
KS: Yeah. 'Cause I always carry my trusty mouth, wherever I go.

SModcast 72: Hello Dere!
Bryan witnesses a very odd fight at the teen club

BJ: At the very tip [of the amusement park] was a nightclub I went to once.
KS: You went to a nightclub there?
BJ: Yeah — I guess it was like a teen club, at the time? And I went there with Mark London and TJ Mendes.
KS: "Hi guys! Let's get some Sarsaparillas and sit around this malt shop!" What did you do? What were you doing at a teen club? "This is scary, London, all these fuckers are gay!"
[Laughter.]
BJ: That's fucking really close, because I remember both of us were standing against this window, and I had lent him my Members Only jacket. And we were standing against this window while this kid TJ went out to talk to girls and shit. And I remember as we left, some black guy was getting thrown out of the club. And I remember he was getting wild and punching… [Dissolves into laughter.]
KS: [Laughing] What?
BJ: [Still laughing] He started punching Mark London.
KS: He started punching your friend? Why?
BJ: I don't know! He just turned on him. I think what happened was, he had

been fighting in the club with somebody…

KS: Someone unrelated to Mark London?

BJ: Yeah — 'cause we were already outside. And the security guards threw him out, so he can't fight with the guy he wants to fight with, now he can't even fight with the security guards, but he wants to still fight with somebody [laughs]…

KS: And the first person he laid eyes on…

BJ: Was Mark London! [Laughs.] And he just starts windmilling, and punching him *so fast*. It was fucking insane! [Begins to cry with laughter.] The way that fucking poor guy was set upon!

KS: What did you do?

BJ: I fucking backed up and went "What the fuck?" And the security guards came out and grabbed the black guy again.

KS: "We can't throw him out of outside! But whatever you do with him, don't be in his line of sight when you stop doing it! That's what happened to poor Mark!"

[Helpless laughter.]

BJ: That's what happened to me. It was a flurry man, it was a flurry!

KS: I would imagine a thing like that really ruins the night.

BJ: Yeah. I mean, it wasn't that great a night anyway. But to cap it off… We were just like, "Shit, are you alright?" When you think the boredom of the night is going to be the worst thing. And then within seconds, it's not even close!

KS: You're just like, "Look, I feel bad for him, but I don't want to get involved in this drama." "Look, are you alright? I'm going to go…" "Wait… my arm!" "Yeah… that sucks. We'll get him. Do you remember his name?"

BJ: "We'll call the club later. We'll get his name. My dad said I can't give you a ride home." The door closes, and no explanation.

KS: Well, that is the explanation. "My dad says I can't drive you home."

BJ: Well, you could get away with that shit back then. What's your friend going to say? You're right — it's just like, "It has nothing to do with me!"

KS: Shit, yeah. Abandon somebody else's child in public twenty-five years ago, and people wouldn't bat an eyelash. Worst case scenario, they'd be like, "Well, they could have dropped you off."

BJ: Yeah, "Why didn't Bryan give you a ride home?" "Well, his dad said he couldn't." "Oh."

From SModcast 78: For Today's Elegant Man
Jaundice and *Star Wars*

KS: He went jaundiced [Kevin's grandfather]. Have you ever seen anyone turn yellow? It was fucked up. It looked like *Sin City*. Did you see that, when they did That Yellow Bastard? He literally was that shade of yellow.
BJ: This was when he was alive?
KS: Yeah. It was over the course of a month that he was that color and dying. It was strange.
BJ: How old were you when you were seeing him like that?
KS: Nine. They tried to explain it to me like, "Jaundice is this condition," but I'm like, "I'm nine motherfucker, he looks like something out of *Star Wars*!" I mean seriously, I'm half expecting Ben Kenobi to jump out and cut his fucking arm off!
BJ: "Thanks Ben!"
KS: "So don't hit me with your clinical description of jaundice, I'm in a different fucking place, and it's creepy and horrible!"

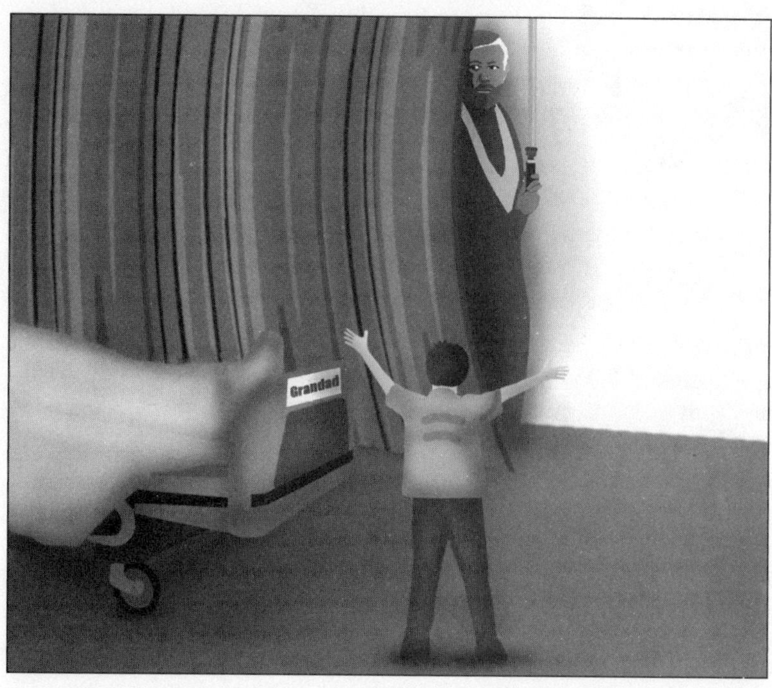

From SModcast 80: RIP
The future dies

KS: How are you man?
SM: I'm good.
KS: I had an adventure of my own this week and I was almost sure that that was what we'd be talking about on SMod but…
SM: I trumped it?
KS: Mosier may have. I was trying to build up to it. Mosier may have trumped it. So I'm on chat with Mosier and I'm like, "Hey man, you want to play some Stick or something?" and he goes, "Maybe later on, in an hour, I've got to go get a vasectomy..." I just typed, "?!?"
SM: You were like, "Do you want to come over later?"
KS: Ironically I was like, "Do you want to come over later and donate healthy sperm?"
SM: I was like, "Well…"
KS: "It's funny you should mention it Kev."
SM: Because Tusk was coming over and you were going to go and see *Watchmen*.
KS: Mark Tusk was in town, the dude who worked in acquisitions in Miramax, he bought *Clerks*. He was the one that found *Clerks*, the guy that championed it at Miramax. Anybody who knows the story of *Clerks* knows this. Mark was in town.
SM: He was coming over to your house and you were like, "Mosier would you like to come over?" I was like, "Well…" I couldn't come because I was about to head over to get a vasectomy.
KS: Dude it wasn't even like, "Well…" It was so nonchalant, matter of fact, it was almost like you were, "Oh I'm going to get my teeth cleaned in about an hour." And even then I'd be like, "He's not putting import on this teeth cleaning, he sounds like he's taking it real lightly," and that was for fucking teeth, the fact that this was about a vasectomy... I was fucking spellbound. "What the fuck is going on?" But I shouldn't have been surprised, knowing you all these years, but oh my god, what the fuck dude? Why?
SM: Why is because I don't want to have kids.
KS: You hate children.

SM: I hate children.

KS: And sperm. The two things you most hate, children and sperm.

SM: Children covered in sperm.

KS: "We all hate that, but I hate it the most."

SM: I've never really wanted kids. Now that I've done it, now that I'm on the other side…

KS: Now that you've had the clip you're all like, [sobs] "I want a child!"

SM: No! I was like, "Why didn't I do this a lot sooner?"

KS: Really? "Why didn't I do this at age twelve?"

SM: Yeah.

KS: "I could have been fucking girls left and right and been like, 'I'm Mr Safe right here kids!'"

SM: "Hey mom, I want to get a vasectomy. I haven't really started producing sperm…"

KS: You're like, "Mom, the more I think about it, if I get a vasectomy now, more girls will probably want to fuck me."

SM: "Even girls that don't like me!"

KS: "I'll get girls that are disgusted by me, but they got to fuck somebody and they're terrified of getting pregnant."

SM: "I won't get you pregnant."

KS: "I'm a hundred percent!" Is it a hundred percent?

SM: Well, there is the *Jurassic Park* nature-finds-a-way where the tube that gets cut, can find its way back.

KS: Is that the cum shaft? Is that what the doctor called it? He's like, "Mosier, I'm cutting your cum shaft."

SM: "Do you feel it?"

KS: You're like, [enjoying the pain] "I love it, cut it!"

SM: "It's hot!" It's the tube that carries your sperm into the area where it hooks up with your ejaculation, where it all comes together.

KS: You will still cum hard.

SM: Ejaculate.

KS: But you just won't…

SM: From the naked eye you won't…

KS: If you're in a porn they'll be like, "Nothing wrong with that dude."

SM: "Yeah, it looks great." But I'm like, "There's no sperm in there."

KS: If you watched porn with a microscope…

SM: Microscopic porn!

KS: You'd be like, "Something's wrong!"

SM: "These fluids aren't hot."

KS: So it was just a matter of you going, "I don't ever want to have kids"?

SM: I didn't really want to have kids, and if you don't want to have kids the idea of an accidental pregnancy is not something that you want to deal with. My wife and I both don't want to have kids, we're both prepared not to have kids, but I think if the accident happened and she was to get pregnant it suddenly becomes different. Not for me but for her.

KS: She'd probably be like, "I might want to keep the kid."

SM: It's a different choice to make.

KS: You'd be like, "Crush it beneath my boot heel! Kill all children!" It's just more complicated.

SM: And even if you still choose not to have a kid, that experience is not fun.

KS: Which one?

SM: Aborting.

KS: Between the two choices it's better for you to have invasive ball surgery rather than her have an abortion.

SM: If you don't want to have kids it's easier to have a vasectomy. Versus all the other measures out there it is so much easier. For a guy it is pretty simple.

KS: And it's also completely reversible.

SM: Not a hundred percent.

KS: Really?

SM: They do warn you that there are cases…

KS: "We can reverse it, but shit can happen."

SM: … where you reverse it, it's basically the same procedure in reverse, then it's the same thing where you bring in sperm into your ejaculation and then they test it for sperm. When I did it they tested it for sperm to check that they're gone.

KS: They test your sperm in advance?

SM: No.

KS: You weren't curious. "Before I let them go…"

SM: "Are there sperm in my sacs?"

KS: "Can you check my cum and see if there is sperm in it?"

SM: He's like, "I can pretty much look at you right now and tell you."

KS: You're like, "No no no, here's the true test, put it in your mouth!"
SM: "Be a real doctor!"
KS: "Run the cum between your teeth and tell me if you feel tails."
SM: "Filter the sperm out with your teeth."
KS: "Act like a giant sperm whale with a mouthful of kelp and find the sperm, find it!" He's like, "Mr Mosier I think..."
SM: I wouldn't get a vasectomy.
KS: "... we need to send you over to the place where they'll give you a lobotomy, as opposed to a vasectomy."
SM: So the decision-making process was just, "Do you want to have it?"
KS: Who brought it up? You or her?
SM: She brought it up.
KS: And you were like, "Uh! Haha uh! Fuck you!"
SM: "That's funny!"
KS: "You have it!"
SM: "You have a vasectomy! Why do I gotta do everything?"
KS: After two hours of this...
SM: It came up, actually, by her gyno.
KS: He was like, "I'm tired of scraping sperm out of your uterus, tell this dude to clip his nuts!"
SM: "This sperm is the grossest sperm ever!"
KS: "Look at it, it's like the ceiling of a poker room, a casino, it's dark and brown. Look at all these dead sperm!"
SM: She brought it up where it came up about birth control and then it became, "Look, if he doesn't want to have kids, then the simplest thing is..."
KS: "To get a puppy."
SM: "...is to get a puppy. And fuck it!"
KS: "Just put baby clothes on it."
SM: "Just always shoot your wad on the puppy." "Get the puppy ready!"
KS: Then you're like, "Is that what it is doctor?" He's like, "Don't be ridiculous, you get a puppy so that it chews your ball sac and you can't produce sperm. It's the poor man's vasectomy."
SM: "You wrap your nuts in ham..."
KS: "This hurts so much, but I love you honey!"
SM: "Yeah, I think this is good for both of us! But Oh My God!"
KS: "I wish we'd chosen the more expensive but less painful option. He's real

Random SModquotes

"Now that I think about it, that was a *very* gay idea; to walk around in robes with no clothes on underneath..."

hungry!"

SM: "Oh, he's moving on to the penis now."

KS: "Stop him!"

SM: "There's no ham on it! What are you doing?"

KS: No ham!

SM: If that was what happened when I came in there, "Well, wrap your balls in ham and this wild dog will eat them," I'd be like, "Honey?"

KS: "Here? In the office?" He'd be, "No, you do it at home." Even weirder.

SM: "We don't want to see this, come on! It's fucked up."

KS: "I don't want to see some dog eating your balls."

SM: So once we decided to do it…

KS: She came home from the gyno and the gyno said, "Tell him to do it."

SM: Well yeah, it's easier to do than for the women to have the other surgery.

KS: The tubes tied?

SM: To go inside of their system and to do it is not as easy.

KS: Before you did that, you had to watch an informational video?

SM: So I went to my general practitioner and was like, "Do you have a urologist?" and he gave me the name of a guy, we'll call him Dr Balls.

KS: Dr Balls? Wait, so did Dr Non-Balls react at all when you were like, "Hey man, can you recommend somebody to give me a vasectomy?"

SM: No.

KS: Or were you like, "Hey man, can you do it?"

SM: "Hey man, you want to see them?"

KS: "You've seen them! Look at my nuts, now cut something there!"

SM: "You want to cut them open?" No, I just threw it out there and he was like, "Yeah."

KS: [Nervous laughter] "Ah ha ha aha ha uh!"

SM: He was scared, a doctor for all those years and suddenly he was like, "You've thrown me for a loop!"

KS: "I have operated on brains and yet…"

SM: "…your balls disgust me!" So I went to the urologist and you go in and I had actually been once before, a year before.

KS: Exploratory visit?

SM: I went to this guy and he had the consultation and I was in the middle of a job and I remember that scheduling it wasn't that easy.

KS: Or he rubbed you the wrong way or something like that. You're like, "What happens to the sperm when you cut the little tube and stuff? Where does it all go?" And he's like, [nonchalantly] "Oh, in my mouth!"

SM: I'm like, "I would like a second opinion."

KS: He's like, "OK, in my ass?"

SM: "Whatever, find a hole."

KS: What would you do if he was like, "It's not a big deal, you'll never see it. I just want to drink your sperm"?

SM: What, if I brought my thing in to test and he just opened the cup and drank it?

KS: Like a shot! You're like, "Here it is," and he's like, "Thank god! I'm parched!!" He tosses it back.

SM: I'm like, "Well, is that how you test it?"

KS: "Sure."

SM: "You can taste sperm?"

KS: "Sure, it's a taste-test. It's the Pepsi challenge, bitch."

SM: "Now bring back another one in a couple of days."

KS: "You got any more? I could go for a double shot, bring friends."

SM: "You've been eating asparagus boy! Get out of here!"

KS: What was the video like?

SM: So when I went into the consultation room, once again you get a consultation then you schedule surgery; the video was from the late-'70s, early-'80s.

KS: They haven't updated the video?

SM: No. It was pretty old.

KS: Did you offer, as a film producer, to update the video?

SM: I could do one better. It was pretty charming. It's a guy and he's just like, "Debbie and I have three kids and we were thinking about contraception." Then they get in the idea of getting the vasectomy, then they go on and have a consultation. It's basically just the doctor going, "I don't want to answer the same fucking questions already so this fucking nimrod in the video is going to ask all the questions so that by the time you're done you know all the answers." Everything, like, "When can I continue exercising?" "When can I continue having sex?"

KS: When *can* you continue having sex? You notice I don't give a fuck about exercise, I'm like, "What about the nookie?"
SM: He said that realistically within a couple of days. But it's based on your own comfort level. Physically, I don't know if I would... I had it Tuesday and today is Friday. I think the thing that is holding me back is that you would definitely be watching out. It's still tender so it's not like you can go to town. You don't want to have impact. I don't want anything to hit my nuts.
KS: She's like, "Stuff your balls in my ass!" And you're like, "Oh, *now* you ask!"
SM: "Not today!"
KS: "Not tonight! You hit me back in a couple of days I'll be ready to pop them right in there!"
SM: "It said a week on the video, they said a week!" I'm still tender enough that, if you really wanted to do it you could be careful, but you would be fine.
KS: I remember when Jen had the baby, which naturally is nothing like you having this, in fact it's the opposite, it's the fucking Bizarro version of having a baby is fucking killing the babies… You're like Auschwitz dude, you've got Auschwitz in your pants, just bulging in your fucking — you wear briefs or boxers?
SM: I was wearing little Swastika panties when I came in.
KS: "I am here to kill millions!"
SM: He's like, "What are those for?"
KS: What happens to the sperm? Did he say?
SM: So I watch the video... let's go through it in order.
KS: Does he sit you down and say, "You're a bit concerned as you don't want your wife to get pregnant. So you could use condoms, have you ever thought of that?" Or he figures you're smart enough to have thought of that.
SM: Yeah, he gave me the benefit of the doubt. "There are these things that are rubber, they used to be made of whale stomach."
KS: "Oh, I was ready for elective surgery, I had no idea I could just put a little plastic bag on it."
SM: "There are other things?"
KS: "Thanks doctor." Does he point out shit like, "If you fuck her in the ass she can't get pregnant"? You're like, "I like the way you think!"
SM: "Thank you!"

KS: “I don’t need a second opinion.”

SM: “Do I have to pay for this?”

KS: “That is my internal opinion.” When I come in to be diagnosed for cancer I want that diagnosis.

SM: “You can fuck her in the ass.”

KS: “Doctor, I’m in.”

SM: “You’re still going to die but…”

KS: “… but at least she won’t get pregnant.” He doesn’t give you options? You’re here, you know what the options are.

SM: It’s not even like he says, “You should go see a therapist to analyze whether you really want to do this.” He’s like, “So you really don’t want to have kids?” So I was like, “No.” He says, “It is reversible.” After I watch the video I go into his office and he was pretty chipper, he was like, “OK, you want to do this? You don’t want kids? You have kids?” I was like, “No.” “You sure you don’t want kids?” “No.” That was about the extent of his psychological evaluation.

KS: “Do you like kids?” “No.” “Have you ever seen kids in a park?” “Yes.”

SM: “From afar.”

KS: “Kids on bikes, how do you feel about that?” “Pretty good.”

SM: “I’m glad that kids are riding.”

KS: “One kid leaves Pittsburgh on a train traveling 900…”

SM: “84!”

KS: “Alright Mr Mosier…”

SM: “You’re ready!” So you just show up, you don’t bring anything.

KS: Can you bring an iPod?

SM: I’m sure you could have.

KS: You didn’t want to whilst you had a laser drill on your nuts?

SM: Exactly, I wanted to hear them go, “Ew!”

KS: Or like, “Ooops!” Or the burn that goes “Ssssss!” Burning fucking ball flesh.

SM: I didn’t know what to expect. The worst that they tell you is that one, it’s reversible but not all the time, and they do tell you that basically once they cut the tube, the sperm just goes in your body and your body absorbs it.

KS: You are shitting me!

SM: No.

KS: So your nuts still continue to…

SM: Once a month you throw up…

KS: He's like, "Mr Mosier, I asked you and your wife to come here to talk about the harsh reality of vasectomy. Everything is fine and good. But, once a month…"

SM: "The sperm cycle."

KS: "Just as your wife is entering into her period, you will be hocking up what probably amounts to a bucketful of sperm."

SM: "So unless you throw up into her pussy you will not get her pregnant."

KS: "The good news is you won't get her pregnant. The bad news is that it could strike anywhere. You could be out to dinner, you could be at the theater and you'll just start hocking up sperm. Imagine this Mr Mosier, stepping out of a mens' room in an airport and suddenly you start barfing buckets of sperm. Do you really want to go and do this?"

SM: "There are still men in jail." So, it gets absorbed by your body.

KS: That's weird man.

SM: It just sort of goes in your body.

KS: Can you chemically burn it? Can you chemically burn your balls to death? So that they don't produce sperm any more? Would that make you a eunuch at that point?

SM: Stopping the sperm production?

KS: What if you were like, "Man, that ain't good enough. The fact that this sperm is floating around… I hate sperm, don't you get it?"

SM: "I'm a walking ejaculation. I'm just a guy filled with sperm."

KS: You're like, "You don't understand, I want to *kill* sperm. This sounds like you're not killing them."

SM: "I don't want them in me any more!"

KS: "If she doesn't want them in her, what makes you think *I* want them in me?" You can chemically castrate yourself, that's what it is right? Your testes produce both sperm and testosterone, correct? Or there is testosterone in sperm. But that's where your testosterone comes from. If you burn your balls out, or chemically altered your nut sac…

SM: If you just OD'd on something?

KS: I was reading an article, I think somebody linked it on the SModcast thread, about some dude in Czechoslovakia, some horrible pederast. They've got a policy over there where you can elect to chemically castrate yourself and sometimes they can sentence you to chemical castration. But they also make it a choice, for people who have raped a kid or have molested a kid, or tried or attempted and know they are going to do it again, then they are, "We'll give you this option." Then they'll chemically castrate themselves and they can never fuck anybody, let alone a kid, again. But then there are the opponents who say, "Pederasty is not in the balls, it's in the brain."

SM: "That is not a cure, that's just the testicles." I was never offered the chemical castration. "You can do it this way, or you can do it like they do in a Czechoslovakian jail. Which one do you want to do?"

KS: "You can do the normal route, Mr Mosier, the way we do it here in Beverly Hills, or we can take the Czechoslovakian package."

SM: "For a thousand dollars we can do it this way, for fifty-five dollars I could chemically castrate you."

KS: "For fifty-five dollars we inject your testes with Listerine and a healthy dose of Windex and then it just goes to work."

SM: I assume that part of the operation is based on the idea that it is reversible. But this is what he said, and he said it quick, and I honestly should probably have been more interested…

KS: "I love you, I'm a cum eater!" "What?"

SM: "What did you say? I turned away for a second I think. Can we have a nurse come in? To monitor?" I think that sometimes because the sperm goes into your body, your body will then create antibodies.

KS: To fight the sperm? That's like a walking contraceptive. You'd be spitting that vaginal foam that women use to kill sperm.

SM: "Patient Zero."

KS: You'll be that guy.

SM: Sperm killer!

KS: Shooting sperm killer everywhere.

SM: People can come and buy my sperm killer.

KS: Or if they are dudes, nobody will want to fuck with you in a bar fight because you can render them sterile for life.

SM: That's what I have going for me people. I think that that is one of the things that makes it hard to reverse it, if that happens.

KS: Public opinion when you become the sperm killer?

SM: Exactly.

KS: "Once you've done that, look, you can reverse the operation…"

SM: "But nobody wants to be Son of Sperm Killer!"

KS: "And also, there is a good chance that people will remember what you did when you were Sperm Killer. People have long-term memories of you. If you hurt the people you love. Say you take some poor dude's ability to reproduce and then you stop being Sperm Killer… you can't give him back his power."

SM: So we did the consultation.

KS: Watch the video. Did you watch it by yourself?

SM: I watched it by myself.

KS: At home or there in the office?

SM: No, there in the office.

KS: Did he leave you there by yourself?

SM: Yeah.

KS: Did he give you popcorn?

SM: No.

KS: It's a big decision. I'd be like, "Here's some popcorn."

SM: I was like, "If this is over ten minutes I should really have some popcorn."

KS: "I have a very short attention span. What am I doing here? Who are you? Get off my nuts!"

SM: "Don't take my children!" Then we agreed and I was like, "I'm totally fine, I'm ready to do it."

KS: I've got to tell you man, this is fucking killing me. I still flashback to the moment where you're like, "Yeah, I've got to get a vasectomy in ten minutes…" and I'm like, "What?!!"

SM: When you go through the process the doctor is just like, "OK, now I want you to really think about what you are about to do."

KS: It's not like you're changing sex.

SM: "You're going to come in, it's going to take half an hour, you can drive yourself, you can drive in and out, it's no big deal." He's like, "It'll take about a day, you'll feel pretty rough for about a day,"

KS: In the office or in the hospital?

SM: Right in the office. I literally went right back to the office, then we scheduled it, and that's when I lost track of it because it was a couple of weeks after that, on the 10th, then the day came and…

KS: "And then I stopped cumming forever…"

SM: Alex was like, "I'll drive you." I was like, "OK."

KS: You were like, "It's the fucking least you can do! Ball Killer!"

SM: "Why do I gotta to do everything?"
KS: "Remember when I said that? I still mean it!"
SM: So she drove me and then she dropped me off, she was going to go get the car washed. I was like, "That's fine."
KS: Think about the implications of that though.
SM: Getting the car washed?
KS: Kinda. You're going to *destroy generations*, and she's going to wash the fucking car. If it had been me, I'd have been holding your hand the whole time. I'd have wanted to hold it the whole time.
SM: They won't let other people in there.
KS: Bullshit, I'd have turned up and been like, "Look!"
SM: Then they'd be like, "We're not going to do it."
KS: "Fine. Mosier, let's go!"
SM: "This is my way of stopping this."
KS: "I want to stop this!"
SM: "Please leave now!"
KS: "I know we're friends but go away now!"
SM: But I think that I didn't care, I would have driven myself if she had anything to do, I would have been, "Whatever, I don't care."
KS: Just to bring this back to me, because it's been about you too much, I'm sitting here thinking that this is one of those things where to you it really ain't a big deal, but to me I would spend, weeks, months, years…
SM: Deciding?
KS: Yeah, it's a big deal. "Oh my god, shutting down potential futures and blah blah blah. Isn't that the only thing I'm here for really, everything else is just window dressing…" Is there anything that *I* do that you're like, "I can't get my head around how that dude can make that decision, live that life, I think I should probably put a pillow over his face like in fucking…"
SM: Do you want to kill me?
KS: Yes! Because I'm, "I've got to stop him from doing this!" No, but is there anything that I do where you're like, "Wow, that's fucked up, I can't even grasp it"?
SM: I don't want kids. I look at people with kids and…
KS: "Why would anyone want that?" But you're a kid yourself.
SM: I am?
KS: Yeah, you're somebody's kid. So you know why somebody wants that.

SM: No. Based on the fact that we all hit a certain age and we can make the choice to have a kid and then lead the life of being a parent, I don't understand. Let me put it this way, I understand why people have kids. I'm just, "No way, not me!" I don't want that.
KS: But what is it? Is it the idea of, "Why would I compromise my existence like that? I've just got it down to a science"? Is it really that? "I'm taking care of myself, how am I supposed to take care of somebody else?"
SM: It's not even fear of too much pressure, I just don't want to make decisions…
KS: What if they could come out as adults, like eighteen or nineteen years old? Would that be OK?
SM: They still might be like, [sarcastic] "Hey *dad*!"
KS: Then you're like, "Oh fuck! Get back in!"
SM: I know everyone is probably sitting there being, "But it's amazing," and all these amazing examples. I get it. I'm not saying that everyday of my life with my children would be miserable, I just choose to not have to deal with it. It occupies a lot of time.
KS: What, having a kid? Oh god yeah. Well, yes and no. To be fair, and you've known me now for many years as a parent, who spends more time with the kid, me or her?
SM: I assume her.
KS: Think about it. Knowing me as you've known me all these years, who do you think probably spends more time with the kid?
SM: She does.
KS: Why? What am I doing?
SM: Because you're working.
KS: Of course, I'm just sitting there trying to figure out what we're doing, what to do next, what we've done.
SM: But still you're not necessarily under pressure, but my point is this, when you get home from working you become a father. Not every day but you generally do.
KS: It depends. If we're shooting? The way I run shit, particularly on set for me when I'm in production since I've had the kid, is that when I get home I'm an editor, and really for forty or fifty days I'm not a parent, or I'm not a very good one. I'm more like the uncle who's like, "Hey, how are you?"
SM: "Nice to meet you."

KS: "Hey yeah, remember me?" Because I'm buried in it. So maybe a good parent is like the way that you're describing, but me? Not really.

SM: But you're talking about something that you do every few years for a very short amount of time. But the general Monday through Sunday existence is that you are putting aside time to be a parent. Most of the time it's not a choice, or because you *want* to, well most of the time you want to, but also that's just part of being a parent — you actually spend time with your kids. I don't want to.

KS: You don't think you would ever find your own kid interesting?

SM: I'll say this, if I had a kid obviously I wouldn't just look at it and be like, "I don't want this."

KS: "Put that in the closet."

SM: "Why are you here?"

KS: "Back under the stairs Harry Potter!" They're like, "Oh man!"

SM: "I've got to make this fun for me somehow! This fucking kid is Harry fucking Potter!"

KS: "But isn't it weird that he chose to play the role of the Dursleys?"

SM: Then when he's eight or whatever I'm throwing envelopes at him pretending to be an owl. "Time to go."

KS: Now he's Dumbledore's owl. Now he's taken on the role of Dumbledore. This kid is never going to understand that. Nah, the kid would have read the book many times, he'd understand that.

SM: So he understands what an idiot his dad is.

KS: "Why are you raising me according to a fictional story of witches and wizards, dad?"

SM: "Because it's awesome!"

KS: "I have no answer for you!"

SM: "We didn't want you, I don't owe you an answer!"

KS: "You want to be here? This is the cost! You want life? Well, life costs and right here is where you start paying. Under the stairs with sweat Harry Potter."

SM: "Now! Say your lines!"

KS: Yeah, I guess rather than put some poor kid through that perhaps it's a positive. So you get into the room, did they shave your nuts?

SM: So the day arrives and this is the procedure, you come in and they take your blood pressure.

KS: Was yours high?

SM: No, mine was fine.

KS: Were they like, "Mr Mosier, yours is uncommonly calm."

SM: "You are a robot."

KS: "As suspected, you are a cock-fucking jerk-ass robot."

SM: "We pulled that from a recent SModcast..."

KS: "... to put it in your terminology, your *patios* if you will." How was your pulse?

SM: It was fine, it was normal.

KS: That's what they say about serial killers when they make their kills, their pulse doesn't rise. Just like you.

SM: Exactly.

KS: As you were like, "Kill them." You're like the Emperor, dude, "Wipe them out! All of them!"

SM: "This will kill *all* of them, right? We're not going for a percentage." I told you I was going to walk into the meeting room with my pants around my ankles, shuffling up to them going, "Take my babies! Take them!" I didn't do that.

KS: You also told me afterwards when you saw me online a day or two later on and I asked how it was and you intimated that you had a rock hard stock boner the whole procedure. I was like, "Get the fuck out of here." The doctor had to work around it and shit. I was like, "No way!" Then you were like, "Nah."

SM: There is no way.

KS: That would have rocked. Some dude is trying to cut your nuts and...

SM: Somebody may get an erection but I will say this, that Dr Balls would probably go down in history as, after me, the male who has touched my scrotum and penis the most. There is me and then there is him.

KS: That's true. I guess if I had to go that way there was a doctor who gave me a physical for *Jay and Silent Bob Strike Back* in Shrewsbury who was the last, and only man I believe, to ever touch my nuts. I think I have to get into nut-touching more now though, as I crest into forty years old.

SM: You get into nut-touching but once you hit forty that's when you get it in the butt.

KS: Are there any female proctologists?

SM: Urologists?

KS: Urologists and proctologists. Proctology, they rock your balls too, not just your ass hole.

SM: Well my general practitioner, when I go in to…

KS: He's the one who juggles your balls?

SM: For hernias.

KS: I've got to tell you, I have real issues with it. Mine aren't deep-seated homophobic or homoerotic issues, I could care less.

SM: "I'm going to cum!"

KS: Yeah, I'm just like, "I don't want to cum in some dude's face." No, I'm just terrified that I'm recognizable. I know I get recognized.

SM: He's under there with his camera-phone?

KS: Yes! Maybe not his camera-phone, not so much that.

SM: "Here's Silent Bob's…"

KS: Yes! It's not so much the camera-phone but I am terrified that I've got a *small* fucking cock, dude, I'm not kidding. And it's accentuated by the weight.

SM: Then why are you worried that people are going to find out that you have a small cock? You keep announcing it.

KS: I don't want people talking about it and shit. Also I feel like it's not a crippling debility because it's a zero-to-sixty cock. When it gets hard, it's presentable.

SM: You should be on Viagra all the time.

KS: I should, I really should. I should just constantly be pumping Viagra so that when…

SM: At the doctors!

KS: "He is a normal sized man who is apparently always aroused."

SM: Just like when you go to the doctors to get the hernia test and you're like, "Wait a second!"

KS: I pop it like spinach and shit.

SM: "Go ahead, check it now."

KS: My fucking boner is like a Popeye muscle in the cartoon with the steamship on it and whatnot, blows smoke out of the tip of it. I'm like, "Go ahead, touch me!" [Makes Popeye laughing noise.] That is what holds me back, I know it, I see my future, I'm one of those dudes… remember Yul Brynner?

SM: You think the doctor would put it on the Internet?

KS: No, it's not about that dude. It's not about him putting it on the Internet. That is part of it, but that is not the big part.
SM: Is it anyone knowing?
KS: Yeah, I just don't want to see the dude's face drop a little bit, you know? Just have any indication like, "Fuck, you said small but this is fucking…"
SM: "Hey man, I've seen a lot… [pause]"
KS: Totally. That would be bad enough, but imagine if he was like, "Uh, come on, I've seen every size, we've got to get you to a specialist. This is dangerously small."
SM: "I've seen a penis this small, on a four-year-old."
KS: He's like, "We're afraid that this penis is going to suck back out of existence. The mushroom cap is traveling closer and closer to your pelvis."
SM: "It could become a genital black hole."
KS: "It may go supernova any minute and drag all of us, including the entire county into it!"
SM: "We're all going to die!!"
KS: "Run!!! He's got the cock hole!" "The cock hole?" "Well, I can't call it the black cock. That just sounds racist. But it's a black hole and it's a cock so it's a cock hole!" "But he always has a…" "Run!!!"
SM: "You don't understand, this is the end of time!!!"
KS: "There is no time for semantics arguments. This man's cock is about to go supernova!" But remember Yul Brynner died, and then they started running a commercial with Yul Brynner from beyond the grave where he was like, [zombie voice] "Brains!" No he didn't say that, but he was like, "I'm Yul Brynner and smoking killed me. Stop smoking now or be dead like me." Or something like that. It was unsettling dude.
SM: "I'm Yul Brynner, I died from smoking."
KS: Yes! You're like, "They taped this in Hell! This was videotaped in Hell!"
SM: "Yul Brynner is in Hell!"
KS: "Yul Brynner burns in Hell and this was taped in Hell!"
SM: "We should go and save Yul Brynner!"
KS: "If they can get into Hell and tape him then why can't we save Yul Brynner from Hell? And if we can in fact save Yul Brynner why can't we save everybody from Hell? This is the moment we've been waiting for people! The war on Hell begins now!!"
SM: So your fear is?

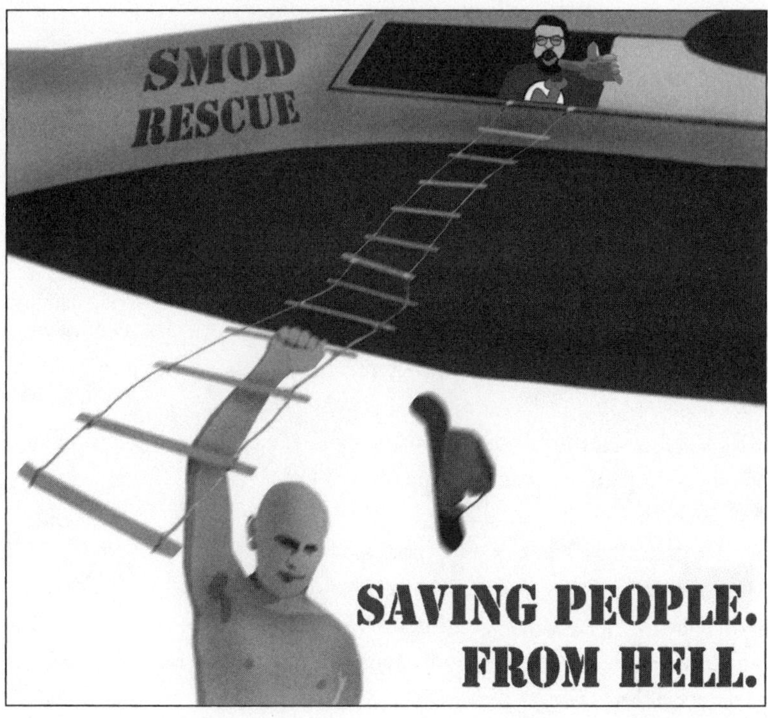

KS: That! That's my fear dude, I don't want to battle Hell. Hell is a tough thing to fight. And it all starts with my nuts.
SM: So your fear is that posthumously somebody will be like, "We want you to do an infomercial for people with small wieners."
KS: No, I'm dying of nut cancer and I've got to go on the commercial and be like, "If I hadn't been such a jerk off, being ashamed of my little dick — I'd be alive today!"
SM: Oh, because you won't get your nuts tested?
KS: Yes. That's what I am getting at. I think it would just be easier with a woman doctor because I'm used to women being disappointed by the size of my dick. It's not so much, "Well, I'd rather a woman saw it." It's just I've seen so many chicks go like, "Yeah whatever man, I've seen smaller."
SM: For me it's pretty different. Alex was asking me…
KS: Did she ask about that?
SM: No, she was asking me if I cared if it was a guy. The doctor who did it,

Dr Balls, was a guy, but if it was a girl…
KS: Would you have cared if it was a girl?
SM: Not really.
KS: I'd almost prefer a blind person to operate on my dick.
SM: I wanted an alien. I was like, "Do you have anybody like a little green man who can just pass his hand over it?"
KS: "Is there anyone from Protus?" "Produce?" "No, Protus, the planet!"
SM: "K-Pax?"
KS: "*Pay It Forward*?" Nah, now you're just naming Kevin Spacey movies.
SM: Nah, it wouldn't have mattered to me. Because the unease is more about a stranger.
KS: But also you're thin, you're in shape dude. Even if you had a small dick... like I remember there was a picture of Brad Pitt.
SM: Yeah, they caught him on the deck.
KS: He didn't have what I would consider a small dick, but he had a fucking skinny dick. It looked like a cigarette.
SM: You're like, "You better feed that dick!"
KS: "Either feed it or let someone smoke it. Like maybe me, because I like cigarettes. Fleshy man cigarettes." How far do I get into that proposal before some bodyguard has cracked my skull open?
SM: He's like, "Look, I didn't really want to talk about it at all."
KS: "It's really uncomfortable that you brought up my dick in that picture but I'm pretty sure you just intimated that you want to suck it."
SM: "To make me feel better."
KS: "And I'm not quite sure who you are."
SM: "You want me to feed it, which is not really possible, and in lieu of that you want to suck it like a cigarette."
KS: It did look very skinny, but Brad Pitt is with Angelina Jolie and he was with Jennifer Aniston. Nobody cares because he looks like Brad Pitt and he is thin and good looking and shit. Dick size, people can work around it. I know this first-hand, women can work around a dick size. But when it is attached to somebody as thin and good-looking as Brad Pitt they're like, "Who gives a shit man? I'll never be in pain." That's what they think.
SM: Generally speaking when you get in there, you get naked, you transfer into a robe, one of those hospital robes that tie at the back.
KS: We're not going to talk about Brad Pitt's dick any more?

SM: No.

KS: I see.

SM: It's not like you go in there and lie on your side like the *Playgirl* centerfold on a fucking polar bear rug.

KS: Stroking your cock and staring at them all fucking creepily.

SM: "Is this it doc?"

KS: "Is this what you want?" He's like, "Not at all."

SM: And he Tasers me.

KS: "Nurse, can you hold him down?" "Doc! No!"

SM: You basically are lying on your back and you have the thing on.

KS: That's not a bad position for me, I could do that.

SM: You're lying on your back and staring up at the ceiling.

KS: But up to that point he's already looked at your dick a lot, touched it.

SM: Nah.

KS: Never? That's the first moment he's touched your dick? Is there a female assistant? Just one dude?

SM: I was alone with the dude.

KS: One on one? Really? They don't feel the need to have a second person there, particularly in that nut area?

SM: No. You mean in case it's inappropriate?

KS: [Makes chewing noises] "Dr Balls is hungry!" You're like, "Excuse me? Who's Dr Whoaohohoh!"

SM: "You *are* hungry!"

KS: "Oh! You're Dr Balls!"

SM: "You know it would be better if you hadn't given me the anesthetic. I can't really feel anything now."

KS: "Are you putting me out?"

SM: "Is this laughing gas? Are you blowing into it?"

KS: "Am I going down?" "Well I am!" "Oh Dr Balls you punster."

SM: You're nude.

KS: "Oh Dr Balls I came!"

SM: "Oh Dr Balls! There's sperm in that. But you knew that, you know that, this is your house."

KS: He's like, "Look I know it may seem a little weird, but before I give dudes

Random SModquotes
"Look, in the world of an Ice Age, we're all fucked."

vasectomies I like to be the last one to eat their sperm."

SM: That would not go over well with me.

KS: That would bug you? What if he was, "I don't have to suck it out of you, couldn't you just masturbate into this cup?"

SM: "So I can drink it."

KS: "It's spiritual, it's tribal, dude. You like to travel."

SM: I'd be like, "Do I get a discount?"

KS: He'd be like, "Sure, man!" Why? Is it expensive?

SM: It's a thousand dollars and the insurance doesn't cover it.

KS: He's like, "Two fifty."

SM: Two fifty off or two fifty for the whole thing?

KS: Two fifty for the whole thing.

SM: And he wants to take a whiskey shot of my sperm?

KS: It doesn't even have to be directly from your dick, it can be into the cup and then passed to him. He's going to drink it, and you guys are going to say a prayer whilst you hold hands over a candle and then he's going to perform the surgery. But he's known as the world's best.

SM: He's like, "I'm one hundred percent."

KS: He's like, "Look, when I get in there, oh my god, I'm the Gretzky of ball-cutting but until that moment…"

SM: "Do you know who Wayne Gretzky is?" "As a matter of fact I know a lot about Wayne Gretzky."

KS: "The confluence of events leads me to tell you…"

SM: "Leave it on the ice!"

KS: "I'm going to the puck doc."

SM: I don't know.

KS: For two fifty?

SM: It would certainly make it the most amazing fucking story ever.

KS: No fucking doubt. Also if anyone was like, "Oh you're gay," you'd be, "No I'm not."

SM: "No I'm not."

KS: "No, I'm smart. I'm fiscally responsible."

SM: "Look at what is happening in the economy right now. You've got to make those hard decisions."

KS: "When I say hard I mean my dick was hard as I jerked off into a cup and some dude ate it."

SM: "Then we prayed."

KS: "And then, he cut my balls. It was a pretty weird day now that I think about it." So you get in there?

SM: You get in there, you're wearing the robe, you lie on your back. He basically pulls the robe up and starts…

KS: [Hysterically laughing] I'm sorry, I'm sorry it's just that as you were starting to say it I was smiling and then you were looking back at me going, "I know exactly what you're thinking." It just sounded kinda sexy for a moment.

SM: He pulls the robe up.

KS: Slowly or fast in one quick motion?

SM: I don't remember the speed, it was medium speed. He didn't do it like a magic trick, "And Pizzow! It's gone! Now it's back!"

KS: It wasn't really slow?

SM: Like creeping up there? He did it and then they started laying towels. Then they move your junk around because they shave the scrotal area where they're going to make the incision.

KS: Where is the incision going to be made?

SM: It's basically between your balls.

KS: And your dick? It's where you dick meets your balls?

SM: It's between your balls. It's farther away.

KS: It's nowhere near your dick? It's at the bottom of your balls? Is it closer to your asshole than your dick?

SM: No, it's closer to your dick, it's on the up-side towards your dick. It's like an inch and a half I think.

KS: OK, this bottle I have here, this is the dick, this is the balls. I guess that don't work. OK, here's the balls and here's the dick and he's holding the dick up like this. So it's this section right here?

SM: Like right between the balls.

KS: What about right here where I'm pointing to on the bottle?

SM: I did not see your diagram.

KS: This is a dick. The balls are the bottom right here.

SM: The dick is pointing up?

KS: Yeah, because the doctor is holding it.

SM: It's like if this is where they meet, where they join?

KS: This is where they meet, clearly.

SM: Yeah, I'm sorry, I didn't realize. It's like an inch below where they meet roughly. So he pulls it up and shaves.

KS: You've never shaved that area before?

SM: No. He uses this plastic shaver.

KS: Does he foam you up?

SM: No, it's a dry shave.

KS: Really? You're like, "Hey buddy, how about a wet shave, huh?"

SM: "Get a hot towel."

KS: "Slap a hot towel on my nuts would you?"

SM: So he does a quick shave of the area, according to him for reasons of infection.

KS: Did it hurt at all, the shave? Not hurt but just like, "Ow Ow Ow."

SM: It didn't really. You could kind of feel it but it didn't hurt.

KS: Because if you pluck a ball hair off it fucking hurts like hell.

SM: But he wasn't pulling them out, he was just shaving them.

KS: Is he talking during this? Is there music?

SM: He's talking.

KS: What's he talking about?

SM: We were talking about *Watchmen*.

KS: Really?

SM: Because it had done well, he was like, "Did you see the *Watchmen*?"

KS: And you're like, "Would you fucking pay attention to my balls!"

SM: Yeah, "Do you see my balls?! Why don't you *watch* the *men* down there and fucking make sure…" Nah, he was asking me about that because he hadn't seen the movie and he hadn't read the graphic novel.

KS: How old was this dude?

SM: He's got two full-grown kids, Dr Balls is probably early or late fifties.

KS: Older than you?

SM: Yeah, older than me. He shaves and then he lays four towels down so that your nuts are the only thing that is sticking up. So he lays the four towels down in a square so there is just a little opening where your nuts are. Does that make sense?

KS: Yes.

SM: One on top, where your penis is underneath that. One under the bottom and two on the sides.

KS: So there is a square with your nuts poking out. What keeps the nuts from not...

SM: They clamp the bottom to push everything up.

KS: Clamp what?

SM: Your nuts.

KS: Oh.

SM: Pushing them up and then clamps the skin so that it is taught. This is what I think he was doing.

KS: You didn't look? "Hey, can I get a mirror?"

SM: He's like, "I'm going to apply some pressure." I'm like, [through gritted teeth] "Oh OK."

KS: You're like, "I like it hard doc!"

SM: He was clamping something, and then I knew I was going to get a local.

KS: Oh wait, I don't know if I want to know this. Tell me he gave it to you in pill form. Please say that.

SM: No. I was going to get the local. I'd never asked where I was going to get it.

KS: [Sounding increasingly queasy] I get the feeling you're going to start talking about needles and balls.

SM: Yeah.

KS: OhmaaaanAAAaaaaggghh! [Bangs table.] Hold on. [Kevin lights up a calming cigarette.]

SM: You know when somebody is about to do something bad and sometimes they just do it, and then tell you they did it?

KS: He tricked you?

SM: He stuck the needle in half a second before he said it. [Makes needle insertion sound] "I'm putting the needle in." I think that was because the idea of it is awful...

KS: Oh god yeah!!

SM: The pain of it is fine.

KS: That just hurts. I don't know what the corresponding hurt part of a woman's body would be, maybe the boobs, but from what I understand not even that.

SM: It was the most painful shot I've ever had.

KS: It might be cramps, you know how when women have really bad cramps, triple that, times it by a hundred and that's what it feels like when somebody kicks you or punches you in the nuts. So the notion of a needle

even coming near it and poking into it!
SM: It doesn't feel that bad. I've had shots before in my ass and my arm.
KS: In your butt cheek, not in your fucking ring-piece or anything.
SM: No. It definitely hurt.
KS: Ow Ow Ow. Did you want to punch him?
SM: Nah, it didn't hurt that bad. It sort of centralizes around it.
KS: Did it feel exactly like what it was, a needle going into one of your balls?
SM: Yeah.
KS: Eurgh! Oh god.
SM: For like sixty seconds it was pretty uncomfortable.
KS: Then after sixty it was like?
SM: You couldn't really feel anything.
KS: Because of the numbing agent? What do you think they're thinking in your balls, "What the fuck?"
SM: "We were doing so well!"
KS: "What's going on? What's that?"
SM: And that's probably kinda it. If you really break it down into its essential elements, that is really the only thing that you need to be prepared for, that they are probably going to jam a needle in your nuts. And it definitely doesn't tickle. But I'll say this, and I'll say it because I know women out there who've had babies and everything, it doesn't hurt.
KS: It doesn't?
SM: It doesn't really hurt. I would not put it anywhere near what a pregnancy must feel like.
KS: You're giving the ladies a pass?
SM: I ain't the guy who is going to go on…
KS: You're like, [singing] "All the single ladies, all the single ladies." You heard that song?
SM: No.
KS: You're like that song.
SM: I'm just saying that I am not in any way, shape or form saying that it is anywhere close to…
KS: You don't want a bunch of people going, "Hey prick, try pushing a baby through it."
SM: "You don't know pain!"
KS: My old lady gave me that rap when I had the fucking anal fissure. That

is the most pain I have ever been in in my life and she was just like, "That is nothing compared to pushing a child out."
SM: I guarantee you that what you had, your anal fissure, was more painful.
KS: Than this?
SM: This was, [deep exhale breath] "OK." It wasn't like, "Oh my god!" I wasn't like…
KS: "Shoot me! Kill me! Shoot me now!"
SM: "Come on! That's a good prophylactic." Yeah, it didn't hurt that bad. That was the only moment where I was kinda breathing through it a little bit. It was not pleasant, but I sprained my ankle once and that hurt more. The idea of it is fucking *horrific*, but the actual feeling was not that bad. Then they start doing their thing. They make an incision, really small, like maybe a quarter of an inch is the actual incision. They make the incision, they go in, they cut it, tie it or cauterize it and then they sow you back up. That's basically it. Then they clean you all up. We were talking the whole time, he finished a thought and was like, "Oh, and we're done." It's really simple.
KS: He's like, "Fifty-six million is a pretty great opening for a movie… Oh, and we're done."
SM: Yeah, "And by the way, we're done." Then what he puts you in is kinda like a jockstrap, but it is basically a nut-sling. It's a small pouch for your nuts and there are four elastic bands, two fasten underneath your butt-cheeks, two are up on your waist. But your cock is out so it's just for your balls.
KS: So your wife is just like, "I want to suck it so bad, you look so hot!"
SM: "I've always wanted you to not have balls!" There was also gauze and some blood.
KS: And that's even more exciting for a woman.
SM: "Ah, bloody nuts!"
KS: "I want to suck the cock of those bloody nuts."
SM: It happened so fast that she was literally walking in from washing the car and I was leaving.
KS: And you're like, "Hey, I'm done. Thanks for nothing!"
SM: "Thanks for nothing! I was crying in there and didn't know where you were!"
KS: "The babies are gone!"
SM: Then we drove home, and then they say for the first four or five hours stay off your feet, so I lay in bed.

KS: And naturally at this point you're not thinking about fucking.

SM: No. It was sore, there was pain below. So I'm sat in bed with an ice-pack on my nuts for like four hours.

KS: What if she was like, "Oddly enough this is the weekend I'd planned to have a fucking threesome with you and here is this fucking way hot bitch that you've always wanted to fuck. We're just going to have to sit and eat out in front of you I guess. Maybe if you can overcome your little boo-boo you can join in."

SM: I'd be really surprised by her meanness.

KS: You're just crying the whole time. You're like, "Stop."

SM: She takes my ice-pack. "Fucking bitch."

KS: Opens it over the other woman's boobs and shit.

SM: I'm like, "I can't move!"

KS: "It hurts! They cut my balls! And I did it for you!"

SM: "I do *everything*!"

KS: So you go home and put your feet up.

SM: I just lay in bed and was playing…

KS: Some EA?

SM: … a little EA.

KS: It hurt big-time.

SM: Anyone who is actually considering it…

KS: I don't know any people who do… they're like, "You're the youngest vasectomy I've ever heard of." You're thirty-eight.

SM: I've just turned thirty-eight.

KS: That's right, we missed your birthday last slot. We didn't even talk about it. The next day was your birthday! Happy belated Birthday! There is a thread up on the board of a bunch of people who, I know you've never visited the board but, there's a Happy Birthday Scott Mosier thread.

SM: Only when you send me things. You're like my filter.

KS: Well I'll send you the link to that because it's four pages of people going, "You fucking rock! Scott Le Rock!" Whatever, they like you, it's clear.

SM: Thanks everyone.

KS: I guess you could have used that over those days when you're like, "My balls hurt and I'm alone."

SM: "My balls hurt, doesn't anybody love me? Doesn't anybody wish me a happy birthday?"

KS: What did you do for your birthday? You went away to the desert, and this is before the ball cutting right? Was this the last hurrah, take the boys on one last trip out into the desert?

SM: "Let's go to the desert, sperm! Where do you guys want to go?"

KS: "I'm spilling my sperm on the fucking desert one last time!"

SM: "Fucking cacti."

KS: "Then fucking burying it in a shallow grave." What do you guys do when you go out there?

SM: Sometimes we hike. It's quiet. Just go somewhere that is quiet. Sometimes we bring the dogs out and just chill.

KS: Did you bring the dogs?

SM: Yeah. We rented a house.

KS: Did you guys fuck?

SM: That did happen.

KS: Was that the last time, or did you fuck at home before you went for the operation?

SM: No. That was the last time.

KS: Last time you fucked like a man, not a eunuch.

SM: Pre-cut.

KS: With empty shots. You're the dream, dude. This is the smart play. The smart play is to have the vasectomy, come here and be able to tell something fucking cool that very few people can. I was full of questions. You answered them all, sadly because now I'm out of them. But now the word is out there, say one day Alex is like, "Fuck you, I want to be with somebody who can impregnate me!" and leaves you, suddenly you're the hottest ticket in town.

SM: Well you are to a percentage of people, but then the percentage of people who want children…

KS: Yeah, but you're hot to the right percentage, the ones who are like, "Take me in this bathroom stall and fuck me, up the ass."

SM: "I don't want to get pregnant."

KS: "But you know that I can't get you pregnant." "Just do it!"

SM: "Why do I gotta do everything!?"

KS: "That's what I used to say."

SM: For anyone who has even thought about doing it, I'm telling you, and I wish I could get paid, I would do a commercial, "I'm not Yul Brynner, I'm not dead. I'm alive! And I'm fucking my wife, and I'm not even thinking about it! I'm not in Hell, this isn't posthumous, this is the height of living! I'm in Heaven people!"

[Kevin laughs himself into a coughing fit.]

KS: "I'm not in Hell"? I would so fucking pay attention to a commercial that started like that with some dude maintaining that he's not in Hell. "What? Did somebody say he was?"

SM: What if he started with the Yul Brynner line, from a totally unconnected commercial.

KS: "If anyone remembers this?" Star wipe to Yul Brynner.

SM: "Yul Brynner didn't go to Heaven, Yul Brynner went to Hell. Because of his decision."

KS: Smash cut to you. Bbrrrrrp! "I'm Scott Mosier, that motherfucker was burning in Hell when he sent you that message. I'm alive! I'm on the planet with you!"

SM: "I'm in Heaven!"

KS: "Get a vasectomy today!" "Ting! Paid for by the National Vasectomy Association." Perhaps a more subtle sell would be in order?

SM: It's good.

KS: It works.

SM: It's not bad.

KS: I think that would be an effective campaign. Or just like, "Vasectomy. It doesn't hurt."

SM: "Don't be a pussy. It doesn't hurt."

KS: A national campaign of testimonials where they cut to you, Scott Mosier.

SM: If you've got a really low threshold of pain…

KS: That's me!

SM: … then it's going to hurt.

KS: But I'm not getting it done. You're *not* going to talk me into it.

That's SModcast for this book...

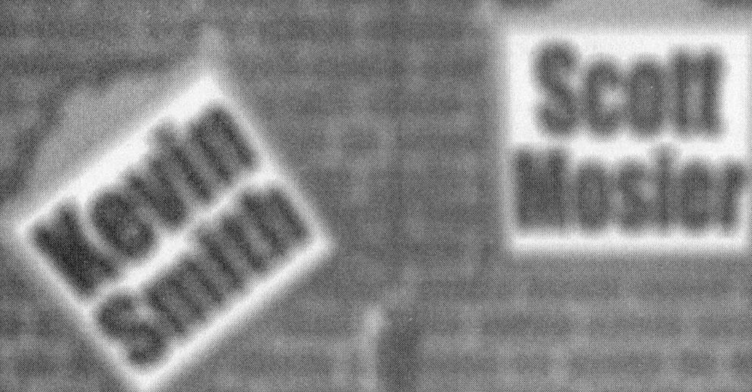

HAVE A WEEK

SMOD

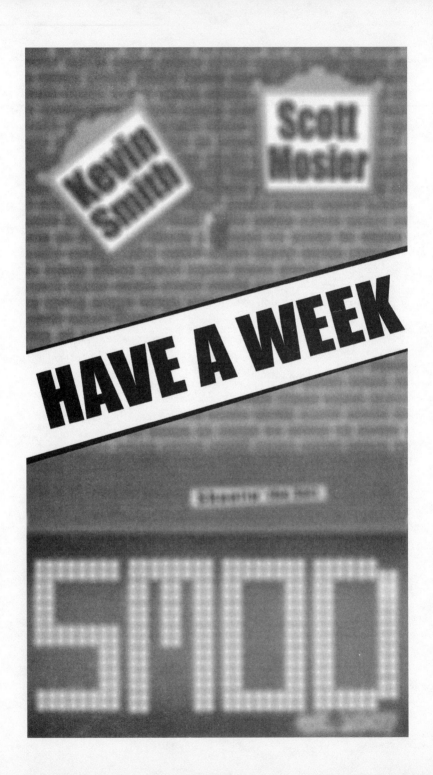

Kevin Smith sold his comic book collection to fund *Clerks*, and after the film became a huge hit he was able to buy them back. Smith was the producer of the Oscar-winning *Good Will Hunting* and has also written and directed *Mallrats, Chasing Amy*, *Dogma, Jay and Silent Bob Strike Back, Jersey Girl, Clerks II* and *Zack and Miri Make a Porno*. He is also a comic book writer, actor, and author. His previous book for Titan, *My Boring-Ass Life: The Uncomfortably Candid Diary of Kevin Smith*, was a *New York Times* bestseller. His next movie as director is *A Couple of Dicks*, starring Bruce Willis.

Selected Index

Air conditioning, lame ass German 29

BEACH!!, BRIDGE 267-271
Blow job noise, rhythmic 327
Blue City (1986), narrative complexities of defeat stoned Kevin 226
BOOBERTY! 323
Bottom, sloppy party 319
Boxing, old-timey, significance to The Second Coming of Christ 157
Brynner, Yul, saved from Hell 350

Cereal, breakfast, bewildering variety of postulated to confuse aging British rocker 271
Combustion, spontaneous 201
Connelly, Jennifer, has better boobs than Mosier 106
Curtains, meat, flappiest you've ever seen in your life 16

Dessert platter, repeated consumption of 212
Dushku, Eliza, visit leads to suspicions of a gay dog 15

Eggs, bukkake 135
EH?! 201, 205, 208
Every Which Way But Loose (1978), importance of in training the returned Messiah 129

Fellatio, used to save lives 331
Fissure, anal 88, 358, 359
Flanagan, Walt
- has fight with seventy-five year-old woman 41-53
- yearns for a clone 238-267

Fräuleins, naked 32
Fuck, the quest for 8
Fucktard, as taught to Helen Keller 82

Ghandi, Mohandas Karamchand 'Mahatma', is pooped on 205
Glenn, Senator John, achievements nothing compared to invention of adult wet wipe 88
Granger, Hermione, engages in candy-related sex play 95-96
Gretzky, Wayne, bigger inspiration than Jesus 128

Hitler, Adolf, amused by dachshunds 282
Human race, subjugation of by chickens 27

Ingram, Malcolm
- accused of toilet misuse 88
- makes rash wager 58

Johnson, Bryan
- disillusioned by stripper 91
- in Greco-Roman death hold 94

Keller, Helen, told not to masturbate in public 74
Kenobi, Ben 'Obi-Wan', poised to attack defenseless grandparent 333

Lasers, eye-mounted, as used by returning Jesus Christ 142
The Lost Legend of Hitler Claus 315
Laughter, hysterical, duration eleven seconds, followed by dizziness 328
Lugers, as Christmas present 317

Masturbation, risky 62
Mewes, Jason
- beats man with pool stick 5
- willing to suck dick for free comic book 140

Mosier, Scott
- drives shitbox 174
- evades shark 290-296
- fights Jesus 156-168
- has needle injected into balls 357
- stars in posthumous porno 113

Selected Index

Penis, fat overweight 122
Pickle, anal insertion of 227
Pig, whipped 94
Pillow baby porn 237

Quarters, roll of, anal insertion of 328

Schwalbach, Jennifer
- gets over-excited about neighbors' kitchen counters 214
- tries to continue applying mascara while Kevin tugs one out 9

Semen
- as slimming aid 19-21
- dog covered in 17

Sexuality, Kevin's web of 115
Sexual organs, angels' lack of 124
Sonic Disruptors, as example of shit comic book Mewes nevertheless thought was 'awesome' 139
Shit
- liquidy 170
- shootin' the 1-364

Smith, Harley
- is embarrassed by her father talking about boys 172-173
- turns to Satan 303-306

Smith, Kevin
- admits to having small penis 11
- does not go in for back door shenanigans 117
- learns hard way not to eat raw meat 168-171
- looks at Mosier's sister in a sexual way 101
- loses any shot of getting together with Alanis Morrisette 7
- runs from a breast 90
- will cry if you hit him 5
- wins *Time* magazine Man of the Year when his brain is transplanted into body of eight year-old girl 303

Squid, giant, pissed off, does not attack New York 314
Stalin, Josef, tries to create monkey soldiers 237
Strippers, Canadian, superiority of 206
Sturluson, Snorri 309

Threesome, inadvisability of immediately following vasectomy procedure 360

Weeney, and puss equals waa-waa 83

Zamboni, fun to say word, like SModcast 3

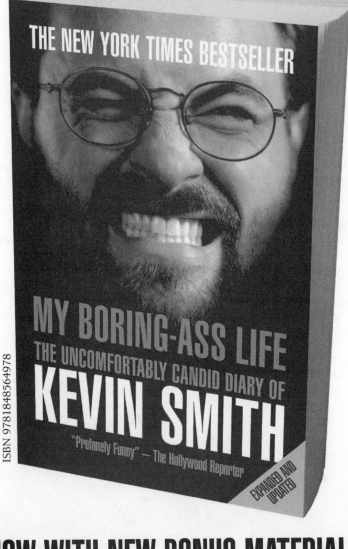